Time Out

Amsterdam Guide

Penguin Books

PENGUIN BOOKS

Published by the Penguin Group
Penguin Books Ltd, 27 Wright's Lane, London W8 5TZ, England
Penguin Books USA Inc., 375 Hudson Street, New York, New York 10014, USA
Penguin Books Australia Ltd, Ringwood, Victoria, Australia
Penguin Books Canada Ltd, 10 Alcorn Avenue, Toronto, Ontario, Canada M4V 3B2
Penguin Books (NZ) Ltd, 182-190 Wairau Road, Auckland 10, New Zealand

Penguin Books Ltd, Registered Offices: Harmondsworth, Middlesex, England

First published 1991
Second edition 1993
10 9 8 7 6 5 4 3 2 1

Copyright © Time Out Group Ltd, 1991, 1993
All rights reserved

Printed by Imprimerie Pollina s.a., 85400 Luçon, France

Edited and designed by
Time Out Magazine Limited,
Tower House,
Southampton Street
London WC2E 7HD
tel: 071 836 4411
fax: 071 836 7118.

Editorial
Managing Editor
Peter Fiennes
Editor
Sarah Guy
Deputy Editor
Caroline Taverne
Indexer
Rosamund Sales

Design
Art Director
Warren Beeby
Designer
John Oakey
Ad Make-up
Martin Harrison

Advertising
Group Advertisement Director
Lesley Gill
Sales Director
Mark Phillips
Advertisement Sales (Amsterdam)
David Pepper
Advertising Assistant
Nana Ocran

Administration
Publisher
Tony Elliott
Managing Director
Mike Hardwick
Financial Director
Kevin Ellis
Marketing Director
Gill Auld
Production Manager
Mark Lamond

Reprographics by Rapida
136-148 Tooley Street
London SE1

Contents

About the Guide

PRACTICAL GUIDE

The *Time Out Amsterdam Guide* is updated every two years. However interesting we've made this Guide, we also want it to be practical. Addresses, telephone numbers, transport details, opening times, admission prices and credit card details are all included in our listings. And, as far as possible, we've given details of facilities, services and events.

All the information was checked and correct when we went to press, but please remember that owners and managers can change their arrangements at any time – it's always best to phone before you set out to check opening times, the dates of exhibitions, admission fees and other important details. In particular, we have tried to include information on access for the disabled, but once again, it's wise to phone first to check your needs can be met.

AMSTERDAM'S AREAS

For every place listed in the Guide, we give an idea of its location: just after the address, and before the telephone number, are some letters which refer to areas of Amsterdam. These areas are highlighted on the map at the back of the Guide, but roughly speaking, **C** (*Central*) covers the area bounded by the River IJ in the north of the city and the Singel and Nieuwe Herengracht canals; **IE** (*Inner East*) is defined by the IJ, Nieuwe Herengracht, Binnenamstel and Singelgracht; **IS** (*Inner South*) by Binnenamstel, Singelgracht and Leidsegracht; **IW** (*Inner West*) by Leidsegracht, Singelgracht, Singel, and back again to the River IJ to the north. Beyond these inner areas are **OE** (*Outer East*), stretching east from Singelgracht and the River Amstel; **OS** (*Outer South*), south from Singelgracht between the River Amstel and Overtoom; and **OW** (*Outer West*) between Overtoom and the River IJ. With areas a long way from the centre of Amsterdam – and beyond the range of our map – we have tried to give a little more information by making the compass directions more specific. For instance, the Metro stations at the far end of the line are

listed as **OSE** (*Outer South East*). Finally, **N** (*North*) indicates those areas north of the River IJ. The majority of the places listed within this guide fall within the C, IE, IS and IW areas.

PRICES

The prices we've listed throughout the Guide should be used as guidelines. Fluctuating exchange rates and inflation can cause prices, in shops and restaurants especially, to change rapidly. If prices or services somewhere vary greatly from those we've quoted, ask whether there's a good reason. If not, go elsewhere. Then, please let us know. We try to give the best and most up-to-date advice, so we always want to hear if you've been overcharged or badly treated.

CREDIT CARDS

Throughout the Guide, the following abbreviations have been used for credit cards: **AmEx**: American Express; **CB**: Carte Bleu; **DC**: Diners' Club; **JCB**: Japanese credit cards; **MC**: Mastercard (linked to Access and Eurocard); **TC**: travellers' cheques in any currency; **fTC**, **£TC**, **$TC**, and so on: travellers' cheques in guilders, sterling, US dollars or other specified currencies; **V**: Visa (linked to Barclaycard).

Introduction

Amsterdam is a paradoxical city. Not as cosmopolitan as London or Paris, it manages to combine olde worlde charm with the faster pace of modern life. Because of its relatively small size, city life never becomes too frenzied. The rhythm is relaxed, the atmosphere liberal.

People from all over the world have grown to love Amsterdam for its tolerant attitude and have settled here. This reputation for tolerance – be it political or religious – goes back to the seventeenth century when refugees, mostly Jews from the Iberian peninsula, sought shelter from persecution. In the sixties, this liberal attitude meant that Amsterdam was dubbed 'hippy capital of the world', and has been trying to cope with 'drugs tourism' ever since. Each summer youngsters from all over Europe flock to cafés in the city where grass is legally sold. Though there has been an increase in hard drug abuse, stories about drug-related criminality tend to be exaggerated.

Wandering along the inner city's beautiful canals, it's not difficult to imagine what Amsterdam looked like in the seventeenth and eighteenth centuries. Over 5,000 gabled canal houses are classified monuments, and some of them are open to visitors. The most spectacular ones, however, are privately owned and have either been turned into banks or are still used as residences. Richly stuccoed ceilings and exquisitely painted wall panels are to be found in many of these grand houses, once the property of wealthy merchants of the Golden Age. Although not ostentatious in their display of prosperity, the original inhabitants fitted their dwellings with all the mod cons of their age; one of the best kept secrets of the canals are the park-like gardens, complete with coach houses and garden follies, at the back.

Amsterdam is renowned for its museums: the most famous ones – the Rijks, the Stedelijk and the Van Gogh – are conveniently grouped around the Museumplein, a large square on the south side of the city. For those who do not only want to enjoy art passively but also want to consume

it actively, there are more than 250 private art galleries, and European and American art buyers still roam the galleries in search of bargains.

While the municipal system of public transport is justly praised by tourists (coming third after the canals and the Amsterdammers' fluency in English in a recent survey of reasons for visiting the capital), one of the nicest and most authentic ways to see Amsterdam is to rent a bicycle and join the thousands of cyclists who monopolise city traffic every day. Whether in winter, when wisps of fog rise from the Amstel river, or on a summer's day when cafés open their terraces and the entire population takes to the streets, Amsterdam is truly a city for all seasons.

Essential Information

All you need to know about the basics, from currency to queuing, tipping or day-tripping.

Most visitors to Amsterdam are swiftly put at ease by the city's compact size, efficient transport system and the linguistic skills of its cosmopolitan inhabitants. A visitor's struggling attempts at Dutch will often be met with a smile, followed by a reply in perfect English. But, as with any city of character, Amsterdam has its own way of getting things done. The following list of essentials is designed for a trouble-free arrival to get your visit off to a good start. For more detailed advice on staying healthy and dealing with emergencies *see chapter* **Survival**, and for details of the abbreviations used within this guide *see chapter* **About the Guide**.

Visas

A valid passport is all that is required for a stay of up to three months in The Netherlands if you are an EC national or from one of the following countries:
*Australia, Czechoslovakia, Cyprus, Finland, Hungary, Iceland, Japan, Malaysia, New Zealand, Norway, Poland, Singapore, Sweden, Vatican City
*Africa: Burkina-Faso, Malawi, Niger, Togo
*The Americas: Argentina, Barbados, Brazil, Canada, Costa Rica, Ecuador, Guatemala, Honduras Republic, Jamaica, Mexico, Nicaragua, Panama, Paraguay, El Salvador, Uruguay, USA, Venezuela.

If you are unsure of visa requirements or know you need a visa, contact your nearest Dutch embassy or consulate at least three months before your departure. For stays of longer than three months EC citizens need a residence permit, available from the **Bureau Vreemdelingenpolitie** (Aliens' Police, *listed below*). For information on work and residence permits *see chapter* **Business**.

Bureau Vreemdelingenpolitie (Aliens' Police)

Bijlmerdreef 90, C (general enquiries 691 9100/visa enquiries 559 3179). Metro Bijlmer. **Open** 8.30am-4.30pm Mon-Fri.

An extension visa is free of charge and can normally be obtained on the day of application. Appointments are not required but queues start at around 7am and you can expect a wait of up to two hours. Once you are through the queue it takes literally minutes for the interviewer to process your application and grant you a visa. You will need to take ID, proof of an address in The Netherlands, and a contract of employment or proof of sufficient funds for a longer stay.

Customs

Since European Unification in 1992, EC nationals over the age of 17 may now import limitless goods for their personal use. However, the following limits apply to tobacco and alcohol:
*800 cigarettes, 400 small cigars, 200 cigars, 1kg (2.2lbs) of tobacco
*10 litres (17.6 pints) of spirits (over 22 per cent alcohol) or 20 litres of fortified wine (under 22 per cent alcohol)
*90 litres of wine
*110 litres (193.6 pints) of beer
For citizens of non-EC countries, the old limits still apply:
* 200 cigarettes or 50 cigars or 250g (8.82oz) tobacco
*1 litre (1.76 pints) of spirits (over 22 per cent alcohol) or 2 litres of fortified wine (under 22 per cent alcohol) or 2 litres of non-sparkling wine
*50g (1.76oz) of perfume
*500g (1.1lb) coffee
*100g (3.52oz) tea
*Other goods to the value of f125
The import of meat, meat products, fruit, plants, flowers and protected animals is forbidden.

Insurance

EC countries have reciprocal medical treatment arrangements with The Netherlands. British citizens will need form E111, which can be obtained by filling in the application form in leaflet SA30, available in all Department of Social Security (DSS) offices. Make sure you read the small print on the back of form E111 and ensure that you know how to obtain medical or dental treatment at a reduced charge, since the

chances are you'll have to explain this to the Dutch doctor or dentist who treats you. If you should need treatment, photocopy your insurance form and leave that with the doctor or dentist who treats you.

Citizens of other EC countries should make sure they have obtained one of forms E110, E111 or E112.

Citizens of the following **non-EC countries** can also receive medical treatment at reduced rates by producing the appropriate form: Austria form O/NL111 or O/NL112; Morocco MN111; Yugoslavia YN111; Tunisia TUN/N111; Turkey TUR/N111; Sweden SV/N111.

Citizens from **all other countries** should take out private medical insurance before their visit. Dutch medical treatment costs about half what it would in the USA, which is still more than enough to make travelling without insurance unwise.

As always when travelling abroad, visitors should take out insurance on personal belongings before leaving for Amsterdam. Such insurance is usually included in package holidays, but be sure to check.

Money

The unit of Dutch currency is the **guilder**, variously abbreviated as f, fl or Hfl. Throughout this guide the abbreviation 'f' is used. The guilder is divided into 100 cents, rather more obviously abbreviated to c. Coins in use are 5c, 10c, 25c, f1, f2.50 and f5. The 5c coin is copper, 10c, 25c, f1 and f2.50 coins are silver and the f5 coin is gold. The 5c coin is also known as *stuiver*, the 10c coin *dubbeltje*, 25c *kwartje* and the f2.50 coin is called *rijksdaalder*. Notes come in f5, f10, f25, f50, f100, f250, f500 and f1,000 denominations. The f5 note is green, f10 blue, f25 pink, f50 yellow and f100 brown. Raised symbols give the denominations for blind people (*see chapter* **Survival: Disabled**).

Since the Dutch no longer have 1c or 2c coins, prices are rounded up or down to the nearest 5 cents, so f1.53 will be charged as f1.55.

Amsterdammers prefer to use cash for most transactions, although the larger hotels, shops and most restaurants will accept one or more of the major credit cards (Access/Eurocard/Mastercard, American Express, Diners Club, Visa) and many will take Eurocheques with guarantee cards, and travellers' cheques with ID such as a passport.

Banks

Banks and bureaux de change offer similar rates of exchange but banks tend to charge less commission. Most banks are open from 9am to

4pm Monday to Friday. As yet no banks open on Saturdays but exchange facilities are available at the bureaux de change listed below. Dutch banks buy and sell foreign currency and exchange travellers' cheques and Eurocheques, but few give cash advances against credit cards. For this you'll need to go to a bureau de change (see below). For a full list of banks in Amsterdam see chapter **Business** or look in the Amsterdam Yellow Pages (*Gouden Gids*), under '*Banken*'. *Gouden Gids* can be found in post offices, hotels and phone centres (see chapter **Survival**).

Bureaux de Change

Bureaux de change can be found throughout the city centre, especially on Leidseplein, Damrak and Rokin. Those listed below give reasonable rates of exchange, although they charge more in commission than the banks. It is wise to avoid using hotel and tourist bureaux exchange facilities (see below **Tourist Information**) as these are generally more expensive.

American Express
Damrak 66, C (626 2042). Tram 4, 9, 16, 24, 25.
Open 9am-5pm Mon-Fri; 9am-noon Sat; 11am-4pm Sun and public holidays.
This office has a 24-hour cash machine for card holders and an automatic travellers' cheque refund service. Mail can also be sent poste restante if you are a cardholder; the service is free. It should be addressed, with your name, to *Client Mail Service, American Express, Damrak*

66, 1012 LM, Amsterdam. When collecting mail you need to show ID and your AmEx card.

Change Express
Damrak 86, C (624 6682). Tram 1, 4, 9, 16, 24, 25.
Open 8am-midnight daily.
Branch *Leidsestraat 106, C (622 1425)*. **Open** 8am-midnight daily.

GWK
Centraal Station, C (627 2731). Tram 1, 2, 4, 5, 9, 13, 16, 17, 24, 25. **Open** 24 hours daily.
Branch *Amsterdam Schiphol Airport (in the railway station) (601 0507)*. **Open** 24 hours daily.

Thomas Cook
Dam 23-25, C (625 0922). Tram 4, 9, 14, 16, 24, 25.
Open *winter* 9am-6pm daily; *summer* 9am-8pm daily.
Branches *Damrak 1-5, C (625 0922)*. **Open** 9am-6pm Mon-Sat; 9.45am-6pm Sun; *Muntplein 12a, C (620 3736)*. **Open** 9am-6pm Mon-Fri; *Van Baerlestraat 40, OS (676 1018)*. **Open** 9am-6pm Mon-Fri.

Tourist Information

The national tourist information organisation is the VVV, which stands for *Vereniging Voor Vreemdelingenverkeer* – the Association for Tourist Traffic – and is pronounced 'Vay Vay Vay'. Although it is a private, non-profit making organisation, many of the individual offices are subsidised by local councils. There are two offices in Amsterdam and about 450 throughout the rest of The Netherlands, all offering services similar to those listed below. In the larger branches all the staff speak English, German and French, and English is spoken by almost all the staff in the smaller offices.

Many phone centres (*see chapter* **Survival: Communications**) run a booking service for theatres, car hire, hotels and excursions.

VVV

Stationsplein 10, C (06340 34066). Tram 1, 2, 4, 5, 9, 13, 16, 17, 24, 25. **Open** *Easter-June, Sept* 9am-5pm daily; *July, Aug* 9am-11pm daily; *Oct-Easter* 9am-6pm Mon-Fri; 9am-5pm Sat; 10am-1pm, 2-5pm, Sun. **No credit cards.**
This is the main office of the VVV. Both here and at the branch listed below English-speaking staff can change money and provide information on transport, entertainment and exhibitions as well as day-trip ideas for the whole of The Netherlands. The VVV can also arrange theatre and hotel bookings for a fee of f3.50, and excursions and car hire for free. There is a comprehensive range of brochures for sale detailing walks and cycling tours as well as cassette tours, maps and, for f1.50, the useful if dull fortnightly English-language listings magazine *What's On*. The VVV runs a general information line on *626 6444* which is open from 9am to 5pm Mon-

Sat and features an English-language service.
Branch *Leidsestraat 106, IS. Tram 1, 2, 5, 6, 7, 10.* **Open** *Easter-June, Sept* 10.30am-4.30pm daily; *July, Aug* 10.30am-9pm daily; *Oct-Easter* 10.30am-5.30pm Mon-Fri; 10.30am-9pm Sat. **No credit cards.**

Dutch Tourist Information Office

Damrak 35, C (638 2800). Tram 4, 9, 16, 24, 25. **Open** 9am-10pm Mon-Sat. **No credit cards.**
Recently opened, this single Dutch office concentrates on a booking service for theatres, car hire, hotels and excursions, rather than the all-round information provision of the VVV. Nevertheless it provides an alternative when the VVV offices are full, especially in high summer.

AUB Uitburo

Leidseplein 26, IS (621 1211). Tram 1, 2, 5, 6, 7, 10. **Open** 9am-6pm Mon-Sat. **No credit cards.**
AUB Uitburo provides information and advance tickets for theatre, concerts and other cultural events. The reservation fee is f2. You can also get the Cultureel Jongeren Passport (CJP) here (f15), which is valid for a year and entitles people under 26 to discounts on museum entrance fees and cultural events nationally. An essential

Vocabulary

The vast majority of Amsterdammers speak good English and are happy to show off their linguistic talents. However, some knowledge of the absolute basics of the language may be useful – and polite – particularly if you intend to venture out of the city. Pronunciations given are the nearest approximation we could find.

Pronunciation

v – pronounced like 'f' in 'for'
w – like 'w' in 'which', with a hint of the 'v' in 'vet' thrown in
j – like 'y' in 'yes'
ch – like 'ch' in 'loch'
g – similar to above (this has to be heard to be imitated)
oo – like 'o' in no
ou, au – like 'ow' in 'cow'
ui – similar to above (has to be heard to be imitated)
oe – like 'oo' in 'book'
ie – like 'ea' in 'lean'
ee – like 'ay' in 'hay'
ÿ – similar to above

do you speak English? – *spreekt u Engels?* (spraykt oo engels)
sir – *meneer* (menayr)
madam – *mevrouw* (mevrow). NB: the progressive Amsterdammers rarely address anyone as 'Miss'
waiter – *ober*
open – *open*
closed – *gesloten*
I want.... – *ik wil graag*....
how much is...? *wat kost...?*
could I have a receipt? – *mag ik een bonnetje alstublieft?*
how do I get to...? – *hoe kom ik in...?*
how far is it to...? – *hoe ver is het naar...?*
left – *links*
right – *rechts*
straight ahead – *rechtdoor gaan*
far – *ver*
near – *dichtbij*
street – *straat*
canal – *gracht*
square – *plein*
good – *goed*
bad – *slecht*
big – *groot*
small – *klein*

Useful Phrases

hello – *hallo* (hullo) or *dag* (darch)
goodbye – *tot ziens* (tot zeens)
yes – *ja* (yah)
no – *nee* (nay)
please – *alstublieft* (als – too – bleeft)
thank you – *dank u* (dank-oo)
excuse me – *pardon* (par – don)
I'm sorry, I don't speak Dutch – *Het spijt me, ik spreek geen Nederlands* (et spate meh, ik sprayk hane nay – der – lants)

Numbers

0 – *nul*; **1** – *een*; **2** – *twee*; **3** – *drie*; **4** – *vier*, **5** – *vijf*, **6** – *zes*; **7** – *zeven*; **8** – *acht*; **9** – *negen*; **10** – *tien*; **11** – *elf*, **12** – *twaalf*; **13** – *dertien*; **14** – *veertien*; **15** – *vijftien*; **16** – *zestien*; **17** – *zeventien*; **18** – *achttien*; **19** – *negentien*; **20** – *twintig*; **21** – *eenentwintig*; **22** – *tweeëntwintig*; **30** – *dertig*; **31** – *eenendertig*; **32** – *tweeëndertig*; **40** – *veertig*; **50** – *vijftig*; **60** – *zestig*; **70** – *zeventig*; **80** – *tachtig*; **90** – *negentig*; **100** – *honderd*; **101** – *honderd een*; **110** – *honderd tien*; **200** – *tweehonderd*; **201** – *tweehonderd een*; **1,000** – *duizend*

stopping-off point for everyone interested in exploring the city's culture, it has chatty and helpful staff, plus a comfortable café area where visitors can leaf through listings guides and brochures at leisure. Centrally located, it's a good place to arrange to meet friends.

Maps

Almost every complimentary brochure or leaflet that you will find in hotels and some bars will provide a sketchy map. But if you require more detail, the *Falk Pocket Book Map* (f10) and the Falk fold-out map (f7) are useful and accurate, and have a full street index. Cheaper and smaller, but perfectly adequate is Falk's small fold-out plan (f5.50). Steer clear of the complicated Falk 'patent-folded' map unless you're keen on origami. All these can be bought from newsagents and bookshops (*see chapter* **Survival**).

What's On

Amsterdam's theatres, cafés, bars and libraries supply Dutch-language freesheets with general entertainment information and display a weekly cinema listing. Such information is easy to follow even without an understanding of Dutch. The fortnightly English-language listings magazine *What's On*, f2.75, is available in hotels, restaurants and information offices.

Time

In spring and summer Amsterdam time is two hours ahead of Greenwich Mean Time (GMT); in the autumn and winter it's one hour ahead of GMT.

Climate

Amsterdam's climate is very changeable and often wet and windy. January and February are the coldest months, with icy winds whipping around the narrow streets from off the canals. It can be very humid in the summer, when mosquitoes thrive on the canals and in campsites. The average minimum and maximum daytime temperatures are: January-February 0.3°C to 4.6°C (32.5°F to 40.3°F); March-May 5.5°C to 12.1°C (41.9°F to 53.8°F); June-September 11.5°C to 19.4°C (52.7°F to 66.9°F); October-December 4.1°C to 10°C (39.4°F to 50°F). If you can speak Dutch there is a 24-hour recorded information weather line on *003*.

Public Holidays

Called *Nationale Feestdag* in Dutch, they are: **New Year's Day**; **Good Friday** 9 April 1993, 1 April 1994; **Easter Sunday** and **Monday** 11 and 12 April 1993, 3 and 4 April 1994; **30 April** (*Koninginnedag*, the former Queen Juliana's

Birthday, *see chapter* **Amsterdam By Season**); **Ascension Day** 20 May 1993, 12 May 1994; **Whit (Pentecost) Sunday** and **Monday** 30 and 31 May 1993, 22, 23 May 1994; **Christmas Day** and **the day after Christmas**.

Opening Times

For all our listings in this guide we give full opening times, but in general shops are open from 1pm to 6pm on Monday; 9am to 6pm on Tuesdays, Wednesdays and Fridays; 9am to 9pm on Thursdays; and 9am to 5pm on Saturdays. Smaller, specialist shops tend to open at varying times; if in doubt phone first. For shops that are open late *see chapter* **Early Hours**.

The city's bars open at various times during the day and close around 1am Monday to Thursday and at 2am on Fridays and Saturdays, reverting to 1am on Sundays. Restaurants are generally open for business in the evening from 5pm until 11pm (though some close as early as 9pm), and for seven days a week, although some close on Sunday and Monday.

Tipping

Although by law a service charge is included in hotel, taxi, bar, café and restaurant bills most Amsterdammers generally also round up the change to the nearest five guilders for large bills and to the nearest guilder for smaller ones, leaving the extra in small change rather than putting it on a credit card. In taxis the most common tip is around 10 per cent for short journeys. Because of the compulsory service charge, never feel obliged to leave a tip; use your discretion and do so only when the service warrants it. Taxi drivers we spoke to say the best tippers are American and British, and the worst, apparently, are the Dutch themselves.

Queuing

A ticketing system is widely used here which cuts out the need for the traditional 'queue'. From supermarket delicatessen counters and information bureaux to doctors' surgeries, you tear off a numbered ticket from a small machine on entry and then wait until your number is either called or appears on an electronic screen. This allows you to seek somewhere comfortable to wait; you can even wander off for a while, but beware, if you miss your turn it will take some persuasive arguments if you are to be served.

Any queues that you do come across, like those at tram stops, tend to be multinational, and so vary in character from tidy to non-existent, depending on who's in them.

Getting Around

Amsterdam has an efficient and cheap public transport system, as well as a large cycling population. We explain how to buy tickets, hail a taxi, hire a bike and avoid getting run down by a tram.

To and From the Airport

Schiphol Airport Rail Service

Schiphol Airport/Centraal Station (information 06 9292).
Times trains daily at 15-minute intervals 4am-midnight;
then hourly 12.45am, 1.45am, 2.45am, 3.45am. **Tickets**
single f5; f1 under-12s with adult; free under-4s; *return* f8;
f2 under-12s with adult; free under-4s. **No credit cards.**
The journey to Centraal Station takes about
20 minutes.

KLM Hotel Bus Service

Main exit Schiphol Airport (649 1393/5651). **Times**
buses at 30-minute intervals 6.30am-3pm, then one at
5pm daily. **Tickets** f15. **No credit cards.**
This service is available to anyone; you don't need to
have travelled on the airline or be staying at one of the
hotel stops. The route starts at Schiphol, then goes to
the Golden Tulip Barbizon (Leidseplein), Pulitzer
(Westermarkt-Keizersgracht), Krasnapolsky (Dam
Square), Holiday Inn and Sonesta (Nieuwe Zijds
Voorburgwal), Barbizon Palace (Zeedijk) and back to
Schiphol again.

Taxis

There are always plenty of taxis outside the main exit.
It's pricey, however: at the time of writing about f45
from the airport into central Amsterdam, and even more
at night. For details of car hire firms operating from
Schiphol Airport *see chapter* **Survival**. For more details
about Amsterdam's taxi service, *see below* **Taxis**.

Airline Information

For general airport enquiries ring Schiphol airport on *601 0966*. The major airlines can be
reached at the following addresses. Staff answering telephone enquiries will speak English.

British Airways

*Stadhouderskade 4, OS (601 5413). Tram 1, 2, 5, 6, 7,
10.* **Open** 8.30am-6pm Mon-Fri; 10am-2pm Sat. **Credit**
AmEx, DC, MC, V.

British Midland

*Ticket desk Schiphol Airport (604 1459/freephone
information 06 022 2426).* **Open** 6am-9.30pm Mon-
Fri; 6am-8.30pm Sat; 8am-9.30pm Sun. **Credit** AmEx,
DC, MC, V.

KLM

Museumplein, IS (474 7747). Tram 1, 2, 5, 6, 7, 10.
Open 8.30am-5.30pm Mon-Fri; 10am-2pm Sat. **Credit**
AmEx, DC, MC, V.

TWA

Singel 540, C (626 2277). Tram 4, 9, 14, 16, 24, 25.
Open 9am-5pm Mon-Fri. **Credit** AmEx, DC, MC, V.

City Transport

Getting around Amsterdam by public transport is
easy. The city has an efficient, reasonably priced
tram and bus system and, because of its compact
size, it's possible to cycle or walk to most places of
interest. Cycling is the method of transport preferred by many native Amsterdammers and, true
to the cliché, the streets are busy with bicycle traffic throughout the day. The canals are also well-used
by pleasure boats, commercial barges and water
taxis. If you are thinking of bringing a car to
Amsterdam for a short stay – don't! Trams, bikes
and buses jostle alarmingly at the larger junctions
and jams are common on the narrow one-way systems around the canals. Parking places are elusive
and expensive. However, public transport provision for those with disabilities is dire and, although
there are lifts at all Metro stations (apart from
Waterlooplein), the staff can't always help people
in wheelchairs. So if you can't do without a car *see
chapter* **Survival** for information on car hire, parking and what to do if the car breaks down. For
details of orientation and maps *see chapter*
Essential Information: Tourist Information.

Public Transport

For information, tickets, maps and an English-
language brochure explaining the city's ticket
system visit the **Municipal Transport
Authority** *(listed below)*. But if all you need is
information on Amsterdam's ticketing system
see below **Tickets**.

takes you to the heart of the city

Berlin
Amsterdam
London
Paris
New York

The insider's guides to the most cosmopolitan cities in the world

Penguin Books

GVB (Amsterdam Municipal Transport Authority)

Stationsplein 15, C (551 4911). Tram 1, 2, 4, 5, 9, 13, 16, 17, 24, 25. **Open** *7am-10.30pm Mon-Fri; 8am-10.30pm Sat.* **No credit cards.**
The GVB runs Amsterdam's Metro, bus and tram services.
Branches *GVB Head Office, Prins Hendrikkade 108, C.* **Open** *8.30am-4.30pm Mon-Fri.* **No credit cards.** *Amstel Railway Station, Julianaplein, OE.* **Open** *7am-8.30pm Mon-Fri; 10.15am-5pm Sat, Sun.* **No credit cards.**

Metro

The Metro (underground) system in Amsterdam uses the same ticketing system as trams and buses (*see below* **Tickets**), but it mainly serves the eastern, south-eastern and southern (the newest line) suburbs and so is mostly used by commuters. There are three lines, all terminating at Centraal Station. Trains run from 6am Mon-Fri (6.30am Sat, 7.30am Sun) to about 12.15am daily.

Trams and Buses

As a visitor to Amsterdam you will find buses and particularly trams a good way to get around the city centre. Tram services run from 6am Monday to Friday, 6.30am on Saturday and 7.30am on Sunday, with a special night bus service taking over after midnight. **Night buses** are numbered from 71 to 77, with numbers 73 to 76 running through the city centre. Night bus stops are indicated by a black square at the stop with the bus number printed on it. Buses run between 1am and 5.30am between Monday and Friday and 6.30am on Saturday and Sunday.

Yellow signs at tram and bus stops indicate the name of the stop and further destinations. There are usually maps of the entire network in the shelters and diagrams of routes on board the trams and buses. Amsterdam's bus and tram drivers are generally courteous and will happily give directions if asked. Like other Amsterdammers, most are sufficiently fluent to do this in English.

The yellow tram is as synonymous with Amsterdam as the red double-decker bus is with London. The vehicles make for fast and efficient travel, but other road-users be warned that they will stop only when absolutely necessary. Cyclists should listen out for the tram's warning bell and motorists should avoid blocking tramlines – cars are only allowed to venture on to them if they're turning right. It doesn't pay to argue with a tram. Those on bikes should also ensure to cross tramlines with the front wheel at an angle in order to avoid getting stuck. It's easily done and can result in a painful and undignified tumble. To get on or off a tram, press the yellow button adjacent to the doors

at the front, middle and rear of the vehicle, which will then open.

In buses there is only one door. There are three doors on trams, most of which serve as both exits and entries. If you want to buy a ticket enter by the door nearest the driver.

Tickets

Strip tickets (strippenkaart). In Amsterdam a strip ticket system operates on trams, buses and the Metro, which is initially confusing but ultimately good value for money. Prices range from f2.75 for a strip with two units to f10.25 for 15 units and f29 for 45 units. Foreign pensioners and the unemployed unfortunately aren't entitled to any reductions on ticket prices but children under four travel free and older children pay reduced fares for two-day tickets (*see below*). Tickets can be bought at GVB offices (*see page 9* **Public Transport**), post offices (*see chapter* **Survival**), at train stations and many tobacconists. The tickets must be stamped on board a tram or bus and on entering a Metro station. The city is divided into five zones: Noord (north), West, Centrum, Oost (east) and Zuid (south); most of central Amsterdam falls, not surprisingly, within zone Centrum.

For travel in a single zone, two units must be stamped, while one is stamped for two zones, four for three zones and so on. In trams you can stamp your own tickets in the yellow box-like machines at the back. Just fold it so the unit you need to stamp is at the end. On buses, drivers stamp the tickets and on the Metro there are stamping machines at the entrance to stations. An unlimited number of people can travel on one card, but the appropriate number of units must be stamped for each person. The stamps are valid for an hour, during which time you can transfer to other buses and trams without having to stamp your card again. If your journey were to take more than an hour you would have to stamp more units, but no single tram journey in central Amsterdam is likely to take more than an hour. There is no time limit on the use of a *strippenkaart*.

Day ticket (dagkaarten). A cheaper option for unlimited travel in Amsterdam, a day ticket costs f11, two days cost f13.60 and three days f16.80, with each additional day costing an extra f3.20. Only Dutch pensioners and the unwaged are eligible for cheaper travel, but for a child (aged 4 to 11) a two-day ticket costs f6.80 and three days f8.40, with each additional day costing a further f1.60. Child day-tickets are not valid on night buses. A day ticket is valid on trams, buses and Metro on the day it is stamped and throughout that night. Only the one-day ticket and the less economical hourly ticket can be bought on board trams and buses from their drivers. The hourly ticket is valid in all five zones for one hour and costs f4.25 for everybody.

Season tickets (sterabonnement). These can be bought from GVB offices and are valid for a week, a month or a year. A weekly pass for zone Centrum costs f13.50, a monthly one f46 and a yearly one f460. Children between the ages of 4 and 11 can get the all passes at half price. You will need a photograph and passport.

Beware of travelling on a bus or tram without a ticket. Uniformed inspectors make regular checks and those without a valid ticket – or an exceptionally good excuse – are liable to be fined f100 on the spot. Foreign visitors professing ignorance of the rules rarely escape penalty.

Taxis

Generally Amsterdam's taxi drivers are an informed and friendly lot though, as in every city, there is the odd rogue. Always check the meter is blank (aside from the minimum charge) and ask the driver for an estimate of how much the journey will cost before setting out. Even short journeys are expensive, working out at f2.60 per kilometre between 6am and midnight and rising to f3.25 per kilometre at night and, particularly on the narrow streets around the main canals, you may get stuck behind an unloading lorry and end up paying a fortune for the privilege. If you feel you have been ripped off, ask for a receipt, which you are legally entitled to see before handing over any money. If the charge is extortionate, refer it to the central taxi office (*677 7777*), or the police. We stress that such rip-offs are rare – taxi drivers have too much to lose if they are caught.

You cannot hail a taxi in the street, but there are ranks dotted around the city. Places you are likely to find a taxi waiting in a rank include Centraal Station (C); next to the bus station at the junction of Kinkerstraat and Marnixstraat (OW);

Rembrandtsplein (IS); and Leidseplein (IS). You generally can't book a cab in advance, but if you call Amsterdam's 24-hour central taxi control on *677 7777* a taxi will arrive almost immediately. The line is busy on Friday and Saturday nights, but there's a telephone queuing system.

Taxis can only take **wheelchairs** if they are folded. If you need to travel in a wheelchair, phone the car transport service for wheelchair users on *613 4134*. The office is generally open between 9am and 6pm, Monday to Friday, although office hours are casual and you might well find someone there outside these times. You need to book one or two days in advance and it costs around f2.80 per kilometre.

Water Taxis

It would be rather extravagant to use this service as a regular taxi – most Amsterdammers use water taxis for special occasions only. However, it is possible to hire out a taxi, with guides, food and drink provided by the company at extra charge, and use it for your own personal canal tour or mobile party. The boats are modern and well-maintained, with both covered and on-deck seating.

For details of canal tours *see chapter* **Sightseeing**.

Water Taxi Centrale

Stationsplein 8, C (622 2181). Tram 1, 2, 4, 5, 9, 13, 16, 17, 24, 25. **Open** 9am-1am daily. **Cost** *8-person boat* f90 for first half hour, then f2 per minute; *16-person boat* f135 for first half hour, then f3 a minute; *35-person boat* f195 for first half hour, then f300 per hour. **Credit** AmEx, DC, MC, TC, V.
Advance booking is advisable as the service is usually busy, particularly in high season. Water taxis can be hailed as they're sailing along a canal – but it's unlikely they'll be free.

Canal Buses

Canal Bus

Nieuwekeizersgracht 8, IE (623 9886). Tram 9, 14. **Open** 9am-5pm Mon-Fri. **Cost** *day ticket* f12.50; f8 under-12s; *two-day ticket* f20; f17.50 under-12s. **No credit cards**.
The 52-seater canal buses are the latest addition to Amsterdam's water transport system. They offer a regular service through the canals from the Rijksmuseum to Centraal Station, stopping at Leidseplein, Leidsestraat/Keizersgracht and Westerkerk/Anne Frankhuis. The service operates every day between 10am and 8pm at 30-minute intervals.

Cycling

Cycling is widely considered the most pleasant, convenient – and Dutch – means of transport around the city. There are bike lanes everywhere, clearly marked with blue circles. At first, cycling on Amsterdam's busy roads may appear a hazardous exercise, but motorists are well-used to the abundance of cyclists and collisions are

Rent a bike, and get around the city the way the Amsterdammers do.

rare. Remember, however, that cycling two abreast is illegal, as is going without reflector bands on both front and back wheels. Never leave your bike unlocked, as there's a thriving trade in stolen bikes. Be sure to use a sturdy lock; some thieves are equipped with powerful cutters which will make short work of thin chains. The police are clamping down hard on bike theft because of its traditional association with raising a fast buck for junkies. If someone in the street offers you a bike for sale ('fiets te koop') don't be tempted: it's almost certainly stolen. There's no shortage of bike hire firms where a good vehicle can be hired for about f10 a day. Below we list three reputable companies; others can be found in the Amsterdam *Yellow Pages* (*Gouden Gids*) under 'Fietsen en Bromfietsen Verhuur' (Bikes and Motorbikes for Hire).

The Bulldog
Oudezijds Voorburgwal 126, C (624 8248). Tram 4, 9, 14, 16, 24, 25. **Open** *May-Sept* 10am-6.30pm daily. **Cost** f10 per day plus f200 deposit and passport. **No credit cards.** *See also chapter* **Cafés & Bars.**

Rent-A-Bike
Pieter Jacobsdwarsstraat 17, C (625 5029). Tram 4, 9, 14, 16, 24, 25. **Open** 9am-6pm daily. **Cost** f12.50 per day plus f50 deposit and passport, or credit card imprint. **Credit** AmEx, DC, MC, TC, V.

Take-A-Bike
Centraal Station, Stationsplein 6, C (624 8391). Tram 1, 2, 4, 5, 9, 13, 16, 17, 24, 25. **Open** 6am-10pm daily. **Cost** f7.50 per day (8am-10pm) plus f200 deposit. **No credit cards.**

Trains

From Centraal Station, one of the biggest stations in Europe, you can get direct trains to many major cities across the continent. But be warned, you must obtain a reservation for international trains and the reservations office gets very crowded during the summer season. Tickets can be reserved over the phone but you must do this seven days in advance. For more information on rail travel *see chapter* **Trips Out of Town.** The ornate station is one of Amsterdam's most imposing structures and gives a bustling first impression of the city. All conceivable needs of the newly-arrived visitor are catered for here, from shower facilities and restaurants inside the station to hotel, travel and entertainment booking services on the Stationsplein just outside. As most of the city's bus and tram services begin and end at the station it is also an ideal starting point for trips around the city. A year-round entourage of flower stalls, street entertainers and hippy buskers singing *Hey Joe* in front of the main entrance adds to its character, though beware of pickpockets and rip-offs.

Centraal Station Information Desk
Stationsplein 13, C (information 069292). Tram 1, 2, 4, 5, 9, 13, 16, 17, 24, 25. **Open** *information desk* 5.15am-10pm Mon-Fri; 9am-8pm Sat, Sun; *reservations office* 8am-8pm Mon-Fri; 9am-5pm Sat, Sun. **Credit** MC, V.

Sightseeing

A tour of the city's unmissable sights and hidden charms, on foot, by bicycle, boat or helicopter.

Amsterdam is small enough to make sightseeing a pleasure rather than an endurance test. The major sights are easily accessible from the city centre, and many pleasant hours can be spent meandering from one to another, following a canal or stopping off in one of the numerous bars. Trying to adhere to a strict itinerary is inadvisable; the city's main asset is its spontaneous, relaxed atmosphere.

Entertainment is everywhere in Amsterdam, not only in the cinemas, clubs and theatres, but most of all on the streets. Tourist spots such as **Leidseplein** and the **Dam** (*both listed under* **Focal Points**) attract every kind of street performer, day and night, throughout the year; but buskers seem to play in every park and lurk on every street corner.

Amsterdam is breathtaking by night. Many of the magnificent canalside buildings and most of the bridges are illuminated and the city is still alive and kicking at two in the morning (most bars close around two at the weekend, clubs usually later). Compared to other major cities, the streets are reasonably safe, provided you take sensible precautions (*see chapter* **Survival: Police and Security**).

Our Sightseeing chapter should be used as a quick reference to Amsterdam's major sights (and some of the less familiar ones as well). Most of the places listed below appear elsewhere in the Guide in greater detail; and the subjects covered (Amsterdam's history, its sights, transport and culture) are dealt with in depth in other chapters.

Focal Points

Like all cities, Amsterdam has several well-known areas where tourists tend to congregate. These have an international flavour – billboards, busking and pavement cafés – so don't expect to find the 'real' Amsterdam there.

Dam
C. Tram 1, 2, 4, 5, 9, 16, 24, 25.
Although tourists tend to cluster here, this square is one of the least atmospheric parts of the city, with few cafés and no worthwhile nightlife. Nevertheless, there are a number of important landmarks on and around it. The west side is flanked by the **Royal Palace** (*see p17* **Heritage**) and the **Nieuwe Kerk** (*see p20* **Churches and Viewpoints**); in the middle of the eastern side is

the **National Monument** (*see also chapter* **World War II**). This 22m (72ft) obelisk is dedicated to the Dutch servicemen who died in World War II. Designed by JJP Oud, with sculptures by John Rädecker, it incorporates 12 urns: 11 filled with earth collected from the then 11 Dutch provinces, the 12th with soil from war cemeteries in Indonesia, which was a Dutch colony until 1945.

Leidseplein
IS. Tram 1, 2, 5, 6, 7, 10.
The area around Leidseplein probably has more cinemas, theatres, nightclubs and restaurants than any other part of the city. Several cafés border the square, dominating the pavements during the summer. You can also take a drink on the terrace of the American Hotel (*see chapter* **Restaurants**), a prominent feature on the south of the square. Leidseplein itself is a stage for every kind of performer. During the summer, fire-eaters, jugglers, acrobats, singers and small-time con-artists fill the square (watch out for pickpockets). In the winter, part of the Leidseplein is transformed into an open-air ice-skating rink (*see chapter* **Sport & Fitness**). The rapid development of the Leidseplein over the last few years and the invasion of 'McDonalds culture' (there's a branch of the burger chain here) has not been unreservedly welcomed by all of the locals, who feel the essential Dutch flavour of the district is being destroyed for a fast buck. Just off the square is the Adamant, a white pyramid-shaped sculpture given to Amsterdam by the city's diamond industry in 1986 to commemorate 400 years of the trade. Designed by Jacob van Saanten at a cost of f75,000, it uses light to create a rainbow hologram.

Red Light District
C. Tram 4, 9, 16, 24, 25.
The lure of Amsterdam's red light district, known colloquially as *de walletjes* because it's the area within the old city walls, proves irresistible to most visitors. Sex for money is on offer in and around one of Amsterdam's oldest streets, Warmoesstraat. Obviously the area attracts more than its fair share of crime, but if you stay away from Zeedijk, the red light district is safe enough. The prostitutes are mainly concentrated along Oudezijds Voorburgwal, Oudezijds Achterburgwal and the small interconnecting alleyways. They take up their shop window positions at about 10am and are still there well into the small hours. While this area is the main tourist attraction, there are smaller red light districts in two other parts of town: along Spuistraat (between Centraal Station and Raadhuistraat) and Singel by the Sonesta Hotel, and along Ruysdaelkade between Ferdinand Bolstraat and Ceintuurbaan. *See also chapter* **Amsterdam by Area**.

Rembrandtplein
IS. Tram 4, 9, 14.
The gloriously tacky Rembrandtplein only comes alive at night. Offerings range from the faded fake elegance of traditional strip-tease parlours to seedy peepshow joints and nondescript cafés and restaurants. Nevertheless, there are a few exceptions to this exuberant display of trash (including the fantastic art deco Café Schiller, *see chapter* **Cafés & Bars**, and Tuschinski

Cinema, *see chapter* **Film**). Just round the corner on the Amstel is a stretch of gay cafés (*see chapter* **Gay Amsterdam**).

Waterlooplein
C. Tram 9, 14/Metro Waterlooplein.
This up-and-coming district is dominated by the ultra-modern **Stadhuis-Muziektheater** (*see p19 under* **Cultural Centres**). It opened in 1985 amid great controversy; protesters were furious that it had been sited on what had for centuries been an important open space (*see chapter* **Post-war**). Also here is the Waterlooplein Flea Market (*see below* **Markets** and *chapter* **Shopping**) and Rembrandthuis (*see chapter* **Museums**).

Heritage

Anne Frankhuis (Anne Frank House)
Prinsengracht 263, IW (626 4533). Tram 13, 14, 17.
Open *Sept-May* 9am-5pm Mon-Sat; 10am-5pm Sun, public holidays; *June-Aug* 9am-7pm Mon-Sat; 10am-7pm Sun, public holidays. **Admission** f7; f3.50 10-17s, over-65s, CJP card holders; free under-10s; group discount. **No credit cards**.
Every tourist to Amsterdam should visit this seventeenth-century canalside house where the young Jewish girl Anne Frank spent over two years in hiding during World War II. It is not a cosy re-creation of a family home; the Nazis destroyed the furniture and the interior has been left bare, although you can still see the diary and the bookcase which concealed the entrance to the annexe where the family hid. The Anne Frank Foundation was founded in 1957 to safeguard the house and combat fascism, racism and anti-Semitism. Regular exhibitions are held, but visit early to avoid the crowds. *See also chapter* **World War II** and *chapter* **Museums**.

Begijnhof
Spui, C. Tram 1, 2, 5.
A quiet backwater hidden behind a doorway just off Amsterdam's noisy main shopping area, the Begijnhof is a group of houses built around a secluded courtyard and garden. It was established in the fourteenth century to provide modest homes for the Begijntjes, a religious sisterhood of unmarried women of good families who, although not nuns, lived together in a close community and often took vows of chastity. They did many charitable works, especially in education and nursing. The last sister died in 1974. Most of the neat little houses were 'modernised' in the seventeenth and eighteenth centuries. In the centre of the courtyard stands the English Reformed Church (Engelsekerk), built in about 1400 and a principal place of worship for Amsterdam's English community (*see chapter* **Music: Classical & Opera** and *chapter* **Survival**). The pulpit panels were designed by Mondrian. You can also see a Catholic church, secretly converted from two houses in 1665, following the banning of the Roman Catholic faith after the Reformation. The wooden house at number 34 is dated 1475 and is the oldest house standing in the city. This is the best known of the city's numerous hofjes; for details of others *see p28* **Hofjes**.

Munttoren (Mint Tower)
Muntplein, C. Tram 4, 9, 14, 16, 24, 25.
On Singel between the floating flower market (*see below* **Markets**) and the start of Kalverstraat (the pedestrianised shopping street), this medieval tower was the western corner of the Regulierspoort, a gate in the city walls in the 1480s. In 1620 a spire was added by Hendrik de Keyser, the foremost architect of the period. Its called the 'mint tower' because the city authorities used it to mint coins for a short period in 1672 when Amsterdam was cut off from its money supply during a war with England, Munster and France. There's a shop on the

ground floor selling fine Dutch porcelain, but the rest of the tower is closed to visitors. The Munttoren is prettiest at night, when it's floodlit; although day-time visitors may be able to hear its carillon, which often plays for 15 minutes at noon (*see chapter* **Music: Classical & Opera/Carillons**).

Koninklijk Paleis (Royal Palace)

Dam, C (624 8698 ext 217). Tram 1, 2, 4, 9, 13, 14, 16, 17, 24, 25. **Open** *June-Sept* 12.30-5pm daily.

The Royal Palace was designed by Jacob van Campens in the seventeenth century along classical lines and was originally intended to be the city hall. The exterior is not particularly impressive for a building of its stature and betrays its municipal origins. Inside it's a different story, with chimney pieces painted by artists such as Ferdinand Bol and Govert Flinck, both pupils of Rembrandt. The city hall was transformed into a royal palace in 1808 after Napoleon made his brother, Louis, King of the Netherlands (*see chapter* **Decline & Fall**). A fine collection of furniture from this period can be seen on a guided tour of the building. The Palace is still used occasionally by the present royal family.

Guided tours June-Sept, 1.30pm Wed (f5, f3 students, over-65s, f1.50 under-12s); group tours (min 10 people) can also be arranged Oct-May, phone for details.

Schreierstoren (Weeping Tower)

Prins Hendrikkade, C. Tram 1, 2, 4, 5, 9, 13, 16, 17, 24, 25.

The most interesting relic of Amsterdam's medieval city wall is the Weeping Tower. Legend relates that the wives of sailors leaving on trade expeditions stood here and waved tearful farewells to their men. Of course, the Dutch have a more pragmatic explanation: *schreier* can also mean 'saddle' and the tower does indeed straddle two canals. Dating from 1487, it was successfully restored in 1966 and its most interesting feature is its gablestone.

In 1927, a bronze memorial plaque was added by the Greenwich Village Historical Society of New York: its English text states that it was from this point on 4 April 1609 that Henry Hudson departed in search of shorter trade routes to the Far East. He ended up colonising a small island in the mouth of a river in North America. The river was later named after him and the colony was called New Amsterdam; only to have its name changed by the English to New York. And there's another, less grandiose, American connection. In 1956 some stones from the Schreierstoren were taken to Chicago and placed into the wall of the *Chicago Tribune* building alongside similar chunks from famous buildings from around the world, including Athens's Parthenon, Paris's Notre Dame cathedral and the Great Wall of China. Visitors are not allowed inside the Schreierstoren.

Beurs van Berlage (Berlage Stock Exchange)

Damrak 277, C (626 5257/fax 620 4701). Tram 4, 9, 16, 24, 25. **Open** *office and enquiries* 9am-5pm Mon-Fri.

Designed in 1896 by Hendrik Petrus Berlage as the city's stock exchange, the Beurs represents an important break with nineteenth-century architecture and prepared the way for the modern lines of the Amsterdam School (*see chapter* **Between the Occupations**). No longer used as a stock exchange, the building has been sensitively converted into a conference and exhibition centre, and two concert halls, with a café and restaurant. Tours can be arranged by Archivise, *see p27*.

Den Waag (Weigh House)

Nieuwmarkt, C. Tram 9, 14/Metro Nieuwmarkt.

The Waag, previously called St Antoniespoort, stands in the centre of the Nieuwmarkt and dates from 1488, when it was built as a gatehouse for the city defences. It's an odd, squat building with turrets protruding from unlikely places. Over the years it has housed various institutions: in 1617 the ground floor was a public weigh house while the first floor held the trade guilds of smiths, bricklayers, painters and surgeons. The surgeons' annual anatomy lectures were the inspiration of Rembrandt's 1656 painting, *The Anatomy Lecture of Dr Jan Deyman*, which hung here from 1691 until it was damaged by fire in 1723. It now hangs in the Rijksmuseum (*see p19* **Cultural Centres**). After 1819, the building was no longer used as a weigh house and has since been put to a variety of uses – it was the Jewish Historical Museum from 1932 to 1986. After ambitious plans to convert it into a cultural centre fell through it has fallen into disuse and remains boarded up at the time of writing.

Attractions

Artis Zoo

Plantage Kerklaan 40, IE (623 1836). Tram 7, 9, 14. **Open** *Apr-Oct* 9am-6pm, *Nov-Mar* 9am-5pm, daily; last Planetarium show 4pm; *children's farm* 9am-5pm, daily. **Admission** *zoo, children's farm, Planetarium and Zoological Museum* f19; f11 under-10s; group discount (min 20 people). **No credit cards.**

Amsterdam Zoo – or Natura Artis Magistra ('nature is the master of the arts'), as it is formally called – was established in 1838, making it the oldest zoo in The Netherlands. It's home to over 6,000 animals. Though popular, it is never too crowded to prevent enjoyment of the beautifully laid out gardens and broad range of exhibits. The liberal use of perspex allows generally unrestricted views, and the aquarium, one of the zoo's best features, boasts over 2,000 fish and a wide variety of species. Don't miss the seals being fed at 11.30am and 3.45pm; or the penguins at 3.30pm. Also recommended

The **Gassan Diamond House**: *one of the many diamond polishing factories in Amsterdam.*

are the reptile house, the luxuriant tropical greenhouse, the young animals' section, the children's farm (*see chapter* **Children & Parents**) and the spectacular planetarium (with Dutch commentary, but an English-language summary is available). Unfortunately, a few of the enclosures, particularly for the big cats, rhinos and hippos, appear cramped. The guidebook is in Dutch.
Café and restaurant. Guided tours by prior arrangement (free). Schools' educational programme. Shop. Wheelchair access and toilets for the disabled.

Diamond workshops

Coster Diamonds *Paulus Potterstraat 2-6, OS (676 2222). Tram 2, 3, 5, 12.* **Open** 9am-5pm daily. **Tours** throughout the day on request, free, duration approx 20 mins.
Gassan Diamond House *Nieuwe Uilenburgerstraat 173-175, C (622 5333). Tram 9, 14/Metro Nieuwmarkt.* **Open** 9am-5pm daily. **Tours** throughout the day on request, free, duration 45 mins-1 hour, free soft drink at end of tour.
Holshuysen-Stoeltie *Wagenstraat 13-17, C (623 7601). Tram 9, 14.* **Open** 8.30am-5pm daily. **Tours** throughout the day on request, free, duration 30 mins-1 hour, free soft drink at end of tour.
Van Moppes & Zoon *Albert Cuypstraat 2-6, OS (676 1242). Tram 16, 24, 25.* **Open** 8.30am-5pm daily. **Tours** throughout the day on request, free, duration approx 30 mins.
Amsterdam has a fascinating association with diamonds dating back to the sixteenth century (*see chapter* **Between the Occupations**). The largest diamond ever found, the Cullinan, and the world-famous Koh-I-Noor, part of the British Crown Jewels, were cut by Amsterdam workers. The smallest 'brilliant cut' diamond (a brilliant cut has 57 facets) was also cut here, a tiny sliver of sparkle – just 0.0012-carat. There are about 24 diamond polishing factories in Amsterdam, and the four bigger ones listed above welcome visitors.

All offer similar tours, lasting from around 20 minutes to an hour. The guides provide a brief history of the diamond industry and Amsterdam's strategic importance in it. You'll probably be shown a worker polishing or setting a diamond, but the real thrill (only offered to those in large groups) is when the guide nonchalantly pours diamonds from a black velvet bag onto a table for your inspection. **Gassan Diamond House**, built in 1879 as a diamond factory, offers one of the more enjoyable tours. There's not much to choose between the others, but be prepared for an unenthusiastic commentary and a very brisk walk around to the sales room if you're not part of a group. Tours can be given in any European language.

Heineken Brewery

Stadhouderskade 78, IS (523 9239). Tram 6, 7, 10, 16, 24, 25.
Beer production here was stopped at the beginning of 1988 amid some outcry – after all, Heineken is virtually the national drink. But the company remained public-spirited and now runs tours round the old brewery (phone for details). The fee is f2, which goes to charity, and snacks and beer are served at the end. No bookings are taken and participants must be over 18 years old.

Madame Tussauds Scenerama

Dam 20, C (622 9239). Tram 4, 9, 14, 16, 24, 25. **Open** 10am-5.30pm daily. **Admission** f17; f11 under-15s, over-65s. **No credit cards**.
The show is housed in the top two floors of the Peek & Cloppenburg department store at the Dam. Replacing the Kalverstraat site, it is Tussauds' only branch outside the UK. An express lift whisks visitors from ground level to be greeted by Amsterdam Man, a five metre figure clothed in windmills, buccaneers, tulips and all those clichés. Visitors walk through a series of elaborate, climatically controlled scenes, many with impressive animatronic scenarios. The emphasis is very much on the

Golden Age of commerce and empire. Merchants and peasants, artists and kings are all depicted. But modern Amsterdam is confined to models of the royal family, a few local celebs and a designer punk.

Cultural Centres

Amsterdams Historisch Museum

Kalverstraat 92, C (523 1822). Tram 1, 2, 4, 5, 9, 14, 16, 24, 25. **Open** 11am-5pm daily. **Admission** f5; f2.50 under-16s; f12.50 family ticket (2 adults, 2 children); free with Museum Card; group discount (min 20 people). **No credit cards.**

The city's elegant historical museum is a wonderful cluster of buildings and courtyards, located on the site of St Lucy's Convent (which was built in 1414). The Museum used to house an orphanage and is one of the most underrated attractions of the city centre. Exhibits are well displayed but not interactive. *See also chapter* **Museums**. *Restaurant.*

Concertgebouw

Concertgebouwplein 2-6, OS (ticket reservations 10am-7pm daily 671 8345/recorded information in Dutch 675 4411). Tram 3, 5, 12, 16. **Open** box office 10am-7pm Mon-Sat; 40 mins before performance for ticket sales and collection. **Tickets** f30-f175; reductions for CJP card holders. **Performances** 8.15pm. **Credit** AmEx, DC, MC.

Amsterdam's venerable Concertgebouw, known as one of the world's three most acoustically perfect concert halls (the others are in Boston and Vienna), was actually outside the city limits when it opened in April 1888. For the event, the 422 horse-drawn carriages bearing the city's élite to the first concert were lined up from Museumplein to the Amstel River. A century later, the hall celebrated its centenary with a face-lift that involved replacing the 100 year-old wooden piles with concrete ones, and the addition of a controversial glass side wing – the performers never missed a beat. Currently about 500 performances a year are given for some half million visitors. *See also chapter* **Music: Classical & Opera**. *Wheelchair access by arrangement.*

Rijksmuseum

Stadhouderskade 42, OS (673 2121). Tram 2, 5, 6, 7, 10/Bus 63, 170. **Open** 10am-5pm Tue-Sat; 1-5pm Sun, public holidays. **Admission** f10; f5 under-18s, CJP card holders, over-65s; free with Museum Card; group discounts (min 20 people). **No credit cards.**

The Dutch national museum is an imposing sight on the otherwise boring Stadhouderskade. It's one of The Netherlands' most prestigious museums and houses a rich collection of paintings by the seventeenth-century greats, such as Rembrandt, Vermeer and Frans Hals. Opened in 1885, the museum building came in for a lot of criticism. People felt it was too French, that it should not have been situated outside the city centre (it was well outside the municipal boundaries at that time) and that it looked too much like Centraal Station or a Gothic church in style. This is not really surprising as architect Paul Cuypers also designed Centraal Station and many churches. As well as paintings, the Rijksmuseum contains thousands of examples of other arts and crafts, including sculptures, gold and silverware, glass, ivory and pottery artefacts, and Delft-ware. There are also changing exhibitions in the Print Room and a huge collection of treasures in the **Museum of Asiatic Art**, which is housed in the same building. Holding approximately seven million works of art, the Rijksmuseum should be visited in palatable time spans rather than in one exhausting day. *See also chapter* **Museums**.

Stadhuis-Muziektheater

Waterlooplein 22, C (625 5455). Tram 9, 14/Metro Waterlooplein. **Open** *box office* 10am-8pm Mon-Sat; 11.30am-8pm Sun. **Tickets** *opera* f17.50-f100; *ballet* f20-f45; reductions for CJP card holders, over-65s. **Performances** *opera* 8pm; *ballet* 8.15pm. **Credit** AmEx, CB, DC, MC.

Dominating the Waterlooplein, the modern Music Hall/City Hall complex is home of the **Netherlands Opera** (*see chapter* **Music: Classical & Opera**) and **Dutch National Ballet** (*see chapter* **Dance**). Designed by Wilhelm Holtzbauer and Cees Dam and opened in 1985, it occupies 30,000 sq m (35,900 sq ft) and cost f300 million to construct. The project has had a troubled history ever since it was first mooted in the twenties, although it was not until 1954 that the City Council selected Waterlooplein as the site and 1979 before the decision was made to combine the civic headquarters with an opera house. The decision was a controversial one – as was the design itself. Indeed, one of Holland's top composers called the proposed building 'a monument of deceit, mediocrity and lack of taste – a European scandal'. Amsterdammers showed their discontent by organising demonstrations and continued to protest during construction (*see chapter* **Postwar: Stopera!**). Finally, in 1982, a riot caused a million guilders' worth of damage to construction equipment. In the passage between the City Hall and the Muziektheater there is a display of geological information, the Amsterdam Ordnance Project. This includes a device showing the NAP (normal Amsterdam water level, *see chapter* **The Golden Age**) and a cross-section of The Netherlands showing its geological structure.

Stedelijk Museum

Paulus Potterstraat 13, OS (573 2911/Dutch recorded information 573 2737). Tram 2, 3, 5, 12, 16. **Open** 11am-5pm daily; 11am-4pm public holidays.

The **Rijksmuseum**.

Once a convent, the elegant **Historisch Museum** *occupies a cluster of buildings and courtyards. See* **review** *page 19.*

Admission f7.50; f3.75 under-17s, CJP card holders; free with Museum Card, under-7s. **No credit cards**. The most lively of the trio of mighty institutions – the others are the Rijksmuseum (*see above*) and the Van Gogh Museum (*see below*) – that dominate Museumplein. A refreshingly light and airy building, it holds art from 1850 to the modern day and includes photographs, video arts, industrial design and posters. Most significant is its collection of the modern art classics by painters such as Cézanne, Chagall, Manet, Matisse, Mondrian, Monet and Picasso. Unfortunately, the Museum doesn't have the space to keep all of these on permanent display. Worth a mention is the excellent café and its courtyard terrace. *See also chapter* **Museums**.

Van Gogh Museum

Paulus Potterstraat 7, OS (570 5200). Tram 2, 3, 5, 12, 16. **Open** 10am-5pm Mon-Sat; 1-5pm Sun, public holidays. **Admission** f10; f5 under-18s; f3.50 with Museum Card; free CJP card holders; group discounts (min 20 people). **No credit cards**.
The Van Gogh Museum opened in 1973 to provide a permanent home for over 700 letters, 200 paintings and 500 drawings by Van Gogh, including *Sunflowers* and several self-portraits. Also on display are works by contemporaries such as Gauguin and Toulouse-Lautrec. In 1990 the Dutch flung themselves into celebrating the centenary of Van Gogh's death with great vigour and everything from Van Gogh wine to Van Gogh potatoes were sold, while a whole Van Gogh village appeared on Museumplein. All of which would have been very gratifying to the great man himself, who suffered agonies of self-doubt and sold just one painting during his lifetime. *See also chapter* **Museums**.

Churches and Viewpoints

Lutheran Church

Kattengat, C (information 621 2223). Tram 1, 2, 4, 5, 9, 13, 16, 17, 24, 25. **Concerts** *classical* 11am Sun; *jazz* 3pm one Sun per month (Sept-Mar). **Admission** f8; f6 under-12s, CJP card holders. **No credit cards**.
Extensive restoration of this seventeenth-century church was completed in the mid-seventies, financed by the national monuments committee, the city of Amsterdam and the hotel, of which it is now part. Since then the outer stairways, fencing and façade have all been restored or replaced in the original style. Its gloriously grand interior is perfect for today's use as a banqueting hall, conference venue and concert hall; original marble tombstones lie beneath the carpet. The church was deconsecrated in 1935 because of a dwindling congregation. The copper dome was replaced in 1950. The organ, still in use, was built in 1830 by the Batz brothers of Utrecht and has recently been restored; the Sunday morning coffee concerts are an inexpensive treat.

Nieuwe Kerk

Dam, C (Nieuwe Kerk foundation 626 8168). Tram 1, 2, 4, 5, 9, 13, 14, 16, 17, 24, 25. **Open** 11am-5pm daily. **Admission** free.
While the Oude Kerk (*p21*) was built in 1306, the Nieuwe Kerk dates from 1408. It is not known how much

damage was caused by the great fires of 1421 and 1452, or how much rebuilding took place, but most of the pillars and walls were erected after that period. Iconoclasm in 1566 left the church intact, although statues and altars were removed in the Reformation (*see chapter* **War & Reformation**). In 1645 the church was completely gutted by fire; the ornately carved oak pulpit and great organ are thought to have been constructed shortly after this. Of interest is the tomb of naval hero Admiral de Ruyter who died in 1676. Behind his black marble tomb is a white marble relief depicting the sea battle in which he died. Poets Pieter Cornelisz Hooft and Joost van den Vondel are also buried here. The Nieuwe Kerk is no longer used as a place of worship, but for exhibitions, organ recitals and state occasions, such as the crowning of Queen Beatrix in 1980.

Oude Kerk

Oudekerksplein 23, C (625 8284/624 9183). Tram 4, 9, 16, 24, 25. **Open** *Mar-Oct* 11am-5pm daily; *Nov-Feb* 1-5pm Fri-Sun. **Admission** f3; f2 students, over-65s. **No credit cards.**
Originally built in 1306 as a wooden chapel and constantly renovated and extended between 1330 and 1571, this is Amsterdam's oldest and most interesting church. All furnishings were removed during the Reformation, but the church retains a wooden roof painted in the fifteenth century with figurative images, a Gothic and Renaissance façade above the northern portal, and stained glass windows, parts of which date from the sixteenth and seventeenth centuries. The church is also noted for its carillon and large organ built in 1738-42, which is still in use; *see chapter* **Music: Classical & Opera.** Rembrandt's wife Saskia, who died in 1642, is buried under the small organ.

Westerkerk

Prinsengracht 281, IW (624 7766). Tram 13, 14, 17. **Open** *church* 10am-4pm Mon-Sat; *tower June-Sept* 2-5pm Mon, Thur, Sat. **Admission** *tower* f3. **No credit cards.**
The neo-classical Westerkerk was built at the beginning of the seventeenth century by Hendrik de Keyser and its 83m (273ft) tower, topped with a somewhat gaudy gold, blue and red crown, dominates the city skyline. The story goes that in about 1500, Maximilian, the Holy Roman emperor, granted the city the right to include this crown on the city arms as a sop to local merchants who had lent him money. An impressive exterior belies a rather featureless interior. Points of interest include Tuscan pillars and an organ built in 1680 by Duyschot with shutters painted by Gerard de Lairesse. It's worth climbing to the top of the tower for the superb view of Amsterdam – and while you recover from the exertion, ponder the fate of one of Amsterdam's most famous sons, Rembrandt van Rijn: it is thought that the painter is buried somewhere in the graveyard here, although no-one knows for certain which grave is his. Rembrandt died a pauper, and though his burial on 8 October 1669

Collapsing Houses

While it is the sea that has been responsible for Amsterdam's development and prosperity, it has also been the city's greatest adversary. Most of Amsterdam is below sea level, making building extremely difficult. Although a system of dikes now protects the whole of the western Netherlands, the water which regularly flooded the Amsterdam area for hundreds of years has left a soft peat layer, preventing usual building methods. The visible evidence of this underground problem is the number of buildings that noticeably lean from the vertical.

During the Middle Ages, houses were made of wood to keep their weight to a minimum and prevent subsidence. After a number of huge fires had reduced parts of the city to ashes, wooden houses were banned in 1669. The use of brick and stone in buildings meant that foundations had to be laid on wooden pilings, which were driven about 11 metres (36 feet) into the ground so they rested on a sturdy layer of sand – quite an achievement when done by hand. An incredible number of pilings were needed: the **Royal Palace** on the Dam (*see page 17* **Heritage**), for example, was built on 13,659 pilings. Amsterdam's buildings are still constructed on pilings, although since World War II concrete has replaced wood, and the pilings are now sunk as deep as 60 metres (195 feet).

Despite the pilings, you won't have to walk far in Amsterdam before you encounter your first collapsing house. Windows have been re-cut to fit into crushed frames; while inside, floors slope, table legs are propped up by slabs of paper and furniture trundles from wall to wall. Any dip in the water table exposes the piles to the atmosphere. Wooden ones start to rot and subsidence sets in.

Solutions to the problem vary. Many grand old houses suffer from little more than an elegant list, and since they have inclined in this way for hundreds of years seem to need no special attention. Others, particularly in less wealthy areas, are propped up or bound together with steel brackets and timbers. Eventually they will have to be restored or rebuilt.

Some of the decrepit buildings may be amusing, but they are inhabited – which illustrates the housing shortage that has been an expensive headache for Amsterdam Council for years.

*Follow the cartoon trail at the **Hortus Botanicus**, one of the oldest gardens in The Netherlands. See **review**.*

was recorded in the church register, the actual spot was not specified. There's a good chance that he shares a grave with his son, Titus, who died a year earlier. Inside the church is a monument to the painter.

Parks and Gardens

Although the local council claims there are 28 parks in Amsterdam, the city really only has a few green spaces worth visiting: **Amster-damse Bos**, **Beatrixpark**, **Hortus Botanicus** (Botanical Gardens), **Vondelpark** and **Amstel-park**. The rest are either small scraps of grass – for a very short period in the spring these are transformed into sheets of colour by beautiful displays of tulips and crocuses – or found in uninteresting residential neighbourhoods. For gardens outside Amsterdam, *see chapter* **Excursions in Holland**. Admission to all the parks listed below is free.

Amstelpark

OS. Bus 8, 48, 49, 60, 158, 173. **Open** dawn-dusk daily. Created for Floriade 1972, a garden festival held in a different location every ten years, this major park offers recreation and respite in the suburb of Buitenveldert (near the RAI Congress and Convention Centre). A formal rose garden and rhododendron walk are among the seasonal floral spectacles. Art shows at the Glass House (Glazenhuis), pony rides, a children's farm, and tours aboard a miniature train are available. The Rosarium

Restaurant serves expensive meals; its outdoor café is somewhat less pricey.

Amsterdamse Bos

OS. Bus 170, 171, 172. **Open** 24 hours daily. Created in the thirties, partly as a job creation scheme to ease what was a chronic unemployment problem, the 2,000-acre (800 ha) Bos (wood) is a favourite retreat for Amsterdam families, especially at weekends. The man-made Bosbaan (canal) is used for boating and swimming and other attractions include a horticultural museum (*see chapter* **Museums**), play areas, jogging routes, a buffalo and bison reserve, a watersports centre, horse-riding stables and a picnic area. In the outdoor pancake restaurant, the peacocks have a habit of flapping noisily from table to table. Bicycles can be hired (March-October) at the main entrance.

Beatrixpark

OS. Tram 5. **Open** dawn-dusk daily. A little off the beaten tourist track, though on the doorstep of the RAI business centre in the elegant south of the city, this is one of Amsterdam's loveliest parks. There are no real amenities, but it is peaceful, and there's a pond complete with ducks, geese and herons, plus a children's wading pool.

Hortus Botanicus

Plantage Middenlaan 2, IE (625 8411). Tram 7, 9, 14. **Open** *Oct-March* 9am-4pm Sat, Sun, public holidays; *April-Sept* 9am-5pm Mon-Fri; 11am-5pm Sat, Sun, public holidays. **Admission** f5; f3 with Museum Card, over-65s. The University of Amsterdam has had its own medicinal plant garden since 1638, and it has been at this location since 1682, making it one of the oldest gardens in The Netherlands as well as one of the most beautiful. Best of all are the greenhouses, which are planted with tropical and subtropical plants: one is filled with various carnivorous plants, while the palm house (which includes a 400 year-old cycad, reputed to be the oldest potted plant in the world) also has several tanks of tropical fish. You can also seek out Van Gogh's favourite plants with the help of a special leaflet. Information and suggested route guides are available in English. Amsterdam boasts another botanical garden, run by Vrije University (*see chapter* **Museums**).

Vondelpark

OS. Tram 1, 2, 3, 5, 6, 12. **Open** dawn-dusk daily.
Named after the city's most famous poet, Joost van den Vondel (1587-1679), this is the most central major park. It was designed in the 'English style' by D Zocher, with the emphasis on natural landscaping. The original 10 acres were opened in 1865. It has several ponds and lakes (no boating), several cafés (the most pleasant being the terrace of the Filmmuseum, which backs onto the park; *see chapter* **Museums** and *chapter* **Film**), and children's play areas. This was once the Mecca of hippiedom, and pop concerts are still held here.

Canals

A stroll along any of Amsterdam's 160 canals is always pleasant, but the four concentric city-centre canals – Singel, Herengracht, Keizersgracht and Prinsengracht – and the tiny streets that connect them (don't miss Reestraat, Hartenstraat, Berenstraat, Runstraat, Huidenstraat, Wolvenstraat and Herenstraat) are the most interesting to wander round. Smaller, connecting canals to seek out for their charm include Leliegracht, Lauriergracht, Egelantiersgracht, Bloemgracht, Spiegelgracht and Brouwersgracht.

Seeing Amsterdam from the water is an unforgettable experience. There are plenty of tours (*see below*), but if you prefer to drift at will, hire a pedal boat or, if money is no object, a water taxi. And don't forget to navigate on the right-hand side of the waterways. *See also chapter* **Canals**.

Canal Bike

Amstel 57, 1018 EG (626 5574). **Open** 10am-6pm Tue-Sun. **Moorings** *Centraal Station; Leidsekade at Leidseplein, between Marriott and American Hotels; Stadhouderskade, opposite Rijksmuseum; Prinsengracht, by Westerkerk; Keizersgracht, on the corner of Leidsestraat.* **Hire costs** *2-person pedalo* f19.50 per hour; *4-person pedalo* f29.50 per hour. **Deposit** f50. **Credit** fTC.
Canal Bike has two- and four- seater pedalos for hire.

Roell

Mauritskade 1, by the Amstel, OE (692 9124). Tram 6, 7, 10. **Open** *Apr-Sept* 8am-10pm Tue-Sun; *Oct-Mar* 9am-6pm Wed-Sat. **Hire costs** *2-person pedalo* f17.50 per hour; *4-person pedalo* f26 per hour; *4-person motor boat* f37.50 for one hour, f60 for two hours. **Deposit** *pedalo* f50; *4-person motor boat* f150. **No credit cards.**
Roell is a general watersport centre which has four-seater pedal and motor boats for hire.

Water Taxi Centrale

Stationsplein 8, C (622 2181). Tram 1, 2, 4, 5, 9, 13, 16, 17, 24, 25. **Open** 9am-1am daily. **Cost** *8-person boat* f150 per hour; *15 and 30-person-boats* f135 for 1st hour, then f180 per hour (inclusive collection charge). **Credit** AmEx, DC, MC, TC, V.
You can't hail a taxi from this company – you have to book by phone. The boats can take up to 30 passengers and charge a tariff based on the duration of your trip (f2 per minute).

Bridges

With so many canals, it's logical that Amsterdam should also have a fair number of bridges – in fact there are over 1,200 of them. There's a point on Reguliersgracht, at the junction with Keizersgracht, where you can see seven parallel bridges, floodlit by night. One of Amsterdam's most unusual bridges is the Magerebrug, also known as the Skinny Bridge, which was originally built in the seventeenth century. Uniquely, it's made from wood and has to be repaired every 20 years. It's opened by hand whenever a boat needs to pass; which tends to be about every 20 minutes. It links Kerkstraat and Nieuwekerkstraat. You should also try to see the Blauwebrug, which was inspired by the elaborate Pont Alexandre III in Paris.

Windmills

Amsterdam's windmills

D'Admiraal *Noordhollandsch Kanaaldijk, near Jan Thoméepad, N. Bus 34, 37, 39.*
De Bloem *Haarlemmerweg, near Nieuwpoortkade, OW. Bus 18.*
De Rieker *Amsteldijk, near De Borcht, OS. Bus 148.*
1200 Roe *Haarlemmerweg, near Willem Molengraaffstraat, OW. Bus 85.*
De Gooyer *Zeeburgerstraat, IE. Tram 10/bus 22, 28.*
1100 Roe *Herman Bonpad, Sportpark Ookmeer, OW. Bus 19, 68.*
Amsterdam is not the best place to see windmills – go to nearby Zaanse Schans to see some more impressive examples in action (*see chapter* **Excursions in Holland**). If you are keen, there are six in the city, but you can only look at them from the outside. All the mills are capable of working, or at the very least turning their sails, and do so on National Windmill Day (*see chapter* **Amsterdam by Season**). With the exception of D'Admiraal, which was built in 1792 to grind chalk and is now empty, all are private homes or shops. The best example is De Rieker, situated on the banks of the Amstel, which can be reached by walking through Amstel Park. Built in 1636 to drain the Rieker polder, it's beautifully preserved and is now a private home. This was a favourite spot of Rembrandt's and there is a small statue close by to commemorate the fact that he used to paint here. There are two mills on the Haarlemmerweg: 1200 Roe (circa 1632) – a roe is an old-fashioned unit used to calculate the distance from the city centre – and the corn mill De Bloem (1768). The other mills are De Gooyer (1725) on Funenkade in the east of the city, which was another corn mill; and 1100 Roe, an old water-mill in a western suburb.

Amsterdam, City of Diamonds!!!

For over 400 years Amsterdam has maintained its well deserved reputation for polishing diamonds. While in Amsterdam, experience the thrill of seeing the famous diamond polishers at their craft, transferring rough diamonds into fascinating brilliants. The five members of the Diamond Foundation Amsterdam (D.F.A) invite you to visit their factories, all situated in the very heart of the city.

While touring the factories, multilingual staff will give you an ample explanation as to where diamonds are found, how they are polished, graded and mounted. Large collections of loose stones as well as comprehensive jewellery collections are available, from modestly priced to extravagantly chosen.

Only after a visit to one of the five D.F.A members, is your Amsterdam Tour complete.

❖ **Amsterdam Diamond Center**
Rokin 1-5, 1012 KK Amsterdam
Phone: (0) 20-624 5787

❖ **Gassan Diamonds B.V**
Nwe Uilenburgerstraat. 173-175,
1011 LN Amsterdam.
Phone: (0) 20-622 53 33

❖ **Van Moppes & Zoon B.V.**
Albert Guypstraat 2-6
1072 CT Amsterdam
Phone: (0)20-676 12 42

❖ **Coster Diamonds**
Paulus Potterstraat 2-6
1072 CZ Amsterdam
Phone: (0) 20-676 22 22

❖ **Holshuysen Stoeltie**
Wagenstraat 13-17
1017 CZ Amsterdam
Phone: (0)20-623 76 01

Markets

Albert Cuyp Markt
Albert Cuypstraat, OS. Tram 2, 16, 24, 25. **Open** 9am-4.30pm Mon-Sat.
The largest general street market in Amsterdam, and bargains can be picked up from stalls selling clothing, shoes, materials, jewellery, spices, fruit and vegetables. The fish and olive stalls are particularly fascinating, offering a staggering choice of varieties. It's best on a sunny Saturday, when the traders are on top form. *See also chapter* **Amsterdam by Area: De Pijp** and *chapter* **Shopping: Markets**.

Bloemenmarkt (Flower Market)
on Singel between Koningsplein and Muntplein. Tram 1, 2, 4, 5, 9, 14, 16, 24, 25. **Open** 9am-7pm Mon-Sat.
You can find a lot more than tulips on Amsterdam's floating Bloemenmarkt, where the stalls are set out on barges. A riot of colour in all seasons, the market has an incredible variety of plants, bulbs and dried flowers as well as a stunning assortment of cut flowers. At night the floating greenhouses are lit with strings of fairy lights. *See also chapter* **Shopping: Flowers**.

Noordermarkt
Noordermarkt, OW. Tram 3/bus 18, 22, 44. **Open** 9am-noon Mon.
Bargain hunters come from far and wide to this Monday morning textile market with its vast selection of material, extending from PVC to fun fur.

Oudemanhuis Book Market
Oudemanhuispoort (off Oudezijds Achterburgwal), C. Tram 4, 9, 14, 16, 24, 25. **Open** 10am-4pm Mon-Sat.
People have been buying and selling books, prints and sheet music on this charming arcade since the nineteenth century. English-language books appear from time to time. When the alley was first built, in 1601, it was the entrance to the homes for the elderly (one each for

men and women); hence the strange name. *See also chapter* **War & Reformation** and *chapter* **Shopping: Books**.

Stamp & Coin Market
Pedestrian island in front of Nova Hotel, Nieuwezijds Voorburgwal 276, C. Tram 1, 2, 5, 13, 17. **Open** 11am-4pm Wed, Sat.
A specialist market for collectors of stamps and coins, old postcards and commemorative medals.

Waterlooplein Flea Market
Waterlooplein, C. Tram 9, 14/Metro Waterlooplein. **Open** 10am-5pm Mon-Sat.
Situated alongside the smart new Muziektheater/City Hall complex (*see p19* **Cultural Centres**), Amsterdam's flea market has a spectacular collection of curiosities, clothing, furniture, household articles and unadulterated junk. *See chapter* **Shopping: Markets**.

Tours

For advice on how to get around town under your own steam, *see page 23* **Canals** and *chapter* **Getting Around**.

Walking

Amsterdam is compact enough to be a great city for walking around, but it isn't the world's best for stilettos, pushchairs or wheelchairs because of its uneven streets and tramlines. The tourist organisation VVV (*see chapter* **Essential Information**) has a series of English-language brochures outlining eight easy-to-follow walks, including ones themed around Van Gogh, sculpture

*One of the enormous dormitories at **Sleep-In Mauritskade**. See **review**.*

a definite bonus, being just a short distance from the Leidseplein nightlife.
Hotel services *Café. Lifts. Wheelchair access with assistance.*

Hotel Kabul
Warmoesstraat 38-42, 1012 JE; C (623 7156/fax 620 0869/telex 15443). Tram 4, 9, 16, 24, 25. **Rates** *10-bed dormitory f26; 6-bed dormitory f29; 4-bed dormitory f32; double f79; triple f116.* **No credit cards.**
Hotel Kabul is within easy walking distance of Centraal Station and on the edge of the red light district. Rooms and dormitories are basic and rather cramped; all have lockers and sheets are included in the price. The bar regularly has live music until the early hours.
Hotel services *Bar. Hotel open 24 hours. Lockers. Restaurant.*

Sleep-In Mauritskade
's-Gravesandestraat 51, 1092 AA; OE (694 7444/fax 663 2649). Tram 6, 10/Metro Weesperplein. **Rates** *80-bed dormitory f15 ; 8-20 bed dormitory f17.50; sheets f3.* **No credit cards.**
Situated close to the Oosterpark, three stops on the metro from Centraal Station. The mixed and single-sex dormitories are vast, though following renovation, some single and double rooms will be available from the summer of 1993. The hostel is closed between noon and 4pm each day for cleaning, but there is no night-time curfew, and the bar is open from 4pm to 2am during the summer. There's a luggage room and free lockers in all rooms. Breakfast costs f6. The Sleep-In also functions as an international youth cultural centre, organising events, live gigs and exhibitions on its premises.
Hotel services *Bar. Garden. Lift.*

Youth Hostels

The Dutch Youth Hostels Association (NJHC) has two hostels in Amsterdam (*listed below*). You have to be a member of the International Youth Hostel Federation (IYHF), but you can enrol in the Dutch Association at the hostel itself; membership costs f30 for non-natives (no concessions available), but Federation membership can be up to 50 per cent cheaper if you join in your own country. It is also possible to become a temporary member at a cost of f5 per night, but full members are given preference during busy periods. From 1993 the NJHC is introducing a classification system, dividing its hostels into three categories: depending on facilities and location, Category 1 will be the most basic, Category 3 the best.

For information on NJHC hostels throughout The Netherlands, contact the **NJHC**, Professor Tulpplein 4, 1018 GX Amsterdam (551 3155); the office is open for enquiries from 9am to 5pm, Monday to Friday.

NJHC Hostels
Vondelpark *Zandpad 5, 1054 GA; OW (683 1744/fax 616 6591/telex 110 31). Tram 1, 2, 5.* **Category** 3. **Rates** f23 NJHC members; f28 non-members; *sheets f6.*

Amsterdam Guide
Advertiser's Index
Please refer to the relevant sections for addresses

Stadsdoelen *Kloveniersburgwal 97, 1011 KB; C (624 6832). Tram 4, 9, 14, 16, 24, 25.* **Category** 2. **Rates** f21.50 NJHC members; f26.50 non-members; **Both** *July-Aug* seasonal supplement f2.50. **Open** 8am-midnight. **No credit cards.**
Multinational staff provide a cheery welcome at both sites, of which the Vondelpark is larger and far more pleasantly situated. Facilities at both sites include communal rooms, non-smoking areas, kitchen, lockers and a bar. There are no lifts or wheelchair access at either. All accommodation is in dormitories, generally mixed, although there is one women-only dorm, for 16 to 40 people in bunk beds. There is also a limited amount of two- and four-bed rooms, intended mainly for group members. Curfew at both sites is 2am. Groups are advised to book at least two months in advance.

Eben Haezer (Christian Youth Hostel)

Bloemstraat 179, 1016 LA; IW (624 4717/fax 623 2282). Tram 13, 14, 17. **Open** 8am-midnight Mon-Thur, Sun; 8am-1am Fri, Sat. **Rates** f15. **Credit** f£TC.
This is perhaps the better of the two Christian hostels because of its pleasant location on the edge of the Jordaan. The same excellent standards of cleanliness apply in both, but the single-sex dormitories here are smaller, with between 18 and 20 beds. Groups of 10 or more should book in advance. The age limit is 35. Alcohol and drugs are forbidden, and the staff organise a programme of religious activities, participation in which is optional.
Hotel services *Exchange facilities. Snack bar (open 7.30-11.30pm daily).*

The Shelter (Christian Youth Hostel)

Barndesteeg 21, 1012 BV; C (625 3230/620 0329/fax 623 2282). Tram 1, 2, 4, 5, 9, 13, 16, 17, 24, 25. **Open** 8am-midnight Mon-Thur, Sun; 8am-1am Fri, Sat. **Rates** *dormitory* f15. **Credit** TC.
No membership is required and religion is optional although you will receive a Christian leaflet on arrival and gentle Christian messages throughout your stay. These will seem a contrast to the 'temptations' of the red light district where the Shelter is located. There are separate male and female dormitories with bunk beds. The larger ones can be rather cramped, with up to 40 beds squeezed in. The smaller dormitories sleep 16. The age limit is 35. Alcohol is absolutely forbidden on the premises, as is anyone under the influence; curfew is midnight on weekdays and 1am at the weekend. The building is spotlessly clean, and pleasant gardens and a fountained courtyard adjoin the building. Weary and hungry backpackers can leave their belongings in lockers, which cost f1 to hire, and have dinner for f6.50.
Hotel services *Café (open 7.30am-11pm). Exchange facilities. Wheelchair access with assistance.*

Barge

Amstel

Steiger 5 (pier number), De Ruijterkade, C (626 4247). Tram 1, 2, 4, 5, 9, 13, 16, 17, 24, 25. **Open** 24 hours daily. **Rates** *single* f47; *double* f36 per person; *twin* f31-f34 per person; *triple* f29-f31 per person; *4-6 bed rooms* f25 per person. **No credit cards.**
It used to be commonplace for back-packers to stumble out of Centraal Station to the city's piers, looking for cheap dormitory accommodation on one of many barges. However, battles with authorities over fire regulations has meant all but one of these floating hotels – the Amstel – has closed. Don't expect a quaint and cosy Dutch barge; this is a large, efficiently run hotel, which just happens to float. Rooms are neat, if rather small, and functional.
Hotel services *Bar (open 10am-1am).* **Room services** *TV in private rooms.*

Campsites

There are a number of camping grounds in and around Amsterdam; we list below four recommended by the VVV. Two are just to the north of the city, a 15-minute bus ride from the centre, two are further out and more rurally situated. If you're intent on staying under canvas, it's worth remembering the climate is very changeable, but you can always hire a cabin should you fall foul of a downpour. During the summer, the weather is reliably mild. Note that the Gaasper, Vliegenbos and Zeeburg sites are classified by the VVV as youth camp-sites; they welcome people of all ages but be prepared for noise and high spirits late into the night.

Gaasper Camping

Loosdrechtdreef 7, 1108 AZ (696 7326). Metro Gaasperplas/Bus 59, 60, 158. **Reception** **open** *June* 8.30am-12.30pm, 1.30-10pm, daily; *July-Aug* 8.30am-10pm daily; *March, Nov-Dec* 9.30am-12.30pm, 1.30-7pm, daily; *Sept-Oct, Jan-Feb, Apr-May* 9am-12.30pm, 1.30-8pm, daily. **Rates** f5; f2.75 under-12s; f4 car; f6.75 caravan; f8 camper; f4.25-f6.25 tents; f2 motorbike; f3.50 electrical connection; f1.25 hot showers; all per night. **Credit** TC.
This campsite is in the south-east of Greater Amsterdam, easily accessible by Metro or bus. It's on the edge of the Gaasperplas park, which has a lake with a watersports centre and a marina. Facilities include shop, café, bar and restaurant.

Het Amsterdamse Bos

Kleine Noorddijk 1, 1432 CC, Aalsmeer (641 6868/fax 640 2378). Bus 171, 172. **Reception** **open** *April-Oct only* 8am-10pm daily. **Rates** *inclusive of car, tent, shower* f7.30 per night per person; f3.65 4-12s; under-4s free; electricity for caravans/campers f3 per night. **Credit** TC.
The site is several miles from Amsterdam, a long and dreary cycle ride. However, bus services for the 30-minute trip into town stop 300m from the grounds, which are on the southern edge of the beautiful Amsterdamse Bos, a large park with facilities for horse-riding and watersports. Wooden cabins sleeping four can be hired for f46 per night; two-person cabins for f27.50. These are equipped with stoves and mattresses, but you will have to provide your own cooking utensils and sleeping bags. Site facilities include phones, a shop, bar and restaurant, lockers, and bike hire in July and August.

Vliengenbos

Meeuwenlaan 138, 1022 AM (636 8855). Bus 32. **Reception** **open** *April-Sept only* 8am-11pm daily. **Rates** f6.75 over-30s; f5.75 14-30s; f4.50 3-14s; under-3s free; car and one person f8.75, motorbike and one person f7.75, camper with two people f15.50, electricity f1.75, all per night; hot showers f1.50. **No credit cards.**
The grounds are close to the River IJ to the north of Amsterdam, a 10-minute bus journey from Centraal Station. Facilities include bar, restaurant, a safe at reception, and a small shop with exchange service. Cabins sleeping up to four people cost f46 per night. Caravans aren't really welcome, as the site is too small.

Zeeburg

Zuider IJ Dijk 44, 1095 KN (694 4430). Bus 37. **Reception** **open** *April-Sept only* 9am-11pm daily. **Rates** phone for details. **Credit** TC.

Facilities at these grounds just north of the River IJ include a bar, a small restaurant, lockers, a shop and bike hire. Caravans can be hired for by the night, as can tents. Cabins sleeping up to four people are also available.

Apartment Rentals

Flat seekers in Amsterdam require two vital commodities: tenacity and luck. Competition for all apartments is fierce, and landlords have little trouble in quickly filling empty properties, whatever their size and location. There follows some basic advice and tips on finding a reasonable place to live as quickly and with as little bother as possible.

Don't count on a cheap flatshare, which is rare here in comparison to London or Paris. The Dutch seem rather shy of sharing their living space, and many of the available properties are simply too small to accommodate more than one person. However, it is common for the Dutch to let their flats during holidays or periods spent working abroad.

The property agencies listed below, and others found in the *Gouden Gids* (Yellow Pages) may be worth contacting, but be prepared for a hefty commission if they find you a flat. You can also try looking in the daily newspapers *De Telegraaf* and *De Volkskrant* under the *Te Huur* (To Let) sections, particularly on Wednesdays, Fridays and Saturdays, when there are more ads. If you spot something you will need to act swiftly. Most desirable properties are usually snapped up within a few hours. Also, don't be surprised if the landlord instantly dismisses your enquiry if you can't speak Dutch.

The noticeboard in the main public library (*see chapter* **Survival**), plus many supermarkets and tobacconists, display cards advertising available lets. If you're having no luck it may even be worth placing a card saying you are looking for a place.

Many people eventually get lucky by trying the above methods, but many more simply find a place through word of mouth. Be sure to let your friends, workmates, associates, everybody, know that you are looking and something may turn up.

When you find a flat, the landlord will probably charge you a *borgsom*, a refundable deposit ranging from a week's to a month's rent. The previous occupants may also attempt to charge an *overname* (key money), to cover the costs of any furniture they leave. Though often unavoidable, such charges are often inflated and can only be recouped by similarly charging the next tenant when you leave. If you already have furniture you may be paying for a lot of unwanted junk, or for little more than light bulbs, paper blinds and toilet roll holders.

When you register with the Aliens' Police (Bureau Vreemdelingenpolitie) on arrival in Amsterdam (*see chapter* **Essential Information**) you will be directed to the Bevolkings Register (Housing Register). Following registration, after a minimum of two years' continuous residence in Amsterdam, you may be eligible for council accommodation at a controlled rent. To prove that you have been in continuous residence, remember to keep getting your visa renewed every three months at the Bureau Vreemdelingenpolitie. When you become eligible for council accommodation you will be given at least two refusals on apartments somewhere within the city limits.

Bevolkings Register
Herengracht 531-537, IS (551 9911). Tram 4, 9, 14. **Open** 8.30am-3pm Mon-Fri.

Amsterdam Apartments
Nieuwezijds Voorburgwal 63, 1012 RE; C (626 5930). Tram 1, 2, 5, 13, 17. **Open** 9am-9pm Mon-Sat. **No credit cards.**
Privately owned furnished, self-contained flats in the centre of town. Rates start from f600 per week for a one-person studio or one-bedroom flat. The minimum let is one week, maximum two months.

GIS Apartments
Keizersgracht 33, 1015 CD; IW (625 0071). Tram 13, 14, 17/Bus 18, 22, 44. **Open** 10am-5pm Mon-Fri. **Credit** AmEx, MC, TC, V.
This agency deals with a wide variety of accommodation, from simple holiday flats whose owners are away, to luxurious canal-view apartments. Most of the flats are in the centre of town, but the agency also handles property in outlying villages and towns. Short-term flats (minimum stay four days) cost between f500 and f1,000 per week including commission. Longer-term rentals (over three months) average at least f1,000 per month, plus a commission of 10% (minimum f350), plus 18% tax on commission. For rentals of more than five months the commission is one month's rent. Bookings should be made one month in advance, but the agency may have something available at short notice.

Intercity Room Service
Van Ostadestraat 348, 1073 TZ; OS (675 0064). Tram 3, 4. **Open** 10am-5pm Mon-Fri. **Credit** DC, MC, TC, V.
The place to try if you're in Amsterdam and require something – anything! – very quickly. This agency specialises in flatshares, and occasionally offers entire apartments. Flatshares in the centre of town cost from f50 per day, self-contained flats from f1,200 per month. The minimum stay is one day, maximum is indefinite. The agency charges two weeks' rent as commission.

Riverside Apartments
Amstel 138, 1017 AD; C (627 9797). Tram 9, 14. **Open** 9am-5pm Mon-Sat; by appointment other times. **Credit** AmEx, DC, MC, V.
These privately owned, luxury furnished flats in central Amsterdam cost around f4,500 per month for two to three people. Services include telephone, fax, laundry, cleaner and linen. The apartments are available for a minimum of one week, a maximum of three months.

History

A city built on land painstakingly reclaimed from the sea, Amsterdam's history is preserved in its architecture. We trace its development, from the earliest days as a fishing village, through the golden age of maritime empire-building, to the present day, where the liberal tolerance of the seventies has given way to the hardline policies of the nineties.

Contents

Early History

Reclaimed from the marshy banks of the River Amstel by the farmers of Utrecht, Amsterdam gradually developed into a thriving centre of trade and of pilgrimage.

Although the Romans occupied other parts of Holland, they didn't reach the north. The water-logged swamp land that changed shape and location every time the tide turned was apparently not the stuff empires were built on, so the legions headed for firmer footholds elsewhere in northern Europe. Archaeologists have come up with no evidence of settlement at Amsterdam before AD 1000, although there are prehistoric remains further east in Drenthe (*see chapter* **The Provinces**).

It looks as though Amsterdam's site was partially under water for most of history, forsaken by all but the birds. The River Amstel had no fixed course in this marshy region until enterprising farmers from around Utrecht began the laborious task of building dikes in the area during the early eleventh century. Once the peasants had done the work, the nobility took over.

During the thirteenth century, the most important place in the newly reclaimed area was Oudekerk aan de Amstel. In 1204, the Lord of Amstel built a castle near this tiny hamlet on what is now the outskirts of Amsterdam. Once the Amstel was dammed (in about 1270), a village grew up on the site of Dam Square, acquiring the name *Amestelledamme*. The Lord of Amstel at this time was Gijsbrecht. A pugnacious man, Gijsbrecht was continually in trouble with his liege lord, the Bishop of Utrecht, and with his nearest neighbour, Count Floris V of Holland.

Tension in this power struggle increased when Floris bestowed toll rights – and thus some independence – on the young town in 1275. Events culminated in Floris' murder by Gijsbrecht at Muiden (where Floris' castle can still be seen, *see chapter* **Excursions in Holland: Castles**). Gijsbrecht's estates were confiscated by the Bishop of Utrecht and given to the Counts of Holland, and Amsterdam has remained part of the province of North Holland ever since. Three centuries later, the Dutch equivalent of Shakespeare, Joost van den Vondel, loosely based his classic *Gijsbrecht van Aemstel* on the life of Gijsbrecht (*see chapter* **Theatre**).

The Count of Holland's overlordship was essentially nominal since Amsterdam, like many European cities with charters of rights, was effectively self-governing throughout this period.

ROLL OUT THE BARREL

The saying goes that Amsterdam's prosperity was launched in a beer barrel. This commercial boost came courtesy of a later Count of Holland, Floris VI, who in 1323 made the city one of only two toll points in the province for the import of brews. This was no small matter at a time when most people drank beer instead of water (drinking the local water was equivalent to attempting suicide). Hamburg had the largest brewing capacity in northern Europe and within 50 years a third of that city's production was flowing through Amsterdam. Because of its position between the Atlantic ports and the Hansa towns (such as Hamburg and Lübeck), Amsterdam increased its trade in a wide assortment of essential goods, including grain. The city's ships became a common sight all over Europe.

Schreierstoren

Prins Hendrikkade, C. Metro Centraal Station. Tram 1, 2, 4, 5, 9, 13, 16, 17, 24, 25.
Dating from 1487, this is one of the few really old buildings in Amsterdam, and is a reminder of the city's maritime prominence. The name roughly translates as the 'Weeping Tower' and it's said to be the place where sailors' wives waved a tearful farewell to their men. But *schreier* also means saddle, and the tower does indeed straddle two canals. The tower was part of the city's medieval fortifications, defending the approaches on the former Zuider Zee (the Ijsselmeer). Nothing else remains of the walls, except the St Antoniespoort (St Anthony's Gatehouse), which dates from 1488, and became the Waag (Weigh House) in 1617. *See also chapter* **Sightseeing: Heritage**.

BUILDINGS AND FIRES

Although a major trading force, Amsterdam remained little more than a village until well into the fifteenth century. In 1425, it consisted of a few blocks of houses with kitchen gardens and two churches, neatly and compactly arranged along the final 1,000-metre (1,094-yard) stretch of the River Amstel and bordered by the present Geldersekade, Kloveniersburgwal and Singel. The buildings, like the Houtenhuis (*see chapter* **Sightseeing: Begijnhof**) were virtually all wooden, so fire was a constant threat. In the great fire of May 1452, three-quarters of Amsterdam was razed.

Not surprisingly, very few buildings predate 1452, and those built later had to be faced with stone and roofed with tiles or slates. Limited urban expansion first occurred around this time. Foreign commerce led to the development of shipbuilding. Numerous craftsmen in related trades set up shop outside the city walls (of which nothing remains) in what is now the Nieuwmarkt quarter.

CATHOLIC CONTROL

It is almost impossible to over-estimate the role of the Catholic Church in early medieval society. It permeated every aspect of life throughout Europe, and Amsterdam was no exception. Contemporary chronicles show that the city became an independent parish sometime before 1334. Documents from this date are the first to refer to the Oude Kerk; the Nieuwe Kerk was built at the start of the fifteenth century (for both *see chapter* **Sightseeing**).

Cloisters proliferated as the city became more prosperous; no fewer than 18 were dotted around the tiny urban enclave. The only remaining example, the Begijnhof (*see chapter* **Sightseeing**), shows their original structure.

Historians haven't come up with any concrete reasons for such a concentration of cloisters, but one explanation could be the 'miracle' which occurred in 1345. A dying man was given the Last Sacrament and later vomited up the host (bread consecrated in the Eucharist). The vomit was thrown into a fire but the host emerged from the ashes undamaged. From that date Amsterdam attracted large numbers of pilgrims (*see chapter* **Amsterdam by Season: The Silent Procession**). The *Heiligeweg* (Holy Way) was the road within the city leading to the chapel that was built on Rokin, close to where the miracle took place. Its length (roughly 70 metres/77 yards) is an indication of just how small Amsterdam was.

The cloisters in Amsterdam were also the main source of social welfare, providing hospital treatment, orphanages and poor relief for both inhabitants and travellers. Nothing remains of these complexes, as the Protestant élite which took over the city after the Reformation obliterated every trace of popery.

Amsterdam's oldest house, the Houtenhuis, is in the **Begijnhof** *courtyard.*

War & Reformation

The religious turmoil of the sixteenth century united the Dutch against the Spanish. The ensuing war and the fall of Antwerp brought commercial gain, as well as a flood of refugees, to Amsterdam.

None of the wealth and glory of Amsterdam's seventeenth-century Golden Age would have been possible without the turbulent events of the sixteenth century. During these hundred years, Amsterdam's population increased five-fold, from about 10,000 (a level low even by medieval standards) to 50,000 by the year 1600. Its first major urban expansion took place to accommodate the growth, yet people flocked to the booming city only to find poverty, disease and squalor in the hastily erected working-class quarters. But Amsterdam's merchants weren't complaining. During this century the city started to emerge as one of the major trading powers in the world.

Amsterdam may have been almost autonomous as a chartered city, but on paper it was still subject to absentee rulers. Through the intricate and exclusive marriage bureau known as the European aristocracy, the Low Countries (today's Netherlands and Belgium) had passed into the hands of the Catholic Austro-Spanish House of Hapsburg. The Hapsburgs were the mightiest monarchs in Europe, owning most of South America and with ties to the English throne – Amsterdam was a comparative backwater among their European possessions. However, events in the sixteenth century soon gave the city a new prominence.

THE REFORMATION HITS HOLLAND

Amsterdam's burgeoning trade led to the import of all kinds of radical religious ideas which were flourishing throughout northern Europe at the time, encouraged by Martin Luther's audacious condemnation of the all-powerful Catholic Church in 1517. The German princelings sided with Luther, but the Hapsburg kings of Spain gathered all the resources of their enormous empire and set about putting the protesters in their place – back in the Catholic Church.

Although Luther's beliefs failed to catch on with Amsterdammers, many people were drawn to the austere and sober creeds of first the Anabaptists and later Calvin. Advocating a revolutionary Christian equality, the Anabaptists insisted on adult baptism. Calvinist doctrine was intertwined with principles of sober, upright citizenship.

When the Anabaptists first came to the city (from Germany) in about 1530, the Catholic city fathers tolerated the new movement. But when they seized the Town Hall in 1534 during an attempt to establish a 'New Jerusalem' on the River Amstel, the authorities clamped down. The leaders were arrested and subsequently executed, signalling a period of religious repression unparalleled in the city's history. Protesters of every persuasion had to keep a low profile – heretics were burned at the stake on the Dam.

Calvinist preachers came to the city from Geneva (where the movement started), or via France (the Principality of Orange, in the south of France, had links with Holland and was one of the few safe pockets of Protestantism outside Switzerland and parts of Germany). Their arrival caused a sweeping transformation in Amsterdam. In 1566, religious discontent erupted into what became known as the **Iconoclastic Fury**, the most severe such outbreak in European history. In the space of two months, a popular, spontaneous uprising led to the sacking of many churches and monasteries in the country. Statues, altar pieces and priceless religious art were dragged into the streets and burned or smashed. The iconoclasm had two major effects: one was that a church in Amsterdam was allocated to the Calvinists; the other was Philip II of Spain's decision to send an army to suppress the heresy.

Zuiderkerk

Zuiderkerkhof, C (Zuiderkerk foundation noon-5pm Mon-Wed, Fri; noon-8pm Thur 622 2692). Tram 9, 14/Metro Nieuwmarkt. **Open** *1 June-15 Oct* 2-5pm Wed, Thur; 11am-2pm Fri; 11am-4pm Sat. **Admission** fl.50. **No credit cards.**

The South Church is Amsterdam's earliest post-Reformation church, and was the first to be built expressly for the Calvinists. The architect was the ubiquitous Hendrick de Keyser, who was able to introduce innovations in design because the religious requirements were no longer Catholic. All De Keyser spires are distinctive; this one is braced with columns and topped with an onion dome. Construction started in 1603 and the first service was held here in 1611.

UNITY AGAINST SPAIN

The **Eighty Years' War** (1568-1648) between the Hapsburgs and the Dutch is often seen as primarily a struggle for religious freedom, but there was a lot more at stake than that. The Dutch were looking for political autonomy from an absentee king who meant little more to them than a continual drain on their coffers, through taxation for his interminable wars. By the last quarter of the sixteenth century, Philip II of Spain was fighting wars against England (to which he sent his Armada) and France, in the East against the Ottoman Turks, and for control of his colonies in the New World. The last thing he needed was a revolt in the Low Countries.

Amsterdam at first stayed on the political fence, ostensibly supporting Philip II until it became clear that he was losing. Only in 1578 did the city patricians declare for the rebels, who were led by William of Orange. A year later the Protestant states of the Low Countries united in opposition to Philip when the first modern-day European Republic was born at the **Union of Utrecht**. The Republic of Seven United Provinces was made up of Friesland, Gelderland, Groningen, Overijssel, Utrecht, Zeeland and, most importantly, Holland. Although lauded as the start of the modern Netherlands, it wasn't the unitary state that William of Orange had wanted, but a loose military federation with an impotent States General assembly (for more information on the political structure after the Union of Utrecht *see chapter* **The Golden Age**).

Each province appointed a so-called *stadhouder*, a rank which in Hapsburg times had been held by the king's deputy. The *stadhouder* commanded the Republic's army and navy and had the right to appoint some of the individual cities' regents or governors. *Stadhouders* of each province sent delegates to the assembly, which was held at the Binnenhof in The Hague (*see chapter* **The Randstad**). The treaty also enshrined freedom of conscience and hence of religion – except for Catholics (until the end of the Republic in 1795). The Union of Utrecht was in part a response to the Union of Arras, encompassing the southern provinces of the Low Countries who had declared for Spain and Catholicism and some which had sided with William of Orange but were later reconquered by the Spanish.

CALVINIST CLIQUE

From its earliest beginnings, Amsterdam had been governed by four burgomasters and a **city council** representing the citizens' interests. This sounds pretty Utopian and it may have begun that way, but by 1500 city government had become an incestuous business. The city council's 36 members were supposed to be both rich and wise, but they were appointed for life and themselves 'elected' the burgomasters from among their own ranks. Selective intermarriage meant that the city was, in effect, governed by a handful of families. When Amsterdam joined the rebels in 1578, the only real change in civic administration was that the formerly Catholic élite was replaced by a Calvinist faction comprising equally wealthy families.

However, **social welfare** was transformed. Formerly the concern of the Catholic Church, it was now incorporated into city government. The Regents, as the Calvinist élite became known, took over the convents and monasteries, establishing charitable organisations including orphanages and homes for the elderly. But the Regents' hard-work ethic and abstemious way of life would not tolerate any kind of excess. Crime, drunkenness and immorality were all condemned and those who found themselves in front of a magistrate for this kind of offence were immediately sent to a house of correction.

Law and order in the city was the province of the civic guard or militia who, fortunately for artists like Rembrandt, had a penchant for having their portraits painted. Street names like *Voetboogstraat* (Bowman's Street) indicate the location of their barracks.

Oudemanhuis

Oudezijds Achterburgwal, C. Tram 4, 9, 14, 16, 24, 25/Metro Nieuwmarkt.
The Oudemanhuis was originally a home for elderly men. It was set up by the Regents, the Calvinist élite who took over responsibility for social welfare after the Reformation. Its gateway, *Oudemanhuispoort*, survives, and provides shelter for second-hand booksellers' stalls. The adjacent buildings of 1754 are now part of the University of Amsterdam.

PROFITING IN WAR

During the two centuries before the Eighty Years' War, Amsterdam had developed a powerful maritime force, expanding its fleet and broadening its trading horizons to include Russia, Scandinavia and the Baltic. Yet until Antwerp was taken by the Spanish in 1589, Amsterdam remained overshadowed by that Belgian port. The Hapsburg Spanish, rather than engaging in pitched battles against the rebellious Low Countries, adopted siege tactics, primarily in what is now Belgium. Thus Amsterdam was unaffected by the hostilities and benefited from the crippling blockades suffered by rival commercial ports. Thousands of refugees fled north, including Antwerp's most prosperous Protestant and Jewish merchants. They brought with them the skills, gold, and most famously the diamond industry, that would set Amsterdam on course to becoming the greatest maritime trading city in the world.

The Golden Age

Amsterdam's pre-eminence during the seventeenth century didn't just extend to the military and political spheres but to those of the arts, learning and oversees trade.

History is cluttered with Golden Ages – any country with the least claim to fame seems to boast one. But in Amsterdam's case, the first six decades of the seventeenth century truly deserve the title. The small city on the River Amstel came to dominate world trade, and established important colonies, resulting in a population explosion and a frenzy of urban expansion. The still-elegant girdle of canals excavated around the city centre was one of the greatest engineering feats of that century. Extraordinarily, this all happened while the city was at war with one of the greatest powers in the world. And equally startling for the period, this growth was presided over not by kings but by businessmen.

THE FIRST MULTINATIONAL

The East India Company doesn't have much of a ring to it – to modern ears it sounds rather like an enterprise specialising in cottons or joss sticks. Yet the name of the mighty *Verenigde Oost Indische Compagnie* (VOC) definitely loses something in translation, as this was the first ever transnational company. The VOC was created by a States General charter in 1602. Its initial purpose was to finance the wildly expensive and hellishly dangerous voyages to the East. Drawn by the potential fortunes to be made out of spices and silk, the shrewd Dutch saw the sense in sending out merchant fleets, but they also knew that one disaster could leave an individual investor penniless. As a result, the main cities set up trading 'chambers' which evaluated the feasibility (and profitability) of ventures, then equipped ships and sent them east. The VOC had enormous powers, including the capacity to found colonies, establish its own army, declare war and sign treaties.

Brouwersgracht warehouses

Brouwersgracht, IW. Tram 1, 2, 3, 5, 13, 17.
North of the Brouwersgracht canal is the former shipping quarter where goods from VOC shipping were unloaded. Brouwersgracht is lined with warehouses: once storerooms for spices and East Indies produce, they've now mostly been converted into luxury apartments. The functional architecture of the warehouses contrasts dramatically with the heavily ornate merchants' houses of the same period.

VOC Headquarters

Oude Hoogstraat at Klovenierburgwal, C. Tram 4, 9, 14, 16, 24, 25/Metro Nieuwmarkt.
The VOC Headquarters was the meeting place for the most influential chamber of the mighty East India Company. Many wealthy Protestant and Jewish refugees settled in the city after the fall of Antwerp and it was their money that helped to finance the lucrative voyages to the East Indies (now Indonesia). Some ships berthed here before unloading; provisions for the ships were stored and the more precious booty (such as rare spices and silk) was laid up to await a rise in prices. The building dates from 1606, shortly after the founding of the VOC, and is now part of the University.

THE STRAITS OF LEMAIRE

The story of Isaac Lemaire, whose name would be immortalised in atlases, is a good illustration of just how powerful the VOC became. Lemaire had fled to Amsterdam from Antwerp in 1589 and became a founder member of the VOC, initially investing f90,000 – about £30 million in today's terms. But, accused of embezzlement, he was forced to leave the company and, in businesslike fashion, cast around for ways to set up on his own. But the Republic had given the VOC a monopoly on trade with the East via the Cape of Good Hope and at that time there was no alternative route.

However, Portuguese seamen claimed the Cape route was not the only passage to the East. They believed the fabulous spice islands of Java, the Moluccas and Malaya could also be reached by sailing to the tip of South America where a strait would lead into the Pacific. In 1615, Lemaire financed a voyage, led by one of his sons, and discovered the strait that still bears his name. His son perished on the voyage home and Isaac died of a broken heart.

While the VOC concentrated on the spice trade, a new company received its charter from the Dutch Republic in 1621. The **Dutch West India Company** (*West-Indische Compagnie, WIC*) was not as successful as its Eastern sister, but it did dominate trade with the Spanish and Portuguese possessions in Africa and America. The WIC was also first to colonise a small island in the mouth of a river in North America in 1623. The settlement on Manhattan Island was laid out on a grid system similar to Amsterdam's and subsequently it adopted the Dutch city's name. New Amsterdam flourished

*The **NAP** (Normaal Amsterdams Peil or normal Amsterdam water level). See **review**.*

and more land was cleared on the banks of the River Hudson and named after other enterprising towns with a stake in the new colony: Haarlem (Harlem) and Breukelen (Brooklyn). Staten Island was so-called in honour of the States General, the 'national' council of the Republic.

But after an invasion by the Duke of York in 1664, the terms of the peace treaty between England and The Netherlands determined New Amsterdam would change its name to New York and come under British control. The Dutch were given Surinam as a consolation prize.

Lelystad

Battavaer Oostvaardijk 0109, Lelystad (032 0061409). Bus 150 from Lelystad station. **Open** 10am-5pm daily. **Admission** f11.50; f7.25 over-65s; f5.75 under-16s; free children under 6. **No credit cards.**
A visit to the shipyard in Lelystad will reveal exactly what kind of vessels the Dutch used to conquer the trading world. Master shipwrights and apprentices – on a new youth scheme for the unemployed – are building a full-size replica of the *Batavia*, one of the VOC's biggest East-Indiamen, lost on its maiden voyage in 1629. Lelystad is about 40 minutes by train from Centraal Station. *Café. Wheelchair access.*

NAP

Off Waterlooplein, C. Tram 9, 14/Metro Waterlooplein.
In the passage between the City Hall and the Muziektheater you can still see the height of the NAP (*Normaal Amsterdams Peil* or normal Amsterdam water level), set over 300 years ago in 1684. This became the basis for measurements of altitude for most of Western Europe. Three glass columns are filled with water; two

indicate the water level at the coastal towns of Vlissingen and IJmuiden – at high tide the water rises well above knee level. In the third column, the water level is far over your head, indicating the height of the North Sea during the disastrous floods in Zeeland in 1953. The real NAP, which is a large bronze plate, can be seen by descending the staircase by the water columns.

Scheepvaart Museum

Kattenburgerplein 1, IE (523 2222). Bus 22, 28. **Open** 10am-5pm Tue-Sat; noon-5pm Sun, public holidays. **Closed** 1 Jan. **Admission** f10; f2.50 CJP card holders; f7.50 6-18s; free with Museum Card, under-6s ; £7.50 over-65s. **No credit cards.**
Located in a restored VOC warehouse (*see chapter* **Museums**), this well-organised museum charts the history of the East India Company and naval history using ship models, period sea charts (works of art in their own right), instruments and paintings. It has a pleasant waterside coffee shop overlooking the harbour. *Café. Wheelchair access.*

MONOPOLY MONEY

Extensive though commerce with the Indies became, it never surpassed Amsterdam's European business. The city became the major European centre for distribution and trade. Grain from Russia, Poland and Prussia, salt and wine from France, cloth from Leiden and tiles from Delft all passed through the port. Whales were hunted by Amsterdam's fleets in the waters round Spitsbergen, generating a flourishing soap trade, and Surinam sugar and spices from Dutch colonies were distributed to ports throughout Scandinavia and the north of Europe. This manifold activity was financed by the Bank of Amsterdam, a bank set up in the cellars of the Town Hall by Amsterdam's municipal council as early as 1609. It was a unique initiative and was considered the money vault of Europe, its notes being freely exchangeable throughout the trading world – the seventeenth-century equivalent of an AmEx Gold Card.

ORANGE AID

The political structure of the young Dutch Republic was complex. When the Treaty of Utrecht was signed in 1579, no suitable monarch or head of state was found, so the existing system was adapted to new needs. The seven provinces were represented by a 'national' council known as the States General. In addition, the provinces appointed a *stadhouder* (*see* chapter **War & Reformation**).

The most popular and obvious choice for *stadhouder* after the treaty was William of Orange, the wealthy nobleman from Holland who had led the rebellion against Philip II of Spain. William was succeeded by his son, Maurice of Nassau, who was as militarily successful against the Spanish as his father had been, securing the Twelve Years' Truce (1609-1621). Although each province could, in theory, elect a different *stadhouder*, in practice they usually chose the same person. It became something of a tradition to elect an Orange as *stadhouder*, and by 1641 this family had become sufficiently powerful for a later William to marry a princess of England. It was their son who, backed by Amsterdam money, set sail in 1688 to accept the throne of England in the so-called Glorious Revolution.

HOLLAND OUT-WITTS ORANGE

But the Oranges weren't popular with everyone. The provinces' representatives at the States General were known as regents, and Holland's (that is, Amsterdam's) representative was in a powerful enough position to challenge the authority and decisions of the *stadhouder*. In 1650 this power was used. The crisis was precipitated by Holland's decision to disband its militia after the end of the Eighty Years' War with Spain. The *stadhouder*, William II of Orange, wanted the militia maintained (and paid for) by Holland. In response to the disbandment, he got a kinsman, William Frederick, to launch a surprise attack on Amsterdam. The attack met with no resistance, but three months later William II died. The leaders of the States of Holland then called a Great Assembly of the provinces, which decided (apart from Friesland and Groningen, which remained loyal to William Frederick) that there should be no *stadhouders*. Johan de Witt, Holland's powerful regent, swore no prince of Orange would ever become *stadhouder* again. This became law in the Act of Seclusion of 1653.

CIVIC PRIDE

Amid all these political machinations, you may wonder how anyone ever got any work done. But the powers that be in Amsterdam, the Lords (Heren) XLVIII (composed of a sheriff, four mayors, a 36-member council and seven jurists) kept a firm grip on all that went on both within and without the city walls. Although this system was self-perpetuating, these people were merchants rather than aristocrats, and anyone who made enough money could, in theory, become a member. The mayors and the council usually came from a handful of prominent families, the most powerful being the Witsen, Bicker, Six and Trip families. Their wives, nieces and daughters made up boards of governesses at the multitude of charitable institutions scattered throughout the city (*see below* **Social Welfare**).

Koninklijk Paleis (Royal Palace)

Dam, C (624 8698 ext 217). Tram 1, 2, 4, 5, 9, 13, 14, 16, 17, 24, 25. **Open** *mid June-7 Sept* 12.30-5pm daily. **Admission** f5; f1.50 under-12s. **No credit cards.**
Although this building has been called the Royal Palace for the past 180 years, it was built in the seventeenth century to be the City Hall. The impressive Palladian design reflects the civic pride of the period. This pride was also expressed when the city élite refused permission for the Nieuwe Kerk to have a tower – in case it detracted from their City Hall's dominance of the Amsterdam skyline. *See also chapter* **Sightseeing**.
Guided tours throughout year 2pm Wed. Guided tours by arrangement throughout year: Mon-Fri f35 for 15-30 people, f50 for 10-15 people.

Trippenhuis

Kloveniersburgwal 29, C. Tram 4, 9, 14/Metro Waterlooplein.
A palatial abode that gives some idea of the opulence enjoyed by the Trip family, one of the powerful merchant clans that ran Amsterdam during the Golden Age. Built in 1662 by Justus Vingboons, the exterior has Corinthian columns and a grandly decorated pediment. The interior – which isn't open to the public – housed the Rijksmuseum collection for most of the nineteenth century.

GUILDS AND PROTECTIONISM

The less elevated folk, the craftsmen, artisans and shopkeepers, were equally active in maintaining their position. A system of guilds had developed in earlier centuries, linked to the Catholic Church, but under the new order, guilds were independent organisations run by their members. The original Amsterdammers were known as *poorters*, deriving from the Dutch for gate (they originally lived within the gated walls of the city). As the city fast expanded, the *poorters* began to see their livelihoods threatened by an influx of newcomers who were prepared to work for lower wages.

Things came to a head when the shipwrights' trade began to be lost to less expensive competitors in the nearby Zaan region. The shipwrights' lobby was so strong that the city regents decreed that Amsterdam ships had to be repaired in Amsterdam yards. This kind of protectionism extended to almost all industrial sectors in the city and effectively meant that most crafts became closed shops. Only *poorters* or those who had married *poorters'* daughters were allowed to join a guild, thereby protecting Amsterdammers' livelihoods.

Werf 't Kromhout

Hoogte Kadijk 147, IE (627 6777). Bus 22, 28. **Open** 10am-5pm Mon-Fri. **Admission** f3.50; f1.50 under-12s. **No credit cards.**
The Kromhout Shipyard Museum is sited in the eastern port area of the city where there were numerous shipyards in the seventeenth century. Old vessels undergo repair and restoration here and the work in progress is open to view. *See also chapter* **Museums**.
Guided tours. Wheelchair access with assistance.

URBAN EXPANSION

In 1600 Amsterdam's population was no more than 50,000 but in the space of about 50 years the figure quadrupled. This increased opportunities for trade and industry, but brought inevitable headaches for the city fathers. The city was obliged to expand. The most elegant of the major canals girdling the city centre was *Herengracht* (gentlemen's canal); begun in 1613, this was where many of the Heren XLVIII had their homes. So that there would be no misunderstanding about who was the most important, *Herengracht* was followed further out by *Keizersgracht* (emperor's canal) and *Prinsengracht* (prince's canal). Immigrants were housed in the Jordaan quarter – built to a more modest pattern.

The frenzy of building also included churches, as the wave of immigrants brought with them

Built by Jacob van Campens as a city hall, the **Koninklijk Paleis** *was transformed into a royal palace in 1808. See* **review** *page 70.*

an amazing range of variations on the Protestant theme. Renaissance influences were already noticeable in Hendrick de Keyser's Calvinist Zuiderkerk (*see chapter* **War & Reformation**), but his classical Westerkerk (*see* **Sightseeing**) marked a watershed in Amsterdam architecture. De Keyser's Noorderkerk followed in 1620-23 to a Greek Cross ground plan, and Dortsman's Nieuwe Luthersekerk (1668-71) (*see* **Sightseeing**) acquired a baroque dome. But the most striking new building was the Palladian City Hall (now called the **Royal Palace**, *see above* **Civic Pride**).

For the first few decades of the century Catholics, Baptists, Lutherans and Jews were obliged to hold services in secret. But towards the end of this period the location of most of the clandestine churches was common knowledge and they were tolerated by the authorities.

Amstelkring Museum, 'Our Lord in the Attic'

Oudezijds Voorburgwal 40, C (624 6604). Tram 1, 2, 4, 5, 9, 13, 16, 17, 24, 25. **Open** 10am-5pm Mon-Sat; 1-5pm Sun, public holidays. **Admission** f4.50; f3 students, CJP card holders; free with Museum Card; group discount. **No credit cards.**

Hidden in the attic of the Amstelkring Museum is one of the two clandestine churches left intact in Amsterdam (the other is in the Begijnhof). During the seventeenth century, Roman Catholic worship was banned in the city, and this chapel, 'Our Lord in the Attic', was one of several used for secret Catholic services. The chapel has three tiers of balconies, a huge organ (which must have been anything but clandestine when played) and an altarpiece by Jacob de Wit. It's an enjoyable place for children, who can try to discover the numerous secret ways to reach the chapel. The rest of the house is preserved in its seventeenth-century state, giving an insight into the domestic life of the period.

Guided tours by prior arrangement.

Museum Van Loon

Keizersgracht 672, IS (624 5255). Tram 4, 9, 14. **Open** 10am-5pm Mon; 1-5pm Sun. **Admission** f5; free under-12s. **No credit cards.**

This museum is housed in a beautifully restored and rather grand seventeenth-century home. The Van Loon family was one of the most powerful in Amsterdam at the time – Willem Van Loon helped to found the VOC (Dutch East India Company) in 1602. The house was built in 1672 by Adriaan Dortsman; the painter Ferdinand Bol was the first tenant. Among the collection of period pieces there is an enormous number of family portraits, all excellent examples of contemporary portraiture.

Guided tours by prior arrangement f4 per person (min 10 people).

SOCIAL WELFARE

Despite the city's wealth, and the reputation of its people as masters of transport, famine hit Amsterdam with dreary regularity in the seventeenth century. Guilds had benevolent funds set aside for their members in times of need, but social welfare was primarily in the hands of the ruling merchant class. Amsterdam's élite

was noted for its philanthropy, but only *poorters* were eligible for assistance and they had to fall into a specific category, described as 'deserving poor'.

Those seen as undeserving were sent to a house of correction. At first these had been rather Utopian places, run on the premise that hard work would ultimately produce reformed, useful citizens. But this soon changed and the institutions became little more than prisons.

Spinhuis

Oudezijds Achterburgwal 28, C. Tram 1, 2, 4, 5, 9, 13, 16, 17, 24, 25.

The Spinning House was a house of correction for women. In the seventeenth century the governors made a bit of cash on the side by allowing sightseers to watch the inmates at work. It is now used as offices by the city and is not open to the public.

ARTS AND SCIENCES

Amsterdam's seventeenth-century Golden Age did not only encompass commercial life, but embraced the arts too. Rembrandt, not to mention hundreds of long-forgotten artists, made a good living during the period. United in the Guild of St Luke, these artists are estimated to have produced no fewer than 20 million paintings. Art historians believe that almost every family had at least three or four paintings in their home. Though Rembrandt died in poverty, he had a remarkably comfortable life – when he managed to keep his temper and not offend his rich patrons. The house where he lived still exists, now as a museum, and it's no garret.

Unlike other European countries, The Netherlands wasn't liberally scattered with ancient universities. In fact, Amsterdam didn't have one at all. The first move towards establishing a centre of higher education came in 1632 when the Athenaeum Illustre (Illustrious School) was opened. It was attended by (male) members of the élite who studied Latin, Greek, law and the natural sciences. But two of the era's scientific pioneers, Anthonie van Leeuwenhoek, who pioneered microbiology, and the physicist Christiaan Huygens, didn't go to a university at all. They did their work in improvised laboratories at home. Amsterdam's guild of surgeons, as Rembrandt records, held public demonstrations of anatomy, using the bodies of executed criminals for practice.

Rembrandthuis

Jodenbreestraat 4-6, C (624 9486). Tram 9, 14. **Open** 10am-5pm Mon-Sat; 1-5pm Sun, public holidays. **Admission** f4; f2.50 over-65s, 10-15s; free under-9s; free with Museum Card; group discount (min 15 people). **No credit cards.**

The great master lived here for around 20 years. The museum includes a good collection of his etchings and paintings by his pupils. *See also chapter* **Museums.** *Guided tours by prior arrangement.*

Decline & Fall

The good times receded as The Netherlands lost supremacy at sea; its trading power faltered and invasion followed.

After Amsterdam's intoxicating Golden Age came the hangover. The city remained one of the wealthiest in Europe until the early nineteenth century, but after 1660 its dominant trading position was lost to England and France. Wars at sea and invasions by land would gradually milk the small country dry.

DUTCH COURAGE

It's no accident that the English language is littered with 'Dutch' adjectives, all of them pretty derogatory. 'Double Dutch' (incomprehensible jargon), 'going Dutch' (each person paying only their share of the bill), 'Dutch Courage' (bravery fuelled by alcohol) –all are indications of how the British viewed their major rivals in maritime trade. The United Provinces spent a couple of centuries bickering about trade and politics with Britain and the other main powers: France, Spain and the Austrian Hapsburg Empire. International relations were only straightforward when war broke out – which it did frequently. Major sea conflicts included battles against the Swedes and there were no fewer than four Anglo-Dutch wars (*see below* **Monuments to Admirals**), from which the Dutch came off slightly the worst.

It wasn't that the Dutch didn't win many of the wars, it was more that the small country ran out of men and money. Amsterdam became the most vociferous opponent of the Orange family's attempt to acquire kingdoms – although it was one of William III's staunchest supporters when this Orange crossed the sea to become King of England in 1688. The city fathers believed a Dutchman on their rival's throne could only be advantageous to them. For a while that proved true, but Billy was soon knocking on the Amsterdammers' door for more money to fight even more wars – this time against France.

Monuments to Admirals

Nieuwe Kerk, NZ Voorburgwal/Dam, C (626 8168). Tram 1, 2, 5, 13, 14, 17. **Open** 11am-5pm during exhibitions only. **Admission** varies.

The admirals who led the wars against Britain are Dutch heroes, and the Nieuwe Kerk (New Church) has monuments to admirals Van Kinsbergen (1735-1819), Bentinck (1745-1831) and, most celebrated of all, Michiel de Ruyter (1607-1676). The most famous incident, though not prominent in British history books, came during the

Second English War (1664-1667). In 1667, de Ruyter cheekily sailed up the river Thames to Chatham naval base, stormed the dockyards and burnt the *Royal Charles*, the British flagship, as it lay at anchor. The *Royal Charles*' coat of arms was stolen, and is now displayed in the Rijksmuseum. In Delft's Oude Kerk are memorials to the equally illustrious admirals Piet Heyn (1577-1629); and Maarten Tromp (1598-1653). Naval battles of this period are a frequent theme of Delftware tiles in the Luis Lambert van Meerten Museum, also at Delft (*see chapter* **The Randstad**).

RICHES AND RIOTS

Despite diminished maritime prowess, Amsterdammers of all classes still had the highest standard of living in Europe well into the eighteenth century. The prestigious Plantage district (*see chapter* **Amsterdam by Area**) was the period's principal city development, of which the sole remaining patrician's villa is Frankendael (*see page 74*). Tradesmen and artisans flourished and their role in society can still be gauged by interpreting the shapes and carvings on gablestones. The cause of improving society through the practice and development of the arts and sciences, and the encouragement of commerce, was promoted by the Felix Meritis brotherhood. The brotherhood included pioneers in anatomy and astronomy.

Unlike the general upheavals elsewhere, civil unrest was rare in Amsterdam. One exception was the Undertakers' riot of 1696, which was provoked by the city's interference in their trade and the imposition of a tax on weddings and funerals. Fifty years later, in 1748, the entire province of Holland was shattered by a series of popular uprisings against the notorious tax farmers.

Felix Meritis Building

Keizersgracht 324, IW (626 2321). Tram 1, 2, 5. **Open** *café* noon-1am Tue-Fri; 5pm-2am Sat **No credit cards.**

Napoleon was once received at this magnificent building, designed in 1787 by Jacob Otten Husly. It was originally constructed for the Felix Meritis brotherhood and has a somewhat chequered past. In the nineteenth century, the fine oval concert hall became the centre of Amsterdam's music scene, until financial problems forced the building's sale to a printing company. In 1932 it was burnt down, but was soon restored. The Dutch Communist Party took up residence here in 1946 (*see chapter* **Postwar**), and in 1956, the building was attacked as a protest against the Soviet invasion of Hungary. Since the late seventies, it has housed the Amsterdam Summer University (*see chapter* **Students**) and the Shaffy Theatre (*see chapter* **Theatre**).

Frankendael
Middenweg 72, OE. Tram 9. **Open** *gardens only* sunrise-sunset daily. **Admission** free.

The only surviving 'country house' in the Plantage area, which was the most significant land development in Amsterdam during the eighteenth century. The area south from Plantage Middenlaan was converted into a residential district where rich businessmen constructed villas like Frankendael. The area had lots of green space which has now been parcelled into Artis Zoo (*see chapter* **Sightseeing**), Oosterpark and Frankendael's grounds (open to the public). You can't enter the villa, but the entrance is rich with Louis XVI ornamentation and there's a fountain with statues of river gods.

The Golden Curve
Herengracht between Leidsegracht and Vijzelstraat, IS. Tram 1, 2, 5, 16, 24, 25.

This stretch of Herengracht contains some of Amsterdam's best examples of eighteenth-century architecture. The buildings are faced with expensive sandstone and are wider than most canal houses. Most notable are numbers 475 (designed by Hans Jacob Husly in 1703); 485 (Jean Coulon, 1739), 493 and 527 (both of Louis XVI design, 1770). At 284 (Van Brienen House, 1728) there's another Louis XVI façade.

BANKING ON NO FUTURE

The Republic began to lag behind the major European powers in the eighteenth century. The Agricultural and Industrial Revolutions were taking off elsewhere, starting in Britain, but they didn't get off the ground in The Netherlands.

Amsterdam was nudged out of the shipbuilding market by England, and its lucrative textile industry was lost to other provinces, but the city exploited its position as the financial centre of the world – until the final and most devastating Anglo-Dutch War (1780-1784). The British hammered the Dutch fleets, both naval and merchant (which also carried heavy guns), crippling the Dutch's profitable trade with their far-eastern colonies. This was the beginning of the end of prosperity, but the death blow would come not from the English, but from the French.

OCCUPATION

The closest organisation the Dutch had to the republican movements of France and the United States was the Patriot Party. The Patriots tried to shake off the *stadhouders'* influence in the 1780s, but were foiled, partly by the intervention of the Prince of Orange's brother-in-law, Frederick William II, the King of Prussia, whose troops actually occupied Amsterdam in 1787. Hundreds of Patriots fled to exile in Paris, where their welcome convinced them of Napoleon's philanthropic intentions towards the wealthy Dutch Republic. The Patriots returned in triumph in 1795, backed by a French army of 'advisers'. With massive support from Amsterdam, they proclaimed the Batavian Republic (named after an early barbarian tribe from the mouth of the Rhine).

IGNOMINY

It sounded too good to be true, and it was. According to one contemporary: 'The French moved over the land like locusts'. Over f100 million (about a billion guilders in today's currency) was extracted from the Dutch people – Amsterdam paid a particularly high toll as it was one of the wealthiest cities. According to the French, this sum was appropriated in 'payment' for advice on the restructuring of the Dutch government along revolutionary, republican lines.

The French also sent a standing army, all 25,000 of whom had to be fed, equipped and billeted by its Dutch 'hosts'. The promised republican ideals seemed increasingly hollow when Napoleon installed one of his numerous brothers as King of The Netherlands. Piling insult on injury, the symbol of Amsterdam's mercantile ascendancy and civic pride, the City Hall of the Dam, was requisitioned as Louis Bonaparte's royal palace, Koninklijk Paleis (*see chapters* **The Golden Age** *and* **Sightseeing**).

However, even Louis was disturbed by the increasing impoverishment of a nation that had recently been one of Europe's most prosperous. After Louis had allowed Dutch smugglers to break Napoleon's blockade of Britain, he was forced to abdicate in 1810 and the Low Countries were absorbed into the French Empire.

Government by the French wasn't an unmitigated disaster for the Dutch. The foundations of the modern Dutch state were laid in the Napoleonic period, a civil code was introduced and there were advances in education. However, trade with Britain ceased and the growing price of Napoleon's wars prompted the Dutch to do something about what was a problem of their own making.

London has its Waterloo Station, and Amsterdam has a Waterloo Square – Waterlooplein – for exactly the same reason. The Dutch joined the revolt against France and after Napoleon's defeat at Waterloo in 1815, Amsterdam became the capital of a constitutional monarchy, incorporating what is now Belgium. This was the unity dreamt of by William the Silent of Orange before the Treaty of Utrecht in 1597, and once again an Orange claimed the throne – William VI of Orange was crowned William I in 1815. Although the Oranges still reign in the northern provinces to this day, the United Kingdom of the Netherlands, as it then existed, was to last only until 1831.

Between the Occupations

The long, slow haul to recovery saw Amsterdam become an industrialised city, with a booming population and attendant problems.

When the French were finally defeated and left Dutch soil in 1813, Amsterdam emerged with a fancy title – the capital of the new kingdom of The Netherlands – but very little else. The city wasn't even the seat of government. With its coffers almost totally depleted and its colonies abroad occupied by the British, Amsterdam would have to fight hard for recovery.

This was made more difficult by two huge barriers. First, Dutch colonial assets had been reduced to present-day Indonesia (then known as the Dutch East Indies), Surinam and the odd island in the Caribbean. Secondly, the Dutch were slow to join the Industrial Revolution. The Netherlands has few natural resources to exploit, and Dutch business preferred to keep

its hands clean by relying on the power of sail. Moreover, Amsterdam's opening to the sea, the Zuider Zee, was too shallow to accommodate the new, larger, steam-powered ships.

In an attempt to link the city to the North Sea port of Den Helder, the circuitous Great North Holland Canal was dug in 1824. But because it had so many bridges and locks, it was slow and thus expensive. Rotterdam gradually took over the capital's position as the most progressive industrial centre.

PROSPERITY RETURNS

Prosperity returned to Amsterdam after the 1860s. The city readjusted its economy to meet modern demands, and its trading position was

One of modernism's embryonic masterpieces: **Beurs van Berlage.** *See* **review** *page 76.*

greatly improved by the building of two canals. The opening of the Suez Canal in 1869 speeded up the passage to the Orient, producing a giant increase in commerce. But what the city needed most was easy access to the major shipping lanes of Northern Europe. Opened in 1876, the North Sea Canal (from Amsterdam to IJmuiden) enabled Amsterdam to take advantage of German industrial trade and to become The Netherlands' greatest ship-building port again – at least temporarily.

Industrial machinery was introduced late to Amsterdam. However, by the late nineteenth century, the city had begun to modernise production of the luxury goods it would become famous for – chocolates, cigars, liquors, beers and cut diamonds.

Although there had been a local railway track between Haarlem and Amsterdam since 1839, the city finally got a major rail link and a new landmark in 1889. Centraal Station (see chapter **Essential Information**) was designed by PJH Cuypers, who was known mainly for his design of neo-Gothic churches. The terminal was initially intended to be in the Pijp, but it was finally decided that the track should run along the Zuider Zee, shutting the city off from its seafront; much local objection ensued. There was also much controversy when the Rijksmuseum (see **Museums**) was sited at what was then the fringe of the city, and about the selection of Cuypers as its architect. Catholics demanded a neo-Gothic style and Protestants neo-Renaissance; the result was, like Centraal Station, uniquely eclectic and led to the museum being ridiculed as a 'cathedral of the arts' – not an entirely inappropriate label, given the contemporary boom in culture.

In 1877, the Carré Theatre opened (see chapter **Theatre**), to be followed a year later by the Concertgebouw (see **Music: Classical & Opera**), then by the neo-Renaissance municipal theatre, the Stadsschouwburg (1894; see **Theatre**), the Stedelijk Museum (1895; see **Art Galleries**) and, in 1926, by the Tropen Institute (now the Tropenmuseum, see **Museums**). The city's international standing improved to the point that in 1928 it hosted the Olympic Games.

Beurs van Berlage (Berlage Stock Exchange)

Damrak 279, C (626 5257/fax 620 4701). Tram 4, 9, 16, 24, 25. **Open** *office and enquiries* 9am-5pm Mon-Fri. Designed by Hendrik Petrus Berlage (1856-1934), this former stock exchange looks like a cross between an Italian *palazzo* and a railway station. It was intentionally experimental in its use of modern technology. Berlage advanced principles that would guide modernism: the building's function was fundamental to the design. Where Berlage departed from the norm was in his use of other arts, such as sculpture and decoration, to sym-

bolise the building's place in society. The Beurs is now revered as one of modernism's embryonic masterpieces, but it aroused outrage when it opened in 1903. It is now used for cultural events and trade fairs.

SOCIAL FACETS

Social welfare in Amsterdam, for so long dependent on the goodwill of the élite, was transformed in the nineteenth century. But until prosperity returned in the last third of the century, the living conditions of the working population were appalling. Amsterdam's solution before 1850 was to follow central government policy and round up the destitute, sending them off to do hard agricultural work. Yet, throughout this period, Amsterdam spent a relatively large amount of money on poor relief.

In the second half of the century, however, the notion that assistance only made the poor lazy gained more ground, and relief was cut back. But towards the end of the 1800s, the newly formed trade unions set up some forms of poor relief for their members. Socialist ideas began to permeate, and the way was paved for the development of one of the best social security systems in the world.

A SHORT CUT TO WEALTH?

The story of diamonds in Amsterdam is also the history of social change in the city (to visit working factories, see chapter **Sightseeing**). Diamond-working in Amsterdam had first been recorded in 1586. Fabulous stones such as the Koh-i-Noor (Mountain of Light) and the giant Cullinan diamond, both among the British crown jewels, were cut by Amsterdammers. But as the industry depended on the discovery of rare stones, it was in a continual state of flux. In the early 1870s, diamond cutters could light cigars with f10 notes (the average weekly wage for the rest of the workforce was then f8) and travel to work in a hansom cab. Yet a decade later, the city would have to issue proclamations prohibiting diamond workers from begging naked in the streets. The working classes, meanwhile, had become more literate and politicised, so the ideas behind the old guild system (see **The Golden Age**) took on a new resonance. Funds were established to protect diamond workers during slumps, and this led to the formation of the first Dutch trade union; numerous other trades soon followed suit.

In the early days of the trade union movement, socialists and the upper classes co-existed relatively harmoniously, but by the 1880s early activists had dispensed with their forelock-tugging ways. The movement needed an articulate leader and it found one in Ferdinand Domela Nieuwenhuis (see below), who also set up a political party, the Social Democratic Union. The SDU faded into obscurity after a

The De Stijl **Openluchtschool.** See **review.**

split in 1894, but a splinter group, the Social Democratic Labour Party (SDAP), later won the first-ever socialist city-council seat for the diamond workers' union chief, Henri Polak in 1901. The SDAP went on to introduce the welfare state after World War II.

Educational reform was perhaps the greatest step forward made in the late nineteenth century. A network of free primary schools was set up to teach the working classes the rudiments of reading, writing and arithmetic.

Ferdinand Domela Nieuwenhuis Museum

Herengracht 266, IW (673 2820 evenings only). Tram 13, 14, 17. **Open** 10am-4pm Mon-Fri; phone first during school holidays as access is through a school. **Admission** free.

The museum pays a touching homage to the man who became the father of Dutch socialism. Once a Protestant pastor, Nieuwenhuis (1846-1919) threw himself into the task of making the lower classes politically aware. His growing influence worried employers, and many of them co-operated in engineering social change. Material includes personal effects, his library, letters, photos and some great posters. Documents focus on the labour movement of the period and on Nieuwenhuis's life. A statue of Ferdinand Domela Nieuwenhuis can be found on Haarlemmerplein (OW).

General Diamond Workers' Union building

Henri Polaklaan, IE. Tram 7, 9, 14.
This building was designed by Berlage to house the offices of The Netherlands' first trade union. Plans are

afoot to convert it into a trade union museum, but no date has been set for its opening.

A NEW METROPOLIS

Amsterdam's population had stagnated at around a quarter of a million for two centuries after the Golden Age, but between 1850 and 1900 it more than doubled. This increased labour force was desperately needed to meet the demands of a revitalised economy, but the major problem facing the council was how to house the new workers. Today, the old inner city quarters are desirable addresses, but they used to be home to many of Amsterdam's poor. The picturesque Jordaan (*see chapter* **Amsterdam by Area**), where riots broke out with increasing regularity, was occupied primarily by the lowest-paid workers. Canals were used as cesspits and the mortality rate was high. Oddly enough, the Jordaan was the first area in the city to have Tarmac streets. The decision wasn't philanthropic; it came after Queen Wilhelmina had been pelted by cobblestones as she was driven through the Jordaan's streets.

Around the old centre, entirely new neighbourhoods were constructed. The new housing developments – the Pijp (*see chapter* **Amsterdam by Area**), Dapper and Staatslieden quarters – weren't luxurious by any means, and most of them were cheaply built by speculators, but they had simple lavatory facilities (though no bathroom). Wealthier city-dwellers found elegance and space in homes built around Vondelpark and in the south of the city.

The expensive fashions for art nouveau and art deco largely bypassed the city, although the Tuschinsky Cinema (*see chapter* **Film**) is a fine example of art deco, and the luxurious café of the otherwise 'Amsterdam School' **American Hotel** of 1900-1902 (*see* **Accommodation**) has both art nouveau and art deco features. Perhaps the paucity of these styles is due to the Dutch inclination towards elegant functionalism, rather than decadent decoration. The purist **De Stijl** movement (*see below* **Openluchtschool**) took modernism to an extreme.

Greenpeace Building

Keizergracht 174, IW. Tram 13, 14, 17/Bus 21, 170, 171, 172.
The former headquarters of the ELHB insurance company is one of the few decent examples of art nouveau in the city. Designed by G van Arkel in 1906, it's now the head office of environmental campaigners Greenpeace.

Openluchtschool (Open-air School)

Cliostraat 36-40, OS. Tram 5, 24/Bus 26.
Amsterdam's main example of the **De Stijl** movement. Started in 1917 in Rotterdam with Theo van Doesburg's journal *De Stijl* (The Style), the movement soon included the painter Piet Mondrian and the furniture-maker and architect, Gerrit Rietvelt. Its design group advocated severe functionalism in order to house large numbers of people. Influenced by Soviet constructivism, it

The Amsterdam school

Mention council housing projects and most people think of cheaply constructed, darkly oppressive tower blocks. However, when the rest of Europe was embroiled in World War I, the Dutch managed to create a model of successful urban planning. The *Amsterdaamse School* produced both superlative public buildings and housing on a human scale with an individualistic touch.

Prevailing socialist thinking elevated the status of the working class, and the council determined that workers' homes should be spacious and of high quality. HP Berlage was the city council's chief architect of the period (*see page 76* **Beurs van Berlage** *under* **Prosperity Returns**) and he implemented its *Plan Zuid* (plan for Amsterdam South). Michel de Klerk and Pieter Kramer, two leading Amsterdam School architects, were commissioned by the council. They came up with an innovative design: long, low housing blocks, culminating in landmark towers, and incorporating expressionist features such as curved and slanted walls, ruffles of brick and playful shapes for windows.

Through his architecture, Berlage hoped to encourage the working classes to adopt a more bourgeois way of living. He designed kitchens to be tiny spaces so people would be obliged to eat in the dining room he provided. Also, he usually set window sills at eye-rather than waist-level, to prevent people from frittering away the day, gossiping with neigh-

bours. One of the best preserved examples of this kind of architecture is at **Hembrugstraat**, OW, built by De Klerk in 1917. The end of the housing block has an extraordinary tower which serves no useful purpose (like most of De Klerk's elaborations). Other examples include the apartments at **Henriëtte Ronnerplein** (1921-23), in Amsterdam South, and housing at **PL Takstraat**, OS (1921-22), which is dominated by the fanciful pleated walls of the Dageraad building. These projects have widely been judged successes by residents as well as architects.

Some of the most distinctive examples of Amsterdam School architecture are not houses, but public buildings. A VVV walking tour takes in many of the prominent buildings of the genre (for details, *see chapter* **Sightseeing**). The earliest example (1911-16) is the peculiar, turreted **Scheepvaarthuis** (Shipping Building), Prins Hendrikkade 8, C. Designed by Kramer and De Klerk, it's decorated with maritime reliefs and is sculpted both inside and out. The **Lydia House**, Roelof Hartplein, OS, is a witty variation by De Klerk on the typical Dutch *buurthuis* (neighbourhood house), a community centre. In the Zaanstraat neighbourhood (OW) is the extraordinary **Spaarndammerbuurt Post Office** (1917-20) Spaarndammerplantsoen, OW. This squat community centre has a ruffled, drum-like tower and eccentrically shaped window frames.

---

was contemporary with the German *Bauhaus*. Characteristic features include rectangular planes and grids in white, black and primary colours, arranged in harmony. Openluchtschool was a typically idealistic project. There are huge windows and classroom-sized balconies for *al fresco* teaching, which embraced the fitness ethic of the period. The best *De Stijl* buildings are JJP Oud's **Café de Unie** in Rotterdam and the **Rietvelt-Schröder House** in Utrecht, which looks like a Mondrian painting projected in 3-D (for both, *see chapter* **The Randstad**).

WAR AND DEPRESSION

The city didn't fare badly in the first two decades of this century, but Dutch neutrality during World War I brought problems. While the élite lined their pockets selling arms, the poor were confronted with continual food shortages. In 1917, with food riots erupting, especially in the Jordaan, the city had to open soup kitchens and introduce rationing.

The army was called in to suppress another outbreak of civil unrest in the Jordaan in 1934. This time the cause was unemployment, endemic throughout the industrialised world after the Wall Street Crash of 1929. In the worst year of the Depression, 1936, historians estimate that 19 per cent of the workforce was unemployed.

Unfortunately, the humiliation of means testing for unemployment benefit meant that many families suffered in hungry silence. Many Dutch workers even moved to Germany where Hitler's National Socialism was creating a mass of new jobs. At home, Amsterdam initiated extensive public works, under the 1934 General Extension Plan, whereby the city's southern outskirts were developed for public housing (*see above* **The Amsterdam School**). The city was just emerging from the Depression by the time the Nazis invaded in May 1940.

World War II

Like much of Europe, Holland was devastated by the war, and the learning and recovery process still continues.

Amsterdam endured World War II without being flattened by bombs, but a lot of its buildings, infrastructure and inhabitants were reduced to a terrible state by Nazi occupation. The Holocaust also left an indelible scar on a city whose population in 1940 was ten per cent Jewish. You can trace these experiences through the photographs and relics of the small World War II collection at the Amsterdams Historisch Museum (*see chapter* **Museums**).

INVASION

Early in the morning of 10 May 1940, German bombers mounted a surprise attack on Dutch airports and military barracks in order to destroy the Dutch air force. The government and people had hoped that The Netherlands could remain neutral, as they had in World War I. Thus the armed forces were unprepared for war. Yet the Dutch aimed to hold off the Germans until the British and French could come to their assistance. This hope was in vain. Queen Wilhelmina and the government fled to London to form a government in exile, leaving Supreme Commander Winkelman in charge of state authority. Many Dutch considered this cowardice, but later the Queen's broadcasts on *Radio Oranje* boosted the morale of the Dutch public and the Resistance. She and the government would not return to The Netherlands until the liberation in summer of 1945 (*see below* **Liberation**).

The centre of Rotterdam was destroyed by bombing, and when the Germans threatened the same for cities like Utrecht and Amsterdam, Winkelman capitulated on 14 May 1940. French and Dutch troops continued to fight in Zeeland, but succumbed three days later.

The Dutch colonies of Indonesia and New Guinea were also invaded (by the Japanese), in January 1942. After their capitulation on 8 March, Dutch colonials were imprisoned in Japanese concentration camps and the Indonesian nationalists Soekarno and Hatta proclaimed an independent republic.

NAZIFICATION

Hitler appointed Arthur Seyss-Inquart, an Austrian Nazi, as *Rijkskommissaris* (State Commissioner) of The Netherlands. His policy was to tie the Dutch economy to the German one

and to Nazify (*nazificeren*) Dutch society. The National Socialist Movement (NSB) was the largest and most important Fascist political party in The Netherlands, although it was much smaller than its counterparts in Italy and Germany. In the 1939 elections the NSB won less than five per cent of the votes, but it was, of course, the only Dutch party not prohibited during the occupation. Its doctrine greatly resembled German Nazism, but the NSB wanted to maintain Dutch autonomy under the direction of Germany. In the beginning the Germans operated very carefully, hoping to reduce resistance to a minimum and win the population over to the National Socialist cause. So not all important posts were delegated to NSB members, because most Dutch rejected them as racists and betrayers of their country.

During the first years of the war, the Nazis allowed most people to continue their normal daily life relatively undisturbed. But because of rationing, the Dutch became vulnerable to the black market; cinemas and theatres eventually closed because of curfews, censorship and disrupted transport, although there were no travel restrictions. This soft approach failed to Nazify the locals, so the Germans adopted more aggressive measures. Dutch men were forced to work in German industry and economic exploitation assumed appalling forms. In April 1943 all Dutch soldiers – who'd been captured during the invasion and then released in the summer of 1940 – were ordered to give themselves up as prisoners of war. In an atmosphere of deep shock and outrage, strikes broke out during April and May throughout the country, only to be suppressed bloodily.

COLLABORATION

Ordinary people, as well as the political and economic élite, at first didn't have to decide between collaboration and resistance. They 'accommodated' their daily routines as much as possible to the new situation. In this cautious atmosphere the Germans took the first measures against the Jews (*see below* **The Holocaust**). As Nazi policies became more virulent, opposition swelled and a growing minority of people were confronted with the difficult choice of whether to obey German measures

*Jan W Havermans' **Apollolaan** sculpture commemorates the death of three members of the Dutch Resistance. See **Resistance Monuments**.*

or to resist. But most of the population were neither collaborators nor Resistance workers.

There were many patterns of collaboration. Some people joined the NSB, others intimidated Jews, were involved in economic collaboration, or betrayed people in hiding or members of the Resistance; a few even signed up for German military service. In Amsterdam several social institutions gave information about Jews to the Germans, who had claimed that the Jews would be employed in the German camps. The most shocking institutional collaboration was by the police, who dragged Jews out of their houses for deportation. Sometimes on these *razzias* (raids) they caught Jews who weren't on their lists. After the war between 120,000 and 150,000 people were arrested for collaborating. Mitigating circumstances – as in the case of NSB members who helped the Resistance – made judgements very complicated and eventually 60,000 people were brought to justice.

RESISTANCE

The Resistance comprised chiefly Calvinist Protestants and Communists. The latter gained much public support, although the Protestant élite ensured that there was no Communist takeover after liberation. Anti-Nazi activities took several forms. Illegal newspapers, unlike the censored press, kept the population properly informed and urged resistance; copies can be seen in the **Verzetsmuseum Amsterdam** (*see below*).

There were many kinds of underground groups, which spied for the Allies, fought an armed struggle against the Germans through assassination and sabotage, or falsified identity cards. A national organisation took care of people who wanted to hide because they refused to work in German industry. It also helped the railway strikers, Dutch soldiers and illegal workers who were being sought by the Germans. Other groups helped Jews into hiding, which was a lot more difficult and risky. By the end of the war, more than 300,000 people had gone underground in The Netherlands.

Resistance Monuments

Apollolaan *at Beethovenstraat, OS. Tram 5, 24.*
H M van Randwijkplantsoen *Singelgracht at Weteringlaan, IS. Tram 6, 7, 10, 16, 24, 25.*
Weteringplantsoen, *IS. Tram 6, 7, 10, 16, 24, 25.*
The **Apollolaan** sculpture is of three men waiting to be shot on 24 October 1944 as a reprisal against the killing of a member of the German Sicherheits Dienst, an espionage organisation, by the Resistance. Sculpted by Jan W Havermans, it was unveiled in 1954. The **H M van Randwijk Pleasure Garden** was named after an important Resistance figure. The 1970 monument, designed by Gerda van der Laan, has the text: 'A people that gives in to tyrants will lose more than body and goods; then the light is extinguished.' Nearby on **Weteringplantsoen** 35 people were shot on 12 March 1945, as punishment for a Resistance attack on Rauter, head of the German police

in The Netherlands. The sculpture of a man shot with a bugle in his hand is by G Bolhuis.

Verzetsmuseum Amsterdam (Museum of the Resistance)

Lekstraat 63, OS (644 9797). Tram 4, 25. **Open** 10am-5pm Tue-Fri; 1-5pm Sat, Sun, public holidays. *Closed* 25, 31 Dec; 1 Jan. **Admission** f4.50; f2 under-16s; f2 CJP card holders; free with Museum Card; group discount (min 15 people). **No credit cards.**

This collection is housed in a former synagogue in the Rivierenbuurt, a part of town where Anne Frank lived between escaping Nazi Germany in 1933 and hiding in the Prinsengracht attic. The permanent collection holds artefacts, documents and interactive displays explaining matters such as sabotage, espionage and the February Strike. You can hear radio broadcasts, look around a mock-up of a hiding place and see a bicycle-powered machine used to print illegal papers. Much of today's Dutch press started underground, namely: *Het Parool* (The Password), *Vrij Nederland* (Free Netherlands), *Trouw* (Loyalty) and *De Waarheid* (The Truth, now called Forum); *see chapter* **Media**. Early editions of these are on display. In addition exhibitions highlight contemporary developments such as extreme right wing Dutch political parties, about which there is general concern. There are other Resistance Museums in Leeuwarden in Friesland (*see chapter* **The Provinces**) and Gouda (*see chapter* **The Randstad**). *Wheelchair access and toilets for the disabled.*

THE HOLOCAUST

'I see how the world is slowly becoming a desert, I hear more and more clearly the approaching thunder that will kill us,' wrote Anne Frank in her diary on 15 July 1944. As well as to Jews, Anne's words applied to the less publicly mourned gypsies, homosexuals, the mentally handicapped and political opponents, who were all severely persecuted during the war (*see below* **Gypsies and Homosexuals**). The genocide of the Jews, especially, was carried out in a hideously accurate and systematic way by means of the latest industrial techniques. Anti-semitism in Holland had not been as virulent as in Germany, France or Austria. Yet most – but not all – of the Dutch closed their eyes to the persecution, and there's still a feeling of national guilt as a result.

There were three stages to the Holocaust. First came measures to enforce the isolation of the Jews: the ritual slaughter of animals was prohibited, Jewish government employees were dismissed, Jews were banned from public places such as restaurants, cinemas and libraries and, eventually, all Jews were made to wear a yellow Star of David. Some non-Jewish Dutch courageously wore the badge as a demonstration of solidarity. Concentration was the second stage. From the beginning of 1942 all Dutch Jews were obliged to move to three areas in Amsterdam, which were isolated by signs, drawbridges and barbed wire.

The final stage was deportation. Between July 1942 and September 1943, most of the 140,000 Dutch Jews were deported, via **Kamp** Westerbork (*see below* **Gypsies and Homosexuals**), to death camps, where over 100,000 were killed. Although some 27,000 went underground, about half of these were in the end captured and sent to the gas chambers. In 1941, public outrage at the first deportations from Amsterdam provoked the most dramatic protest against the anti-semitic terror, the impressive **February Strike** (*see below* **Dokwerker statue**). *See also* chapter **Museums: Joods Historisch Museum.**

Anne Frankhuis

Prinsengracht 263, IW (626 4533). Tram 13, 14, 17. **Open** *Sept-May* 9am-5pm Mon-Sat; 10am-5pm Sun, public holidays; *June-Aug* 9am-7pm Mon-Sat; 10am-7pm Sun, public holidays. *Closed* 25 Dec, 1 Jan, Yom Kippur. **Admission** f7; f3.50 10-17s; free under-10s; group discount. **No credit cards.**

Anne Frankhuis is one of the city's most visited sights. Having already fled from persecution in Germany in 1933, Anne Frank, her sister Margot, her parents and four other Jews went into hiding on 5 July 1942. Living in an annexe behind Prinsengracht 263, they were sustained by friends who risked everything to help them. Eventually, on 4 August 1944, the occupants of the annexe were arrested and transported to concentration camps, where Anne died along with Margot and their mother. Her father, Otto Frank, survived and decided that Anne's moving and perceptive diary should be published. The archive here contains a photo album of Mr Dussel, one of the Jews in hiding with Anne, which was found in 1978 at Waterlooplein Flea Market. There's also an exhibition on the Jews, and their persecution in the war, and a display of different editions of the diary (known as *Het Achterhuis* – The Annexe – in The Netherlands). Exhibitions chart current developments in racism, neo-Fascism and anti-semitism; there are explanatory texts in English. The museum is managed by the Anne Frank Foundation, whose aims are to combat prejudice, discrimination and oppression. The Educational Service devises special programmes for schools and other groups. A **statue of Anne Frank** by Mari Andriessen (1977) stands where Westermarkt and Prinsengracht meet.

Documentation department: Keizersgracht 192, IW (626 4533). Tram 13, 14, 17. Open 1-5pm Mon-Fri for reference.

Dokwerker statue

Jonas Daniel Meijerplein, C. Tram 9, 14.

The **Dokwerker statue**, sculpted by Mari Andriessen, commemorates an anti-Nazi protest unparalleled in occupied Europe. In February 1941, members of the Jewish Resistance fought with Dutch Nazis, who had been intimidating and terrorising Jews. When one of the Fascists was killed, the SS and the 'Grüne Polizei' (Dutch Police) rounded up 400 Jews here on J D Meijerplein and deported them to Mauthausen for execution. In protest, the local population started a general strike on 25 February, led by dockers and transport workers. After just two days, the strike was suppressed with brutal violence. As a warning against future anti-semitism, a ceremony is held at the statue each year on 25 February.

Hollandse Schouwburg (Dutch Theatre)

Plantage Middenlaan, IE. Tram 14.

For about 50,000 Jews the Hollandse Schouwburg was their last residence in Amsterdam and there's a monument here to all those deported between 1940 and 1945.

The Germans had formed the Jewish Council, a so-called interest group for Dutch Jews, whose members were forced to prepare the deportations of their own people. One member was Etty Hillesum, whose published diary, *Etty: A Diary*, recounts her voluntary decision to go to Westerbork (she ended up at Auschwitz), explaining the fatalistic submissiveness of so many Dutch Jews as a refusal to play the role of victim in an unequal fight. Jews who didn't show up voluntarily for 'work' in Germany were dragged out of their houses or hiding places and brought to this building, which had been a Jewish theatre since 1941. In the theatre there was a Resistance group led by Walter Süskind, who helped Jews – children above all – to escape deportation, and there's a plaque here to his memory.

Holocaust Monuments

Ravensbrückmonument *Museumplein, OS. Tram 2, 3, 5, 12, 16.*
Jewish Resistance Monument *Zwanenburgwal at Amstel, C. Tram 9, 14.*
The **Women of Ravensbrück** memorial by J van Santen, G Eckhardt and F Nix was unveiled in 1975. Light flickers from a central silver column to illuminate metal panels set in a semi-circle; the text runs, 'For women who to the utmost kept saying no to Fascism'. The memorial to the dead of the **Jewish Resistance**, designed by JJ Glatt and made by EM Glatt, is a column of black marble which bears the quote from the Bible: 'If my eyes were a well of tears I would cry day and night for the fallen fighters of my beloved people'.

GYPSIES AND HOMOSEXUALS

The Nazis wanted to eliminate Dutch gypsies in as systematic a way as they had dealt with German gypsies much earlier. On 16 May 1944 the Dutch police were ordered to arrest all the gypsies in the country. They deported 578 to **Westerbork** transit camp (*see below*), but 279 of them were returned home because, according to Nazi race laws, they weren't gypsies. More than 200,000 European gypsies, about 200 of them Dutch, were exterminated in concentration camps. The Nazis exploited the prejudices of many of the Dutch against gypsies, whose slaughter was virtually ignored.

Homosexuals were also threatened with extermination, but because they were not easily recognisable their persecution was less systematic. Public morality acts prohibited homosexual behaviour and gay pressure groups ceased their activities. Gays were sometimes arrested in bars and sent to the German labour service, and men arrested for other activities were punished more severely if they were discovered to be gay. Amsterdam has the world's first memorial to persecuted gays, the **Homo-monument** (*see chapter* **Gay Amsterdam**), which incorporates pink triangles in its design, turning the Nazi badge of persecution into a symbol of pride.

Gypsy monument

Museumplein, OS. Tram 2, 3, 5, 12, 16.
The *hel van vuur* (hell of fire) sculpture by Heleen Levano, unveiled in 1978, was the world's first monument to gypsy persecution by the Nazis. The gypsies hold a commemoration ceremony here on 1 August each year.

Kamp Westerbork

Herinneringscentrum (Remembrance Centre)
Oosthalen 8, Hooghalen, Drenthe. **Getting there** Car *Centre and site of Kamp are signed from A28 between Hoogeveen and Assen (05939 2600).* No public transport. **Open** *Centre 1 Apr-31 Oct* 9.30am-5pm Mon-Fri; 1-5pm Sat, Sun; *1 Nov-31 Mar* 9.30am-5pm Mon-Fri; 1-5pm Sat. *Site of Kamp* 24 hours daily.
Admission *Centre* f3.50; f1.50 8-18s, CJP card holders; free under-8s; group discount (min 10 people); *Site of Kamp* free. **No credit cards.**
Westerbork transit camp was originally built in 1939 to handle Jews who fled to The Netherlands from Nazi Germany. Between 1942 and 1945, Jews and gypsies passed through the camp and were treated relatively well, because the Germans wanted them to believe they were going to Germany to work, not to die. Today, the site is parkland. With the aid of text panels, you can see the house of a camp commandant, a cellar, a small pill-box bunker, a reconstruction of a watch-tower and traces of canals, although the housing sheds have been demolished. A monument by Ralph Prins symbolises the ascension of the prisoners' souls using railway track (from the line to the death camps) bent up towards the sky. The Remembrance Centre is a 2½km (1½ mile) car drive away (the centre has just three cycles and there are no buses). It has several exhibitions: on Westerbork Camp; on World War II in The Netherlands, stressing the Holocaust; on the history of Dutch Jewry; and a duplicate of the Netherlands display in Poland's Auschwitz Museum. You can also see some drawings by two young Westerbork prisoners.
Books for reference and sale. Tours by prior arrangement. Wheelchair access; toilet for the disabled.

HUNGER WINTER

The 'Hunger Winter' of 1944 was the result of three developments. The supply of coal had ceased after the liberation of the south (*see below* **Liberation**), and a railway strike, called by the Dutch government in exile in London to hasten German defeat, was disastrous for the supply of food. In retaliation for the strike, the Germans damaged Schiphol Airport and the harbours of Rotterdam and Amsterdam, and resorted to stealing cars, bicycles, ships, machines, food, textiles, fuel and so on. In Amsterdam, walking became the only means of transport, domestic refuse was no longer collected, sewers overflowed and the population, suffering malnutrition and cold, was vulnerable to disease.

There were three survival strategies. The first was stealing fuel. More than 20,000 trees were cut down and 4,600 buildings were demolished. Floors, staircases, joists and rafters were plundered, causing the collapse of many houses, particularly those left by deported Jews; Jodenbreestraat and Sint Antoniesbreestraat were ruined. The second scheme was black marketeering. At the end of the war the Dutch were given vouchers for food, clothes and fuel. But supplies were scarce and many people couldn't even afford to buy their allowance, let alone the expensive produce on the black market. The last resort was 'hunger expeditions', whereby citizens took pushcarts to the countryside and tried to buy food from farmers. By the end of winter, 20,000 people had died of starvation and disease and much of the city was damaged.

LIBERATION

The Allies liberated the south of The Netherlands on 5 September 1944, *Dolle Dinsdag* (Mad Tuesday). But celebrations in the north were premature because the Allies' priority was to reach Germany. Complete liberation came after the Hunger Winter (*see above*) on 5 May 1945, when it became apparent that The Netherlands was the most badly hit country in Western Europe. In spite of the chaos, destruction, hunger and the loss of so many lives, there were effusive celebrations. But in Amsterdam tragedy struck on 7 May, when German soldiers opened fire on a crowd gathered on Dam Square to welcome their Canadian liberators, killing 22 people.

Nationaal Monument

Dam Square, C. Tram 1, 2, 4, 5, 9, 13, 14, 16, 17, 24, 25. Unveiled on 4 May 1956, ts national memorial was erected for all the Dutch who lost their lives in the war. The 22m (72ft) obelisk decorated with sculpted figures was designed by De Stijl architect JJP Oud and sculptor John Raedecker. It's fronted by two lions (national symbols) and embedded in the wall behind it are urns containing soil from each province and from the colonies of Indonesia, Surinam and The Netherlands Antilles. Every year, on 4 May, all the Dutch war victims are commemorated here in a remembrance ceremony (liberation feasts take place on 5 May); *see chapter* **Amsterdam by Season**.

National War and Resistance Museum

Museumpark 1, Overloon, Noord Brabant; 35 miles south of Nijmegen (04781 41820). **Open** *June-Aug* 9.30am-6pm daily; *Sept-May* 10am-5pm daily. **Closed** 24, 25, 31 Dec; 1 Jan. **Admission** f6; f4 13-19s, CJP card holders; f3 4-12s; free under-4s, with Museum Card; group discount (min 20 people). **No credit cards.** Overloon was the site of intense fighting (27 Sept-14 Oct 1944) as the Allies pushed towards Germany; east of the town is the British war cemetery. Set in parkland, the Nationaal Oorlogs- en Verzetsmuseum displays relics of both Allied and German militaria. There are some fascinating documents and photographs, plus tanks, aircraft and a V-1 flying bomb.

Nieuwe Oosterbegraafplaats Cemetery

Kruislaan 126, OS (694 0074). Tram 9/Bus 69, 169. **Open** 8am-4pm Mon-Fri; 10am-4pm Sat, Sun. This cemetery has several Allied war graves, many of soldiers only 'known unto God'. The three most notable memorials are in section 76. The **Buchenwald Monument** is a flat, white stone with two hands holding an urn which contains soil from every country whose citizens were among those killed at Buchenwald concentration camp. The famous Dutch writer-sculptor Jan Wolkers made the **Never Again Auschwitz** memorial with the words *nooit meer Auschwitz* standing in glass letters on a plate of glass. In a sunken urn containing the ashes of Jews from Auschwitz are three broken mirrors, so that heaven will never again be reflected perfectly. A statue of a woman waving a flag represents **Resistance** fighters whose deaths, says the text, teach us that tyrants cannot prevail where people refuse to be slaves.

The Nieuwe Oosterbegraafplaats Cemetery *contains many Allied war graves. See* **review.**

Post-war

Years of rebuilding Amsterdam were followed by a period of radical action and grass-root 'happenings'.

The Netherlands was deeply scarred by the German occupation, losing about ten per cent of all housing, 30 per cent of industry and 40 per cent of its total production capacity. The transport system had been immobilised and some of the country's dikes had been blown up, leaving large areas flooded. Amsterdam tried to put a brave face on its pains. Although it had escaped the bombing raids which devastated Rotterdam, it had borne the brunt of the deportations, and only 5,000 out of a pre-war total Jewish population of 80,000 remained.

NATIONAL REVIVAL

Despite intense poverty and drastic shortages of food, fuel and building materials, the Dutch tackled the massive task of post-war recovery and restoration with the spirit of the Resistance. There was a strong sense of optimism, excitement and unity, which was sustained until the end of the forties. In 1948, people threw street parties, firstly to celebrate the inauguration of Queen Julianna and later the achievements of Amsterdam athlete Fanny Blankers-Koen, who'd won four gold medals at the London Olympics.

For a time, the Dutch political tendency to *verzuilen* (divide up into small, competing interest groups) threatened to undermine this heady mood. Some Dutch flirted briefly with Communism directly after the war, but in 1948 a compromise was struck between the Catholic party KVP and the newly created Labour party PvdA. The two governed in successive coalitions until 1958. Led by Prime Minister Willem Drees, the government resuscitated pre-war social programmes and laid the basis for the country's lavish welfare state. Under the firm but benevolent hand of Drees, the Dutch reverted to the virtues of a conservative, provincial society: decency, hard work and thrift.

The country's first priority after the war was economic recovery. The Amsterdam city council concentrated on reviving the two motors of its economy: Schiphol Airport and the port of Amsterdam, which was boosted by the opening of the Amsterdam-Rhine Canal in 1952. Joining Belgium and Luxembourg in the Benelux bloc brought the country trade benefits and The Netherlands was the first to repay its Marshall Plan loans – $133 million out of a total $978 million received in aid. The authorities dusted off pre-war development plans and embarked on a period of rapid urban expansion. To the west, garden cities were created, such as Slotervaart, Geuzenveld and Osdorp. The architecture was sober, but the setting was airy and spacious. But as people moved out to the new suburbs, businesses moved into the centre, worsening congestion on the already cramped roads, which had to deal with an explosive growth in car traffic on top of the trams, buses and bicycles. Road casualties soared.

A quite unanticipated blow to the economy was the flood disaster of 1953. An unusually high spring tide broke the sea defences in Zeeland, flooding large sections of south-west Netherlands, claiming almost 2,000 lives and causing billions of guilders worth of damage. The Delta Works (*see chapter* **The Provinces: Zeeland**) was built to prevent a repetition of the disaster.

COLONIES AND CULTURE

Directly after the war, the Dutch colonies of Indonesia and New Guinea (now West Irian), liberated from Japanese occupation, pushed for independence. With Indonesia accounting for 20 per cent of their pre-war economy, the Dutch were unwilling to hand over power and launched military interventions on 20 July 1947 and 18 December 1948. These could not prevent the transfer of sovereignty to Indonesia on 27 December 1949. The dispute with New Guinea dragged on until 1962, and did much to damage The Netherlands' international reputation. Colonial immigrants, including the later arrival of Surinamese, and of Turkish and Moroccan 'guest workers', now comprise 16 per cent of the population. Although poorer jobs and housing have usually been their lot, racial tension has been relatively low. Only those from The Moluccas, denied independence from Indonesia, have not integrated so well: the Dutch train hijacks in the seventies were by Moluccan separatists.

By the end of the fifties the economy was reviving and the welfare state was in place, but memories of the war lingered and there was much civil unrest. Strikes flared at the port, and council workers defied a ban on industrial action. In 1951, protesters clashed violently with police outside the Concertgebouw (*see*

Fort van Sjakoo *stocks the iconography of radical politics. See* **review** *page 86.*

chapter **Music: Classical & Opera**), angered by the appointment of the pro-Nazi Paul van Kempen as conductor of the Concertgebouw Orchestra. In 1956, demonstrators also besieged the Felix Meritis Building, the base of the Dutch communist party CPN from 1946 until the late seventies and now the Shaffy Theatre (*see chapters* **Decline & Fall, Dance** *and* **Theatre**), hurling stones in outrage at the Soviet invasion of Hungary.

As the fifties progressed, Amsterdammers began to turn back to pre-war pursuits: fashion and interviews with celebrities filled the newspapers and cultural events mushroomed. In 1947, the city had launched the prestigious **Holland Festival**, which is still held every June (*see chapter* **Amsterdam by Season**). The élite held annual events called 'Boekenbal', where writers met royalty and other dignitaries. New avant-garde artistic movements emerged, notably the COBRA art group (*see* **Art Galleries**), whose 1949 exhibition at the Stedelijk Museum caused an uproar. The *vijftigers*, a group of experimental poets led by Lucebert, also sent shock waves through the literary establishment. Many of these writers, intellectuals and artists gathered in brown cafés around Leidseplein, particularly **Café Eijlders** (*see* **Amsterdam by Area: Leidseplein**).

SIXTIES HEYDAY

The sixties must go down as one of the most colourful and intoxicating decades in Amsterdam's history. There were genuine official attempts to improve society and make it more prosperous. The IJ Tunnel eased communications to North Amsterdam and the national economy took off. There were high hopes for vast rehousing developments, such as the Bijlmermeer (*see below* **Housing Crisis**), and there was influential new architecture by Aldo van Eyck and Herman Herzberger; *see chapter* **Students** for the latter's University Arts Faculty and Weesperstraat Student Flats and Restaurant.

Yet the generous hand of the welfare state was being bitten: 'Welfare is not well-being', ran a common slogan of the day. Discontent began early in the decade on a variety of issues: the nuclear threat; rampant urban expansion and industrialisation; the consumer society and authority in general. Amsterdam saw the creation of popular movements similar to those in other West European cities, but with a zaniness and creativity not found elsewhere. Because protest and dissent have always been a vital part of The Netherlands' democratic process, and the Dutch have a habit of keeping things in proportion, many popular demonstrations took a playful form.

Design for Netherlands Railway and ptt Post

Designers in Amsterdam and The Hague have set the world pace in graphics, drawing on the Dutch appetite for avant-garde, spartan design with a touch of fun. You'll encounter their work whether travelling, posting a letter or spending money. International attention was drawn by Gert Dumbar's sixties' redesign of **Netherlands Railways**, from their distinctive colour scheme and signs to the timetable, which is one of the best-selling books in The Netherlands. Dumbar's studio also created a new corporate identity for the **Rijksmuseum** in the eighties and in 1977, with Total Design (the first Dutch design consultancy, set up in 1963 and famous for the Schiphol Airport sign system), for **ptt Post**, including many stamps. Since the sixties, the head of ptt Post's design branch, RDE Oxenaar, has modernised Dutch **banknotes**, introducing vivid colours and the first use of relief points for the blind (*see chapter* **Survival**).

Municipal Orphanage

IJsbaanpad 3, OS (676 9753).
Built in 1960-61 behind the Olympic Stadium, this is one of Van Eyck's most important works. Low-level and on a human scale, its modular units were inspired by African styles and in turn became an international model of school architecture. Unfortunately poor construction has threatened its existence, but it may become the College for Visual Arts. In 1981 Van Eyck designed a similarly sensitive building for the **Moederhuis** (*see chapter* **Survival**).

PROVO HAPPENINGS

The feeling of discontent gained focus in 1964, when *ludiek* (happenings) around **'t Lieverdje statue** (*see below*), at Spui, highlighting political or social problems, became the springboard for a new radical subculture, the Provos (from *provocatie* – provocation). Founded by Roel van Duyn, a philosophy student at Amsterdam University, the Provos only numbered about two dozen, but they appealed to a wide group of young people. When police cracked down heavy-handedly on a *ludiek* in 1965, clashes followed, culminating in two serious bouts of civil disorder which drew international attention.

On 10 March 1966, protests about the cost of Princess Beatrix's wedding to Claus von Amsberg at the Westerkerk, and about the fact that her groom was German, turned into a riot. Demonstrators threw smoke bombs at the wedding procession and fought police throughout the city. On 13 June, during a demonstration by building workers, the (false) assumption that a marcher's death was caused by police resulted in four days of violent clashes. After a month, Amsterdam's police chief was forced to resign, followed a year later by the city's mayor.

As opinion turned against the council's large-scale planning, the Provos gained increased public support, winning 2.5 per cent of the municipal vote and a seat on the council in 1966. However, their manifesto – the so-called **White Plans** (*see below* **Amsterdam Collection**) – tended towards the naïve and Utopian and by May 1967 the Provos had outgrown themselves and disbanded. Van Duyn's next move was to lead the Kabouters, named after a helpful gnome in Dutch folklore. They set up an alternative 'Orange Free State', with its own 'ministers' and policies, and had considerable success in the early seventies, adopting some of the more realistic White Plans and winning seats in six municipalities (five in Amsterdam). The movement described its form of socialism as 'not of the clenched fist, but of the intertwined fingers, the erect penis, the escaping butterfly…'. It disintegrated in 1981 amid quarrels about ideology.

The Provo actions somewhat overshadowed the beginnings of the Dutch feminist, gay rights and pacifist movements; for details of these, *see chapters* **Gay Amsterdam**, **Women's Amsterdam** *and* **Students**. The changing mentality on the street also affected national politics. New parties emerged such as the pacifist party PSP and the eclectic Democrats 66 (D66), which today is enjoying a popular resurgence. However, they forced little change on the traditional, substantially conservative power-base.

Amsterdam Collection

Centrale Bibliotheek, Prinsengracht 587, IW (525 0900). Tram 1, 2, 5, 7, 10. **Open** 1-9pm Mon; 10am-9pm Tue-Thur; 10am-5pm Fri, Sat.
A department of the Central Library which holds reams of documents and press clippings on the city's history.

With the courteous assistance of the staff, you can refer to, but not borrow, items relating to the city's radical movements. The most significant and publicised radical initiative was the Provo's White Plans. They proposed that the council ban cars from the city centre and provide 20,000 white bicycles for citizens to pick up free of charge and then leave for someone else's use. This evolved into the White Car Plan, which proposed that small, economical cars would be available at suburban 'stations'. Given a trial run in 1974, it didn't catch on (although Georgetto Guigaro, designer of the VW Golf and Fiat Panda, is reviving the idea). They also hoped to stop reckless driving by placing a white plaster cast of every road victim where their accident occurred. For full library details, *see chapter* **Survival**.

Fort van Sjakoo

Jodenbreestraat 24, C (625 8979). Tram 9, 14/Metro Waterlooplein. **Open** 11am-6pm Mon-Fri; 11am-5pm Sat. **No credit cards.**
Radical politics of the kind championed in the sixties and seventies is the lifeblood of this shop. It stocks books, pamphlets, badges, iconography and other paraphernalia of interest to activists, squatters and right-on browsers.

't Lieverdje statue

Spui, C. Tram 1, 2, 4, 5, 9, 14, 16, 24, 25.
The Lovable Rascal, or 't Lieverdje statue, became famous as the site of the first Provo happenings in 1964. Sculpted by Carel Kreulman, the little figure was donated to the city in 1960 by a cigarette manufacturer. It was proclaimed the emblem of 'tomorrow's addicted consumer' by window-cleaner turned self-proclaimed 'anti-smoke sorcerer and medicine man of the Western asphalt jungle', Jasper Gootveld. He was a founder of the Provo movement, whose happenings on Saturday evenings became a focal point for anti-establishment protest. No longer a hotbed of revolution, Spui, flanked by cafés, is still a meeting-place.

HIPPY SLEEP-INS

Meanwhile, foreign hippies flocked to the city, attracted by its tolerant attitude to soft drugs. Although the possession of up to 30 grammes (1oz) of hash wasn't decriminalised until 1978, the authorities turned a blind eye to its use in the sixties, preferring to prosecute dealers, who increasingly pushed hard drugs. Amsterdam subsequently suffered a heroin (and AIDS) epidemic and has since developed a well-defined drugs policy (*see chapter* **Survival**). The hundred or so smokers' bars selling soft drugs (*see* **Cafés & Bars**) are very much left alone, so long as they don't become too conspicuous, foster civil disorder or sell hard drugs.

The focal points of hippy culture were the **Melkweg** (Milky Way) and **Paradiso** (*see* **Music: Rock, Folk & Jazz** *and* **Night-clubs**), from both of which the pungent aroma of marijuana could allegedly be smelled hundreds of metres away in Leidseplein. Set up in 1969 in a former church, Paradiso became famous for its psychedelic slide shows. In March 1969 John Lennon and Yoko Ono gave the subculture global publicity through their 'sleep-in' for peace in the Amsterdam Hilton.

Towards the end of the decade, with the Dam and Vondelpark becoming unruly camping sites, public tolerance of the hippies waned. After a group of off-duty marines evicted hippies from Centraal Station, the hippy population went into decline. In the seventies, along with most West European cities, Amsterdam's popular culture shifted towards a rougher, tougher expression of disaffected urban youth. Yet Vondelpark, the Melkweg and the Dam remained a Mecca for ageing hippies, even into the eighties.

HOUSING CRISIS

Perhaps the most significant catalyst for discontent in the seventies – which exploded into full-scale civil conflict by the eighties – was housing. Amsterdam's compact size and historic city centre had always been a nightmare for city planners. There was a dire housing shortage and many inner city homes were in need of drastic renovation. The population had swelled during the sixties, reaching its peak (nearly 870,000) by 1964 (later dipping to 673,000). The numbers were swelled by immigrants from The Netherlands' last major colony, Surinam, who came to settle in Amsterdam anticipating the country's independence in 1975. Many of the Surinamese immigrants were dumped in the forbidding **Bijlmermeer** high-rise housing project (*below*) which quickly degenerated into a ghetto.

The **Metro** link to the Bijlmermeer is itself a landmark to some of the most violent protests in Amsterdam's recent history. Passionate opposition erupted against the proposed clearance

in February 1975 of a particularly sensitive site – the Jewish quarter of the **Nieuwmarkt**. Civil unrest culminated in 'Blue Monday', 24 March 1975, when heavy-handed police tactics once again sparked off violent clashes with residents and over 1,000 supporters. Police fired tear-gas into the homes of those who had refused to move out and battered down doors with armoured cars. Thirty people – over half of them police – were injured and 47 arrested. Despite further clashes a few weeks later, the plans went ahead and the Metro was opened in 1980, though only one of the four lines planned for the city was every completed.

Faced with inner city problems, the city planners were shocked by the fervent opposition to their schemes for large, airy suburbs and the wholesale demolition of old neighbourhoods. It was simply not what people wanted; they cherished the narrow streets, the small squares and cosy corner cafés. The shortage of residential space in the city centre made it a target for property speculators. The public felt very strongly that the council was selling out to big business and complained that the city centre was becoming unaffordable for ordinary people. Eventually, in 1978, the council decided to improve housing through small-scale development, renovating houses street by street. But with an estimated 90,000 people (13 per cent of the city's population) still on Amsterdam's housing list in 1980, there was growing public concern about the shortages.

*The building of **Nieuwmarkt Metro station** provoked some of the most violent protests in Amsterdam's recent history.*

Bijlmermeer

Amsterdam OE. Metro Bijlmer.
The city council intended this futuristic estate in the south-east of the city to solve its housing problems. But as so often happens with such ambitious schemes, it fast became a very undesirable address. Designed to the principles of Le Corbusier, the housing blocks had decent interiors and stood in parkland. People were separated from traffic, but they were also separated from each other: it wasn't a community and didn't even get a town centre until the mid-eighties. Rents ended up higher than planned and many people understandably refused to move here from the city centre – however dilapidated their houses were. The city council has since planned to improve some parts and demolish other sections of it – and if you take a Metro ride out there, you'll see why.

Nieuwmarkt Metro Station

Nieuwmarkt, C (GVB Information 020 5514911).
Tram 9, 14/Metro Nieuwmarkt. **Open** 6am-midnight Mon-Fri; 6.30am-midnight Sat; 7.30am-midnight Sun.
As a genuine gesture of tribute, the council dedicated this station to those who fought against its existence. It uses bricks from the demolished houses of what was the city's oldest quarter, and sculptures and photographs of the protests decorate the platform. The modern community buildings now surrounding the Nieuwmarkt have been widely judged a success and the area has a lively character.

SQUAT THRUST

Speculators who left property empty for many years caused acute resentment, which was soon mobilised into direct action – vacant buildings were occupied illegally by squatters. The squatting movement took off through two significant events in 1980. In March, police turned against the squatters for the first time and used tanks to evict squatters from a former office building in Vondelstraat; the ensuing battle attracted hundreds of demonstrators and flung the city into chaos. The building was quickly resquatted, and the movement was further strengthened by the riots on Coronation Day a month later (*see below* **Spuistraat mural**). Defeat and the expense of eviction forced the council to rethink its tactics.

In 1982, while the squatting movement reached its peak with an estimated 10,000 members in Amsterdam and a highly organised structure, clashes with police escalated. The eviction of Lucky Luyk, a lavish villa in the select museum area of the city, was the most violent and expensive. Riots went on for three days as demonstrators destroyed property and wrecked cars, forcing the mayor to declare a state of emergency. A year later, Amsterdam had a dynamic new mayor, Ed van Thijn, who took tough action to eradicate the squatters. One of the last of the city's important squats, Wyers, fell amid tear-gas in February 1984. It was pulled down to make way for a Holiday Inn hotel, despite the squatters' coherent plans for a community-oriented refurbishment. The squatters were no longer a force to be reckoned with, although their ideas of small-scale regeneration have become absorbed into official planning.

Café Huyschkaemer

Utrechtsestraat 137, IS (627 0575). Tram 4. **Open** *bar* 3.30pm-1am Mon-Thur, Sun; noon-2am Fri, Sat; *kitchen* 6-10pm daily.* **No credit cards.**
The polarisation of Amsterdam society in the eighties is typified by this coffee house. Once a major haunt of squatters, it has since become a super-trendy café (*see chapter* **Cafés & Bars**). More authentic is the bar **PH31** (*see* **Music: Rock, Folk & Jazz**), housed in an ex-squat, where class warriors are still consoled by political bands.

Spuistraat mural

Spuistraat, opposite Wijdesteeg, C. Tram 1, 2, 5, 13, 14, 17.
Painted on one of the few surviving squats, the exuberant Spuistraat Mural illustrates the squatters' alternative lifestyle. The movement forged links with other anti-establishment groups at home and abroad, even organising its own communications system, radio station and newspaper. The self-sufficient communities had their own crèches, shops, hairdressers, theatre groups and cafés. Given the lack of council housing, there was outrage at the huge cost of Queen Beatrix's investiture, so her inauguration day – 30 April 1980 – was declared the National Day of Squatting. When revellers joined in with the protest, the festivities degenerated into a full-scale riot.

Tetterode

Bilderdijkstraat 165, OW. Tram 3, 12.
One of Amsterdam's biggest squats, Tetterode was bought by the city council in the eighties and rented to the original squatters for a minimal sum, but it still retains its 'squatted' atmosphere. Like the squats of the movement's heyday, this large, rambling former Linotype factory has sprouted numerous small businesses, including hairdressers, a bicycle repair shop, an art gallery, a café called *Het Varkentje* (The Piglet) and **Trut** night-club (*see chapter* **Gay Amsterdam**). A similar example of urban renewal is **Leeuwenberg**. Although some historic buildings suffered at the hands of squatters, this former thirties milk factory on Zwanenburgwal was rescued from demolition as part of the **Stopera!** construction (*see below*). It is now refurbished, brightly painted and occupied mostly by its original squatters.

DOWN TO BUSINESS

Born and bred in Amsterdam, Ed Van Thijn embodied a new approach to Dutch politics, and launched a two-pronged plan to raise the city's international profile. Although a socialist, he took tough action against 'unsavoury elements' – hard drug traders, petty criminals, squatters – and upgraded facilities to attract new businesses and tourists. A new national political era also emerged, with the election in 1982 of Rotterdam millionaire Ruud Lubbers as leader of the then centre-right coalition government of Christian Democrats and right-wing Liberals (VVD). He saw to it that the welfare system and government subsidies were trimmed to ease the country's large budget deficit, and aimed to revitalise the economy, which had been flagging since the 1973 oil crisis, with more business-like policies (*see chapter* **Business**).

*A **peace sculpture** marks the site of mass demonstrations against the placing of Cruise missiles on Dutch soil. See **review**.*

The price of Amsterdam's new affluence (among most groups, except the poorest) seems to be a definite swing towards commercialism. Van Thijn has found it hard to live down a clumsy remark he made about turning Amsterdam into a 'pleasure park'. Yet the evidence can be seen in the new casino, luxury apartments and shopping complex at the Leidseplein and the massive redevelopment of its docklands (for both, *see chapters* **Amsterdam by Area** *and* **Amsterdam Today**).

NMB Postbank headquarters

Bijlmerplein 888, OS. Bus 59, 60, 61, 62, 137/Metro Bullewijk. **Open** 9am-4pm Mon-Fri.

The vast NMB Postbank headquarters is a monument to Amsterdam's current financial prowess, but is probably the city's oddest building. Unlike a conventional office 'block', it has no right angles; instead there are organic forms and running water in every room, and it's the world's most energy-efficient building. Opened in 1987, it was designed by Ton Alberts and Max van Huut to the anthroposophical theories of George Steiner, and is more clearly described by the public as a cross between a sandcastle and a herd of galloping dromedaries. It seems a happier place to work in than the characterless glass towers that were also built in this southern suburb to relieve pressure on the cramped city centre. Group tours can be booked (563 9111), but there's a six-month waiting list.

STOPERA!

The scruffy hordes of squatters have been largely supplanted by the well-groomed yuppie. Flashy cafés, galleries and *nouvelle cuisine* restaurants replaced the alternative scene and a mood of calm settled on the city – with just the occasional glimpse of Amsterdam's dissenting spirit. Apart from housing, the other great issue of the eighties was the Peace Movement, with its attendant anti-Americanism. Van Thijn also pushed through plans to build the **Stadhuis-Muziektheater** (City Hall-Opera House) complex, dubbed 'Stopera!' ('Stop the Opera') by the campaign waged against it (*see chapter* **Sightseeing**). Another classic example of Dutch free expression was provoked by the city's campaign in the mid-eighties to host the 1992 Olympics. Amsterdam became the first city ever to send an (ultimately successful) official anti-Olympics delegation.

Peace Sculpture

Museumplein, OS. Tram 3, 5, 10, 12, 16/Bus 63, 170, 179.

Europe's largest anti-nuclear demonstrations were held in Amsterdam (November 1981) and The Hague (October 1983). This white sculpture commemorates the site where 400,000 people protested against the placing of NATO Cruise missiles on Dutch soil, supported by a petition of over four million signatures – 35 per cent of the population. It depicts two human figures embracing in such a way that they resemble a nuclear warhead. The Dutch insistence on neutrality was mocked by the Americans as 'Hollanditis' and the resultant anti-American sentiment is tattooed on Keizersgracht (between Leliegracht and Brouwersgracht) in graffiti demanding 'US out of everywhere!' A Cruise base was built at Woensdrecht, but USA-USSR arms negotiations aborted the missiles' deployment.

Amsterdam Today

Economic realities are biting as Amsterdam squares up to problems familiar to cities across Europe.

Amsterdam suffers the same problems as many other major Western European cities, but differs drastically in its approach to them – alternative solutions and pragmatism are features of Amsterdam life.

Two of the most obvious examples of this alternative approach concern the attitude towards drugs and prostitution. Soft drugs are technically illegal, but are tolerated in small quantities for personal use. Despite pressure from the rest of Europe to tighten their restrictions on soft drugs, the Dutch have so far refused to budge. They cite the lack of evidence linking the use of hash and marijuana to hard drug abuse, and have managed to hold off the EC for the moment. However, the pressure has meant that it is becoming increasingly difficult to get a licence to open a coffee shop (*see chapter* **Cafés & Bars**).

Petty theft, vandalism and other symptoms of hard drug use are as much in evidence in Amsterdam as in other cities. Once there were pockets of junkies, concentrated mostly in the older areas of the city; now the problem is more widespread. Mainly as a result of the *stadswacht* (city watchers), who patrol the tourist areas in light blue uniforms, the drug addicts have moved on. So far the official solution has included access to drug substitutes, acquittal from petty criminal sentences in exchange for addicts agreeing to treatment, as well as needle exchange programmes. A familiar sight in most neighbourhoods is the van from the local health authority (GG&GD) where addicts can exchange needles and collect methadone. However, some Amsterdammers feel that this understanding approach is not enough. At the end of 1992, Metro employees took matters into their own hands by forcibly evicting junkies loitering in the underground stations.

Prostitution is also under discussion – but Amsterdammers have a more relaxed attitude to prostitution than they do to drugs. The prostitutes union, De Rood Draad (the Red Thread) has been campaigning to list 'sex worker' as a legal profession and thus ease the problems many prostitutes have with the tax system,

health insurance and social security. November 1992 saw De Rood Draad, politicians, sex workers, brothel owners and tax officials discussing the inherent inequalities in the present system. Although owners and workers are currently treated as independent workers, in reality brothel and club owners treat the women as employees and charge exorbitant prices for their rooms and facilities.

THE GROWTH OF THE FAR-RIGHT

'Live and let live' may be a Dutch characteristic, but the resurgence of racism felt in France, Germany and Belgium is also in evidence in Amsterdam. There are estimated to be over 100 different cultures trying to live harmoniously in this relatively small area. Though on the whole they seem to be succeeding, cracks in traditional Dutch tolerance are appearing under pressure of economic hardship and the increase in immigration. There are currently two extreme neo-Fascist parties, the Centrumdemocraten and the Centrumpartij '86, each with one seat on the local council, and both the frequent butt of criticism in the local press.

Almost 16,000 immigrants arrived in Amsterdam in 1991. Immigrants make up 23 per cent of the total population, estimated to rise to 31 per cent by the year 2000. They come from eastern and southern Europe, as well as Africa, The Antilles, Turkey and Asia. Discrimination is not only insidious, but increasingly violent as well. Mosques in The Hague and Amersfoort have been bombed, and physical attacks are on the increase.

EVERGREEN TOPICS

Amsterdammers don't talk much about the weather – they simply endure it. But they do talk about the lack of bicycle racks, green issues within the city, the IJ-Oevers development and of course, dog mess.

Environmentally, Amsterdam leads the way in The Netherlands and in Europe (*see chapter* **Green Issues**). A big issue within the city, concerning locals and environmental groups, is the

massive development along the docklands, the IJ-Oevers. The f6 billion redevelopment of the southern IJ bank will create four waterfronts along the six-kilometre stretch, together with a series of islands, connected by corridors of public space. With plans for low-cost housing, huge new office blocks and business premises, a Metro extension, a four-lane motorway and new bridges, the development will change the face of Amsterdam's harbours forever. At present the area consists of squats, cheap housing and artists' studios. Amsterdammers protest that the IJ-Oevers is not being built for them, citing the council's desire to attract foreign capital as an argument.

CUTS AND SQUEEZES

The pressure for economic competition within Europe, and the changing economic climate, mean inevitable changes. As the city council looks towards the Europe of the future, funding choices are threatening many of the infra-structures which made Amsterdam famous in the seventies and eighties.

An important loss is the Museum Fodor. The Fodor kept track of trends and selected and exhibited new, young artists: its functions and funding (f275,000 a year) are to be handed over to the Stedelijk Museum. Many Amsterdammers worry that this will endanger the access of more experimental artists to exhibition space, and limit the range of art supported in Amsterdam.

Also hard hit in the race for economic self-sufficiency are feminist, lesbian and gay organisations. For example, The Netherlands has pioneered experimental new therapies for women, conducting and publishing original research. Now, the last of these centres, Stichting De Maan, has lost funding and is to be closed. De Maan specialised in health care for prostitutes, lesbians, older and minority women as well as victims of sexual violence. Feminists fear that these new methodologies will not be absorbed within the existing structures and will be lost. As less than ten per cent of the existing institutions use these new therapies, there is a realistic fear that it will be much harder for women to get the help they need in the future.

Gay and lesbian organisations are also under threat, particularly small ones that are funded by incidental subsidies (those that must be applied for yearly). At present, large organisations receiving automatic, yearly subsidies, such as the COC, are safe. While the government has official policies on supporting both minority and gay and lesbian emancipation, and Amsterdam is the only city in the world to have a *homoemancipatie* (gay emancipation) alderman, the funding for Strange Fruit (the country's only ethnic minority gay group) and MVS Radio (one of the few gay stations in the world) are under threat. The alderman, Jeroen Saris, has been severely criticised during the debate, protesters claiming that the push for tourist dollars is damaging the self-proclaimed 'gay capital of Europe'.

The problems Amsterdam faces are shared by most European cities; but addressing these difficulties means a radical readjustment for Amsterdammers used to the liberal, free-spending ways of the last two decades.

Green Issues

The Netherlands is one of the most environmentally-aware nations in Europe, and Amsterdam is at the forefront of the greening process.

Environmental awareness in the Netherlands began in earnest in the eighties, after Lekkerkerk, and other new towns – *nieuwbouwwijken* – built on former chemical dumping sites had to be destroyed. In 1989 The Netherlands' government became the first to be toppled on a green issue. Disagreement over how to pay for the comprehensive National Environment Policy Plan clean-up programme (NMP – an EC first) split open an already fissured coalition government.

By the summer of 1990, the new environment minister, Hans Aders, had produced the even more stringent 'NMP-Plus'. Estimated to cost about f1.17 billion, the NMP and NMP-Plus aim to cut pollution in water, air and soil by between 70 and 90 per cent, though, as the Greens point out, these goals are being shifted as being 'green' loses its political lustre.

LOCAL INITIATIVES

While the Dutch are front runners in Europe on environmental issues, Amsterdam leads The Netherlands. A founding member of the ICLEI (International Council of Local Environmental Initiatives), Amsterdam was also the first city in the Netherlands to structure environmental plans systematically by combining costs and

priorities (*see page 93* **Priorities 1993-1994**). The Dutch arm of Friends of the Earth – Vereniging Milieu Defensie – and Greenpeace International are well-supported locally and nationally.

Groen Links, the first major 'green' political party, was formed by a coalition of four small left-wing parties in 1989. It is one of the fastest growing political parties in Amsterdam, with seven seats on the city council as well as representation in the national parliament. **De Groenen**, the only environmental group to protest about the massive developments along the docklands of Amsterdam – the IJ-Oevers (*see chapter* **Amsterdam Today**) – originally won two seats on the city council. But, at the end of 1992, a split within the party led to the formation of a new party, **Eco 2000**, which retained one of the seats. Within Amsterdam, one of the most important organisations working to safeguard the eco-system of the city as a whole is the **Milieudienst** (Environmental Service). Responsible for the proposal and development of new laws and ordinances and the preparation and dissemination of advice to councils, civil servants, companies and citizens of Amsterdam, it is an important source of information on all aspects of the environment.

Causes for Concern

Some of the areas of major concern for both Milieudienst and Amsterdammers are:

Cars

The large volume of traffic that passes through Amsterdam takes up public space and causes air and noise pollution. In 1990 the Milieudienst brought out a 'Verkeersmilieu' (traffic environment atlas), which gave levels of air and noise pollution, and showed that many Amsterdam streets were over the legal limit. The atlas also detailed the volume of traffic and gave alternative routes through the city which would bring the air and noise pollution down to legal levels. Following a referendum in the spring of 1992, when Amsterdammers voted to reduce the number of cars in the city, the Milieudienst have been cooperating with other services and the pressure group 'Autovrij Binnenstad' (auto-free inner city) to bring about drastic reductions by 1995.

Chemical spills

Companies whose manufacturing processes or services can cause accidents that endanger the environment (like chemical spills), are legally required to file a safety report. In the Netherlands there are over 80 companies that are legally required to do this, six of which are based in Amsterdam.

Water

Water is obviously vital to Amsterdam, and the importance of maintaining quality and quantity is crucial. The Milieudienst is responsible for monitoring both the water-level in canals (waterstand), its movement (doorstromen) and what is dumped into the sewer system. It runs an information line which gives up-to-date information on water-quality (including places where it's safe to swim) in and around Amsterdam.

Soil

Soil damage is also a recognised problem – in some places an acute one. It is simply not practical to replace the contaminated soil, as this would require excavating the whole town which would soon become re-contaminated. All government building projects, and in particular housing projects, are required to test soil quality.

RECYCLING

Yellow and grey containers for paper, old batteries and glass are found throughout the city, lined to reduce noise. Offices have special bags for the disposal of waste paper and there are special depots for used car oil. Two of the most interesting initiatives are *biobak* and *chemicar*. The biobak containers are small composting installations for fruit, vegetables and garden waste which can be found in some of the outlying neighbourhoods. The chemicar collects small-scale chemical waste, like old paint tins and spirits, throughout Amsterdam. There are regular collection days, and its arrival is signalled by a bell which sounds like an ice-cream van.

PRIORITIES 1993-1994

Milieudienst have come up with a list of 88 priorities to help improve the quality of the environment in Amsterdam. They range from introducing more compost installations for fruit, vegetable and garden waste to the removal of graffiti. They also cover such diverse topics as underwater plants, sewage filtering, environmental toxicity, reducing nitrates, phosphates and chlorides, paintwork on the bridges and limiting the number of cars in the city.

The comprehensive priorities were decided using Milieudienst's system of 'environmental scoring', which is based on criteria such as how much the micro (city) or macro (outside) environments are affected, the scale of the problem and the effectiveness and cost of the solution. While the programme is based on the idea that polluters foot the bill, and includes measures like increased taxes on petrol and higher sewerage levies for business, the scheme is still expected to cost the government in the region of f200 million.

Milieudienst Amsterdam

Visitors' address: *Weesperplein 4, OE. Tram 6, 7, 10/Metro Weesperplein*. Postal address: *Postbus 922, 1000 AX (551 3888; information line 551 3838; complaints 620 7976).*

Amsterdams Natuur Milieu-Educatie Centrum

Plantage Middenlaan, IE (622 5404). Tram 7, 9, 14. **Open** 10am-5pm Mon-Fri.
This new educational centre has an information desk for visitors, as well as an extensive library with information in English on all aspects of the environment and nature. Worth combining with a visit to the Hortus Botanicus, the gardens of the University of Amsterdam (*see chapter* **Museums**). Also on site is **Milieu Boek** *(624 4989/9am-6pm Mon-Fri; 11am-5pm Sat*. Billed as the best environmental bookshop in the Netherlands, it has an incredibly large selection covering all aspects of the subject, in many languages.

Eco 2000

Huigenbos 714, 1102 KA Amsterdam (552 2107).
Formed after a split with De Groenen (*see below*) in June 1992, this group has taken over a seat on the city council. At the time of writing policies were still being developed, but the general aims of the party are to enhance the environment in a democratic, humane and sustainable manner through integration and economic policies.

De Groenen

Postbus 3244, 1001 AA Amsterdam (617 9543).
Following a split which led to the formation of Eco 2000 (*above*), De Groenen's two city council seats have been reduced to one. It also has six seats on the district council. The party is mounting protests against the proposed building of a coal-fired power station near Amsterdam, and the pollution of drinking water from the Rhine. It wants offending pesticide manufacturers to pay for filters, which cost Amsterdam householders an estimated f70 million a year.

Groen Links

Postbus 700, 1000 AS Amsterdam (624 5515/620 2212).
A coalition of four small left-wing parties, formed in 1989. In the September 1989 elections, it won six seats (out of a total of 150) in the Dutch national parliament. Its manifesto included a commitment to the clearance and cleansing of polluted soil, the promise of more money to build and maintain cycle paths, and a pledge to reduce speed limits.

Stichting Greenpeace Nederlands

Keizersgracht 174, 1016 DW (626 1877; fax 622 1272).
Greenpeace Nederlands was founded in 1978, when its major campaign was against whaling. It has now grown into the country's largest environmental organisation.

Over the past decade, chemical land pollution and nuclear-waste dumping in the North Sea have been among the most pressing issues. Many of Greenpeace's protest ships, including the replacement for *Rainbow Warrior*, are registered in Amsterdam.

Vereniging Milieu Defensie
Damrak 26, 1012 LJ (622 1366/helpline 9am-2pm Mon-Fri 626 2620).
The Dutch branch of Friends of the Earth can advise on environmentally sound products and on how to recycle various kinds of waste.

Alternative Energy

There is some scepticism among environmentalists on the viability of the wind and sun as a commercial energy source. One has claimed that it is only for the 'geiten wollen sokken' – wearers of goats'-wool socks. None the less, serious money is being spent by both industry and the government on alternative energy, ranging from solar (demonstrated at Zonnehuis) and wind power, to biomass (vegetable matter).

There are over nine hundred windmills in the Netherlands – more than in any other country – and the current wind development programme aims to meet 30 per cent of the Dutch energy needs by the middle of the next century. The Dutch government has set a target of 1000 megawatts of electricity supplied by wind power by the year 2000.

Amsterdam's regional generating board, the Provinciaal Electricteitsbedrijf van Noord-Holland (PEN) has built wind farms along the Noordhollands Kanaal near Alkmaar and at Enkhuizen to supply 300 megawatts of this total. However, wind energy is expensive and to become commercially viable after 1996, when subsidies stop, these sleek, statuesque turbines (technically called aerogenerators) will have to be made bigger. The largest aerogenerator can be found at Wieringermeerpolder near Medemblik. Also of interest are the windmill cooperatives in Noord Holland which are based on a Danish scheme. Amsterdam has one turbine at Oostzaan, called Skoon, meaning beautiful in the local dialect. It is located on the way to the museum village of Zaanse Schans (*see chapter* Excursions in Holland) and includes a windmill museum.

Zonnehuis (Sun House)
Het Lageland 1, off Laan van Alberthoeve, Castricum, near Alkmaar (information and appointments 023 143 665). **Open** by appointment (usually Fri).
Though seemingly identical to its neighbours, this housing estate is unique in being powered by solar energy. There are guided tours in English.

PEN wind farms
Information: PEN, Postbus 150, 2060 AD, Bloemendaal (023 222514; fax 023 222173).
Burgervlotbrug *along Noordhollands Kanaal.* 50km (31 miles) north-west. **Callantsoog** *along Noordhol Kanaal.* 50 km (31 miles) north-west. **Enkhuizen** *along a dike into the IJsselmeer lake.* 45km (28 miles) north-east/by train direct to Enkhuizen.

Skoon wind turbine
Oostzaan; visible 20m (66ft) from Kolkweg; or from A10 motorway. 5km (3 miles) north-east.

Windmill co-operatives
Camperduin *between Alkmaar and Burgervlotbrug wind farm (above). Information 072 155446.* One turbine, 55km (34 miles) north-west. **Venhuizen** *near Enkhuizen (information 02284 2540).* Three turbines, 45km (28 miles) north-east. **De Waal** *Texel Island (information 02223 673).* One large, 250kw turbine, 80km (50 miles) north.

Recycling containers can be found throughout the city. See **Recycling** *page 93.*

Eating & Drinking

What it lacks in gourmet tradition, Amsterdam makes up for in the variety and quality of its restaurants and picturesque cafés and bars. From Indonesian restaurant to haute cuisine, brown café to designer bar, there's something for every pocket.

Contents

CAFE PACIFICO
Mexican Restaurant-Cantina

AMSTERDAM Warmoesstraat 31
Tel: 6242911 Fax: 6274539

LONDON
5 Langley Street., WC2.Tel: 071 379 7728

PARIS
50 Blvd. Montparnasse.Tel: 45486387

KÖLN
Neuhöfferstraße 32.Tel: 814755

Restaurants

Eat your way around the world in the restaurants of Amsterdam, and you won't even notice the lack of a native cuisine.

The dichotomy between capital and country is nowhere more pronounced than in The Netherlands. Amsterdam is a bustling and cosmopolitan melting pot which probably has more in common with New York or London than with the rest of the country. This difference is best appreciated when it comes to eating out, for unless you specifically seek out a Dutch restaurant, you are likely to be making your choice between, say, Filipino, Indonesian, Thai or Caribbean cuisines. Restaurants with no nationality tag are most likely to serve French food interpreted by Dutch chefs. French kitchens are still considered the best, as they have been ever since the days of the Napoleonic occupation, but even the most *haute* of cuisines is subject to international influences. Almost all the celebrated chefs listed below borrow from Japanese, Indian and Italian cuisines.

The Chinese and Indonesians from the Far East, 'guest workers' from the Mediterranean and hippies with a penchant for Indian and vegetarian cooking have also contributed to the internationalising of menus. As the capital of a post-colonial country with continuing links to Indonesia, Amsterdam has an abundance of Indonesian restaurants – in fact, the food has been adopted to such an extent that it is almost considered a national speciality.

In the past few years, Thai, Japanese and Filipino cooking have been in vogue, while Surinam cuisine is on the verge of mass discovery. Surprisingly, despite the number of Surinamers in Amsterdam, very few restaurants feature Surinam cuisine, a spicy blend of mainly Chinese, Hindustani and African flavours reflecting the country's mix of nationalities. The best place to look for this style of food is in cafés and takeaways in the Albert Cuypmarkt area. Restaurants serving Surinam food tend to offer *bami* (noodle) and *nasi* (rice) dishes and typical snacks such as *roti* (a stuffed, Indian-style

Drop into the glorious art nouveau **Café Americain** *for coffee and pastries. See* **review** *page 99.*

pancake), *bojo* (a quiche-like mix of cassava and coconut) and *telo* (baked cassava with peanut sauce). *Pitjil*, baked vegetables with peanut sauce, is said to be a contribution from the Japanese. The largest eating place, and one frequented by members of the Surinam community, is Marowijn (Albert Cuypstraat 68-70, 662 4845; open noon to 10pm daily). It's not a top-of-the-range place, but it's pleasant, with linen table-cloths and Chinese lanterns.

GOING DUTCH

There is little in the way of a distinctive Dutch cuisine and no restaurants serve exclusively Dutch food. Such traditional dishes as there are, are designed to stick to ribs in winter. Typical are potatoes, sausage and curly kale (*boerenkool met rookworst*), meat and vegetable stew (*stamppot*) and thick split-pea soup (*erwtensoep*). Correctly made, the soup is thick enough to hold a spoon upright and is normally eaten with thick slabs of rye bread and raw bacon. Dutch breakfast is also hearty, including several types of bread, cheese, cold meat, a boiled egg and coffee or tea.

Before World War II, meat was mainly reserved for special occasions. Fish and dairy products, especially cheese, were the primary sources of protein. Herring and onions, both eaten raw, are still a national delicacy available on every street corner. Best is the new herring in May, the same month that asparagus from the province of Limburg is served with butter and nutmeg as a meal in itself.

Apple cake, cream cakes and pancakes are the sweet treats. The Pancake Bakery, in a seventeenth-century warehouse (Prinsengracht 191, 625 1333), is the premier stop for plate-size pancakes with a choice of some 30 toppings.

FINDING YOUR WAY AROUND

Several of Amsterdam's streets are lined with restaurants from around the globe. Those on Warmoesstraat (near Centraal Station) and Utrechtsestraat are among the more moderately priced, while those on Reguliersdwarsstraat, parallel to the flower market, and around Leidseplein, tend to be pricier. Most recently, Van Baerlestraat (in the museum area) entered the gourmet sweepstakes with a number of former local shops now transformed into restaurants. The Jordaan is also liberally sprinkled with eating places.

Dining in Amsterdam is leisurely, and most meals are cooked to order. The Dutch eat early (about 6pm at home, 7pm to 9.30pm in restaurants), and many kitchens close at about 10pm, but customers are welcome to linger over coffee and dessert until about midnight. Restaurants open late into the night are listed in **Early Hours**. It is always advisable to book (at least early in the

day) for dinner at leading restaurants. If you do, turn up on time – the Dutch prize punctuality.

For a decent meal out consisting of a starter, main course and dessert you can expect to pay upwards of f30. In haute cuisine establishments the sky really is the limit, although in eetcafés (literally cafés where you can eat) you can pay a lot less, *see chapter* **Cafés & Bars**. In the past decade, most restaurants have started to accept credit cards; many of the smaller ones still do not, however, so check before ordering. Bills always include 17½ per cent tax and a 15 per cent service charge. It is customary to leave the small change as well, if the service merits it. We have indicated any special facilities, such as wheelchair access and high chairs for children, but if you intend to make use of them you should phone ahead to let the restaurant know your needs.

Prices listed below are based on the average cost of a starter, a main course and dessert, WITHOUT drink. You could spend less – or a lot more – depending on what you order and how much you drink.

City Landmarks

1e Klas

Platform 2B, Centraal Station, C (625 0131). Tram 1, 2, 4, 5, 9, 13, 16, 17, 24, 25. **Open** 9.30am-11pm Mon-Wed; 9.30am-11.30pm Thur-Sat; 10.30am-10.30pm Sun. **Lunch served** noon-2pm daily. **Dinner served** 5.30-10pm Mon-Wed, Sun; 5.30-10.30pm Thur-Sat. **Average** f40. **Credit** AmEx, DC, MC, V.

The lofty 1e Klas, restored in grand turn-of-the-century style, is in Centraal Station's former first class waiting room. Its menu offers excellent à la carte nouvelle cuisine; Dutch specialities are featured in season. As the trains roll by outside, you can imagine yourself back in the heyday of rail travel.

Book 6-8pm. Children welcome; children's menu; high chair. Vegetarian dishes. Wheelchair access to restaurant; toilets for the disabled in the station.

De Blauwe Parade and Blauwe Poort

Hotel Port van Cleve, NZ Voorburgwal 178-180, C (624 4860). Tram 1, 2, 4, 5, 9, 14, 16, 24, 25. **Meals served** *Parade* noon-2pm, Mon-Fri; 6-10pm Sat, Sun; *Poort* noon-9.30pm daily. **Average** *Parade* f65; *Poort* f45. **Set menu** *Parade* f65; *Poort* f41.50. **Credit** AmEx, MC, V.

In the 1890s, Brietner, Witsen and Klos were among the renowned artists who gathered regularly at this beer house which later expanded into two restaurants and, in 1954, the Hotel Port van Cleve. The pricier Blauwe Parade (Blue Parade) is quintessentially Dutch, with walls of antique Delft tiles. The companion Blauwe Poort (Blue Door) across the hall has murals of old Amsterdam cityscapes and serves authentic Dutch dishes, including pea soup. Both are famous for their numbered steaks (more than 5½ million have been sold since the place opened in 1870).

Booking advisable. Children welcome; high chair.

Café Americain

Leidseplein 28, IS (623 4813). Tram 1, 2, 5, 6, 7, 10. **Open** 7am-1am daily (non-guest breakfast from 10am). **Lunch served** 11am-2pm. **Dinner served** 6-11.30pm.

Average f45. **Buffet** (served throughout the day) f30. **Credit** AmEx, DC, EC, MC, V.

One of a kind, the glorious *Jugendstil* (art nouveau) interior of the Café Americain is a listed monument decorated with murals and marbled amber lampshades. Theatrical personalities, the *après*-theatre crowd and tourists meet under the high vaulted roof. Some pop in for coffee and pastries, while the f30 buffet entitles you to help yourself to as much as propriety allows.
Booking advisable. Babies and children welcome; high chairs; reduced-price children's portions. Vegetarian menu.

Dikker en Thijs
Prinsengracht 444 (625 8876). Tram 1, 2, 5. **Dinner served** 7-10pm Mon-Sat. **Average** f75. **Set menu** f85 (four courses). **Credit** AmEx, DC, MC, V.

This old and distinguished Dutch restaurant has received mixed reviews in recent years. The classically furnished second-floor dining room overlooking Prinsengracht offers haute cuisine. Other options are a Franco-Dutch meal in the cellar restaurant, Prinsenkelder, where seasonal game is a speciality; a light à la carte meal in the ground-floor brasserie; or takeaway dishes from the adjoining delicatessen of the same name. All are under the same management and chef.
Booking essential; Fri, Sat a week in advance. Vegetarian dishes by arrangement.

Keuken van 1870
Spuistraat 4, C (624 8965). Tram 1, 2. **Meals served** noon-8pm Mon-Fri; 4-9pm Sat, Sun. **Average** f10. **Credit** AmEx, DC, EC, MC, V.

Probably the best value in town, this no-frills old-fashioned establishment was set up as a soup kitchen in 1870 (the name means 'Kitchen from 1870') and still serves copious, plain meals for less than f10. Note the early closing times.
Bookings not accepted. Children welcome.

Keyser's Bodega
Van Baerlestraat 96, OS (671 1441). Tram 3, 5, 12, 16. **Open** 9am-midnight Mon-Sat. **Meals served** noon-11.30pm Mon-Sat. **Average** f60. **Set menu** f55 three courses incl coffee. **Credit** AmEx, DC, MC, V.

Musicians from the Concertgebouw next door have been hanging out at this café-restaurant since 1903, and Amsterdam's literary set favours it as well. The décor and Oriental wool table coverings (an Amsterdam tradition) haven't changed since then – only central heating has been added. Some of the formally dressed waiters could have been here just as long. Sole meunière and smoked eel are specialities, in addition to classic French dishes. Many local business people lunch here, and shoppers tend to stop in for tea; newspapers are available. The place is really busy between 7pm and 8pm, before concerts next door.
Booking advisable. Vegetarian dishes.

Celebrated Chefs

Beddington's
Roelof Hartstraat 6-8, OS (676 5201). Tram 3, 5, 12, 24. **Lunch served** noon-2.30pm, **dinner served** 6-10.30pm, Mon-Sat. **Average** f70. **Set lunch** f55 three courses. **Set dinners** from f80. **Credit** AmEx, DC, MC, V.

Meals at Englishwoman Jean Beddington's establishment are a sumptuous feast. French cuisine is complemented by original touches gleaned from a long trip through the Far East. Reflecting the Japanese influence, the menu includes beautifully presented fish dishes, whilst desserts betray Mrs Beddington's Derbyshire origins. Some diners find the starkly modern décor with almost no colour a bit sterile.
Babies and children welcome; children's portions on request. Book dinner always. Separate room for

parties, seats 16 (with balcony view over gardens). Vegetarian dishes.

Le Ciel Bleu
Okura Hotel, Ferdinand Bolstraat 333 , OS (678 7111). Tram 12, 25. **Dinner served** 6-11pm daily. **Average** f100-f125. **Credit** AmEx, DC, MC, V.

For the height of elegant dining, try the Okura Hotel's twenty-third floor restaurant. Great views of the city, French/Japanese creations by chef Dick Sinnema and soft music make this a place for special occasions. Drinking in the sights at the adjoining bar is less costly.
Booking advisable. Dress: jacket and tie.

Excelsior
Hotel l'Europe, Nieuwe Doelenstraat 2-8, C (623 4836). Tram 4, 9, 14, 16, 24, 25. **Breakfast served** 7-11am daily. **Lunch served** 12.30-2.30pm Mon-Fri, Sun. **Theatre dinner served** 6-11pm daily. **Dinner served** 7-10.30pm daily. **Average** f65. **Set breakfasts** f20-f50. **Theatre menu** f65. **Set dinner** f85 four courses. **Credit** AmEx, DC, MC, V.

Imko Binnerts took over the kitchen at this famous establishment in 1988 – his influence shows in the inclusion of Oriental starters as well as traditional French dishes. Grand style, views of the Amstel and 40,000 bottles in the wine cellar are other reasons for the Excelsior's Michelin star.
Booking essential. Children welcome; children's portions on request; high chairs. Dress: jacket and tie. Vegetarian dishes. Wheelchair access.

De Kersentuin
Garden Hotel (separate entrance), Dijsselhofplansoen 7, OS (664 2121). Tram 16. **Lunch served** noon-2.30pm Mon-Fri. **Dinner served** 6-10.15pm Mon-Sat. **Average** f125. **Set lunch** f50. **Set dinner** f100 four courses. **Credit** AmEx, DC, MC, V.

Lekker Eten, the premier Dutch guide to cuisine, ranks Jon Sisterman among the top ten chefs in the country. His wizardry with nouvelle cuisine and the sophisticated Oriental cherry garden setting here have been attracting Amsterdam's *beau monde* since the early eighties.
Booking essential. Dress: jacket and tie.

De Molen 'de Dikkert'
Amsterdamseweg 104A, OS (641 1378). Bus 175. **Lunch served** noon-3pm, **dinner served** 6-10pm, Mon-Sat. **Average** f100. **Credit** AmEx, DC, MC, V.

A windmill built in 1672, 5km (3miles) south of the city centre, is the setting for the classic French dishes of chef Didier Besnard, served in a spacious traditional dining-room. A good place for expense account dining.
Booking essential. Dress: smart, no jeans.

't Swarte Schaep
Korte Leidsedwarsstraat 24, IS (622 3021). Tram 1, 2, 5. **Meals served** noon-11pm daily. **Average** f60. **Credit** AmEx, DC, MC, V.

Based in this 300 year-old building since 1937, the 'black sheep' is noted for its excellent wines (especially reds), authentic antiques and chef Ton van der Boogaard's subtle blend of classic, nouvelle and post-modern cuisine. Even Prince Willem-Alexander dines here. The window tables have great views of Leidseplein below (the restaurant is on the second and third floors, up a long, steep staircase).
Booking essential. Children admitted.

Tout Court
Runstraat 13, IW (625 8637). Tram 7, 10. **Lunch served** noon-5.30pm Mon-Fri. **Dinner served** 6-11.30pm daily. **Average** f50. **Set lunch** f39.50. **Credit** AmEx, DC, MC, V.

Another stop on the circuit of beautiful people is the Jordaan restaurant of John Fagel, the eldest of six Dutch

brothers who are all celebrated chefs. The nouvelle-based menu changes every four or five weeks, and a range of set menus offers good value. Some critics find the butcher-aproned waiters too slow, but people still come in droves to see and be seen.
Booking advisable Fri, Sat. Children welcome; children's portions on request. Vegetarian dishes. Wheelchair access with assistance.

Moderate

Crignon Culinaire
Gravenstraat 28, C (624 6428). Tram 1, 2, 4, 9, 14, 16, 24, 25. **Dinner served** 6-10.30pm daily. **Average** f35. **Credit** AmEx, DC, MC, V.
'Intimate' best describes this cheese restaurant located in a sixteenth-century building in a narrow street by the Nieuwe Kerk. Previously the mezzanine annex of a local cheese shop (now closed), where customers sampled some of the 140 varieties on sale, the restaurant now specialises in fondues. It also offers meat and fish dishes, including a marinated salmon made to an old (Scandinavian) family recipe. The staircases are impossibly narrow and winding, typically Dutch, though the owner has a dumbwaiter to help.
Booking advisable.

De Impressionist
Keizersgracht 312, IW (627 6666). Tram 13, 14, 17. **Dinner served** 6-10.30pm daily. **Set menus** f30-f50. **Credit** AmEx, DC, MC, V.
Roy Verwey gave his small cellar restaurant a name that people of all nationalities would remember, and the menu reflects this international approach. A team of British cooks produces English, American, Chinese, Japanese and Italian dishes, along with imaginative vegetarian selections.
Book a day in advance. Children welcome; children's portions on request. Vegetarian dishes.

Jean Jean
1e Anjeliersdwarsstraat 12-14, IW (627 7153). Tram 3, 10/Bus 18. **Dinner served** 5-11pm Tue-Sun. **Average** f20-f30. **No credit cards.**
A simply decorated and popular establishment where excellent crêpes (from f8), soups, salads and main courses are served. The pastries are authentic and tempting – try the lemon tartlets.
Children welcome. Vegetarian dishes.

Pier 10
De Ruijterkade, Steiger 10, C (624 8276). Tram 1, 2, 5, 13, 17. **Dinner served** 6.30-11pm daily. **Average** f50. **Credit** AmEx, DC, MC, V.
A former shipping line office behind Centraal Station houses one of Amsterdam's most unexpected restaurants. An unusual combination of functional décor, candlelight, shipside vistas, innovative food and a casual atmosphere attracts a regular following. The three waterside tables are the most coveted.
Children welcome; children's portions on request. Booking advisable. Tables outdoors (terrace, seats 50). Vegetarian dishes.

Piet de Leeuw
Noorderstraat 11, IS (623 7181). Tram 16, 24, 25. **Meals served** noon-10.30pm Mon-Fri; 6-10.30pm Sat, Sun. **Average** f30. **Credit** DC, MC, V.
Most of the customers at this small, friendly steakhouse come for the inexpensive steaks and french fries. People tend to mix and mingle (they may ask to sit at your table if there's space), which makes it a good place to meet the Dutch.
Children admitted.

Salad Garden
Weteringschans 75, IS (623 4017). Tram 6, 7, 10. **Meals served** 8am-11pm daily. **Average** f30. **Salad bar** f18.50. **Credit** AmEx, DC, MC, V.
On the Singel near Leidseplein, this restaurant has a covered garden popular with locals for lunch. French onion soup, salmon on toast and pâté can be accompanied by one of the excellent salads that give the place its name. Hard-to-find English, American and Continental breakfasts are also available, and robust evening dishes include steaks, lamb cutlets and trout.
Book in summer 7-10pm. Children welcome; children's portions on request. Tables outdoors (covered terrace, seats 40).

De Smoeshaan
Leidsekade 90, IS (627 6966). Tram 1, 2, 5, 6, 7, 10. **Open** *café* 10am-1am Mon-Thur, Sun; 10am-2am Fri, Sat; *restaurant* 5pm-1am Mon-Thur, Sun; 5pm-2am Fri, Sat; last orders 10pm. **Average** *restaurant* f40; *café* f20. **Credit** AmEx, DC, MC, V.
There's an old Dutch café-bar downstairs, which is usually busy, and a slightly more formal restaurant upstairs, with a more varied menu (and higher prices). Both serve the same tasty Franco-Dutch food, with lots of fresh vegetables and salads, and both attract a young, lively crowd, including performers from the nearby theatres. An excellent venue for a casual supper.
Booking advisable after 6pm. Children welcome; children's portions on request. Vegetarian dishes.

Cafés and Brasseries

Bern
Nieuwmarkt 9, C (622 0034). Metro Nieuwmarkt. **Open** 4pm-1am Mon-Thur, Sun; 4pm-2am Fri, Sat. **Dinner served** 6-11pm daily. **Average** f32. **No credit cards.**
A popular brown café-restaurant with a reputation for its delicious cheese fondue made, of course, to a secret recipe. Peppered steak is also recommended.
Booking advisable 7-10pm. Children admitted. Tables outdoors (pavement, drinks only). Vegetarian dishes.

Brasserie van Baerle
Van Baerlestraat 158, OS (679 1532). Tram 3, 5, 12, 16. **Meals served** noon-11pm Mon-Fri, Sun. **Average** f55 lunch, f60 dinner. **Credit** AmEx, DC, MC, V.
The media crowd have been hanging out at this turn-of-the-century town house brasserie since it opened about ten years ago. The food is strictly modern: Oriental salads and home-made soups. The table at the rear window gives the most privacy. On warm days, the garden is delightful. Sunday brunch is served here too.
Booking advisable. Vegetarian dishes.

Gerrit van Beeren
Koningsstraat 54, C (622 2329). Metro Nieuwmarkt. **Dinner served** 5-10pm daily. **Average** f24. **No credit cards.**
On a side-street off the Nieuwmarkt, this cheerful neighbourhood café-restaurant has been run by the same person since 1936, though only recently in its present form. It was a greengrocer's first, then a bar, and was refurbished in 1989. The steak and fish dishes (particularly bouillabaisse) are very reasonably priced. The owner is accommodating, but some of the staff can be a bit off-hand.
Bookings not accepted. Children welcome; children's portions on request. Tables outdoors (terrace, 20 tables). Wheelchair access with assistance.

*Ask for a window seat and watch the boats go by at the **Sea Palace**. See **review** page 104.*

Grand Café Beurs van Berlage

Beursplein 3, C (638 4639). Tram 4, 9, 16, 24, 25.
Dinner served 6pm-midnight daily. **Average** f65.
Credit AmEx, MC, V.
A modern, informal café-bar-restaurant, opened in the former stock exchange designed by Amsterdam architect HP Berlage (*see* chapter **Between the Occupations**). Jan Toorop tile murals called 'Past', 'Present' and 'Future' depict the changing roles of workers and women at the turn of the century. The city's money-makers congregate in the restaurant, shoppers and tourists in the café. Both venues offer an international menu (French, Dutch, Spanish and Italian dishes) cooked by Dutch and British chefs.
Booking advisable. Children welcome; children's portions on request; high chairs with reservation. Tables outdoors (terrace). Vegetarian dishes.

Witteveen

Ceintuurbaan 256-258, OS (662 4368). Tram 3.
Dinner served 5-11pm daily. **Average** f55. **Credit** AmEx, DC, MC, V.
Deeply Dutch, this popular working class café-restaurant attracts all ages. Its lengthy menu is supplemented by Cajun dishes from the Cajun Louisiana next door (*see below* **International**), which shares the same owner.
Children welcome; children's portions on request; high chairs. Booking advisable. Tables outdoors (pavement, drinks only). Vegetarian dishes.

Budget

De Blauwe Hollander

Leidsekruisstraat 28, IS (623 3014). Tram 6, 7, 10.
Dinner served 5-10pm daily. **Average** f22.
No credit cards.
People come here for the slightly musty Dutch ambiance

and the simple, inexpensive Dutch cooking; this is the only restaurant in Amsterdam which you could legitimately label as Dutch. The four big tables – there's no separate seating – are always busy, but small parties seldom have to wait long to be seated.
Bookings not accepted.

De Schutter

Voetboogstraat 13-15, C (622 4608). Tram 1, 2, 5, 14, 16, 24, 25. **Meals served** 11am-1am Mon-Thur, Sun; 11am-2am Fri, Sat. **Average** f20. **No credit cards.**
This upstairs bar has a marvellous atmosphere: students, musicians, yuppies and hippies mingle in the two bars and lean out of the enormous stained glass windows in summer. At lunch-time, there are French bread sandwiches (*stockbrood*), salads and pancakes for about f5. From 6pm to 9pm, the smaller bar has a selection of meals for f10 to f20, including delicious steaks and other good bar food, and lots of strong Belgian beers.

Small Talk

Van Baerlestraat 52, OS (671 4864). Tram 3, 5, 12, 16. **Open** *coffee shop* 9am-6pm Mon-Sat, 11am-6pm Sun; *restaurant* 11am-8.30pm Mon-Sat, 11am-6pm Sun; *traiteur* 10.30am-8pm Mon-Sat. **Average** f30. **Credit** AmEx, DC, MC, V.
Two cafés side by side offer some of the most pleasant people-watching opportunities in town. Located halfway between the Concertgebouw and the PC Hoofstraat, Small Talk attracts a fairly well-heeled clientele but the lunches and snacks remain reasonably priced. Dinners upstairs carry rather steeper tariffs. No-one will object if you linger, especially in the tiny corner café, which serves heavenly apple cake and hot chocolate.
Booking advisable for dinner.

Fish

Julia
Amstelveenseweg 169, OS (679 5394). Bus 146, 147, 170, 171, 172, 173. **Dinner served** 5-10pm daily. **Average** f35. **Set menu** f32.50. **Credit** AmEx, DC, MC, V.
For a real neighbourhood Dutch dinner, head out of town to Julia's. It's a zany suburban place that encourages diners to let their hair down – patrons may occasionally burst into song. It's probably the platter with ten kinds of fish, three vegetables, potatoes and salad for f32.50 that generates all this energy – and draws people from all over the region.
Children welcome; children's menu; high chairs.

Lucius
Spuistraat 247, C (624 1831). Tram 1, 2, 5, 13, 14, 17. **Dinner served** 5.30-11pm daily. **Average** f50. **Set menus** f30-f75. **Credit** AmEx, DC, MC, V.
Lucius is a fish-eater's paradise. Fish in wall aquariums (not for eating) form a backdrop for a dinner of fresh ocean fish (as opposed to the normal North Sea variety), poached, grilled or fried, and shellfish when in season. Lobster should be ordered in advance. The décor's old-fashioned Dutch, right down to the tiles.
Booking advisable. Children welcome; children's portions on request; high chairs. Tables outdoors (pavement). Vegetarian dishes on request. Wheelchair access.

Oesterbar
Leidseplein 10, IS (626 3463). Tram 1, 2, 5, 6, 7, 10. **Meals served** noon-midnight daily. **Average** f70. **Credit** AmEx, MC, V.
Some regulars have been coming to this 100 year-old fish restaurant every week for decades. There's an ancient (heated) pavement terrace with views on Leidseplein, a ground floor ringed by aquariums, or an upstairs dining-room with soft music. All three serve fresh North Sea fish (nothing is imported). Specialities are delicate Zeeland oysters in season, herring in May and mussels in June.
Book in summer. Children admitted. Vegetarian dishes on request.

Sluizer
Utrechtsestraat 45, IS (626 3557). Tram 4. **Meals served** noon-midnight Mon-Fri; 5pm-midnight Sat, Sun. **Average** f50. **Credit** AmEx, DC, MC, V.
The old-fashioned flavour of this restaurant is hard to beat: marble-topped tables, fringed lampshades, good service, friendly atmosphere. The menu lists a dozen or more fish cooked in every conceivable way, but dishes of the day offer the best of the catch from the morning market. The meat restaurant of the same name next door is less impressive.
Book 7-10pm. Children welcome; children's menu f13.50; high chair. Tables outdoors (terrace, seats 40). Vegetarian dishes.

International

Cajun

Cajun Louisiana
Ceintuurbaan 260, OS (664 4729). Tram 3. **Dinner served** 5-11pm daily. **Average** f37.50. **Credit** AmEx, DC, MC, V.
A light and airy restaurant serving good southern American cuisine to a mainly trendy clientele. Blackened catfish is a speciality.
Book for 7pm. Children welcome; children's portions on request; high chairs. Vegetarian dishes.

Caribbean

Rum Runners
Prinsengracht 277, IW (627 4079). Tram 13, 14, 17. **Open** 4pm-1am Mon-Fri; 2pm-2am Sat; 2pm-1am Sun. **Dinner served** 6-11pm Mon-Thur, Sun; 6pm-midnight Fri, Sat. **Average** f27.50. **Credit** AmEx, DC, MC, V.
A cocktail spot with a tropical feel to it, right down to the caged parrots. In keeping with the theme you can dine on Caribbean cuisine (spicy stews a speciality), but expect to be surrounded by much bustle and noise.
Booking advisable. Children welcome; children's portions on request. Tables outdoors (terraces). Vegetarian dishes. Wheelchair access.

Chinese

Sea Palace
Oosterdokskade 8, C (626 4777). Bus 22, 44, 47. **Meals served** noon-10.30pm daily. **Average** f60. **Credit** AmEx, DC, MC, V.
Oriental gourmets don't rush to this floating Chinese temple in Amsterdam's inner harbour, but lots of tourists, including those from the Dutch provinces, go for the Peking duck and rijsttafels. A dim sum buffet, served from noon to 3.30pm, includes many Chinese delicacies. Ask for a window table for views of the old sailing ships.

Filipino

Adobo
Utrechtsestraat 42, OS (625 9251). Tram 4. **Dinner served** 5-10.30pm Tue-Sun. **Average** f55. **Rijsttafel** f42.50. **Set dinner** f47.50. **Credit** AmEx, DC, MC, V.
Adobo is a classy choice if you want to experience Filipino cuisine. The rijsttafel, a selection of various dishes, is a good way to experiment. The service is friendly and attentive, and the cooking authentic. Every November the restaurant celebrates its anniversary with entertainment, gifts and a special menu.
Book Fri-Sun. Children welcome; children's menu. Vegetarian dishes on request.

At Mango Bay
Westerstraat 91, IW (638 1039). Tram 3, 10. **Dinner served** 6-10pm Mon-Wed, Fri-Sun. **Average** f45. **Set meal** f39.50. **Credit** AmEx, MC, V.
A variety of distinctive sweet and spicy dishes which use a lot of exotic fruits are served. The restaurant is both tiny and popular so reservations are necessary. Live music is a feature on Wednesday and at weekends.
Booking advisable. Children welcome; children's portions on request. Tables outdoors (pavement). Vegetarian dishes by arrangement.

French

Bartholdy
Van Baerlestraat 35-37, OS (662 2655). Tram 2, 3, 5, 12, 16. **Open** noon-midnight Tue-Sun. **Lunch served** noon-2.30pm, **dinner served** 6-9.30pm (11pm if concert) Tue-Sun. **Average** f55. **Set lunch** f60 three courses. **Pre-theatre dinner** f50 three courses. **Credit** AmEx, MC, V.
Located in a recently converted fire station, and named after the composer Felix Mendelssohn-Bartholdy, this restaurant continues the musical theme in its décor, including a grand piano and portraits of major composers. Upmarket, elegantly served French food is its forte.
Book one week in advance if there's a concert. Children admitted. Tables outdoors (pavement, seats 40). Vegetarian dishes on request. Wheelchair access.

*Crusty pizzas are cooked in the wood-fired oven at **Casa di David**. See **review** page 106.*

Bordewijk

Noordermarkt 7, IW (624 3899). Tram 3. **Dinner served** 6.30-10.30pm Tue-Sun. **Average** f75. **Set menus** f55-f75. **Credit** AmEx, MC, V.
You probably need to be a yuppie at heart to fully appreciate the qualities of this restaurant. Dutch designer Rob Eckhardt conceived the flamingo walls and black furniture décor; Wil Demandt and Hans Mosterd are responsible for the 'French-oriented' menu.
Book 7-9pm. Children welcome; children's portions on request. Vegetarian dishes on request. Wheelchair access.

De Gouden Reael

De Zandhoek 14, Westerdok, IW (623 3883). Tram 3/Bus 28. **Lunch served** noon-2pm Mon-Fri. **Dinner served** 6-10pm daily. **Average** f67. **Set menu** f50 three courses. **Credit** AmEx, DC, MC, V.
Slightly out of the centre, on Reael Island in the western docks, is a seventeenth-century gabled house. It holds this portside split-level restaurant with a bar on the ground floor, wainscoting on the walls and boats at anchor at the door. The young chef Miek Blommestein is gaining renown for her regional French food. A new region is introduced every three months, along with new art displays. To make the trip to the island an occasion, take a water taxi (*see chapter **Essential Information**).
Booking essential. Children welcome; children's portions by arrangement. Tables outdoors (waterside terrace, seats 25). Vegetarian dishes by arrangement.

Kikker

Egelantiersstraat 128-130, IW (627 9198). Tram 3, 10. **Dinner served** 6-10pm Tue-Sun. **Set meals** f75 four courses; f90 five courses. **Credit** AmEx, DC, MC, V.
This two-storey restaurant is tucked away in the Jordaan. The cooking is best described as 'almost French': French with strong Japanese and Italian influences. Chef Theo

Koster changes the menu every day, depending on that day's market produce. There's live music and Dutch cabaret at weekends.
Booking advisable. Children admitted. Vegetarian dishes.

Van Hale

Saenredamstraat 39, OS (676 2495). Tram 16, 24, 25. **Dinner served** 6-10pm Tue-Sat. **Average** f40. **No credit cards.**
Light colours, black marble tables, an interesting menu and an open kitchen identify this pleasantly trendy, modern restaurant; the home-made desserts, however, are old-fashioned treats.
Bookings not accepted. Children welcome; children's portions on request. Vegetarian dish. Wheelchair access with assistance.

Greek

Aphrodite

Lange Leidsedwarsstraat 91, IS (622 7382). Tram 1, 2, 5, 6, 7, 10. **Dinner served** 5pm-midnight daily. **Average** f30. **No credit cards.**
Aphrodite is the result of a mixed marriage. Run by Costas Perandonis and his Dutch wife, it offers a balanced mix of Mediterranean hospitality and northern European simplicity of style. The bill won't break the bank.
Booking essential. Children welcome; children's portions on request. Tables outdoors (pavement). Vegetarian dishes.

Indian

Mayur

Korte Leidsedwarsstraat 203, IS (623 2142/625 0776). Tram 1, 2, 5, 6, 7, 10. **Lunch served** 12.30-2.30pm Mon, Wed-Sun. **Dinner served** 5-11pm daily. **Average** f30. **No credit cards.**

A friendly, casual atmosphere makes this a good family restaurant, while the well-prepared and varied selection of dishes will satisfy the most knowledgeable palate. *Children welcome; children's menu f16; high chairs. Vegetarian dish. Wheelchair access.*

Pakistan

De Clerqstraat 65, IW (618 1120). Tram 3, 12, 13, 14. **Dinner served** 5-11pm daily. **Average** f35. **Credit** AmEx, DC, MC, V.

At first glance this restaurant doesn't appear particularly special, but Pakistan is a cut above the rest and has a Michelin star to prove it. British tourists will find few surprises, but in a city with few good curry houses, this one is worth the slight detour.
Book weekends. Children admitted. Vegetarian dishes. Wheelchair access.

Tandoor

Leidseplein 19, IS (623 4415). Tram 1, 2, 5, 6, 7, 10. **Dinner served** 5-11pm daily. **Average** f20. **Credit** AmEx, DC, MC, V.

When it opened in 1970, the Tandoor was Amsterdam's first commercial Indian restaurant (as opposed to some sixties' hippy co-operatives). The excellent quality of the food, the varied menu and reasonable prices go a long way towards making this one of the most popular Indian restaurants in the city. It is famous for tandoori, but many other regional dishes are offered as well. The Tandoor looks out on Leidseplein – it's worth booking a window seat, as the passing crowds and street performers provide great entertainment.
Children welcome; children's menu f13.

Indonesian

Lonny's

Rozengracht 48, IW (623 8950). Tram 13, 17, 24. **Dinner served** *Easter-Sept* 6-10.45pm daily; *Oct-Easter* 5-9.45pm daily. **Average** f35. **Credit** AmEx, MC, V.

Lonny's has a good kitchen which has earned it a loyal clientele. Small and personal, with a cheery but elegant décor, it offers reasonably priced, authentic meals in a peaceful, pleasantly unhurried environment.
Children welcome; children's portions on request. Vegetarian dishes.

Sama Sebo

PC Hooftstraat 27, OS (662 8146). Tram 2, 3, 5, 12. **Lunch served** noon-1.45pm, **dinner served** 6-9.45pm, Mon-Sat. **Average** f30. **Rijsttafel** f42.50. **Credit** AmEx, DC, MC, V.

One of the first restaurants to serve rijsttafel, Sama Sebo is now suffering from a surfeit of visitors; booking is essential. Good Indonesian nibbles can be ordered at the bar. There are two evening sittings, one at 6pm and one at 8pm, so ask for the latter if you like a leisurely meal.
Children welcome; children's portions on request. Booking essential. Tables outdoors (terrace, drinks only).

Speciaal

Nieuwe Leliestraat 142, IW (624 9706). Tram 10, 13, 14, 17. **Dinner served** 5.30-11pm daily. **Average** f40. **Rijsttafel** f39.50. **Credit** AmEx, DC, MC, V.

No discussion of Indonesian food in Amsterdam is complete without mention of the Special. Be sure to book because the food is appreciated by Amsterdammers and tourists alike, although not all reports we've had recently have been rave ones. The rijsttafel, however, is a sight to behold.
Book Fri, Sat. Children welcome; high chair. Tables outdoors (pavement). Vegetarian dishes on request.

Tempo Doelo

Utrechtsestraat 75, IS (625 6718). Tram 4. **Dinner served** 6-11.30pm daily. **Average** f55. **Rijsttafel** (vegetarian, meat, fish) f47.50. **Credit** AmEx, DC, MC, V.

Another Indonesian institution – here you can test your taste buds on the hottest food in town. The waiters, however, can be relied on to warn you in advance about the dangerous dishes. Unusually for an Indonesian restaurant, fish is a speciality.
Booking essential. Children welcome; children's portions by arrangement. Vegetarian dishes. Wheelchair access with assistance.

Italian

Casa di David

Singel 426, C (624 5093). Tram 1, 2, 5. **Dinner served** 5-11pm daily. **Average** f40. **Credit** AmEx, DC, MC, V.

A romantic, dark-wooded and beamed restaurant that's popular with visitors as well as locals. The pasta is made on the premises and is first-rate; the crusty pizzas are made in a wood-fired oven. Tables by the window give a good view of the canal.
Book weekends. Children admitted. Vegetarian dishes.

Cirelli

Oude Zijskolk, C (624 3512). Bus 100, 104, 105, 106, 110, 111, 112, 114, 115. **Dinner served** 5-10pm Mon-Thur, Sun; 5-11pm Fri, Sat. **Average** f50. **Credit** AmEx, MC, V.

Located in the now cleaned-up Zeedijk where formerly many feared to tread, Cirelli is an elegantly but outrageously furbished restaurant – look out for the leopard skin table legs and bizarre chandeliers. A tempting menu and home-made pasta make Cirelli's good for a special night out. Occasionally there's live music.
Booking advisable. Children welcome; half portions available (for adults too). Vegetarian dishes.

Da Damiano

Jan Pieter Heijestraat 139, OW (685 0795). Tram 1, 6, 7, 17. **Dinner served** 5-10.30pm daily. **Average** f30. **No credit cards.**

Though out of the city centre (just north of Vondelpark), this popular neighbourhood Italian is a find – a true piece of Italy with excellent pizzas (plus pasta and more substantial main dishes) and a house red to match. For those staying in the area it's one to return to again and again.
Booking advisable. Children welcome; children's portions on request. Vegetarian dishes.

Mirafiori

Hobbemastraat 2, OS (662 3013). Tram 1, 2, 5, 6, 7, 10. **Lunch served** noon-3pm, **dinner served** 5-10.30pm Mon, Wed-Sun. **Average** f45. **Credit** AmEx, MC, V.

Located in a grandiose building at the Leidseplein corner of Vondelpark, this is reputed to be the classiest Italian in town. For all its elegance and the excellence of the food, it isn't outrageously expensive, and two can dine very well on three courses with house wine for not much more than f100. Veal dishes are deliciously tender and the service is attentive for a middle-range establishment.
Children welcome. Vegetarian dishes.

Pizzaria Capri

Lindengracht 63, IW (624 4940). Tram 3, 10/Bus 18. **Meals served** 10am-11pm Mon, Sat; 3-11pm Tue-Fri, Sun. **Average** f25. **No credit cards.**

Angela and Nicola Tritatepe give the impression of having been magically transported from central Italy, pizza ovens and all. They make their own ice-cream, and their version of Dutch apple cake is just the thing to complement an espresso or cappuccino. Simple home-made pastas and pizzas, well-chosen robust Tuscan wines and an unpretentious setting are other attractions.

Japanese

Aska
Handweg 1-5, Amstelveen (647 1740). Bus 68. **Lunch served** noon-2pm, **dinner served** 6-10pm, Mon-Sat. **Average** f80. **Credit** AmEx, DC, JCB, MC, V.
It's worth making the short trip south to Amstelveen to come here, as the many Japanese who eat here (mostly business executives), attest. The purpose-built octagonal building, made of wood and natural materials, offers customers a choice of teppan-yakki tables (where customers can watch as chefs prepare the food), lake-view tables or tatami seating (upstairs). Tempura, sashimi and sushi are superbly presented.
Booking essential. Children welcome; children's menu for over-4s. Vegetarian dishes by arrangement.

Shizen
Kerkstraat 148, IS (622 8627). Tram 1, 2, 5. **Dinner served** 5-10pm Tue-Sun. **Average** f35. **Credit** AmEx, DC, MC, V.
Turn right for a conventional western table and chair, left for authentic tatami seating. Shizen is a classy and convincing Japanese restaurant that justifiably takes great pride in producing affordable macrobiotic food. There's no meat on the menu, but the fish is varied and excellent, and the vegetable dishes unbeatable.
Booking advisable. Vegetarian and vegan dishes. Wheelchair access.

Teppan-Yaki & Yamazato
Okura Hotel, Ferdinand Bolstraat 333, OS (678 7111). Tram 12, 25. **Lunch served** noon-2.30pm Mon-Fri. **Dinner served** 6-10pm daily. **Average** f75. **Set menus** from f86. **Credit** AmEx, DC, JCB, MC, V.

These sister restaurants are among the finest purveyors of Japanese fare. Customers at the Teppan-Yaki are treated to amazing showmanship by master Japanese chefs, while at the Yamazato, chefs sliver fish with the same dexterity. The artfully presented sushimi-sushi can be a meal in itself; sukiyaki is downright ceremonial. Tatami rooms are available.
Booking essential. Children welcome; children's portions on request; high chairs. Vegetarian dishes. Wheelchair access.

Mexican

Burrito
De Clerqstraat 14, IW (618 9807). Tram 10, 13, 14, 17. **Meals served** 4-10.30pm Mon-Thur, Sun; 4-11pm Fri, Sat. **Average** f30. **Credit** MC, V.
A small café-style place, a little out of the centre but worth visiting if you're in the area. Owner Ali actually comes from Egypt, but he and his staff offer a better approximation of the cuisine than many of the Tex-Mex factories in town, and certainly a friendlier welcome.
Children admitted. Vegetarian dishes. Wheelchair access.

Pacifico
Warmoesstraat 31, C (624 2911). Tram 4, 9, 16, 20, 24, 25. **Meals served** 5.30-11pm Tue-Thur, Sun; 5.30pm-midnight Fri, Sat. **Average** f30. **Credit** MC, V.
Both the décor (whitewashed stone walls and old Sol ads) and the location (in an ancient, narrow, bustling street on the edge of the red light district) make Pacifico the most authentically Mexican-style bodega in Amsterdam. The crowded bar and cramped eating area add to the effect, and the food has enough of a genuine edge to keep this place in the forefront. Tuesday is marguerita night (f5 a glass), Thursday rib night (f20 for as many as you can eat).
Booking advisable. Children admitted. Separate room for parties, seats 45. Vegetarian dishes. Wheelchair access.

Pacifico, *in a bustling street on the edge of the red light district, is Amsterdam's most authentic Mexican bodega. See* **review**.

The only Spanish restaurant in Amsterdam to offer a reasonable selection of tapas is
El Naranjo. See **review** page 110.

Rose's Cantina
Reguliersdwarsstraat 38, IS (625 9797). Tram 16, 24, 25.
Dinner served 5.30-11pm Mon-Thur; 5-11.30pm Fri, Sat;
5-11pm Sun. **Average** f23. **Credit** AmEx, MC, V.
Rose's is so crowded you have to keep an eye on whose
sauce you are dipping your tacos into. It's definitely not
the place for a quiet night out, and not particularly authentic either; but the ingredients are top-quality and the portions more than generous. It gets our vote for the best
margueritas in town.
*Bookings not accepted at weekends. Children welcome;
children's portions on request. Vegetarian dishes.*

North African

Hamilcar
Overtoom 306, OW (683 7981). Tram 1, 6. **Dinner**
served 5-10.30pm Wed-Sun. **Average** f30; couscous
f17-f34. **Credit** AmEx, DC, MC, V.
Just outside the centre of town, Hamilcar is definitely worth
the walk up Overtoom. Delicious dishes, including couscous, are prepared by owner-chef Kamoun and served by
his Dutch wife in a relaxed and spacious setting.
*Book Fri-Sun. Children welcome; children's portions on
request; high chair. Vegetarian dishes.*

Marakech
*Nieuwezijds Voorburgwal 134, C (623 5003). Tram 1,
2, 5, 13, 17.* **Meals served** 3-11pm daily. **Average**
couscous f18. **Credit** MC, V.
Genuine couscous is served at reasonable prices here.

Mint tea with honey and luscious pastries brought on
a tiered silver stand make the experience even more
enticing. The obligatory cat is enormous, orange, and
very cuddly.

Portuguese

Portugalia
Kerkstraat 35, IS (625 6490). Tram 1, 2, 5. **Meals**
served noon-11pm daily. **Average** f30. **Credit** AmEx,
DC, MC, V.
Piri-piri sauce, cataplana, stuffed squid and – rare in
Amsterdam – grilled swordfish are some of the delica-
cies served here. Portuguese crafts and frescoes con-
tribute to the authentic feel of the restaurant.
Vegetarian dishes.

Spanish

Centra
Lange Niezel 29, C (622 3050). Tram 4, 9, 16, 24, 25.
Meals served 11am-11pm daily. **Average** f20.
No credit cards.
Known for good, wholesome, homely cooking, this
restaurant doesn't look very inviting at first glance.
Cafeteria tables and fluorescent lighting aren't very
atmospheric, but you know you're in the right place
because of the large, satisfied Spanish clientele. House
wines are very good value. It's in the heart of the red light
district, so read your map carefully if you go after dark.
Vegetarian dishes.

The Menu

Most restaurant staff speak English, and many menus are printed in several languages. A few Dutch words are helpful, however: *ober* (waiter); *kellnerin* (waitress); and *mag ik de rekening, graag?* (may I have the bill, please?). This basic list picks out the terms that are hard to recognise even with a combination of English and common sense.

Snacks

Boterham sandwich
Broodje roll
Eieren eggs
Erwtensoep pea soup (with bacon or sausage)
Kaas cheese
Suiker sugar
Stokbrood French bread
Uitsmijter ham or cheese, with fried egg on bread

Drinks

Anijsmelk warm milk flavoured with aniseed
Huis wijn (wit/rood) house wine (white/red)
Jenever Dutch gin; **bessenjenever** blackcurrant-flavoured *jenever*
Pils Dutch beer
Sinaasappelsap orange juice
Spa Rood (brand name) fizzy mineral water
Thee tea
Vrisdranken soft drinks

Main meals

Voorgerechten starters
Hoofdgerechten main courses
Visgerechten fish dishes
Vleesgerechten meat dishes
Nagerechten desserts

Culinary terms

Gebakken fried or baked
Gebraden roast
Gekookt boiled
Gerookt smoked
Gestooft stewed
Vers fresh

Meat

Bitterballen small meatballs (eaten with aperitif)
Eend duck
Gehakt minced meat
Kalkoen turkey
Kalfsvlees veal
Kip chicken
Kroket meat croquette
Lamsvlees lamb
Spek bacon
Varkensvlees pork
Worst sausage

Fish

Garnalen prawns
Haring herring
Kabeljauw cod
Paling eel
Schol plaice
Zalm salmon

Vegetables

Groenten vegetables
Aardappelen potatoes
Bloemkool cauliflower
Bonen beans
Champignons mushrooms
Erwten peas
Knoflook garlic
Patates frites chips
Prei leek
Sla salad; **gemengde sla** mixed salad
Zuurkool sauerkraut
Uien onions

Desserts

Fruit: Aardbei strawberry; **druiven** grapes; **framboos** raspberry; **kers** cherry; **peer** pear; **perzik** peach; **pruim** plum/prune; **swarte bessen** blackberries
Gebak tart, pastry; **Appelgebak** Dutch apple tart
Ijs ice-cream
Pannekoeken pancakes
Poffertjes small doughnut-like pancakes
Slagroom whipped cream
Vlaai fruit tart
Vla custard

Iberia

Hoogte Kadijksplein 16, IE (623 6313). Tram 1.
Meals served 5-11pm daily. **Average** f45. **Credit** AmEx, DC, MC.
Flamenco music sets the scene at Iberia, the first authentic Spanish restaurant in Amsterdam when it opened 27 years ago. The paella, zarzuela (fish stew) and tapas are still popular with the new breed of residents moving into the old dock area conversions.

El Naranjo

Boomstraat 41A, IW (622 2402). Tram 3, 10/Bus 18.
Meals served 5pm-1am Wed-Sun. **Average** f40.
No credit cards.
The only Spanish restaurant in Amsterdam to offer a reasonable selection of tapas. The Spanish owner is friendly and helpful, as are the staff. Friday nights feature live

Spanish music which attracts a real sing-and-clap-along crowd. There are probably better places for food, but not for sheer enjoyment and fun.

Vegetarian

Bolhoed

Prinsengracht 60, IW (626 1803). Tram 13, 14, 17.
Meals served noon-10pm Mon-Fri; 10am-10pm Sat, Sun. **Average** f20. **No credit cards.**
Choose hearty vegan dishes à la carte or from the daily-changing set-price menu. The restaurant is licensed, and there's a sumptuous selection of pastries; the banana cream pie is a *tour de force*, properly tackled by two. The restaurant's style is a pleasantly eccentric mix of folk, new age and modern. *Vegan dishes.*

Imaginative vegetarian food is served in simple surroundings at **The Egg Cream**. *See* **review**.

The Egg Cream
St Jacobsstraat 19, C (623 0575). Tram 1, 2, 5, 13, 17.
Meals served 11am-8pm Mon, Wed-Sun.
Unlicensed. Average f23. **Credit** EC.
Good, imaginative vegetarian food has been served in these simple surroundings for over 20 years. Several cooks of different nationalities work a rota, and the menu changes every day. Vegan dishes are available occasionally.
Bookings not accepted. Children admitted.

Hemelse Modder
Oude Waal 9, C (624 3203). Metro Nieuwmarkt.
Dinner served 6-10pm Mon, Wed-Sun. **Average** f35.
No credit cards.
Booking is the only way of getting a table here. The creative mixed meat and vegetarian menu is based on French and Italian-inspired dishes, and the friendly service makes for a cheerfully upbeat atmosphere. The *pièce de resistance* is a rich chocolate mousse, which goes by the name of Heavenly Mud (*Hemelse Modder*). The restaurant is licensed.
Booking essential. Children welcome; children's portions on request.

Klaverkoning
Koningsstraat 29, C (626 1085). Metro Nieuwmarkt.
Dinner served 5.30-10pm Tue-Sat. **Average** f35.
Credit DC, MC.
A light, airy atmosphere and friendly service set this vegetarian and fish restaurant apart. All vegetables are organically grown. Desserts are always a highlight – the ice-cream is made from fresh cream: fattening but delicious. The restaurant is licensed.
Children welcome; children's portions on request; high chairs. Tables outdoors (terrace). Vegan dis

Sisters
Nes 102, C (626 3970). Tram 4, 9, 14, 16, 20, 24, 25. **Meals served** noon-9.30pm Mon-Fri; 2-9.30pm Sat, Sun. **Average** f25. **Unlicensed.**
No credit cards.
Even committed carnivores are converted by the Sisters' range of wholesome, value-for-money food, and by the informal, friendly atmosphere here. Culinary influences run from Italian to eastern and there's no skimping on portions.
Booking advisable. Children admitted. Vegan dishes. Wheelchair access.

De Waaghals
Frans Halsstraat 29, OS (679 9609). Tram 16, 24, 25.
Dinner served 5-9pm Tue-Sat. **Average** f28. **No credit cards.**
Popular and inexpensive, this dedicated vegetarian establishment serves organically grown food and organic wine. As at The Egg Cream (*see above*) customers here don't believe in eating late and the place empties by around 9pm. A few vegan dishes are usually on the menu, but phone to check and give details of other special dietary requirements.
Children admitted.

Cafés & Bars

One of the city's greatest assets, from the traditional brown café to the more recent smoking coffee shop.

Amsterdam has 1,402 cafés and bars (approximately one per 700 residents), according to the statistic-obsessed VVV, and they are certainly one of the city's major assets. A gentle tipple, a quiet read on a rainy afternoon or a sustained drinking bout – most bars offer congenial surroundings for all three activities.

Except for the most glaringly tourist-oriented joints around Damrak, Rembrandtsplein and Leidseplein, they're relaxed places with a regular and characteristic clientele – gilded youth, tarnished hippies, beautiful 'meedja' people, solid burghers or solitary *pils* drinkers who have occupied the same stool since Liberation Day in 1945. It's worth seeking out the good ones: they have a unique atmosphere that will draw you back time and again.

DESIGNER V. BROWN
Roughly speaking, there are two types of bar in Amsterdam: the 'brown café' and the 'designer bar'. The first, as the name suggests, are small,

dark, smoke-stained, invariably friendly watering-holes where the prevailing activity – except on Friday and Saturday nights – will be quiet, with more or less considered conversation accompanied by equally quiet and considered drinking. The second are the bright, chrome-and-glass alternatives: call them what you will, in Amsterdam they can be hi-tech, post-modernist, new realist or functionalist. In them one tends to be seen and certainly hopes to be talked about.

Almost all bars have a selection of newspapers and magazines – although not often, unfortunately, in English. Several also provide large, central reading tables at which you can spread out luxuriously for a whole afternoon.

GOING DUTCH
Drinking in Dutch is a straightforward matter. Lager beer (Heineken, Amstel, Oranjeboom, Grolsch, Ridder) is called *pils* and is usually served in a small, thin glass with a two-finger head skimmed flat with a plastic knife. (Complaints

*A popular and atmospheric grand café, **Du Lac** has live jazz on Sunday afternoons. See* **review** *page 118.*

about the foam/liquor ratio are generally met with blank incomprehension.) It should cost around f2.50, although in some places – particularly those with waiter service – this can reach f3, and bars featuring live music might charge even more.

More exciting alternatives are *witbier* (Dentergem, Raaf, Hoengaarden), a light, lemon-flavoured beer recommended for summer; or darker beers, either draught or bottled, which tend to be Belgian. Perhaps most popular is De Koninck, widely available and a welcome respite for determined English bitter drinkers; Duvel is a lighter-tasting but considerably stronger alternative. The remaining Belgian bottled beers (Trappist, Kriek – cherry flavoured – and several dozen others) should be treated with extreme caution. Most are brewed by monks with a seemingly perverse sense of humour: one bears the accurate name of Mort Subite (Sudden Death).

Except with their meals, the Dutch are not big wine drinkers. While you shouldn't expect to find many wine bars, or a particularly wide range of wines, most bars will have a tolerable dry white or red, often of indeterminate origin. Ask for *wijn*, either *rood* or *wit*.

Almost all bars stock a considerable variety of foreign spirits (starting at f4) along with the cheaper locally produced hooch: *jenever* (or *genever*) and *vieux*. The former is known as Dutch gin, although it's actually made from molasses and only flavoured with juniper berries. It comes in a variety of ages (*jong*, *oud* and *zeer oud*: young, old and very old), its flavour mellowing progressively up the scale. It also comes in more exotic flavours: *citroenjenever* (lemon), *bessenjenever* (blackcurrant) and in the form of an old North Holland fisherman's drink, a *schelvispekel*. This herb-flavoured *jenever* has its equivalent in all the regions of The Netherlands; the Limburg version, for example, is *els*. If you want to sound truly *Amsterdams*, ask for a *jonge* or *oude borrel* (young or old *jenever*). Those prepared to wake up with amnesia should ask for a *kopstoot* (pils with a *jenever* chaser).

Vieux is a rather weak and insipid Dutch brandy. Drink it only if you can't afford the French version, or if you don't want to get drunk in a hurry. *Advocaat* needs no explanation.

BAR FOOD

Solid refreshment is also available at many bars. Apart from meals, there is a traditional range of pre-prandial nibbles. Particularly worth trying in winter are *bitterballen*: puréed meat deep-fried in breadcrumbs and served with mustard – much more delicious than they sound. Common alternatives include chunks of

cheese with mustard, unshelled peanuts, chorizo sausage, *osseworst* (raw minced beef in sausage form) or insipid tortilla chips with throat-clearing sauce.

More serious sustenance is often available: a roll at lunch-time, a cheap and cheerful meal in the evening, or a full three-course menu. Generally speaking, *eetcafés* (sort of brasseries) are excellent alternatives to restaurants; some serve remarkably imaginative food at more than reasonable prices (starting with *dagschotel*, or dish of the day, from as little as f10).

Unless we've indicated otherwise, the bars and cafés listed don't accept credit cards.

Brown Cafés

A selection of convivial cafés: places for an afternoon read or an evening drink. Where indicated, the *eetcafés* among them serve lunch-time snacks and/or an evening meal of varying degrees of sophistication – but be warned, most brown café kitchens close at around 9pm.

Aas van Bokalen
Keizersgracht 335, IW (623 0917). Tram 1, 2, 5. **Open** *bar* noon-1am Mon-Thur; 4pm-1am Fri-Sun; *kitchen* 5.30-10pm daily.
A stunningly unpretentious little bar serving some of the best-value food in town. It has a fine collection of seventies' tapes and a varied, largely young clientele.

Café Nol
Westerstraat 109, IW (624 5380). Tram 10. **Open** 9am-3am Mon-Thur, Sun; 9am-4am Fri, Sat.
An over-the-top Jordaan bar which is always crowded with lustily singing locals and the occasional stray tourist. Something of an institution and not to be attempted unless you're happy to lose every inhibition you ever had.

De Doffer
Runstraat 12, IW (622 6686). Tram 1, 2, 5. **Open** *bar* 11am-2am Mon-Thur; 11am-3am Fri, Sat; noon-2am Sun; *kitchen* noon-2pm, 6-10pm, daily.
A scruffy, friendly, down-to-earth bar with billiards at the back and cheap, filling food from f16. Much patronised by students.

De Druif
Rapenburgerplein 83, C (624 4530). Tram 1/Metro Waterlooplein/Bus 22, 31. **Open** 11am-1am Mon-Thur, Sun; 11am-2am Fri, Sat.
A little-known bar of immense charm, situated on the water's edge behind the harbour. If you make it out there you'll be the only non-local – but they're a very friendly bunch.

Engelbewaarder
Kloveniersburgwal 59, C (625 3772). Metro Nieuwmarkt. **Open** noon-1am Mon-Thur; noon-2am Fri, Sat; 2pm-1am Sun.
A 'literary café' featuring Sunday live jazz, this is a scruffy but attractive dive whose clientele (including students, retired American hippies and perspiring writers) will welcome you providing you have something intelligent to say. There is additional outdoor seating on a barge moored outside.

Frascati

Nes 59, C (624 1324). Tram 4, 9, 14, 16, 24, 25. **Open** *bar* 4pm-1am Mon-Thur, Sun; 4pm-2am Fri; noon-2am Sat; *kitchen* 5.30-10pm daily.

The Frascati is more Victorian purple than brown, with a large mirror behind the bar and excellent, cheap food. Popular with students and theatrical types from the numerous fringe venues in the street.

Gollem

Raamsteeg 4, C (626 6645). Tram 1, 2, 5. **Open** 4pm-1am Mon-Thur, Sun; 4pm-2am Fri, Sat.

An unbelievably wide range of lethal bottled beers explains this small, crowded bar's popularity. For obvious reasons, early evening is the best time to go if you want anything resembling conversation.

Het Hok

Lange Leidsedwarsstraat 134, IS (624 3133). Tram 1, 2, 5. **Open** 9am-1am Mon-Thur; 9am-2am Fri, Sat; noon-1am Sun. **Credit** AmEx, DC, MC, V.

A friendly chess and board games café with a dedicated local clientele. On the edge of the neon-lit Leidseplein night-life scene, this place couldn't be further removed in mood.

Heuvel

Prinsengracht 568, IS (622 6354). Tram 1, 2, 5, 16, 24, 25. **Open** 10am-1am Mon-Thur; 10am-2am Fri, Sat; noon-1am Sun.

A dark but cheerful and unpretentious bar in a lovely location at the edge of two canals. It's generally full of locals who tend to get rather raucous late at night. The 'terrace' (pavement) catches the sun till late into the afternoon.

Hoppe

Spui 18-20, C (623 7849). Tram 1, 2, 4, 5, 9, 14, 16, 24, 25. **Open** 11am-1am Mon-Thur, Sun; 11am-2am Fri, Sat.

An Amsterdam institution, Hoppe allegedly dates from 1670. Always popular, it becomes impossibly crowded from 5pm to 6pm, when it's filled with stripy shirts and braces on their way home from the office.

De IJsbreker

Weesperzijde 23, OE (668 1805). Tram 3, 6, 7, 10. **Open** *bar and snacks* 10am-1am Mon-Thur, Sun; 10am-2am Fri, Sat.

The bar at this contemporary music centre (*see chapter* **Music: Classical & Opera**) is well worth the bike or tram ride for its terrace on the Amstel, off-beat clientele and good music. Food is available all day, and it's one of the few places open for breakfast on Sunday.

De Kalkhoven

Prinsengracht 283, IW (624 8649). Tram 13, 14, 17. **Open** 11am-1am Mon-Thur; 11am-2am Fri, Sat; noon-1am Sun.

An unremarkable but very pleasant brown bar, generally less crowded than other Prinsengracht alternatives. The clientele is relaxed and friendly, as is the service.

Koophandel

Bloemgracht 49, IW (623 9843). Tram 10, 13, 14, 17. **Open** 4pm-very late daily.

A late-night bar for the very dedicated. Situated in a former warehouse beside the Jordaan's prettiest canal, it remains virtually empty until midnight, when things get steadily livelier. Closing time is flexible but isn't usually much before dawn.

Luxembourg

Spuistraat 22, C (620 6264). Tram 1, 2, 5, 13, 17. **Open** *bar* 10am-1am Mon-Thur, Sun; 10am-2am Fri, Sat; *kitchen* 11am-11pm daily.

Still going strong as *the* place to be seen for the trend-conscious and generally monied Amsterdammer, the

De Jaren, *where an impressive range of beers and spirits is matched with down-to-earth service. See* **review** *page 117.*

Luxembourg is elegant, high-ceilinged and serves an excellent range of high-quality snacks (the dim sum are delicious, the club sandwiches colossal).

Het Molenpad

Prinsengracht 653, IW (625 9680). Tram 1, 2, 5, 7, 10. **Open** *bar* noon-1am Mon-Thur, Sun; noon-2am Fri, Sat; *kitchen* noon-3.30pm, 6-10.30pm, daily.
One of the pleasures of Prinsengracht, this place is long, dark and narrow with a large reading table at the back, good tapes, changing art exhibitions and exceptionally fine food.

Nieuwe Lelie

Nieuwe Leliestraat 83, IW (622 5493). Tram 10, 13, 14, 17. **Open** 2pm-1am Mon-Thur; 2pm-2am Fri, Sat.
A charming split-level Jordaan brown bar, one of the few where you can be sure of a table until quite late in the evening. It's very quiet and relaxed, and chess boards are often unoccupied.

Oosterling

Utrechtsestraat 140, IS (623 4140). Tram 4. **Open** noon-1am daily.
A stone-floored, unpretentious local that doubles as an off-licence. Good for a drink before or after a meal in one of the street's many restaurants; popular at office closing time with BP and Nederlandsche Bank slaves.

Orangerie

Binnen Oranjestraat 15, IW (623 4611). Tram 3/Bus 18, 22, 44. **Open** 3pm-1am Mon-Thur; 3pm-2am Fri; 1pm-2am Sat, Sun.
A delightful, relaxed and very brown bar a stone's throw from Brouwersgracht and its converted warehouses; good for quiet evenings and private conversations.

De Prins

Prinsengracht 124, IW (624 9382). Tram 13, 14, 17. **Open** *bar* 10am-1am Mon-Thur, Sun; 10am-2am Fri, Sat; *kitchen* 6-10pm daily.
Not to be confused with De Prinses, a little way down the canal, De Prins is usually full of students and a good bet if you're young and feeling in need of company. The pretty setting is matched by excellent food.

Van Puffelen

Prinsengracht 377, IW (624 6270). Tram 1, 2, 5, 7, 10. **Open** *bar* 2pm-1am Mon-Thur, Sun; 2pm-2am Fri, Sat; *kitchen* summer 6-10pm daily; winter 4-10pm daily.
A popular, sawdust-strewn brown bar at the front and a high-ceilinged, up-market restaurant at the back. A haunt of the beautiful people, particularly on summer evenings when you can sit on a barge moored outside.

De Reiger

Nieuwe Leliestraat 34, IW (624 7426). Tram 10, 13, 14, 17. **Open** *bar* 11am-1am Mon-Thur, Sun; 11am-2am Fri, Sat; *kitchen* 6-10.30pm daily.
The style-conscious alternative to the Nieuwe Lelie (*see above*) down the street, this is a light and airy brown bar and one of the most popular in the Jordaan. Get there early, particularly if you want to eat.

Reynders

Leidseplein 6, IS (623 4419). Tram 1, 2, 5, 6, 7, 10. **Open** 9am-1am Mon-Thur, Sun; 9am-2am Fri, Sat.
With its neighbour Eylders, Reynders is probably the only bar worth considering on Leidseplein. Both are survivors of a bygone era, with white-aproned waiters and high-ceilinged, antique interiors.

Scheltema

Nieuwezijds Voorburgwal 212, C (623 2323). Tram 1, 2, 5, 13, 17. **Open** 8am-11pm Mon-Sat.

Once thronged with journalists from the national dailies based down the road, this bar has become quieter now they've all moved out to the concrete wilderness. It retains an attractive, slightly highbrow atmosphere.

't Smackzeyl

Brouwersgracht 101, IW (622 6520). Tram 1, 2, 5, 13, 17. **Open** 11.30am-1am Mon-Thur, Sun; 11.30am-2am Fri, Sat.
About as brown as you could wish for, this perfectly situated bar on the corner of two canals is one of the few to serve draught Guinness.

't Smalle

Egelantiersgracht 12, IW (623 9617). Tram 10, 13, 14, 17. **Open** *bar and kitchen* 11am-1am Mon-Thur, Sun; 11am-2am Fri, Sat.
Small, cosy and almost impossible to get a seat in. The terrace is wonderful in summer; in winter it's all candles and calm.

De Tap

Prinsengracht 478, IS (622 9915). Tram 1, 2, 5, 6, 7, 10. **Open** 4pm-1am Mon-Thur, Sun; 4pm-2am Fri, Sat.
A long, narrow, wood-panelled bar not far from the frantic Leidseplein, serving abundant pre-dinner snacks – mainly of unshelled peanuts. It's popular for student reunions and office parties.

De Tuin

2E Tuindwarsstraat 13, IW (624 4559). Tram 3, 10, 13, 14, 17. **Open** 10am-1am Mon-Thur; 10am-2am Fri, Sat; 11am-1am Sun.
One of the Jordaan's classic bars, 'the garden' is stone-floored, dark and always lively. Generally frequented by slightly alternative locals, excellent apple tarts are served in the afternoons, and there's always someone to challenge to a game of chess or backgammon.

Twee Prinsen

Prinsenstraat 27, IW (624 9722). Tram 3, 10. **Open** 11am-1am Mon-Thur, Sun; 11am-2am Fri, Sat.
Opposite the Vergulde Gaper (*see below*), this is an exceptionally friendly bar full of young and vaguely off-beat locals. The outdoor terrace is heated on chillier evenings.

Twee Zwaantjes

Prinsengracht 114, IW (625 2729). Tram 13, 14, 17. **Open** 3pm-1am daily.
A slightly (but only just) less rowdy version of the Café Nol (*see above*), this is a tiny bar usually crammed to bursting point with accordion playing, yodelling Jordaaners.

Vergulde Gaper

Prinsenstraat 30, IW (624 8975). Tram 3, 10. **Open** 11am-1am Mon-Thur, Sun; 11am-2am Fri, Sat.
An up-market and larger version of the Twee Prinsen (*see above*), the Vergulde Gaper is much reviled by the locals of the former as the 'yuppie pub across the road'. All that can truthfully be said is that the skirts are shorter and the braces more colourful. It also has a heated terrace.

De Wetering

Weteringstraat 37, IS (622 9676). Tram 6, 7, 10, 16, 24, 25. **Open** 4pm-1am Mon-Thur; 4pm-2am Fri, Sat; 4.30pm-1am Sun.
A split-level, very brown student bar tucked away in a side-street off Prinsengracht. It boasts friendly locals, a huge roaring fire in winter and an antiquated television turned on for vital football matches.

In De Wildeman

Kolsteeg 3, C (638 2348). Tram 4, 9, 14, 24, 25. **Open** noon-1am Mon-Thur; noon-2am Fri, Sat.

In De Wildeman, *where over 200 brews from various countries are always available. See* **review** *page 116.*

Around 200 bottled brews from various countries are always available here, and if you're missing your favourite pint, this is where it's most likely to be found: of the 18 draughts always on tap, most are a regularly-changing selection of international beers. The place is usually packed with a noisy, friendly mix of locals and visitors. Unusually in this tobacco-infused city, the quieter side bar is strictly non-smoking.

Wildschut
Roelof Hartplein 1, OS (673 8622). Tram 3, 5, 12, 24, 25. **Open** *bar 9am-1am daily; kitchen noon-5pm, 6-10pm, daily.*
The Wildschut tries hard to be a brasserie rather than a bar, serving snacks from around f10. It's very popular with well-dressed office folk and crowded to overflowing when the terrace is open in summer.

Designer Bars

Designer bars tend to serve good but often quite expensive food, and though you won't be thrown out for being underdressed, it's worth bearing in mind that designer bars attract would-be designer people.

De Balie
Kleine Gartmanplantsoen 10, IS (624 3821). Tram 1, 2, 5, 6, 7, 10. **Open** *July, Aug 5pm-1am Tue-Thur, Sun; 5pm-2am Fri, Sat; Sept-June 11am-1am Tue-Thur, Sun; 11am-2am Fri, Sat.*
Part of the cultural/political centre of the same name, the Balie is a slightly sterile, marbled place full of more-or-less active activists watching the riff-raff of Leidseplein from large windows. Reasonably good food is served upstairs (from f17).

De Beiaard
Herengracht 90, IW (625 0422). Tram 1, 2, 5, 13, 14, 17. **Open** noon-1am Mon-Thur, Sun; noon-2am Fri, Sat.
A beer drinkers' paradise: a high-ceilinged bar with a fifties' atmosphere, stocking a huge assortment of draught and bottled beers, served by a beer connoisseur.

Café Americain
American Hotel, Leidseplein 28-30, IS (624 5322). Tram 1, 2, 5, 6, 7, 10. **Open** 11am-1am daily. **Credit** AmEx, DC, MC, V.
Still the haunt of the rich and would-be famous, though beginning to lose out to some aggressive rivals, the Americain is worth visiting if only for the amazing art nouveau interior. The price of the drinks and food (from f25) reflects the surroundings. *See also chapter* **Restaurants: International**.

Huyschkaemer
Utrechtsestraat 137, IS (627 0575). Tram 4. **Open** *bar 3.30pm-1am Mon-Thur, Sun; 3.30pm-2am Fri, Sat; kitchen 6-10pm daily.*
Transformed from a former existence as an old-style brown bar, the Huyschkaemer is now all rag-rolled pastels and intricate mosaics. Popular with the gilded youth of the up-and-coming Utrechtsestraat, it serves excellent food (from f20).

De Jaren
Nieuwe Doelenstraat 20, C (625 5771). Tram 4, 9, 14, 16, 24, 25. **Open** 10am-1am Mon-Thur, Sun; 10am-2am Fri, Sat; *kitchen 5.30-10pm daily.*
A beautifully restored old building overlooking the Amstel, with exposed brickwork and a tiled mosaic floor, De Jaren serves snacks downstairs and a full restaurant menu upstairs (main courses from f20). With sunny balconies on both floors, down-to-earth service and an

Coffee shops

The pragmatism which stems from Holland's liberal tradition has also affected its laws surrounding recreational drugs. Since Holland amended the Opium Act in 1976, the use and sale of up to 30 grams of soft drugs has no longer been regarded as a criminal offence. This liberal attitude has seen the rise of the 'smoking' coffee shop, as a retail outlet for hash and marijuana, as well as the standard coffee and tea (for old-style coffee shops, see page 120 **Cafés**).

Until 1980 coffee shops were still frequently raided by the police; then the Minister of Justice drew up new guidelines for the Public Prosecuter, and the Mayor of Amsterdam publicly stated that a 'relatively low enforcement priority' would be taken, as long as coffee shops didn't advertise, or have hard drugs on the premises. Now there are more than 300 such premises in the city of Amsterdam alone. The police make sporadic, semi-serious efforts to keep the sale of cannabis under control, and coffee shops respond accordingly; some have eliminated references to getting high in their names, others have taken the signs of marijuana leaves off their shopfronts or keep their hash menus behind the bar. Other don't mind paying the token fine for these offences.

With coffee shops now part of the establishment, they are as varied as any other café or bar in town. We list a selection below. Visitors should be aware, however, that getting stoned is only accepted in coffee shops. Respectable cafés and bars will politely ask you to refrain from smoking on their premises.

The Bulldog
Leidseplein 13-17, IS (627 1908). Tram 1, 2, 5, 6, 7, 10. **Open** 9am-1am daily.

One of the oldest coffee shops, the Bulldog is big, plush and loud, with sometimes over-enthusiastic bouncers.

Chocolata
Spuistraat 51, C (622 6241). Tram 1, 2, 5. **Open** 11am-midnight daily.
Small and cosy, this place specialises in hash-laced chocolates and space cakes.

The Grasshopper
Oudebrugsteeg 16, C (626 1529). Tram 4, 9, 16, 24, 25. **Open** 8am-1am daily.
On the edge of the red light district, this place sells 'skunk', the Dutch-grown hybrid 50-times stronger than normal grass.

The Other Side
Reguliersdwarsstraat 6, C (625 5141). Trams 1, 2, 5. **Open** 10am-1am daily.
One of the few gay coffee shops.

The Pooldog
Hekelveld 7, C (627 7032). Tram 1, 2, 5. **Open** 10am-1am daily.
A pool hall cum coffee shop.

Reflex
Kerkstraat 51, C (639 1154). Trams 1, 2, 5. **Open** 10am-midnight daily.
The Reflex is a cosy, cheap coffee shop with a good atmosphere.

Rusland
Rusland 16, C (627 9468). Tram 4, 9, 14, 16, 24, 25. **Open** 11am-9pm daily.
Small and intimate, this place attracts a local crowd.

Siberia
Brouwersgracht 11, C (623 5909). Tram 1, 2, 4, 5, 13, 17. **Open** 11am-11pm daily.
The attractions are a large selection of board games, plus a changing exhibition of the works of local artists.

Tweede Kamer
Heisteeg 6, OW (627 5709). Tram 1, 2, 5. **Open** 11am-11pm daily.
At present, the ultimate insider's coffee shop.

---

impressive range of beers and spirits, it's the most elegant and unpretentious of Amsterdam's new 'grand cafés'.

Kapitein Zeppos
Gebed Zonder End 5, C (624 2057). Tram 4, 9, 14, 16, 24, 25. **Open** *bar* 4pm-1am Mon-Thur, Sun; 4pm-2am Fri, Sat; *kitchen* 6-10pm daily.
Tucked away at the end of a cul-de-sac, this bar has a cobbled courtyard for summer evenings and loud music (live on Sunday afternoons). The tortilla chips have flavour; the menu is interesting and wide-ranging (from f20).

Du Lac
Haarlemmerstraat 118, IW (624 4265). Bus 18, 22, 44. **Open** 4pm-1am Mon-Fri; 4pm-2am Fri, Sat; 2pm-1am Sun.
A beautiful grand café fitted out in a quirky art deco style

that includes heaps of greenery. At peak times, it packs in trendies by the hundred, each of whom has their favourite spot, be it one of the cosy snugs, the raised gallery, or the glass-walled conservatory. Live jazz adds to the atmosphere on Sunday afternoons.

Land van Walem
Keizersgracht 449, IW (625 3544). Tram 1, 2, 5. **Open** *bar* 9am-1am Mon-Thur; 9am-2am Fri, Sat; 9.30am-1am Sun; *kitchen* 9.30am-10.30pm daily.
Land van Walem is one of the earlier designer bars: long, narrow and bright. The seriously self-important clientele is worth braving for the food; although it can be pricey (from f17) it's good and comes in large portions. Excellent vegetarian quiches and big salads are among the dishes.

*There's a good atmosphere at **Reflex**, a coffee shop that prides itself on being one of the cheapest in town. See **review** page 118.*

Malvesijn

Prinsengracht 598, IW (638 0899). Tram 1, 2, 5, 6, 7, 10. **Open** *bar and snacks* 10am-1am daily; *kitchen* 5.30-10pm daily.
Not very designer, but certainly not brown, this convivial, recently opened bar looks like a Habitat ad and serves good value food at lunch-time and in the evenings (from f17). It's rarely full.

Morlang

Keizersgracht 451, IW (625 2681). Tram 1, 2, 5. **Open** *bar* 10am-1am Mon-Thur, Sun; 10am-2am Fri, Sat; *main kitchen* 5.30-10pm daily; *snack kitchen* 10am-11pm daily.
Next door to Land van Walem (*see above*) and a competitor in the style stakes. There's an awesome selection of foreign spirits, and good food downstairs (from f18).

L'Opera

Rembrandtsplein 27, IS (627 5232). Tram 4, 9, 14. **Open** 10am-1am Mon-Thur, Sun; 10am-2am Fri, Sat; *kitchen* 11am-10pm daily. **Credit** MC, V.
Another 'grand café', with an imposing Parisian-style interior full of mirrors and gilt. Unfortunately the overall sense of style is not matched by the service, which is slow. There's a good range of hot snacks until late into the evening (from f10).

Paris Brest

Prinsengracht 375, IW (627 0507). Tram 1, 2, 5, 7, 10. **Open** *bar* 2pm-1am Mon-Fri; 2pm-2am Sat, Sun; *kitchen* 6pm-midnight Mon-Fri; 4pm-midnight Sat, Sun.
A hi-tech stainless steel and glass *eetcafé* that's now an established haunt of those who consider themselves too cool for (or can't get into) the Van Puffelen next door (*see above* **Brown Cafés**). Excellent food costs from f30 for two courses.

Schiller

Rembrandtsplein 26, IS (624 9846). Tram 4, 9, 14. **Open** *bar* 4pm-1am Mon-Thur, Sun; 4pm-2am Fri, Sat; *kitchen* 6-9.30pm daily. **Credit** AmEx, DC, MC, V.
This beautiful bar is a reminder of how things were on Rembrandtsplein before neon was invented. A legendary art deco Amsterdam bar, it belongs to the hotel of the same name.

Tisfris

St Antoniesbreestraat 142, C (622 0472). Metro Nieuwmarkt. **Open** *bar* 10am-1.30am daily; *kitchen* 5.30-9.30pm daily.
A hi-tech but undaunting split-level bar with good and wholesome food (from f16) and a young and largely arty clientele, Tisfris is a good bet if you're in the Jordaan/Waterlooplein area.

Proeflokalen

Generally little larger than a wardrobe, *proeflokalen* or tasting houses were originally taphouse annexes where a distiller or importer would serve potential clients a selection of his flavoured *jenevers* and liqueurs before persuading them, several hours later, to buy a bottle. The free sample element disappeared long ago, but *proeflokalen* remain a feature of early-hours drinking. Most close at around 8pm: probably a good thing given the potency of their wares.

De Admiraal
Herengracht 319, IW (625 4334). Tram 1, 2, 5. **Open** 4pm-midnight Mon-Fri; 5pm-midnight Sat.
A large *proeflokaal* offering – uniquely – sofas and armchairs so you can get sozzled in comfort. Bizarre-sounding liqueurs from Amsterdam's only remaining independent distillery, De Ooiyevaar, line the bar. Unusually, it stays open till midnight.

De Drie Fleschjes
Gravenstraat 16, C (624 8443). Tram 1, 2, 4, 5, 9, 13, 16, 24, 25. **Open** noon-8.15pm Mon-Sat.
There's virtually nowhere to sit here: just knock back your liqueur (ask for the barman's recommendation) and come back for more in the company of large numbers of locals, the odd student and office workers – some of whom have their own reserved cask on the wall.

Het Hooghoudt
Reguliersgracht 11, IS (625 5030). Tram 4, 9, 14, 16, 24, 25. **Open** noon-10pm Mon-Fri; for groups at other times by arrangement.
The Hooghoudt is more of a brown bar than a *proeflokaal*, really, although it still calls itself one. Casks are stacked high around the walls, but this dark, appealing hole also has a reading table – not the idea of a *proeflokaal* at all.

Cafés

The word 'coffee shop' is open to misinterpretation in Amsterdam: as well as being a café for genteel afternoon tea or coffee and cakes, it can also denote the kind of place gran would sniff at: the hash bar or 'smoking' coffee shop (*see page 118*). The two are in fact pretty easy to tell apart; one look at the customers should be enough, but if in doubt, ask the staff. Here we list a selection of Amsterdam's best places for cakes and snacks, and we've called them cafés, to distinguish them.

While not succumbing to the orgies of gâteaux and whipped cream common in Germany and Austria, the Dutch are no mean cake eaters. Coffee is by far the best option to accompany your *taart* (cake): no one would claim that the Dutch make good English-style tea (and if you must have tea, don't expect to get milk without asking for it). The best place to go for afternoon tea is PC Hooftstraat, Amsterdam's most elegant street, which is littered with up-market tearooms catering to shoppers trying not to look concerned about the f400 they've just spent on a shirt. There are few sandwich bars, but a number of the chic eateries provide light lunches or afternoon snacks.

Backstage
Utrechtsedwarsstraat 67, C (622 3638). Tram 4. **Open** 10am-6pm daily.
Run by Greg and Gary, the eccentric Christmas twins,

Backstage is a friendly, relaxed café and boutique. The twins will amuse you with gossip while you eat cake or one of their famous mega tuna sandwiches, accompanied by a cappuccino or espresso. The psychedelic décor matches the range of knitwear on sale.

Berkhoff
Leidsestraat 46, IS (624 0233). Tram 1, 2, 5. **Open** 9am-6pm Mon-Fri; 11am-5pm Sat.
Still one of the best for chocolate- and calorie-laden pastries and cakes, the Berkhoff has a small salon attached. It's usually full of little old ladies who seem to manage, astonishingly, to remain so.

Caffé Esprit
Spui 10A, C (622 1967). Tram 1, 2, 5, 9, 14, 16, 24, 25. **Open** *café* 10am-10pm Mon-Wed, Fri; 10am-midnight Thur; 10am-7pm Sat; *kitchen* 10am-9pm Mon-Wed, Fri; 10am-10pm Thur; 10am-6.30pm Sat. **Credit** AmEx, MC, V.
Owned by the next-door fashion store of the same name, this ultra-modern café serves a full menu of Californian-style food as well as classy rolls and salads. It's at its best in summer, when the large terrace catches the sun and provides a welcome break from traipsing up Kalverstraat looking for bargains.

Lanskroon
Singel 305, C (623 7743). Tram 1, 2, 5. **Open** 8.30am-4.30pm Tue-Sat. **Credit** DC, MC, V.
For many people's money the most refined *banketbakkerij* (patisserie) in town, Lanskroon makes mouthwatering fruit pies and chocolate cakes. Devour them on the premises in the rather cramped tearoom.

Metz
Keizersgracht 455, IS (624 8810). Tram 1, 2, 5. **Open** 11am-6pm Mon-Fri; 9.30am-5pm Sat; 11am-5.30pm Sun. **Credit** AmEx, DC, MC, V.
A post-modern café on the sixth floor of the famous department store, offering one of the best views of Amsterdam. Prices for the more *gourmet* than *gourmand* snacks reflect its location. Food includes smoked salmon on toast and pastrami on rye plus soups and, for larger appetites (and wallets) entrecôte, Metzburgers and so on. Metz claims to serve English afternoon tea: we've yet to be convinced.

Noord Zuid Hollands Koffiehuis
Stationsplein 10, C (623 3777). Tram 1, 2, 4, 5, 9, 13, 16, 17, 24, 25. **Open** *café* 9am-9pm Mon-Sat; 10am-9pm Sun; *kitchen* 9am-8.30pm Mon-Sat; 10am-8.30pm Sun. **Credit** AmEx, DC, MC, V.
Most people shoot straight past this on their way out of Centraal station, which is a shame because, while not worth a special journey, it's pleasantly relaxed, has a fine waterside terrace and serves reasonably-priced, light food.

PC
PC Hooftstraat 83, OS (671 7455). Tram 2, 3, 5, 12. **Open** 10am-7pm Mon-Fri; 10am-6pm Sat, Sun.
A pleasant and relaxed coffee shop, low-ceilinged and with wicker furniture, serving a good-value range of rolls, cakes and toasted sandwiches. Less imposing than some of its competitors.

Pompadour
Huidenstraat 12, IW (623 9554). Tram 1, 2, 5. **Open** 1-6pm Mon; 9am-6pm Tue-Sat.
Chocolatiers of distinction in a remarkable gilt and mirrored interior: your chance to follow Marie Antoinette's instructions in appropriate period surroundings.

Shops
& Services

Lacking the space for hypermarkets, Amsterdam is crammed instead with tiny, quirky shops. We cover the range, from the fashion boutiques of PC Hooftstraat, to flea markets and flower stalls, as well as the famous diamonds, Delftware and tulips.

Contents

You haven't been in Amsterdam, if you didn't visit 'de Bijenkorf'.

For that special gift or souvenir, for the latest fashion or for the latest trends in home decoration, you can't do better than shop in Amsterdam's leading department store 'de Bijenkorf'.

Our opening times: Monday from 11.00 till 18.00, Tuesday, Wednesday and Friday from 9.30 till 18.00, Thursday from 9.30 till 21.00 and Saturday from 9.00 till 18.00.

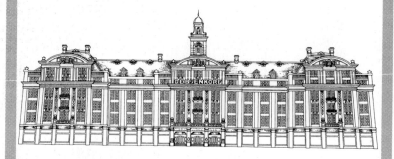

Every visit you'll discover something new in the Bijenkorf.

Shopping

Amsterdam has an enormous range of shops crammed into a small area. From those selling tea or tobacco, to those with nothing but clogs or condoms, we assess the best.

Amsterdammers love to shop. They particularly love the intimacy of small shops, which is just as well because their city has a significant lack of department stores and an abundance of tiny, quirky shops.

SHOPPING BY AREA

The best shopping street for fashion in Amsterdam is PC Hooftstraat (IS), though it's also the priciest. Beautiful window displays and smartly turned-out customers grace this ultra-chic street. Nearly every store carries top-name designer labels for men, women and children. Quality footwear is another strength. Most shops on the street offer tax-free shopping to tourists and it is worth taking advantage of this – Dutch VAT (called BTW) is an extra 17½ per cent on most goods. The tax is included in the price tag.

Van Baerlestraat (IS) has a junction with PC Hooftstraat and is beginning to rival it for smart shopping. The most interesting stretch of this long street is within the four-block area between Jan Willem Brouwersstraat and Vossiusstraat.

If you're on the look-out for unusual or hand-crafted gifts or clothing, wander through the Jordaan (IW). The small side streets running parallel to Rozengracht, such as 1e and 2e Bloemdwarsstraat and their extensions, and Elandsgracht, will divulge a wealth of tiny, interesting businesses. Antiques can be found around Looiersgracht and also in the area around the Rijksmuseum, notably Spiegelgracht, IS.

If you're aiming to go on a spending spree, plan your visit to coincide with the sales. These are mostly in January and February, and again in July and August. And don't neglect the markets if you're looking for bargains. The Dutch claim that a guilder at a market will buy 2½ guilders' worth of merchandise, and this tends to be true.

Most tourists who want to do all their shopping in one area flock to Kalverstraat (IW), but

Nieuwe Spiegelstraat, *near the Rijksmuseum, is clustered with antique shops.*

When in Amsterdam, a visit to Magna Plaza is a must. Seeing is believing.

Magna Plaza by Night.

Magna Plaza. One of the world's most exceptional shop-pingcentres. And it may well be the most beautiful.

The building was designed by architect Cornelis Hendrik Peters and built nearly a century ago. Today this architectural masterpiece houses an entire range of first-class shops. Clothing, sports & leisure wear, music, children's toys and the list goes on. Naturally you can also take a break from shopping to enjoy a light meal or something to drink. We've even provided child-care facilities.

Magna Plaza is all this and more. Come and see for yourself. We look forward to welcoming you. Magna Plaza is conveniently located behind the Royal Palace on the Dam Square.

MAGNA
PLAZA

N.Z. Voorburgwal 182, Amsterdam.

Magna Plaza *on Spuistraat is one of the biggest mall projects the city has ever seen.*
See **Virgin** *page 140.*

it can get very crowded and merchandise is generally very run of the mill. Leidsestraat (IW) is full of bogus souvenirs, and Damstraat (C) has many souvenir shops, but as many pickpockets. Beethovenstraat (OS) is clean, uncrowded and has an attractive array of better, more diverse shops.

General opening hours are 9am to 6pm on weekdays. Many stores are closed on Mondays or are only open in the afternoon (1-6pm). On Saturdays, most businesses close by 5pm and some as early as 3pm. Late-night shopping is on Thursday evenings, when many stores are open until 9pm, but phone first to be certain. Credit cards were slow to catch on in Dutch shops, but these days most large stores and many small shops accept them.

CLASSIC DUTCH

Certain industries and goods are inextricably linked with The Netherlands, and their stories are an intrinsic part of the country's history. They include flowers, cut diamonds, pottery and glassware, and although they are sold in cities across the world, nowhere offers the variety found here. A lesser-known speciality is pewter, made by several Dutch companies. It comes both in traditional forms, similar to utensils seen in seventeenth-century paintings, and in sleek modern shapes. Goods range in size from spoons to tankards, trays, tea sets and

samovars. There's a range of pewter at **Focke & Meltzer** (*listed under* **Pottery**); gift shops and some department stores (*see below* **One-stop**) also carry selections.

Antiques

Most antique dealers can be found in the Spiegel quarter around the Spiegelgracht and the Nieuwe Spiegelstraat near the Rijksmuseum.

Amsterdam Antiques Gallery
Nieuwe Spiegelstraat 34, OS (625 3371). Tram 1, 2, 5, 16, 24, 25. **Open** 11am-6pm Mon-Sat. **Credit** AmEx, DC, MC, V.
Ten antique dealers under one roof. Among their hoards of booty are icons, nineteenth- and twentieth-century paintings, lamps, vases, bronze figurines, silverware and Dutch tiles.

De Haas
Kerkstraat 155, IS (626 5952). Tram 16, 24, 25. **Open** 11am-5.30pm Tue-Sat. **Credit** AmEx, DC, MC, V.
A repository for glass (including famous Dutch designs), pottery, silver articles and bronze figurines created between 1890 and 1940. Art nouveau and art deco vases, figurines and china are a speciality.

Artists' Supplies

J Vlieger
Entrances on Halvemaansteeg 4-6 (nr Rembrandtsplein) and Amstel 52, IS (623 5834/624 5741). Tram 4, 9, 14.

Open noon-5.30pm Mon; 9am-5.30pm Tue-Fri; 9am-5pm Sat. **Credit** AmEx, MC, V.
An inspiring collection of brushes, pigments, pens and paper, plus artists' portfolios and book-binding materials is sold here.
Branch: Van Woustraat 102, OS (671 3733).

Auctions

Sotheby's (627 5656) and Christie's (664 2011) each have a branch in Amsterdam, but their Dutch counterpart is Gijselman's.

L Gijselman

Overtoom 197, OW (618 4470). Tram 1, 6. **Open** 9am-5pm Mon-Fri. **Auctions** usually 10am, 2pm, Tue, Wed. **No credit cards.**
'The only thing we don't auction are human beings', we were told by Gijselman's. The firm was established in 1813, making it one of the oldest auctioneers in The Netherlands; it is still owned by the Gijselman family. Recent specialised auctions have included sales of African and Asian art. When an international public is expected, the catalogue is printed in English. Once a month, household goods are auctioned. This is a particularly good source of art deco furnishings.

Books

General Bookshops

Athenaeum Nieuwscentrum

Spui 14-16, C (624 2972). Tram 1, 2, 5. **Open** 8am-10pm Mon-Sat; 10am-6pm Sun. **Credit** (minimum f50) AmEx, MC, V.
A favourite hang-out of highbrow browsers, Athenaeum stocks newspapers from all over the world, as well as magazines and quality books in many languages. There is a section for fiction, but the shop's strength lies in its non-fiction collection.

The Book Exchange

Kloveniersburgwal 58, C (626 6266). Tram 9, 14/Metro Nieuwmarkt. **Open** 10am-6pm Mon-Fri; 10am-5pm Sat. **No credit cards.**
Second-hand English and American books, mostly paperbacks, both fiction and factual, are bought and sold. There is also a selection of books in Dutch, German and French.

The English Bookshop

Lauriergracht 71, IW (626 4230). Tram 7, 10/Bus 25, 65, 66, 67, 170, 171, 172. **Open** 11am-6pm Mon-Fri; 11am-5pm Sat. **No credit cards.**
English books (both fiction and non-fiction) share shelf space with a selection of British magazines, including *Time Out.*

Oudemanhuis Book Market

Oudemanhuispoort (off Oudezijds Achterburgwal), C. Tram 4, 9, 14, 16, 24, 25. **Open** 10am-4pm Mon-Sat.
A fabulous collection of printed matter finds its way onto the stalls of this market. Old magazines and postcards, second-hand books, sheet music, antique tomes – all in a variety of condition, a mélange of subjects and in multifarious languages. *See also chapter* **War & Reformation.**

De Slegte

Kalverstraat 48-52, C (622 5933). Tram 4, 9, 14, 16, 24, 25. **Open** 11am-6pm Mon; 9.30am-6pm Tue, Wed, Fri; 9.30am-9pm Thur; 9.30am-5pm Sat. **No credit cards.**
One of the city's largest bookshops, De Slegte carries a vast number of volumes in English, Dutch and other languages (including textbooks and children's books, fiction

Lambiek *stocks thousands of comics from all over the world. See* **review** *page 127.*

and non-fiction). It is mainly an antiquarian shop, but there are always some new titles on special offer. Prices are usually low.

W H Smith
Kalverstraat 152, C (638 3821). Tram 4, 9, 14, 16, 24, 25. Open 9am-6pm Mon-Wed, Fri; 9am-9pm Thur; 10am-6pm Sat; 11am-5pm Sun. Credit AmEx, MC, V.
A large, attractive establishment where you can take your pick from a great many titles (fiction and non-fiction) all in English. It also carries all the major English-language magazines.

Specialist Bookshops

For other specialist bookshops, *see chapters* **Theatre, Music: Classical & Opera, Gay Amsterdam, Women's Amsterdam,** *and* **Students.**

Architectura & Natura
Leliegracht 44, IW (623 6186). Tram 13, 14, 17. Open noon-6pm Mon; 9am-6pm Tue-Fri; 9am-5pm Sat. No credit cards.
The name says it all: architecture and nature. The stock includes photographic books of buildings, field guides and animal studies. Many of the books are in English.

Canon Bookstore
Leidsestraat 79 (upstairs from Canon Gallery), IS (625 4494). Tram 1, 2, 5, 6, 7, 10. Open noon-5.45pm Mon-Sat. Credit AmEx, MC, V.
Every aspect of photography is covered in beautiful volumes at Canon, including technique. Many are in English. The shop is above the Canon Photography Gallery (*see chapter* **Galleries**).

Intertaal
Van Baerlestraat 76, OS (671 5353). Tram 3, 5, 12, 16. Open 9.15am-5.30pm Mon-Fri; 9.15am-5pm Sat. Credit AmEx, MC.
Grapplers with Dutch grammar might gain some succour from the language books, records and teaching aids kept at Intertaal. Students of English and other languages are also provided for.

Jacob van Wijngaarden (Geographische Boekhandel)
Overtoom 97, OW (612 1901). Tram 1, 6. Open 1-6pm Mon; 10am-6pm Tue-Fri; 10am-5pm Sat. No credit cards.
Every part of our planet comes up for inspection in the geography books, maps and travel guides sold at Wijngaarden. A great deal of the stock is in English.

Lambiek
Kerkstraat 78, IS (626 7543). Tram 1, 2, 5. Open 11am-6pm Mon-Fri; 11am-5pm Sat. Credit AmEx, MC, V.
Lambiek claims to be the oldest comic shop in the world (established in 1968) and has thousands of comic books from all over the world: some are collector's items. There's a cartoonists' gallery with a new exhibition of comic art for sale every two months. A brochure is given free to customers.

Camera Supplies

Foto Professional
Nieuwendijk 113, C (624 6024). Tram 4, 9, 14, 16, 24, 25. Open 10am-6pm Mon-Wed, Fri; 10am-9pm Thur; 10am-5pm Sat. Credit AmEx, DC, MC, £E$DMTC, V.
This is an official dealer for Hasselblad, Leica, Nikon,

American Discount Book Centers

The American Discount Book Center *has a large stock of English and American titles. See chapter* **Students**.

Minolta, Canon, Pentax, Sony and Olympus. Cameras, camcorders and audio-visual equipment are sold new and second-hand.

Candles

Kramer
Reestraat 20, IW (626 5274). Tram 13, 14, 17. Open 10am-6pm Tue-Fri; 10am-5pm Sat. No credit cards.
Candles in a multitude of shapes and sizes find space at Kramer. Naïve forms from Swaziland, sleek art deco designs and ornamental showpieces (up to f285) are among the more interesting goods.

Children

Babies

Prénatal
Kalverstraat 79, C (626 6392). Tram 4, 9, 14, 16, 24, 25. Open 1-6pm Mon; 9.30am-6pm Tue, Wed, Fri; 9am-5.30pm, 6.30-9pm, Thur; 9.30am-5pm Sat. Credit AmEx.
Four floors of goods for expectant mothers and small children (new-borns to five year-olds). There are stacks of clothing, toys and furniture, plus cotton nappies for babies.

Books

De Kinderboekwinkel
Nieuwezijds Voorburgwal 344, C (622 7741). Tram 1, 2, 5. Open 10am-6pm Tue-Fri; 10am-5pm Sat. No credit cards.
The large selection of books in English and other languages is attractively displayed and arranged according to age. **Branch** 1e Bloemdwarsstraat 21 (622 4761).

Children's Clothes

't Schooltje
Overtoom 87, OW (683 0444). Tram 1, 2, 5, 6. Open 1-6pm Mon; 9am-6pm Tue-Fri; 9.30am-5pm Sat. Credit AmEx, DC, MC, V.
The well-heeled, well-dressed child is fitted out here. The clothing and shoes for babies and children aged up to 16 are attractive but expensive.

Second Time
Frans Halslaan 31, Amstelveen, OS (647 3036). Bus 66. Open 10am-3pm Mon; 10am-5pm Tue-Sat. No credit cards.

Art Film

Theatre

Sport

Music

Books

Television

Clubs

Time Out

Time Out magazine

*The insider's guide to what's happening
in London every day, every night. Every week.*

Wonderful bargains in second-hand clothes for babies and children can be unearthed at this shop. Outfits are top brands and in good condition.

Wampie
2e Anjeliersdwarsstraat 19, IW (627 1675). Tram 3, 10. **Open** 11am-5pm Mon, Sat; 11am-6pm Tue-Fri. **Credit** AmEx, MC, V.
Original fashions at affordable prices. Partners Henny and Lillian create casual clothing in brightly coloured fabrics (mostly cotton) for children aged up to seven. There are toys to amuse the kids while you browse.

Toys

The Bell Tree
Spiegelgracht 10, IS (625 8830). Tram 6, 7, 10. **Open** 1-6pm Mon; 9am-6pm Tue-Fri; 9am-5pm Sat. **Credit** AmEx, MC, V.
Old-fashioned dolls and toys in natural materials are stocked at The Bell Tree, along with children's books in various languages. The shop is run by a devotee of Rudolf Steiner.

De Speelmuis
Elandsgracht 58, IW (638 5342). Tram 7, 10. **Open** 10am-6pm Tue-Fri; 10am-5pm Sat. **No credit cards.**
There's a nostalgic atmosphere here created by the wide collection of wooden toy furniture, vehicles and garages. You can also buy handmade doll's house miniatures and teddy bears, musical instruments, Victorian-style gifts for adults, unusual wrapping paper, cards and child-size cooking utensils that really work. Children are allowed to play with many of the toys in the shop.

Diamonds

Amsterdam has had a lively relationship with these gems since the sixteenth century when refugee diamond workers from Antwerp settled here. By the 1920s, some 10,000 people, many of them Jewish, were employed in the city's jewellery business. The workforce was severely depleted during World War II (*see chapter* **World War II**); but the subsequent rebirth of the trade has been remarkable. If you are interested in a carat or two, do some careful comparative shopping and only buy from long-established, reputable firms such as those listed in *chapter* **Sightseeing**, where you can also see how a rough stone is transformed into a precious jewel.

Fabrics and Trimmings

Capsicum
Oude Hoogstraat 1, C (623 1016). Tram 4, 9, 16, 24, 25/Metro Nieuwmarkt. **Open** 10am-6pm Tue, Wed, Fri; 10am-9pm Thur; 10am-5pm Sat. **Credit** AmEx, MC, V.
Capsicum is dedicated to natural fibres and splendid textures: cotton woven in India and Thai silk in glowing shades are highlights.

HJ van de Kerkhof
Wolvenstraat 9, IW (623 4084). Tram 1, 2, 5. **Open** 9am-6pm Mon-Fri. **No credit cards.**
Trimmings (*passementerie* in Dutch) of every type are

Kerkhof's speciality – stock includes lace collars, feather boas, fringes, sequins, and satin rosettes.

Het Kantenhuis (The Lace House)
Kalverstraat 124, C (624 8618). Tram 1, 2, 4, 5, 9, 14, 16, 24, 25. **Open** 11.45am-6pm Mon; 9.15am-6pm Tue, Wed, Fri; 9.15am-9pm Thur; 9.15am-5pm Sat. **Credit** AmEx, DC, MC, V.
In business for 90 years, 'Holland's only linen shop' sells reasonably priced table-cloths, place-mats, doilies and napkins that are embroidered, appliquéd or printed with Delft blue designs. There are also lace curtain material and kits to make cross-stitch pictures of Amsterdam canal houses.

McLennan's
Hartenstraat 22, IW (622 7693). Tram 1, 2, 5. **Open** 1-6pm Mon; 11am-6pm Tue, Wed, Fri; 11am-9pm Thur; 11am-5pm Sat. **No credit cards.**
Imperial Chinese silks are sold by the metre at McLennan's. They also come ready-made as kimonos, scarfs, lingerie or ever-blooming tulips (f3 each).

TIKAL Native Expression
Hartenstraat 2A, IW (623 2147). Tram 1, 2, 5. **Open** 11am-5.30pm Mon-Fri; 11am-5pm Sat. **Credit** AmEx, MC, V.
Folk fabric from Guatemala is the speciality here. The hand-dyed, hand-woven, hand-washable cotton comes in pleasant patterns and harmonious hues. It's available by the metre (90cm-1m/about 1yd wide) from f25 to f50 per metre, or fashioned into clothing and accessories (shirts from f130 to f200).

Fashion

Accessories

Body Sox
Leidsestraat 35, IS (627 6553). Tram 1, 2, 5. **Open** noon-6pm Mon; 9.30am-6pm Tue, Wed, Fri; 9.30am-9pm Thur; 9.30am-5pm Sat. **Credit** AmEx, MC, V.
Step out in the latest designer tights from Mary Quant, Pierre Cardin and others. There's a large assortment of socks, tights, body stockings and lingerie.

The English Hatter
Heiligeweg 40, C (623 4781). Tram 1, 2, 5. **Open** 1-5.30pm Mon; 9am-5.30pm Tue-Fri; 9am-5pm Sat. **Credit** AmEx, DC, JCB, MC, V.
Hats, caps and other headwear at a variety of prices find shelf space at this shop, as do jumpers, shirts and ties. Goods are directed at men, but are popular with women.

Bespoke Tailoring

Paul Neve
Bilderdijkkade 70, OW (618 1129). Tram 7, 12, 13, 14, 17. **Open** 10am-6pm Mon-Fri; 10am-5pm Sat. **Credit** AmEx, fTC.
Paul Neve has been making trousers at this site for 21 years and he believes he's the last tailor in Amsterdam to specialise in them. Denim trousers cost around f175 and wool mohair between f300 and f350. Everything is made to the client's specifications.

Clubwear

The Fabulous Shop
Eerste Jan Steenstraat 149, OS (664 0180). Tram 24, 25, 16. **Open** 11am-6pm Mon-Wed, Fri, Sat; 11am-9pm Thur. **No credit cards.**
A chic clubwear shop intended for the well-heeled end

Amsterdam's fantastic floating flower market blooms all year round. See **Bloemenmarkt** *page 132.*

of the house music and designer-dressed market. Contains a good selection of one-off items by Benelux designers as well as a large selection of hats.

New Image
Nieuwezijds Voorburgwal 351, C (625 2157). Tram 1, 2, 5. **Open** 10am-6pm Mon-Wed, Fri, Sat; 10am-9pm Thur. **Credit** AmEx, DC, EC, MC, V.
A club shop with an in-house designer who will run you up a nifty little party number within days. The shop also sells photographs and jewellery, and there are permanent photo exhibitions by young local artists, as well as the ubiquitous rave ticket sales.

WILD!
Kerkstraat 104, IS (626 0749). Tram 1, 2, 5. **Open** 11am-6pm Mon-Wed, Fri, Sat; 11am-9pm Thur. **Credit** AmEx, MC, V.
WILD! sells club and sportswear, much of it made by local designers. There's also a hair-dressing salon at the back of the shop which is cheaper than most. Tickets for raves and events are also sold. *See also chapter* **Services: Hairdressers**.

Designer Fashion

Antonia
Gasthuismolensteeg 12, IW (627 2433). Tram 1, 2, 5, 13, 14, 17. **Open** 11am-6pm Tue-Sat. **Credit** AmEx, DC, MC, V.
The top young Dutch designers find a showcase at Antonia, including Gletcher, Imps, Orson and Bodil. There's also underwear and swimwear from True Falsies and fantastic footwear from Lola Pagola (suede and crocodile). Men's garments include shirts, suits and underwear.

Puck and Hans
Rokin 62, C (625 5889). Tram 4, 9, 16, 24, 25. **Open** 1-6pm Mon; 10am-6pm Tue-Fri; 10am-5pm Sat.

Credit AmEx, EC, V.
This shop sells young designer fashion from the likes of Jean Paul Gaultier and Katharine Hamnett, and has one of the best collections in town.

Haute Couture

Edgar Vos
PC Hooftstraat 132, OS (662 6336). Tram 2, 3, 5, 12. **Open** 9am-6pm Mon-Wed, Fri; 9am-9pm Thur; 9am-5pm Sat. **Credit** AmEx, DC, MC, TC, V.
Many of Mr Vos's customers are internationally fashionable businesswomen. His good-looking suits are often severely tailored, made in gorgeous natural fabrics.

Frank Govers
Keizersgracht 500, IS (622 8670). Tram 1, 2, 5. **Open** 10am-6pm Mon-Sat. **Credit** AmEx, fTC, V.
Given the prices of the clothes here, Frank Govers attracts a surprisingly wide variety of clients, ranging from a priest-ess wanting vestments to a diamond heiress after a million guilder, diamond-embroidered wedding dress. Ready-to-wear starts from f1,000 and haute couture from f3,000.

High-street Fashion

Khymo
Leidsestraat 9, IS (622 2137). Tram 1, 2, 5. **Open** 10am-6pm Mon-Wed, Fri; 10am-9pm Thur; 10am-5.30pm Sat. **Credit** AmEx, DC, MC, V.
Trendy fashions for trendy twenty- and thirtysomethings, both male and female. Labels include Katharine Hamnett and Jean Paul Gaultier.

Mac & Maggie
Kalverstraat 8, C (628 1039). Tram 1, 2, 5. **Open** 1-6pm Mon; 10am-6pm Tue, Wed, Fri; 10am-9pm Thur. **Credit** AmEx, EC, V.

A sort of slightly upmarket and better quality version of Miss Selfridge or H&M with good-quality and mass-produced high street fashion. What is seen on the catwalks is reproduced within weeks for this store, and the clothes seem to date quickly as a result.

Onadur
Spiegelgracht 6, IS (626 3735). Tram 1, 2, 5, 6, 7, 10. **Open** 10.30am-6pm Tue-Fri; 10.30am-5pm Sat. **Credit** AmEx, MC, V.
This boutique carries beautiful, timeless, women's fashions in colours that compensate for the lack of sunlight in northern climates and look good on every type of figure. Only natural fabrics are used. There's a full range of clothing, including knitwear and large sizes.

Large Sizes

Duco
Overtoom 167A, OW (683 0184). Tram 1, 6. **Open** 1-5.30pm Mon; 10am-5.30pm Tue-Fri; 10am-5pm Sat. **Credit** AmEx.
Attractive women's clothing in bright colours comes in size 46 up to 60 (American size 16 to 30; British size 18 to 26).

G & G Special Sizes
Prinsengracht 514, IW (622 6339). Tram 1, 2, 5. **Open** 9am-5.30pm Tue, Wed, Fri; 9am-5.30pm, 7-9pm, Thur; 9am-5pm Sat. **Credit** AmEx, DC, MC, V.
A full range of men's clothing from size 58 up to 75 (American and British size 48 to 65) is stocked by G & G. Staff also tailor garments to fit.

Lingerie

Tony Tolo
Kinkerstraat 161, OW (612 0940). Tram 7, 17. **Open** noon-6pm Mon; 9am-6pm Tue, Wed, Fri; 9am-9pm Thur; 9am-5pm Sat. **Credit** AmEx, DC, MC, V.
The last word in lingerie shops. You'll find garments from every designer imaginable, ranging in price from f25 to f500. Cocktail dresses cost between f1,000 and f1,500.

Shoes

Big Shoe
Leliegracht 12, IW (622 6645). Tram 13, 14, 17. **Open** 10am-6pm Tue, Wed, Fri; 10am-9pm Thur; 10am-5pm Sat. **Credit** AmEx, DC, MC, V.
Need a pair of red stilettoes a foot long? Big Shoe specialises in fashionable footwear for large sizes only. Every shoe on display is available in size 46 to 50 for men (American size 12 to 16; British size 11 to 15) and size 41 to 46 for women (American size 10 to 15; British size 8½ to 13½). Designs include modern, sporty, classical and chic styles in the latest colours; high heels, sandals, boots and gym shoes are all available.

Jan Jansen
Rokin 42, C (625 1350). Tram 4, 9, 14, 16, 24, 25. **Open** 11am-6pm Tue-Sat. **Credit** AmEx, DC, MC, V.
Jan Jansen brings out two collections a year, and has fashionable footwear produced for him in Italy. Comfortable walking shoes have been a best-seller for years, but many other styles are available.

Roxanne
St Antoniebreestraat 126, C (638 4788). Metro Nieuwmarkt. **Open** 10am-6pm Mon-Wed, Fri; 10am-9pm Thur; 10am-5pm Sat. **No credit cards.**

One of the many great shoe shops in town specialising in very fashionable, mainly Italian and English, shoes.

Sacha
Kalverstraat 161, C (627 2160). Trams 1, 2, 5. **Open** 10am-6pm Mon-Wed, Fri; 10am-9pm Thur; 10am-5pm Sat. **Credit** AmEx, MC, V.
The Dutch branch of the English shoe shop of the same name stocks a good selection of reasonably priced shoes. **Branch:** Van Baerlestraat 12, OS (673 1345).

Vintage and Second-hand

Daffodil
Jacob Obrechtstraat 41, OS (679 5634). Tram 2, 16. **Open** noon-6pm Tue-Fri; noon-5pm Sat.
No credit cards.
Second-hand haute couture for women – including clothing, shoes, hats, shawls, and jewellery – finds its way to Daffodil. Names such as Hermès, Cardin and Kenzo sell for one quarter or half the original price.

Rose Rood
Kinkerstraat 159, OW (618 2334). Tram 7, 17. **Open** 11.30am-6pm Mon; 9.30am-6pm Tue, Wed, Fri; 9.30am-9pm Thur; 9.30am-5pm Sat. **No credit cards.**
Period women's clothing, from 1700 to the 1960s, is given rail space at Rose Rood. Take a look at the Victorian undergarments, or the long, luscious evening dresses. Accessories and some new fashions are also sold. Prices are on the low side.

Flowers

Each year countless packets of bulbs are bought by foreign travellers. Unfortunately, many are confiscated by customs officers because import regulations either prohibit the entry of bulbs entirely or require them to have a phytosanitary (health) certificate.

The following information was valid at time of writing; however, regulations often change. No certificate is needed to take less than 2 kilograms (4½ pounds) of bulbs into the UK. Bulbs with a phytosanitary certificate can be carried into the USA, Canada and the Irish Republic. Australia will not allow them in even with a certificate; and New Zealand's regulations are too fuzzy to give firm advice. You are allowed to bring one bunch of cut flowers into Britain (not gladioli or chrysanthemums); regulations on cut flowers vary from state to state in the USA. The best way to find out your entitlements is to ask as you leave your home country.

To avoid disappointment, get Dutch wholesale dealers to ship the bulbs to your home. This can be done at the annual Keukenhof flower show (late March to late May), or by mail order from the Frans Roozen Nurseries (the minimum order varies depending on where you live). For both these, and for details of nurseries and gardens, *see chapters* **Excursions in Holland** *and* **Services: Florist.**

The Dutch consume an enormous amount of cheese – and there are plenty of types to choose from.

Bloemenmarkt (Flower Market)

Singel, between Muntplein and Koningsplein, C. Tram 1, 2, 5, 16, 24, 25. **Open** 9am-6pm Mon-Sat.
Amsterdam boasts the world's only floating flower market. This fascinating collage of colour stretches four blocks along the southern side of the Singel canal. Some 15 florists and garden shops are permanently ensconced there on large barges. They offer a wide assortment of fresh and dried blooms, plants for the house or garden, flower bulbs, packets of seeds, novelty plants and souvenirs – including plastic tulips. Rufina van Zoomeren, Singel 526, and A Smit, Singel 502, can provide packets of bulbs with phytosanitary certificates.

Food and Drink

In addition to an abundance of shops selling every kind of food and drink, fast-food counters and stalls offering native and exotic nibbles flourish on practically every street-corner. The favourite national snack is Belgian-style chips (*patates-frites*), eaten with mayonnaise. Don't knock it until you've tried it. The best stall is Vlaamsfrites at Voetboogstraat 33, off Spui. Fresh raw herring is popular, too – it's served with raw onions and purists eat it head first in one gulp, dangling it by the tail. Amsterdam's best herring stall is **Bloemburg Vis Specialiteiten** (*listed under* **Fish**).

Laws regarding the import of foods and alcoholic beverages vary from country to country. In general, most foods, except for dairy produce and unprepared meat products, can be freely imported within the EC, and you can almost always ship non-perishable items anywhere without problems. The best way to find out your allowances is to ask customs officials as you leave your home country. Your embassy (*see chapter* **Survival**) should also be able to help.

Bakeries

There are two kinds of bakeries. For bread, rolls and packaged biscuits, go to a *warme bakker*; for pastries and wickedly delicious cream-cakes, you need a *banketbakker*. *See also* **Chocolate** *below*.

Harrison's

Kinkerstraat 339, OW (612 2380). Tram 7, 17. **Open** 10am-6pm Tue-Fri; 10am-5pm Sat. **No credit cards**.
The place to go should you ever require a huge, multi-tiered and elaborately decorated wedding cake that will feed 3,000. You can custom-order a cake in any shape, colour or flavour – and even have it sent abroad. There is also a mouthwatering selection of French pastries and American cheesecakes, available in individual servings, and a wide choice of marzipan flowers and other edible cake decorations.

Hendrikse

Overtoom 472, OW (618 0472). Tram 1, 6. **Open** 8.30am-5.30pm Mon-Fri; 8.30am-4.30pm Sat. **Credit** AmEx, MC.
Cake suppliers to the Dutch royal family, Hendrikse is unequalled for quality. More than 20 types of tart are sold, including advocaat, plus cream cakes and a wide choice of traditional Dutch pastries and biscuits from all over the country. No chemical additives are used.

Oldenburg

PC Hooftstraat 97, OS (662 8363). Tram 2, 3, 5, 12. **Open** 8.30am-6pm Mon-Wed, Fri; 9am-9pm Thur; 8.30am-5.30pm Sat. **No credit cards**.
This is one of two Oldenburg *banketbakker* in Amsterdam, specialising in fancy dessert cakes, bavarois and chocolate mousse tarts. You can also buy home-made chocolates and marvellous marzipan confections in winter and chocolate eggs and bunnies at Easter. A different theme is featured in the window each month, and the displays much admired.
Branch: Maasstraat 84, OS (662 2840).

Paul Anneé

Runstraat 25, IW (623 5322). Tram 1, 2, 5, 7, 10. **Open** 8am-5pm Mon-Fri; 9am-3pm Sat. **No credit cards**.
Everything at this *warme bakker* is freshly baked daily and made from organically grown grains. Try the popular sour-dough bread and the cakes. There is a display of (non-edible) bread decorations for which the shop is famous. Unfortunately, these must be ordered at least one week in advance. There are also health food products for sale.

Pool

Ceintuurbaan 278, OS (662 1409). Tram 3, 12, 24, 25. **Open** 8am-5.30pm Mon-Fri; 8am-5pm Sat. **No credit cards**.
One of the best bread bakeries in Amsterdam; on Saturday mornings there's often a queue right around the block. Choose from white or wholemeal loaves baked from a variety of grains. Particularly recommended is *roggevloer* (rye bread). You can also buy sandwiches.

Cheese

There are plenty of varieties to choose from. In general, the younger (*jong*) cheeses are creamier and milder. Riper cheeses (*belegen* or even *extra belegen*) will be drier and sharper-tasting. The most popular cheeses are called *Goudse* (from Gouda), followed by *Leidse*, which is flavoured with cumin seeds, and *Edammer*, with its red rind. Some interesting cheeses to try include *Friese nagelkaas*, a ripe cheese, the sharp flavour of which is enhanced by cumin seeds and cloves; *Kernhem*, a good dessert cheese; *Leerdammer* and *Maaslander*. These last two differ slightly from each other, but both are mild, with holes. For cheese-producing towns, *see chapter* **Excursions in Holland**.

Kef, French Cheesemakers

Marnixstraat 192, IW (626 2210). Tram 3, 10. **Open** 10am-6pm Tue-Thur; 9am-6pm Fri; 9am-4pm Sat. **No credit cards.**
French cheesemaker Abraham Kef set up shop over 35 years ago: the shop still imports the finest selection of French cheeses – more than 70 – in Amsterdam. The range of goats' cheeses is particularly good. The shop looks its age in the nicest possible way; it's tiny, dark and wood-furnished, and there are tastings until an hour before closing time. You'll receive expert advice. There is also an assortment of good French wines, pâtés, sausages and baguettes.

Wegewijs Kaas

Rozengracht 32, IW (624 4093). Tram 13, 14, 17. **Open** 8.30am-6pm Mon-Fri; 8.30am-5pm Sat. **No credit cards.**
An authentic Dutch cheese shop, run by the Wegewijs family at the same address for the past 100 years. The Rozengracht, now an avenue, was then still a canal and cheese was delivered by boat. On offer are 50 foreign cheeses and over 100 domestic varieties, including *gras kaas*, a grassy-tasting cheese only available in summer. You can taste the Dutch cheeses before making your selection. They also sell sandwich fillings, bread and wine, and will send cheeses abroad.

Chocolate

Hendrikse Le Confiseur

Overtoom 448-450, OW (618 0260). Tram 1, 6. **Open** 8.30am-noon, 1-5.30pm, Tue-Fri; 8.30am-4.30pm Sat. **No credit cards.**

Special Occasion Food

Certain foods have long been associated with special celebrations in The Netherlands, but many of these traditions are now falling by the wayside. This has the dubious advantage that the more popular delicacies are becoming available year-round as they gradually metamorphose into tourist novelties.

December is a big month for sweet-giving. The excesses of the Christmas season have in the past centred around St Nicholas Day (5 December), with Christmas Day itself reserved for more reverent celebrations, but recently the commercial jamboree has extended to Christmas proper (*see chapter* **Amsterdam by Season**). Exchanged as St Nicholas gifts are chocolate letters (you would give someone their initial), while artistically executed marzipan (*marsepein*) models are given throughout December. These are imaginative, detailed and varied; you can get pigs complete with a litter of piglets, money, cartoon characters and joints of meat.

It's customary for adults to play tricks on each other at St Nicholas and they often buy (or commission) joke *marsepein* figures such as anatomically correct human figures (with or without fig leaf). Another seasonal sweetmeat is *banket staf*, marzipan covered in butter pastry, either shaped into large letters or small rods meant to represent St Nicholas' staff. Models of St Nick himself are made out of *taai-taai*, a heavy gingerbread decorated with candied fruit and nuts. This tradition is dying: the figures used to be moulded on special wooden biscuit boards (still sold as souvenirs), but now they are mass-produced.

There's no respite from tooth-rot in the New Year, which is celebrated with *oliebollen* – large, deep-fried balls of dough coated in sugar. The story goes that doughnuts originate from a misshapen *oliebol*.

Birthdays are important occasions in The Netherlands: celebrants are expected to treat their friends, family and co-workers to cream cakes. Marzipan-filled cakes in the shape of Abraham and Sarah are given as gifts. Tiny pancake puffs called *poffertjes* are associated with the celebrations for the Queen's birthday, when there used to be lots of stalls and competitions for the best *poffertje*. Now they are available all year round; there's an old-fashioned stand on Weteringcircuit at the top of Vijzelstraat.

When a baby is born, *muisjes op biscuit* (candied aniseeds on rusks) or *kandeel* (a heavenly mixture of warm wine with milk, sugar, egg yolks and cinnamon) is distributed to close friends of the family. *Kandeel*, originally given to the pregnant mother to keep evil spirits away, is a dying tradition, but there's still at least one shop in Amsterdam where you can buy it:

Van Gelder Fruitgeschenken

Parnassusweg 3, OS (662 8322). **Open** 8.30am-6pm Mon-Fri; 8.30am-1pm Sat. **No credit cards.**
VG's principal business is in fruit hampers, but it also sells *kandeel*, made and bottled specially. It comes in 50cl bottles (f14.50) lying in miniature ruffled pink or blue bassinets. A great gift for expectant parents.

De Bierkoning *stocks around 750 different brands of beer. See* **review** *page 135.*

Hendrikse specialises in the finest hand-made chocolates. Try *gianduja*, a fudge-like chocolate log made with ground hazelnuts and almonds. Marzipan figures are also a speciality (and can be designed to order). Delicious fruit preserves are also sold.

Delicatessens

Dikker & Thijs
Prinsengracht 444, IW (626 7721). Tram 1, 2, 5. **Open** 11am-6pm Tue-Sat. **Credit** AmEx, DC, MC, V.
Frequented by foodies in search of gourmet ingredients, Dikker & Thijs is the last word in food shops. Expensive and exotic goodies such as truffles can be bought here, as well as complete take-away meals made to recipes served at their three top restaurants (*see chapter* **Restaurants**).

Eicholtz
Leidsestraat 48, IS (622 0305). Tram 1, 2, 5. **Open** 10am-6pm Mon; 9am-6pm Tue, Wed, Fri; 9am-9pm Thur; 9am-5pm Sat. **Credit** (minimum f32) AmEx, V.
Lots of imported foods, notably from the USA and Britain, are available here, as well as Dutch souvenirs (chocolate tiles and so on).

Ethnic

Most general markets have stalls offering authentic foreign snacks such as Vietnamese or Indonesian egg rolls (*loempia*), filled Indian pancakes (*roti*) and Surinam chicken pasties (*kippepasteitje*). Favourite takeaway foods available at snack bars are Chinese-Indonesian rice (*nasi*) and noodle (*bami*) dishes, Indonesian skewered meat with spicy peanut butter sauce (*sateh*) and the ubiquitous pizza.

Florence Exotic Catering
Noordermarkt, IW (699 0868 after 6pm; home phone number, so please ring at reasonable times). **No credit cards.**
Once you've sampled the spicy, authentic Surinam takeaway snacks from Florence's food stall at the Noorderkerk end of the Noordermarkt, you will probably come back for more. She also cooks wonderfully exotic dinners and buffets for any number. Prices are reasonable and the food is delicious. The delivery charge is f30, and a week's notice is preferred. For those who like their food hot, ask for the red sauce. For a description of Surinam cuisine, *see chapter* **Restaurants**.

Hellas
Hobbemastraat 26A, OS (662 7238). Tram 6, 7, 10. **Open** 9am-6pm Mon-Fri; 9am-5pm Sat. **No credit cards.**
Greek delicacies and wines, freshly-made snacks and salads, cheeses, filo pastry and vine leaves fill the shelves.

Meidi-Ya
Beethovenstraat 18-20, OS (673 7410). Tram 5. **Open** 10am-6pm Mon-Wed, Fri; 10am-9pm Thur; 9am-5pm Sat. **No credit cards.**
A Japanese supermarket with every food and condiment necessary to the Japanese kitchen including fresh greens, flown in specially, and saké. Snacks can be eaten at the sushi bar and there are hot dishes and snacks to take away.

Smeraglia
Kinkerstraat 21, OW (616 6895). Tram 7, 17. **Open** 11am-6pm Mon-Fri; 10am-5pm Sat. **No credit cards.**
The friendly staff at Smeraglia can provide customers with northern and southern Italian food, wines and spirits.

Toko Ramee
Ferdinand Bolstraat 74, OS (662 2025). Tram 16, 24, 25.
Open 9am-6pm Tue-Fri; 9am-5pm Sat. **No credit cards.**
All the spices and ingredients used in Indonesian cooking are sold, as well as Chinese and Thai ingredients and take-away dishes. Fresh tropical greens are available on Fridays only.

Fish

Bloemberg Vis Specialiteiten
Van Baerlestraat, across from Concertgebouw and between Stedelijk Museum and the corner. Tram 2, 3, 5, 12, 16. **Open** 9am-5pm Tue-Sat. **No credit cards.**
This famous herring stall is a must for anyone wishing to sample Dutch herring or mackerel. The owner is a recipient of the coveted 'Golden Herring of Amsterdam' award for his delicious cured fish and fish sandwiches. Food can be taken away, or eaten at one of the outdoor tables.

Viscenter Volendam
Kinkerstraat 181, OW (618 7062). Tram 7, 17. **Open** 8am-6pm Mon-Sat. **Credit** AmEx, MC, V.
The family that runs this popular shop commutes from the fishing village of Volendam. It offers a large selection of freshwater and sea fish, shellfish, cured fish (try the smoked eels – *gerookte paling*), take-away snacks and seafood salads.

Health Food

Frica
middle tunnel, Centraal Station C (626 1842). Metro Centraal Station. **Open** 8am-7.45pm Mon-Sat. **No credit cards.**
Prices are reasonable at this health food shop, despite the touristy location. Homoeopathic medicines, herbs and natural cosmetics are sold alongside vitamins and drinks.

Manna
Spui 1, C (625 3743). Tram 1, 2, 5. **Open** 1-6pm Mon; 9am-6pm Tue, Wed, Fri; 9am-9pm Thur; 9am-5pm Sat. **No credit cards.**
Amsterdam's most popular organic food store. Fresh, bottled and frozen foods, wine, beer, cosmetics and aromatherapy oils are all guaranteed free of artificial additives. Bread and pastry are baked daily on the premises and there are take-away meals and a café.

Mineral Water

Waterwinkel
Roelof Hartstraat 10, OS (675 5932). Tram 3, 12, 24.
Open 9am-6pm Mon-Fri; 9am-5pm Sat. **No credit cards.**
Owner Jan Willem Bakker boasts of stocking 100 bottled mineral waters from around the world. Customers are encouraged to sample before buying, and bottles can be gift-wrapped and shipped. There is even mud from the Dead Sea; you don't drink it, you apply it as a balm for acne and arthritis.

Off-licences

The legal age for buying or being served beer is 16, and for wine and spirits it's 18. Beer (*pils*) and Dutch gin (*jenever*) are the most popular alcoholic drinks, although many people enjoy a good glass of wine. Wines often cost less at an off-licence than at the airport tax-free shopping centre. This is also true of spirits if they are on special offer.

De Bierkoning
Paleisstraat 33, C (625 2336). Tram 1, 2, 5, 13, 14, 17. **Open** 1-6pm Mon; 11am-6pm Tue, Wed, Fri; 11am-9pm Thur; 11am-5pm Sat. **No credit cards.**
'The Beer King', named for its location opposite the Royal Palace, stocks approximately 750 different brands of beer from around the world, as well as beer glasses.

De Cuyp
Albert Cuypstraat 146, OS (662 6676). Tram 4, 16, 24, 25. **Open** 9am-6pm Mon-Sat. **No credit cards.**
Specialising in miniature and giant bottles, De Cuyp stocks more than 3,000 miniatures. Huge bottles include an eight-litre bottle of *jenever* and a 21-litre bottle of champagne. There is a large international assortment of wines and spirits, including unusual Surinam drinks such as tropical fruit spirits.

Wijnkoperij Woorts
Utrechtsestraat 51, IS (623 7426). Tram 4. **Open** 1-6pm Mon; 9am-6pm Tue-Fri; 9am-5pm Sat.
No credit cards.
A wine lover's paradise, offering over 600 varieties, with the emphasis on those from Italy. Tasting sessions are held all day on Saturday and qualified advice is available. Some of the bottles have unique labels depicting the work of contemporary Dutch artists, and are becoming collectors' items.

Tea and Coffee

Keizer
Prinsengracht 180, IW (624 0823). Tram 13, 14, 17.
Open 9am-5.30pm Mon-Fri; 9am-5pm Sat.
No credit cards.
The tea and coffee specialist. In business at the same address since 1839 and featuring much of the original tiled décor, Keizer carries everything and anything to do with brewing and serving. For f20 you can buy a decorative tile made of pressed tea. In ancient China, these were used as currency when buying horses from Mongolia. No home should be without one.

Games and Models

Compendium
Hartenstraat 14, IW (638 1579). Tram 13, 14, 17.
Open 1-6pm Mon; 10am-6pm Tue, Wed, Fri; 10am-8pm Thur; 10am-5pm Sat. **Credit** AmEx, DC, MC, V.
Come here for games galore, including fantasy roleplaying from the USA and Britain (Dungeons and Dragons, War Hammer Citadel). Tin soldiers, chess sets, computer games and the Japanese board game Go are also available.

Miniature Furniture
Prinsengracht 293, IW (626 7863/622 1113 private number; please ring at reasonable time). Tram 13, 14, 17. **Open** noon-4.30pm Saturday and by appointment.
No credit cards.
The remarkable assortment of diminutive furnishings is made on a one-twelfth scale by Dutch craftspeople. Ring Mrs Louise Meertens for an appointment to see them.

Scale Train House
Bilderdijkstraat 94, OW (612 2670/fax 612 2817).
Tram 3, 12, 13, 14. **Open** 9.30am-6pm Mon-Fri; 9.30am-5pm Sat. **No credit cards.**
With a do-it-yourself kit from the Scale Train House you

MODERN PAINTERS

A QUARTERLY JOURNAL OF THE FINE ARTS

can build yourself a replica of Moscow's onion-topped St Basil's Cathedral or the Leaning Tower of Pisa (height 44cm/17in). The ready-made parade includes electric trains (with steam or diesel engines and all kinds of rolling stock) plus tracks, European railway stations, houses and scenery, and modern and vintage vehicles in various sizes.

Gifts

Holland Gallery De Munt
Muntplein 12, C (623 2271/fax 638 4215). Tram 4, 9, 14, 16, 24, 25. **Open** 9am-6pm Mon-Fri; 9am-5pm Sat. **Credit** AmEx, MC, V.
Stockists of Royal pottery (Makkum and Porceleyne Fles) plus other hand-painted objects such as traditional tiles and beautifully decorated wooden trays and boxes. Other highlights include miniature ceramic canal houses and dolls in traditional Dutch costumes. You'll find De Munt in the Munttoren (*see chapter* **Sightseeing**).

Poppette Doll Studio
WG Plein 425, OW (683 8862). Tram 1, 3, 6, 12. **Open** by appointment. **Credit** AmEx, V.
Jonette Stabbert is an American artist with a flair for caricature. Her unique handmade gifts include miniature teddy bears, ethnic dolls and life-size soft sculpture car companions – popular in the USA with women drivers travelling alone, as the dummies are sufficiently life-like to fool potential trouble-makers.

Silverplate
Nes 89, C (624 8339). Tram 4, 9, 14, 16, 24, 25. **Open** 11am-6pm Mon-Fri; 11am-5pm Sat. **Credit** AmEx, DC, MC, V.
A good place for gift ideas: wine coolers, cocktail shakers, trays, serving dishes, candlesticks, photo frames and much more, all in silver; also damask napkins and tablecloths made to measure.

Glass and Crystal

Royal Leerdam, one of the oldest glassworks in The Netherlands, is world-famous for its contemporary – and remarkably inexpensive – collections of glassware. Its 'Guild' wine goblet, created in co-operation with the Association of Dutch Wine Merchants in 1930, is still one of the company's most popular products. Amsterdam's better gift shops, such as **Focke & Meltzer** (*listed under* **Pottery**) carry Leerdam's lead crystal 'Unica' one-of-a-kind pieces. Cheaper glassware can be found at household furnishing stores throughout the city.

Glasgalerie Kuhler
Prinsengracht 134, IS (638 0230). Tram 13, 14, 17. **Open** 12.30-6pm Tue, Wed, Fri; 12.30-9pm Thur; noon-5pm Sat. **Credit** AmEx, MC, V.
A large, lustrous collection of contemporary European glass and crystal is kept at Kuhler. All pieces are unique, dated and signed by well-known artists, including two from The Netherlands. Glass-blowing is well represented, along with *pâte de verre* (a method of pouring molten glass into moulds) and cold laminated sculptures. Prices range from f85 to f17,000.

Handicrafts

Cedille
Lijnbaansgracht 275, near Spiegelgracht, IS (624 7178). Tram 6, 7, 10. **Open** Mar-Sept 1-6pm Mon; 11am-6pm Tue-Sun; Oct-Dec 1-6pm Mon; 11am-6pm Tue-Sat; Jan, Feb 11am-6pm Tue-Sat. **Credit** AmEx, DC, JCB, MC, TC, V.
On one side Cedille sells fashion jewellery, mostly handmade in The Netherlands. The other half has handmade wooden toys, including handsome, one-off puppets. There's also a large collection of music boxes.

Tesselschade – Arbeid Adelt
Leidseplein 33, IS (623 6665). Tram 1, 2, 5, 6, 7, 10. **Open** 10am-6pm Tue-Fri; 10am-5pm Sat. **No credit cards.**
The handcrafted gifts here are all made in The Netherlands. Toys, decorations and more utilitarian items (including tea cosies and decorated clothes' hangers) are made and sold on a non-profit basis by an association of Dutch women. This association (its name is that of the shop; a rough translation is 'work ennobles') was founded in 1871 to give women the chance to work from home and make some money, and it's still going strong.

Health and Beauty

The Body Shop
Kalverstraat 157-159, C (623 9789). Tram 4, 9, 14, 16, 24, 25. **Open** 11am-6pm Mon; 9.30am-6pm Tue, Wed, Fri; 9.30am-9pm Thur; 9.30am-5pm Sat. **Credit** AmEx, MC, fالسTC, V.
Great aromas, attractive displays and knowledgeable staff make it hard to resist entering this British export. Natural ingredients are used for the assortment of shampoos, soaps and lotions.

Jacob Hooy & Co
Kloveniersburgwal 12, C (624 3041). Tram 4, 9, 14, 16, 24, 25/Metro Nieuwmarkt. **Open** noon-6pm Mon; 8.30am-6pm Tue-Fri; 8.30-5pm Sat. **No credit cards.**
Established in 1743, this old-fashioned chemist's sells kitchen and medicinal herbs, spices, natural cosmetics, organically-grown grains and other health foods and homoeopathic remedies.

Palais des Parfums
Van Baerlestraat 74, OS (662 5781). Tram 2, 3, 5, 12. **Open** 1-6pm Mon; 9am-6pm Tue, Wed, Fri; 9am-9pm Thur; 9am-5pm Sat. **Credit** AmEx, DC, MC, fSTC, V.
A good, if pricey, place for both men and women to be pampered. Top brands of cosmetics and all the major perfumes are sold. Upstairs there are salons, which offer one-hour facials for f70, a manicure for f27.50 and massage for f70.

Leather and Luggage

Carina Lederwaren
Nieuwendijk 95, C (623 3305). Tram 1, 2, 4, 5, 9, 13, 16, 17, 24, 25. **Open** noon-6pm Mon; 10am-6pm Tue, Wed, Fri; 10am-9pm Thur; 10am-5pm Sat. **Credit** AmEx, DC, MC, V.
Leather bags, cases and luggage for a variety of budgets are kept here. Additional lines include umbrellas, aluminium cases, rucksacks and school briefcases. Samsonite, Delsey, Jolly Bag and Knirps are among the brands.

Façade

PC Hooftstraat 79, OS (676 4440). Tram 2, 3, 5, 12.
Open 1-6pm Mon; 9am-5.30pm Tue-Fri; 9am-5pm Sat.
Credit AmEx, DC, MC, V.
Top labels such as Cardin and Gucci are found at Façade: travel articles, gloves, diaries and wallets are stashed along with umbrellas, men's ties, key rings, cufflinks and briefcases.

Hester van Eeghen

Hartenstraat 1, IW (626 9212). Tram 1, 2, 5, 13, 14, 17. **Open** 11am-5.30pm Tue-Fri; 11am-5pm Sat. **Credit** AmEx, DC, MC, V.
Ms van Eeghen designs all her own goods, which are then made in The Netherlands. Only leather is used, even for linings. Beautiful briefcases for women come in luscious shades including peach and light blue, and there are also items for men – knapsacks and wallets. Be prepared to join a long waiting list if you insist on a custom-made article.

Zumpolle

PC Hooftstraat 103, OS (664 8334). Tram 2, 3, 5, 12.
Open 1-6pm Mon; 9.30am-6pm Tue, Wed, Fri; 9.30am-6pm, 7-9pm, Thur; 9.30am-5pm Sat. **Credit** AmEx, DC, MC, V.
The chic Zumpolle supplies the opulent with the top names in suitcases – Rimowa (hi-tech aluminium), Rodelle (light-weight, dent-resistant), Modler (leather-trimmed canvas), Marco Tabini (crocodile) and Lark (carry-on hold-alls). There is a wide choice of briefcases and small leather goods, jewellery kits, British picnic hampers and leather writing folders.

Markets

General Markets

Albert Cuyp Markt

Albert Cuypstraat, OS. Tram 2, 16, 24, 25. **Open** 9am-5pm Mon-Sat.
The international atmosphere of this market makes it the most popular in Amsterdam. There are many exotic foodstuffs for sale, a variety of fish, shellfish, fresh herbs, clothing, fabrics and houseplants. Interesting shops line the street.

Lapjesmarkt

Westerstraat, IW. Tram 3, 10. **Open** 9.30am-1pm Mon.
As well as the colourful fabrics displayed at this superior market, you can also pick up fantastic bargains in clothing and accessories. There's a small but fascinating flea market near Prinsengracht, plus some exotic take-away foods, and a large stall with houseplants.

Organic Farmers' Market

Westerstraat/Noorderkerkstraat, IW. Tram 3, 10. **Open** 10am-3pm Sat.
All the fresh fruits, vegetables and herbs sold here are organically grown. Health foods and ethnic craft goods can also be bought.

Ten Kate Markt

Ten Katestraat, OW. Tram 7, 17. **Open** 9am-6pm Mon-Fri; 9am-5pm Sat.
A very good market for fresh fruit and vegetables, clothing, cut flowers and houseplants.

Flea Markets

Waterlooplein

Waterlooplein, C. Tram 9, 14/Metro Waterlooplein.
Open 10am-5pm Mon-Sat.

The contents of other people's attics will be revealed to you at Waterlooplein market. A few genuine antiques nestle next to hopeless rubbish. Beware of rip-offs.

Zwarte Markt (Black Market) & Oosterse Markt (Eastern Market)

Industriegebied aan de Buitenlandenden, Beverwijk-Oost. Train to Beverwijk; N202 to A9, then Beverwijk junction. **Open** *Zwarte Markt* 7am-5pm Sat; *Oosterse Markt* 8am-6pm Sat, Sun.
The Zwarte Markt announces itself as 'the largest indoor flea market in Europe'. New goods, old goods, foreign goods – you name it, you'll find it here. Bargains abound and your guilder will go far. The adjoining Oosterse Markt is exactly that – crammed full of Oriental merchandise from pottery and carpets to Vietnamese spring rolls and fresh produce: it's hard to believe you're in The Netherlands.

One-stop

De Bijenkorf

Dam 1, C (621 8080). Tram 1, 2, 4, 5, 9, 13, 14, 16, 17, 24, 25. **Open** 11am-6pm Mon; 9.30am-6pm Tue, Wed, Fri; 9.30am-9pm Thur; 9am-5pm Sat. **Credit** AmEx, DC, MC, V.
De Bijenkorf (The Beehive) is the best-known department store in The Netherlands. It has good clothing for all ages, jewellery, shoes and accessories, a fine book department, household furnishings and linens. The restaurant La Ruche is a good place for lunch.

Gelderlandplein

Gelderlandplein, OS. Bus 148, 149.

Osdorpplein

Osdorpplein, OW. Tram 1/bus 19, 23, 68.
Both these shopping centres incorporate a large selection of chain-stores for one-stop shopping.

Hema

Reguliersbreestraat 10, C (624 6506). Tram 4, 9, 14, 16, 24, 25. **Open** 9am-5pm Mon-Sat.
No credit cards.
The Dutch answer to an American five-and-dime store. Prices are very low and the quality is surprisingly high. Goods include casual clothing and underwear, accessories, household wares, tools, stationery and assorted foods. Decent wines are sold cheaply. Hema has many branches around town.

Metz & Co

Keizersgracht 455, IS (624 8810). Tram 1, 2, 5. **Open** 9.30am-6pm Mon-Fri; 9.30am-5pm Sat. **Credit** AmEx, MC, V.
A great place to shop for gifts. You'll find trendy, modern, attractive furniture alongside small gift items such as ornaments and scented soaps. The top-floor restaurant is popular for business lunches and has a terrific view of the city *(see also chapter* **Cafés & Bars***)*.

Vroom and Dreesman

Kalverstraat 201, C (622 0171). Tram 4, 9, 14, 16, 24, 25. **Open** 11am-6pm Mon; 9.30am-6pm Tue, Wed, Fri; 9.30am-9pm Thur; 9am-5pm Sat. **Credit** AmEx, MC, V.
Prices are a step up from Hema (*above*) but the range of goods is more extensive in this large branch of the V&D chain. Furniture, appliances, gardening supplies, sporting goods, records, inexpensive fashions, cosmetics and tableware are all stocked.

Discover the contents of other people's attics at **Waterlooplein flea market**. *See* **review** page 138.

Parties

Center Stage
Nieuwezijds Voorburgwal 150, C (622 4903). Tram 1, 2, 5, 13, 17. **Open** 1-5pm Mon; 10am-6pm Tue, Wed, Fri; 10am-9pm Thur; 10am-5pm Sat. **Credit** AmEx, MC, V.
Three Californians offer a jolly variety of 2,500 items for every kind of party at Center Stage. They stock decorations, disposable eating utensils, balloons and a huge variety of chocolate figures including horses and carousels.

Christmas World
Nieuwezijds Voorburgwal 137-139, C (622 7047). Tram 1, 2, 5, 13, 17. **Open** *Sept-Easter* 8.30am-6.30pm Mon-Wed, Fri, Sat; 8.30am-9pm Thur; *Easter-Aug* 9am-6pm Mon-Sat. **Credit** MC, TC, V.
Cheery Yuletide decorations, made in the USA and Britain, are sold here all year round. The selection includes personalised stockings for Santa to fill, table linens and old-fashioned tree ornaments.

Party House
Utrechtsestraat 90, IS (620 8304). Tram 4. **Open** 10am-6pm Tue-Fri; 10am-5pm Sat. **No credit cards**.
A multitude of masks – weird, funny, fantastic – hangs from the ceiling in this shop. There are also costumes and accessories for sale or hire and a plethora of practical jokes.

Posters and Prints

Art Unlimited
Keizersgracht 510, IS (624 8419/fax 623 6524). Tram 1, 2, 5. **Open** 11am-6pm Mon; 10am-6pm Tue-Fri; 10am-5pm Sat. **Credit** AmEx, DC, MC, V.
Among the large collection of posters are reproductions of modern paintings, 400 black and whites (no film subjects), thousands of postcards and photos of famous and obscure poets, actors and other international personalities.

Cine-Qua-Non
Staalstraat 14, C (625 5588). Tram 4, 9, 14, 16, 24, 25. **Open** 1-6pm Tue-Sat. **Credit** MC.
Film fanatics flock here for posters (mostly Italian and French), photos and second-hand books concerning their hobby, plus videos of cult films such as Warhol's *Chelsea Girls*. Note that different signal formats prevent the use of European videos in North America.

Pottery

Early in the seventeenth century, merchant ships of the Dutch East India Company (VOC, *see chapter* **The Golden Age**) sailed home with beautifully decorated porcelain from China. Seeing their livelihood threatened, Dutch potters began imitating those popular imports. That was the origin of today's **Delftware**, with its distinctive blue designs on an off-white background. By the middle of the century, there were over 30 small potteries in Delft alone. One of them, **De Porceleyne Fles** (The Porcelain Jar), is still in business. Traditionally, Delftware is made from white baking clay imported from Cornwall, and the pieces are formed on a potter's wheel or in plaster moulds. After one firing, each piece is dusted with a charcoal outline of its decoration and artists paint every detail, including their initials and the article's code number next to the company's trademark. The future heirloom is then given a transparent glaze coating and fired once more. Cheaper, machine-made imitations are only partially hand-painted. The decorations are usually applied by transfer or printed on the surface: look closely and you'll see the tiny dots.

For non-specialist pottery and craft shops, *see above* **Gifts.**

Focke & Meltzer

PC Hooftstraat 65-67, OS (664 2311). Tram 2, 3, 5, 12. **Open** 11am-6pm Mon; 9.30am-6pm Tue, Wed, Fri; 9.30am-9pm Thur; 9.30am-5pm Sat. **Credit** AmEx, DC, MC, V.
Established in 1823, Focke & Meltzer specialises in elegant European china, crystal, silver and figurines. Its Dutch range includes the four Royals: Holland pewter, Leerdam crystal, Makkum pottery and Porceleyne Fles Delftware. Prices start at f20 for cups and saucers and rise to f15,000 for one-off vases.
Branch: Tax-free Shopping Centre, Schiphol Airport (601 5205).

Galleria d'Arte 'Rinascimento'

Prinsengracht 170, IS (622 7509/fax 623 3431). Tram 13, 14, 17. **Open** 9am-6pm daily. **Credit** AmEx, DC, MC, V.
The collectable pottery here ranges from a f40 thimble to an antique tile mural for f30,000. Both old and new Delftware, Porceleyne Fles and Makkum are featured and there's an amazing variety of ceramic clock cases (complete with timepieces). Also on sale are authentic copies of early seventeenth-century vases specifically designed to display precious tulips during Holland's 'tulipmania' – an orgy of speculation that took place in the 1630s, when the price of a tulip bulb rocketed to over f1,500.
Export scheme. Packing and shipping, including insurance.

Kleikollektief (Clay Collective)

Hartenstraat 11, C (622 5727). Tram 13, 14, 17. **Open** 1-5pm Wed-Sat. **No credit cards.**
This showroom is shared by a group of Dutch ceramicists whose studios are scattered throughout the city. View examples of their work here and pick up an English-language folder that tells you where to find the individual artists.

De Porceleyne Fles

Rotterdamseweg 196, Delft (015 569214). **Open** 9am-5pm Mon-Sat. **Credit** AmEx, JCB, MC, V.
The Porceleyne Fles pottery dates from the seventeenth century and uses traditional methods to produce vases, bowls, tiles, candlesticks, display plates and many other pieces with modern as well as traditional motifs. Prices range from f65 to f3,000 for large vases. Except for some slightly flawed pieces (sold only at the factory) you'll pay the same as in shops in Amsterdam. A certificate of authenticity is supplied with every item that bears the Porceleyne Fles symbol.

Tichelaar's Royal Makkum Faience

Turfmarkt 57, Makkum (05158 1341/telex 46424TKM). **Open** 9am-5.30pm Mon-Sat. **Guided tours** 10-11.30am, 1-4pm, Mon-Thur; 10-11.30am, 1-3pm, Fri. **Cost** f3; group discount (min 20 people) f2.50. **Credit** AmEx, DC, MC, V.
As well as traditional Royal Makkum ware, Tichelaar makes intricately patterned blue and white pottery, attractive ceramic brooches and striking art deco vases.

A few pieces of Royal Makkum are found in Amsterdam's best gift shops, but dedicated collectors should visit the factory for the best range. Prices are similar wherever you shop: tiles from f25 to f100, plates from f100 to f3,000.

Records

Boudisque/Boudisque Black Beat

Haringpakkerssteeg 10-18, C (623 2603). Tram 1, 2, 4, 9, 13, 16, 17, 24, 25. **Open** 1-6pm Mon; 10am-6pm Tue, Wed, Fri; 10am-9pm Thur; 10am-5pm Sat. **Credit** AmEx, MC, V.
A wide selection of pop, rock, heavy metal and world music goes on sale at Boudisque. The Black Beat section features funk, disco, soul, jazz, hip hop and dance music.

Concerto

Utrechtsestraat 54-60, IS (626 6577/624 5467/623 5228). Tram 4. **Open** 10am-6pm Mon-Fri; 10am-5pm Sat. **Credit** AmEx, MC, V.
Concerto sells new and second-hand albums and CDs for music-lovers of every persuasion. This is where to look for historic Bach recordings, odd Beatles items, that favourite Diana Ross album that got lost in the move. There are also new releases for slightly less than the usual prices. You can listen to your find before buying it.

Falstaff

Muiderstraat 11, C (626 0988). Tram 9, 14/Metro Waterlooplein. **Open** 1-6pm Mon; 10am-6pm Tue-Fri; 10am-5pm Sat. **Credit** DC, EC, V.
Only classical CDs are stocked at Falstaff, but the shop lays claim to selling the cheapest in town. Staff are friendly, and helpful if you're unsure of what you want.

Forever Changes

Bilderdijkstraat 148, OW (612 6378). Tram 3, 12, 13, 14. **Open** 1-6pm Mon; 10am-6pm Tue-Fri; 10am-5pm Sat. **No credit cards.**
Named after a hippy album by the band Love, this shop stocks mostly pop music imported from the USA and England. There are many second-hand records and CDs, plus collector's items from the sixties, seventies and eighties.

Jazz Inn

Vijzelgracht 9, IS (623 5662/620 4313). Tram 6, 7, 10, 16, 24, 25. **Open** 10am-6pm Mon-Fri; 10am-5pm Sat. **Credit** AmEx, MC.
Unsurprisingly, jazz is the speciality here. You'll find the full spectrum, from thirties' stompers through to modern and Afro jazz. **Branch:** Spuistraat 15, C (no phone).

Outland

Zeedijk 22, C (638 7576). Tram 1, 2, 4, 5, 9, 13, 16, 17, 24, 25. **Open** 10.30am-6pm Mon-Sat. **Credit** AmEx, MC, V.
Bang in the middle of the Zeedijk, this shop specialises in house music. The décor is distinctly unusual, with a selection of paintings by Herman Brood brightening the interior.

Virgin

Magna Plaza, Spuistraat 137, C (622 8929). Tram 1, 2, 5. **Open** 9am-6pm Mon-Wed, Fri; 10am-9pm Thur; 10am-5pm Fri. **Credit** AmEx, EC, V.
The megastore recently opened in one of the biggest mall projects the city has ever seen. The old post office behind Dam now houses a variety of other stores, too. Looking firmly to the future, Virgin doesn't bother stocking vinyl – it sticks to more profitable products like CDs and videos.

All shapes and sizes: the **Condomerie** is the only shop in The Netherlands to specialise in condoms. See **review**.

Speciality Shops

Amsterdam has hundreds of specialist shops – usually small, fascinating places where the owners can indulge an obsession. Below we have listed a selection of the more interesting stores, but there are plenty more all over town: try, for example, wandering around the Jordaan (*see chapter***Amsterdam by Area**) and the area around Utrechtsestraat.

Condomerie Het Gulden Vlies
Warmoesstraat 141, C (627 4174). Tram 1, 2, 4, 5, 9, 13, 16, 17, 24, 25. **Open** 1-6pm Mon-Fri; noon-5pm Sat. **No credit cards.**
Opened in 1987 by two Dutch women, The Golden Fleece was the first shop of its kind in the world. It's still the only one in The Netherlands to specialise in condoms. They come in all shapes, colours, textures, flavours and sizes, with different kinds of lubrication. Besides laboratory-tested, officially approved types, there are novelty sheaths (fluorescent or edible) and others packaged as chewing gum, sweets, or tucked into walnut shells. The illustrated English-Dutch catalogue costs f5.

Fifties-Sixties
Huidenstraat 13, IW (623 2653). Tram 1, 2, 5. **Open** 1-6pm Tue-Fri; 1-5pm Sat. **No credit cards.**
Every available inch of space in this shop is choc-full of authentic period pieces – toasters, blenders, lamps and even vacuum cleaners – all in good working condition (220 volts). Non-electrical goods include floor-standing chrome ashtrays.

P G C Hajenius
Rokin 92-96, C (625 9985). Tram 4, 9, 14, 16, 24, 25. **Open** 10am-6pm Mon; 9am-6pm Tue-Fri; 9am-5pm Sat. **Credit** AmEx, DC, MC, V.
Hajenius was established as a tobacconist's in 1826, but has recently been bought by British tobacco giants Gallagher. The interior has been refurbished to resemble a photo of the shop taken in 1915. Famed for its own brand of cigars, Hajenius also stocks a splendid variety

of pipes including the traditional Dutch clay pipe with either a 14-in or 20-in (35cm or 50cm) stem. The staff will organise the shipping of gifts.

De Witte Tanden Winkel
Runstraat 5, IW (623 3443). Tram 1, 2, 5. **Open** 1-6pm Mon; 10am-6pm Tue-Fri; 10am-5pm Sat. **Credit** AmEx, DC, MC, V.
The White Teeth Shop has all you need for a sparkling smile, from junior-size toothbrushes with a Mickey Mouse or banana handle to champagne or whisky-flavoured toothpaste and electric brushing/ rinsing equipment.

Wooden Shoe Factory
Nieuwezijds Voorburgwal 20, C (623 0632). Tram 1, 2, 5. **Open** *1 Apr-15 Sept:* 10am-10pm daily; *16 Sept-31 Mar* 10am-6pm daily. **Credit** AmEx, DC, MC, V.
Wooden shoes (*klompen*) may not be the highest fashion in footwear, but are very useful for gardeners. Buy them large enough to wear over heavy socks and tell children the Dutch only wear *klompen* outside the house.

Sports

Perry Sport
Kalverstraat 93-99, C (624 7131). Tram 4, 9, 14, 16, 24, 25. **Open** 11am-6pm Mon; 9.30am-6pm Tue, Wed, Fri; 9.30am-9pm Thur; 9.30am-5pm Sat. **Credit** AmEx, DC, MC, TC, V.
An all-purpose sports shop supplying tents, sport shoes, tennis racquets, exercise aids and winter and summer jackets.

Stamps and Coins

Outdoor Market
Pedestrian island in front of Nova Hotel, Nieuwezijds Voorburgwal 276, C. Tram 1, 2, 5, 13, 17. **Open** 11am-4pm Wed, Sat. **No credit cards.**
You don't have to be a philatelist to enjoy this gathering of some 20 local dealers selling currency, stamps, old postcards and commemorative medals.

Services

Where to hire a tuxedo, have that trendy hair cut, or simply get your holiday snaps developed.

Amsterdam is not the most service-oriented of cities. Employment law makes it difficult to get fired, so staff have no personal stake in pleasing their customers. The Dutch penchant for taking things literally can also lead to problems. You often have to be persistent and make sure you ask exactly the right question: enquire if your hotel does dry-cleaning and you may be told no. Only after you have trekked around the city with your grubby shirt crumpled in your bag will you find out that there was a great express dry-cleaners just around the corner that staff hadn't thought to mention.

HOTEL AND SHOP SERVICES

These differ greatly, but the more expensive the hotel or shop, the more services it will offer. However, you'll find that even at budget hotels the staff will be able to recommend baby-sitters and other services if asked. Every department

You can have a same-day service-wash done at the **Clean Brothers**' laundry. See **review**.

store (*see chapter* **Shopping**) has a customer service division (*klantenservice*), which will advise on packaging and shipping arrangements.

Business-related services are listed in our **Business** chapter. For police, fire, ambulance and other emergency services, veterinary services and car hire companies, *see chapter* **Survival**. Bicycle hire shops can be found in the **Essential Information** chapter.

Alternative Health

Natuurlijk Gezondheidscentrum

Shackletonstraat 2, OW (616 4942). Tram 13. **Open** 9am-5pm Mon-Fri. **Consultations** f75-f90 an hour. **No credit cards**.
This respected training centre offers consultations in tarot, astrology, acupuncture, foot reflexology, physiotherapy, iriscopy (the analysis of illness through examination of the irises), fasting, hypnosis and psychotherapy.

Beauty

Beauty Form

1E Oosterparkstraat 101, OE (694 4957). Tram 3. **Open** 9.30am-5.30pm Tue-Sat; evenings by appointment. **No credit cards**.
There's a full range of services for both sexes at reasonable prices. The 1½-hour 'traveller's special' (f55) is aimed at replenishing dehydrated skin and includes epilation, peeling, massage, a mask and compresses. All skin problems are handled by the multi-lingual Shirley Bueno-Bibaz.

Camera, TV and Radio Hire

Ruad Foto

Overtoom 371, OW (697 8191). Tram 1, 5. **Open** 10am-6pm Mon; 9am-6pm Tue-Fri; 9am-5pm Sat. **Credit** AmEx, MC, V.
Cameras, computers, camcorders and video recorders are hired out on a short or long-term basis. A steep security deposit is required (f1,000 for a video recorder, for example), payable by credit card or cheque as well as in cash.

Clothing Care

Clean Brothers

Jacob van Lennepkade 179, OW (618 3637). Tram 3, 12, 17. **Open** 8am-8pm Mon, Tue, Thur, Fri; 8am-6pm Wed; 9am-5pm Sat. **No credit cards**.
You can have a same-day service-wash done at this launderette run by the white-suited British 'Clean Brothers'. If you prefer to wash your own things, the branches listed below are self-service only: the centrally-located Kerkstraat branch is open every day from 7am to 9pm. **Branches**: Rozengracht 59, OW (623 7718); Kerkstraat 56, IS (no phone).

For pizzas delivered to your door on the double, phone **Pizzalijn La Botte**. *See* **review**.

Cleaning Shop Express
Huidenstraat 22, IW (623 1219). Tram 1, 2, 5. **Open** 8.30am-6pm Mon-Fri; 8.30am-1pm Sat. **No credit cards.**
A full range of services, including dry-cleaning, laundering, leather and carpet cleaning, repairs, alterations and invisible mending are offered here. Staff will also hand-launder, and press shirts and sheets. Same-day service on request. You can trust them with your designer originals.

Florist

Ivy
Leidseplein 35, IS (623 6561). Tram 1, 2, 5, 6, 7, 10. **Open** 9am-6pm Mon-Fri; 9am-5pm Sat. **Credit** AmEx, MC, V.
An expensive shop where wonderful flower arrangements are put together. Ivy can arrange to send flowers by Interflora. *See also chapter* **Shopping: Flowers**.

Food Delivery

Heuft's First Class Night Shop
Rijnstraat 62, OS (642 4048). Tram 4, 25. **Open** 4pm-1am daily. **Credit** AmEx, DC.
The place to call when you've got the midnight munchies. It has a huge selection of delicacies and ready-made meals for take-away or delivery: everything from champagne and oysters to full meals or the ingredients to create an authentic Mexican feast. Heuft's is expensive, but quality and service are excellent. Staff will vacuum-pack Dutch cheeses for you to take home.

Pizzalijn La Botte
Lijnbaansgracht 120, IW (623 5539). Tram 3, 10. **Open** 4-11pm daily. **No credit cards.**
Phone Pizza Line for super-quick delivery of pizza and

other fast-food meals. There's no delivery charge to the centre of the city and on orders over f25.

Formal Dress Hire

Joh. Huijer
Weteringschans 153, IS (623 5439). Tram 6, 7, 10. **Open** 9am-5pm Tue, Wed, Fri; 9am-9pm Thur. **No credit cards.**
Men's formal dress hire: all clothing is from the German label Lacerna in Dutch sizes 46 to 60 (British and American sizes 34 to 50). A complete outfit, including cufflinks and bow tie, can be rented for f125. Pick up your outfit in the afternoon, return it the following morning.

Maison Van Den Hoogen
Sarphatipark 88-90, OS (679 8828). Tram 3. **Open** 9am-5pm Mon-Wed, Fri; 9am-9pm Thur; 9am-4pm Sat. **No credit cards.**
A women's formal dress hire outlet where you'll find a choice of cocktail and evening dresses in Dutch sizes 36 to 40 (British 8 to 12; American 5 to 9). The deposit is f100 and the price range from f85 to f125.

Hairdressers

Forum
Weteringschans 167, IS (626 3430). Tram 6, 7, 10. **Open** 9am-5pm Mon-Fri. **No credit cards.**
You can get an inexpensive, good hair cut at this hairdressers' training institute. Cuts are done by advanced students and cost from f9. Ten other locations in Amsterdam are staffed by graduates and so prices are higher, but still reasonable. No appointment necessary.

Hair Studio Scissors

Jodenbreestraat 52, C (626 3444). Tram 9, 14/Metro Waterlooplein. **Open** 10am-6pm Tue, Wed, Fri, Sat; 10am-9pm Thur. **Credit** AmEx, MC, V.

Situated just behind the Waterlooplein market, this is a small and friendly hairdressing salon that specialises in classic cuts.

Images, Hair and Beauty

Hilton Hotel, Apollolaan 138-140, OS (679 0599). Tram 5, 24. **Open** 9am-7pm daily. **No credit cards.**

Styling for men and women. Expensive but excellent, and open to non-guests. Phone for details of the four other locations in town.

Wild! Cuts

Kerkstraat 104, IS (626 0749). Tram 1, 2, 5. **Open** 11am-6pm Mon-Wed, Fri, Sat; 11am-9pm Thur. **Credit** AmEx, MC, V.

At the back of a clubwear shop, this is one of the cheapest and trendiest hairdressers in town. Hair cuts cost from f35; colouring from f45. *See chapter* **Shopping: Fashion/Clubwear.**

Jewellery Repairs

Elke Watch Cy

Kalverstraat 206, C (624 7100/623 6386). Tram 1, 2, 4, 5, 9, 14, 16, 24, 25. **Open** 9am-5.30pm Mon-Fri; 9am-4.30pm Sat. **Credit** AmEx, DC, MC, V.

Elke carry out quick repairs to jewellery and watches, and offer a 24-hour service for simple jobs.

Luggage Repairs

Wentholt Exclusive Luggage Repair Shop

Nieuwezijds Kolk 4, C (624 3252). Tram 1, 2, 4, 5, 9, 14, 16, 24, 25. **Open** 9.30am-5.30pm Thur, Fri. **No credit cards.**

Staff here are used to dealing with people on the hop; Wentholt is frequently used by hotels and airlines. Specialities are leather repair, and repairs or replacement locks on luggage and handbags.

Packing and Removals

De Gruijter

Industrieweg 11-13, 2382 NR Zoeterwoude (071 89 9313). **Open** 8.30am-5pm Mon-Fri. **No credit cards.**

Accustomed to dealing with fragile and expensive items, De Gruijter will package and send your purchases or household belongings anywhere in the world by sea or air and also offers storage facilities. Service is friendly.

Philosophy

Amsterdam is home to the world's first Association of Practical Philosophy, whose members offer the public private consultations with a philosopher. Some clients have specific problems, often regarding their careers; others have more existential concerns and others just want a natter about philosophy. The headquarters are at the Hotel de Filosoof (*see chapter* **Accommodation**), where staff can put you in touch with any of the 16 practising philosophers in The Netherlands. The Association also hosts regular lectures, courses and intellectual gatherings (all in Dutch).

Dries Boele

Spaarndammerplantsoen 108, OW (686 7330 private number, please ring at reasonable times). Bus 22, 28. **No credit cards.**

Mr Boele can advise on the philosophical aspects of important life decisions, such as career changes and make-or-break relationship dilemmas. Many of his clients have tried psychiatry and are now looking for a wider perspective. He is multi-lingual and charges about f120 for a 75-minute session (those on low incomes can negotiate a lower fee).

Photocopying

Grand Prix Copyrette

Weteringschans 84A, IS (627 2703). Tram 6, 7, 10. **Open** 9.30am-5.30pm Mon-Fri; 11am-4pm Sat. **No credit cards.**

Come here for all your photocopying needs. Quick, friendly service – while you wait or DIY. Prices are low and the quality high. Colour copies, enlargements, spiral-binding, and a fax service are available. For more copy shops *see chapter* **Business.**

Photo Processing

Capi

Leidsestraat 77, IS (623 3019). Tram 1, 2, 5. **Open** 9am-5.30pm Mon-Wed, Fri; 9am-9pm Thur; 10am-5pm Sat. **Credit** AmEx, DC, MC, V.

Capi offers a one-hour service for colour film, three or four days for black and white and two days for slides.

"S" Color

Singel 356, IW (624 9102). Tram 1, 2, 5. **Open** 8am-10pm Mon-Fri; 2-5pm Sat; 4-8pm Sun. **No credit cards.**

This is the film laboratory used by top professional photographers, producing quality work in a hurry (black and white ready in two hours). "S" Color is more expensive than other places, but it's the fastest and the best.

Pipe and Lighter Repair

Han Schellings

Reguliersdwarsstraat 47, IS (627 8286). Tram 1, 2, 4, 5, 9, 14, 16, 24, 25. **Open** 9am-4.30pm Mon-Fri. **No credit cards.**

Mr Schellings is regarded as one of the best in the business and deals with customers world-wide by post. He offers a same-day service.

Shoe Repairs

Luk's Schoenservice

Prinsengracht 500, IS (623 1937). Tram 1, 2, 5. **Open** 8.30am-5.30pm Mon-Fri; 9am-1pm Sat. **No credit cards.**

A complete repair and cleaning service, Luk's is professional and quick – top-quality work which can usually be completed in a day. Trust him with your satin evening shoes.

Mr Minit

Leidsestraat 189, IS (624 8368). Tram 1, 2, 5. **Open** 11am-6pm Mon; 9.30am-6pm Tue, Wed, Fri; 9.30am-9pm Thur; 9am-5pm Sat. **No credit cards.**

The service here is fast; usually while you wait. Repairs to shoes, handbags and other small leather goods are done by machine.

Galleries
& Museums

Although works by the Dutch masters attract millions of visitors each year, Amsterdam also has a multitude of specialist museums – covering anything from piggy banks to maritime history – as well as a thriving gallery scene.

Contents

Galleries

A guide to Amsterdam's galleries, where artists and dealers make maximum use of minimum space, producing works of an astonishing range and variety.

The variety of Amsterdam's art life is astounding, given the city's size and its neighbourhood atmosphere. Tourists may teem around the Van Goghs and Rembrandts in the city's museums, but there is also a wealth of more contemporary art, with over 1,500 artists working in the city. Much of their work can be seen in the privately owned galleries which now total more than 250 throughout Amsterdam.

A country of painters, The Netherlands is very strong in graphics, printmaking, meticulously executed small paintings and clean, approachable sculpture. Amsterdam's galleries always have a broad variety of both figurative and abstract work on show.

Modern Dutch art, and gallery tastes, follow two major directions. One is orderly, continuing the traditions of De Stijl (*see chapter* **Between the Occupations: The Amsterdam School**) and Piet Mondrian; the other is anarchic, exemplified by Cobra, the abstract movement of the fifties. The style of Cobra is quite unlike the clean lines of Mondrian. Carel Appel is its hero in The Netherlands, though Corneille, Lucebert, Lucassen, Constant and others may be better respected elsewhere. Cobra has become a respected, virtually institutionalised tradition. Amsterdam remains the focal point for its art, and some of the artists are still doing excellent work.

Space is a major consideration for Amsterdam's art world. The genius of the artists, galleries and buyers in getting the maximum use out of the minimum of space is taken for granted. There is an enormous selection of unobtrusive but concentrated art in a small place – and in small spaces.

DOUBLE DEALERS

Some confusion is caused over the difference between a gallery and a *kunsthandel*. A *kunsthandel* (or art dealer) is more likely to buy and resell art, to carry multiples of paintings as prints, and to go for established names. A gallery, strictly speaking, acts as a sort of agent to the artist, exhibiting and selling art and taking a commission, though not buying the art outright. But to complicate matters, many *kunsthandels* started to call themselves galleries when 'galleries' became fashionable in the sixties, so there is considerable overlap between the two terms.

Glass, ceramics and pottery are the focus at **Gallery In Art**. *See* **review** *page 148.*

A BUYER'S MARKET

At the beginning of the nineties, new movements, new stars and new names are lurking in the wings. The last important changes occurred a decade ago (when a dozen or so new Dutch artists came to prominence), so artists and galleries are awaiting the next outburst. It is difficult to predict what form this will take, and which galleries will sense it first and reap the rewards, but there is no shortage of galleries showing new and unknown artists.

An extraordinary number of internationally-known artists are shown here first. They are often picked up by big-name galleries from New York and elsewhere, bringing fame and sky-rocketing prices. Artists often stay loyal to the Amsterdam gallery which first believed in them, but prices stay at reasonable levels (measured in hundreds, rather than thousands of guilders).

Despite these bargain prices, artists – thus far – show in Amsterdam and sell elsewhere, as The Netherlands has few private collectors. The main market here is the government and the museums. As an incentive for individual buyers, the government has introduced new subsidies and loans to facilitate the buying of art. Foreigners may be eligible: information on this is available at the galleries.

ART IN MUSEUMS

Relationships between museums and galleries are always convoluted. In The Netherlands, the art world is dominated by five of the world's best museums. The Haags Gemeentemuseum (in The Hague, *see chapter* **The Randstad**), Amsterdam's Stedelijk Museum (*see chapter* **Museums**), the Rijksmuseum Kröller-Müller (Otterlo, *see chapter* **The Provinces: Gelderland**), the Groningen Museum (Groningen, *see chapter* **The Provinces**) and the Van Abbe Museum (Eindhoven, *see chapter* **The Provinces: Noord Brabant**). All 'discover' relatively new artists and are known for their 'eye' for art which will be in demand. They provide a standard and sometimes a market for privately-owned art galleries, but they are a very hard act for the galleries to follow, without access to public funding.

The Amsterdam gallery guide, *Alert* (available at all galleries) is in Dutch, but has maps of all districts, with gallery locations clearly marked, and is very helpful when finding your way around. Custom-made guided tours of galleries are run by Amsterdam Gallery Guide (*see chapter* **Sightseeing**). Many of the galleries listed below close for a month some time between June and September, so it's best to phone before setting out.

Unless otherwise stated, galleries do not take credit cards.

Galleries

Apunto
Damrak 30, C (623 9172). Tram 4, 24, 25. **Open** 1-5pm Tue-Sat.
A young gallery with young artists, Apunto is a place to watch. You won't find abstract expressionists, rather a space-age propensity for clean-cut, hard-edged irony and humour. The gallery was Amsterdam's first to show baroque fantastic artists. It also shows installations. Apunto is in a spacious building and the location couldn't be more central, but it's above a store and easy to miss.

Art Affairs
Wittenburgergracht 313, OE (620 6433). Bus 22, 28. **Open** 1-6pm Wed-Sat; also by appointment.
Art Affairs shows 'concrete' art (with solid, strong forms) in all materials. It inclines towards elementary forms concerning nature. Art Affairs emphasises and excels in sculpture, but also shows painters with related strong concepts.
Wheelchair access.

Art & Project
Nieuwesluizerweg 42, Slootdorp (02277 375/fax 02277 385). **Open** 1pm-5pm Fri-Sun; also by appointment.
Although this is technically not an Amsterdam gallery (it's based in a western suburb), Art & Project is the oldest conceptual gallery in the Amsterdam area and is also the best. Struycken, Schuil, Van Elk and Geurts are a few of the top names.
Wheelchair access with assistance.

Aschenbach
Bilderdijkstraat 165C, OW (685 3580). Tram 13, 17. **Open** 1-6pm Wed-Sun.
Aschenbach was the first Amsterdam gallery to show Russian artists, but also concentrates on new German expressionist painters and shows a mixture of famous and new names, including AR Penck and J Jonkers. Its lack of concern about being 'established' gives the gallery added charm.
Wheelchair access with assistance.

Asselijn
Lange Leidsedwarsstraat 198-200, IS (624 9030). Tram 1, 2, 5, 6, 7, 10. **Open** noon-5pm Tue-Sat.
A typically Dutch gallery which has been around for over 20 years. It is consistent and representative of prevailing trends, preferring the soft approach to the shocking and adventurous.
Wheelchair access.

Barbara Farber
Keizersgracht 265, IW (627 6343/fax 627 8091). Tram 13, 14, 17. **Open** 1-6pm Tue-Sat.
A top gallery and a phenomenon in Amsterdam, having put paid to certain myths (such as the need to survive for a decade before being taken seriously). Ms Farber shows new avant-garde work and has an eye for unlaunched artists, particularly young Americans. The gallery has been responsible for an entire list of discoveries who have shot to the top, and also carries established artists like Merz, Paolini, Qucka and Lewitt.

Brinkman
Rozenstraat 59, OW (622 7493/fax 638 4558). Tram 13, 14, 17/Bus 21, 47, 67, 170, 171, 172. **Open** noon-6pm Tue-Sat.
Considered important in the Amsterdam art world, the gallery is a frequent exhibitor at art fairs, and shows Dutch and foreign artists – the sort of art you can live with. Quality is a little variable, but Brinkman has done some good things.

Collection d'Art
Keizersgracht 516, IS (622 1511). Tram 1, 2, 5. **Open** 1-5pm Tue-Sat.
An relatively old gallery (founded in 1969) which has cornered the market in good, established Dutch artists: Armando, Constant, and a stable of big names.

D'Eendt
Spuistraat 272, C (626 5777). Tram 1, 2, 5. **Open** noon-6pm Wed-Sat.
Once a trendsetter, d'Eendt has had its ups and downs in recent years. The gallery features paintings and installations by young international artists; some shows are exciting, some aren't. Modern and good naïve figuratives are the strongest work. D'Eendt is another Dutch miracle of space utilisation.

Espace
Keizersgracht 548, IS (624 0802). Tram 1, 2, 5, 16, 24, 25. **Open** noon-5.30pm Tue-Sat.
Based in Amsterdam since 1960, Eva Bendien is one of Amsterdam's *grande dames* of art. Her gallery shows

The ICAA: three floors of modern exhibition space, a café and a bookshop. See review.

Lucassen, Lucebert and Pierre Alechinsky. Co Westerik's popular, odd, Dutch realism is another highlight. **Branch:** Kerkstraat 276 (638 6034).

Galerie A

Johannes Verhulststraat 53, OS (671 4087/fax 675 2602). Tram 2, 16. **Open** 2-5pm Tue-Sat; also by appointment.
Situated behind the Concertgebouw, this highly specialised gallery shows Fluxus art (an international movement of the sixties) and international conceptualists. The accent is on editions, so sales are often negotiated through catalogues, over the telephone or by fax. However, Galerie A also shows artists such as Wim T Schippers who are still producing new work. Prices are relatively low.
Wheelchair access.

Gallery In Art

Paulus Potterstraat 22-24, C (664 1881) Tram 1, 2, 5. **Open** 11am-5pm Wed-Sat; 1-5pm first Sunday of each month.
Glass, ceramics, pottery and porcelain are the focus here. Gallery owner Carla Koch deftly mixes exhibitions by established names with work by new artists of all nationalities. On permanent exhibition are pieces by renowned artists but limited works are also available at very reasonable prices, all in friendly, welcoming surroundings.

Van Gelder

Planciusstraat 9A, OW (627 7419). Tram 3/Bus 22, 44. **Open** 1-5.30pm Tue-Sat and first Sunday of each month.
Kees van Gelder shows young up-and-coming artists. He has a good, appreciative eye and reacts quickly to new talent, although he's been accused of ignoring young Dutch artists. Conceptual art is the latest trend at this gallery.

ICAA

Nieuwe Spiegelstraat 10, IS (620 1260). Tram 1, 2, 4, 16, 24, 25. **Open** 11am-5pm Tue, Wed, Fri-Sun; 11am-9pm Thur. **Admission** f7; free Tue, 5-9pm Thur; group discounts (min 10). **No credit cards**.
Opened in late 1991, the ICAA (Institute of Contemporary Art Amsterdam) offers what is probably Amsterdam's largest gallery space. An impressive building just off the famous 'golden curve' of Herengracht (*see p74*) has been tastefully converted to provide a large, modern and bright exhibition area covering three floors. The Institute's shows take full advantage of these facilities, offering retrospectives of important modern artists and movements that are definitive in both breadth and depth. Recent major presentations from American beat generation pioneer Wallace Berman and Dutch thematic artist Pieter Laurens Mol typify ICAA's scope. In addition, the building contains a bookshop which also stocks a range of international art magazines, and a café.

KunstHaar

Berenstraat 21, IW (620 0274). Tram 1, 2, 5. **Open** 10am-6pm Tue, Wed, Fri; 10am-8.30pm Thur; 9am-6pm Sat. **No credit cards**.
The names means 'art-hair', which sums up what this place is about – a small hair-studio and gallery in one. Instead of reading tattered mags under the blow-dryer, you can admire the paintings arranged around the walls. And it's no gimmick either: owner Ton Verdegaal changes the exhibition monthly, usually selecting interesting young Dutch artists who can genuinely be said to be a cut above the average (and are reasonably priced). He also offers a friendly welcome to browsers who don't want a hair-do thrown in...

Kunsthandel Leeman

Keizersgracht 556, IS (627 4142). Tram 1, 2, 5, 16, 24, 25. **Open** 11am-5pm Thur-Sat; also by appointment.
An enthusiastic, proud example of the traditional *kunsthandel* (art dealer), Leeman buys and resells works of Cobra artists, associated abstract expressionists of the fifties and sixties, and 'informal' art.

The Living Room

Laurierstraat 70, IW (625 8449). Tram 13, 14, 17. **Open** 2-6pm Tue-Sat.
A top spot, often thought to carry only Dutch artists, but which also has international work that Bart van de Ven feels challenges Dutch artists. The gallery actively promotes artists such as HW Wearther and Peer Veneman abroad and specialises in installations.
Wheelchair access.

Lumen Travo

Paulus Potterstraat 38, OS (675 5010). Tram 5. **Open** 1-6pm Tue-Sat.
Marianne van Tilborg is extremely ambitious and on the look-out for up-and-coming artists (both Dutch and foreign) who break new ground. The gallery began with design (functional or applied art) but has moved to more spatial work and installations. It's a trendy place, Guillaume Bijl and Thom Puckey being two talked-about names.

Marcus & Marcus

Keizersgracht 521, C (625 1416). Tram 1, 2, 5. **Open** noon-6pm Wed-Sat.
Marleen Marcus deals in realism (and occasionally magic realism), and regularly travels abroad to seek out material. An exciting gallery, as the owner has an eye for style, and unerringly produces worthwhile shows. Paintings are the main deal, but sculpture is sometimes featured.
Wheelchair access.

Mokum

Nieuwezijds Voorburgwal 334, C (624 3958). Tram 1, 2, 5. **Open** noon-5pm Tue-Sat; 2-4pm Sun.
Mokum specialises in Dutch realism, an extremely well-developed school of its own here. Magic (or fantastic) realists are also represented. 'Mokum' is the popular Jewish nickname for Amsterdam.

Nanky de Vreese

Keizersgracht 22, C (627 3808). Tram 1, 2, 4, 5, 13, 17. **Open** 10am-5.30pm Tue-Sat; also by appointment.
Nanky de Vreese shows lyrical abstract and contemporary work inclining towards decorative, milder art. She has had good shows and a fair amount of sculpture as well as drawings, prints and paintings, but is not always consistent.
Wheelchair access to ground floor.

Onrust

Prinsengracht 627, IW (638 0474). Tram 1, 2, 5. **Open** 2-6pm Tue-Sat.
A little gallery, run by Milco Onrust, an inscrutable, respected fellow who says he likes boring art. Artists represented are young, poetic, sensual and conceptual. Prints and drawings are particular strengths, but paintings are also featured. An important gallery, at least locally.

Paul Andriesse

Prinsengracht 116, IW (623 6237). Tram 13, 14, 17. **Open** 10am-12.30pm, 2-6pm, Tue-Fri; 2-6pm Sat.
This gallery, which has been around since 1977, is one of the best at promoting both Dutch and foreign artists of repute, and is one of the few Amsterdam galleries doing well overseas. Marlene Dumas' big and discon-certing faces, Guido Geelen's outrageous ceramics and Henk Visch's sculptures are all noteworthy.

Reflex Modern Art Gallery

Weteringschans 83, C (627 2832). Tram 10, 17 . **Open** 10.30am-5.30pm Tue-Sat.
Enterprising gallery owners Lex and Ria Daniels show the best of modern art. As well as an exciting new exhibition changing each month and featuring top international artists such as Arman, Ben, and Kriki, the gallery always has an excellent selection of graphics and lithos by Corneille and Appel. The gallery also exhibits at all major art fairs both in Holland and abroad.
Wheelchair access.
Branch: Spiegelgracht 8 (639 1917).

Van Rooy

Kerkstraat 216, IS (622 9621). Tram 16, 24, 25. **Open** 1-6pm Wed-Sat.
Luce van Rooy shows contemporary architectural work and what she describes as 'related forms of visual art' in this upstairs gallery. The definition is broad, and not exclusive, but there is a consistent thread and identity. This is the Mondrian side of Dutch art, resisting anarchy. Van Rooy has good shows and her own following.

Suzanne Biederberg

Oudezijds Voorburgwal 223, C (624 5455). Tram 4, 9, 16, 24, 25. **Open** 2-6pm Wed-Sat; also by appointment.
Suzanne Biederberg, an Australian, has had a gallery here since 1985. Her list includes competent, appealing Dutch and foreign artists, if no resounding names. Take a look at Nan Hoover's work, when she is showing.

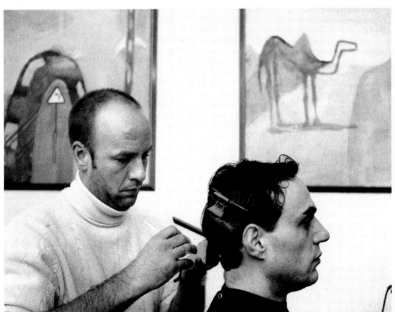

A hairdresser's and an art gallery form an unlikely partnership at **KunstHaar**. *See* **review** page 148.

Swart
Van Breestraat 23, OS (676 4736). Tram 2, 3, 5, 12, 16. **Open** 2-6pm Wed-Sat.
Riejke Swart is the undisputed *grande dame* and god-mother of the Amsterdam art scene. She began in 1964 with constructivism and didn't show women because she didn't consider them aggressive enough (she does show them now, occasionally). Nowadays nobody's sure how to classify her style, but it's always good. She is critical, opinionated and is looking for young people because 'no one buys expensive artists here'. Artists love her and galleries admire her. She showed Donald Judd first (nobody came) and couldn't sell Lucio Fontana's work, so she bought it herself.
Wheelchair access.

Torch
Prinsengracht 218, IW (626 0284/622 4195). Tram 13, 14, 17. **Open** 1-6pm Thur-Sat.
Adriaan van der Have says he has the most international gallery in Amsterdam. Torch majors in current developments in photography and includes video, installations and sculpture. It is classy by local standards, with artists like Joel Peter Witkin and Cindy Sherman. A trendy gallery operating from a small space up a flight of narrow Amsterdam stairs.

Wetering Galerie
Lijnbaansgracht 288, IW (623 6189). Tram 3, 10. **Open** 12.30pm-5.30pm Wed-Sat.
The Wetering Galerie has a reputation for showing sculpture. Michiel Hennus searches for individuals, not 'school' trends, and believes there is a serenity and neatness to Dutch art in the De Stijl (Peter Struycken) tradition – flashiness is equated with foreign influence and insincerity.

Specialised Galleries

Ceramics

De Witte Voet
Kerkstraat 149, IS (625 8412). Tram 1, 2, 5. **Open** noon-5pm Tue-Sat.
Annemie Boissevain hesitates to use the term ceramics to describe her exhibits – people still seem to think in terms of pots, not sculpture. But this is *the* ceramics gallery, mounting solo shows of predominantly Dutch artists.

Interior and Industrial Design

Galerie Binnen
Keizersgracht 82, IW (625 9603/fax 627 2654). Tram 1, 2, 5, 13, 17. **Open** noon-6pm Tue-Sat.
Amsterdam's foremost gallery for industrial and interior design and the applied arts (*binnen* means 'inside' or 'indoors'). The owners have a great roomy space to show new work by Dutch designers, including installations and spatial projects, plus glass, ceramics, jewellery and Czechoslovakian design. Surprisingly, Binnen is the only gallery of its kind and calibre in Amsterdam.
Wheelchair access.

Jewellery

RA
Vijzelstraat 80, C (626 5100). Tram 4, 9, 14, 16, 24, 25. **Open** noon-6pm Tue-Fri; 11am-5pm Sat. **Credit** AmEx, V.
Although Ra isn't the only jewellery gallery, it's the place everyone recommends. There is a thin line between sculpture and jewellery these days, as a look

Marcus & Marcus: *an exciting gallery which unerringly produces good shows. See* **review** *page 148.*

around this gallery will show – you may prefer putting these works on your mantelpiece to wearing them. Opened in 1976, the gallery is now well established. The artists/designers aren't only Dutch, and a wide variety of materials are used.

Wheelchair access to ground floor.

Media Art

Montevideo/Time Based Arts

Singel 137, C (623 7101). Tram 1, 2, 5, 13, 17. **Open** *Montevideo* 1-6pm Tue-Sat; *gallery* 1-6pm Tue-Sat.

Amsterdam's two major media artists' organisations merged in 1992 to provide a single forum for this genre, important to the local scene. The gallery features consistently excellent shows of electronic media work, photography, sculpture and installations. The archives and library may be visited by appointment.

Photography

2½ x 4½ Fotogalerie

Prinsengracht 356, IW (626 0757). Tram 13, 14, 17. **Open** 2-6pm Thur, Fri; noon-5pm Sat.

Together with Canon *(see below)*, this is the survivor of a number of photography galleries which have come and gone. There is a broad range of solo shows.

Canon Image Centre

Leidsestraat 79, IS (625 4494). Tram 1, 2, 5. **Open** noon-5.45pm Tue-Fri; 11am-4.45pm Sat. **Credit** AmEx, MC, V.

The Canon Image Centre is based in a multi-storey building, with exhibition space – large by Amsterdam standards – on the ground and first floors. It's run by a team of well-informed staff. The exhibitions, which change every three weeks, are good, sometimes great. Two photographers, one Dutch, one foreign, are usually shown at the same time, and shows range from exhibitions of portraits of Dutch personalities and news photography to experimental, abstract works. There's also a changing show of vintage photography, and an excellent bookshop.

Print-making

De Expeditie

Leliegracht 47, IW (620 4758). Tram 13, 14, 17. **Open** 2-6pm Wed-Sat.

The one-man shows at De Expeditie take months of preparation. Siguidur Gudmunsson, Tony Cragg, Barry Flanagan and a number of Dutch artists have all worked and exhibited here.

Galerie Clement

Prinsengracht 845, IS (625 1656). Tram 16, 24, 25. **Open** 11am-5.30pm Mon-Sat.

Galerie Clement (previously called Printshop) is the grand-daddy of the printmaker's studio-galleries – it has been an atelier since 1958, a gallery since 1968. Artists do their own prints and the gallery also exhibits their drawings and paintings. Standards are mixed.

Steendrukkerij Amsterdam

Lauriergracht 80, IW (624 1491). Tram 13, 14, 17. **Open** 1-5.30pm Wed-Sat.

Steen is stone; *drukker* is printer, and the *drukkerij* is the place where printers print. The gallery, not surprisingly, shows lithos, woodcuts, and experimental prints.

Sculpture

Fons Welters

Bloemstraat 140, OW (622 7193). Tram 13, 14, 17.

Open 1-6pm Wed-Sat.

The only gallery dedicated exclusively to sculpture, and one of the top ten galleries in the city. It shows everything from multiples to spatial projects and installations. Welters considers Dutch sculptors to be the most international (and eclectic) in the world, and he has the pick of them.

Subsidised Spaces and Collectives

Amsterdam has about half a dozen subsidised exhibition spaces apart from its museums, but funding has been reduced in the past decade, with predictable results. Recent subsidies for open studios and weekend art events no doubt means that artists will prefer annual events to maintaining co-operative spaces all year round. Several non profit-making private and co-operative initiatives throughout The Netherlands organise outstanding exhibitions. Oddly, not many of these are in Amsterdam, but that may change.

Sculptors' Collective

ABK/Amsterdams Beeldhouwers Kollektief

Zeilmakerstraat 15, IW (625 6332). Tram 3. **Open** 1-6pm Wed-Sun.

Amsterdam's sculptors' collective was not big, flashy or exceptionally professional, but it has now greatly expanded its space and taken on new artists. It shows a spectrum of figurative sculptors, in particular.

Wheelchair access.

Subsidised Art Spaces

De Appel

Prinseneiland 7, OW (625 5651). Tram 3. **Open** 1-5pm Tue-Sat.

An Amsterdam institution, dating from 1975, De Appel presents films, lectures and exhibitions, with the accent on theoretical approaches to contemporary art.

Arti et Amicitiae

Rokin 112, C (623 2092/3508). Tram 4, 9, 14, 16, 24, 25. **Open** noon-5pm Tue-Sun.

This beautiful building houses Amsterdam's oldest and most elegant club for artists and their patrons. It has a beautiful, large upstairs exhibition space. Occasionally, this is rented out, but primarily it hosts excellent theme shows and projects by members.

Nieuwe Vleugel Stedelijk Museum (New Wing Stedelijk Museum)

Paulus Potterstraat 13, OS (573 2911/Dutch recorded information 573 2737). Tram 2, 3, 12, 15, 16. **Open** 11am-5pm daily; 11am-4pm public holidays.

Admission f7; f3.50 under-17s, CJP card holders; free under-7s; free with Museum Card; group discounts (min 50 people).

A monument to Amsterdam idealism, the new wing of the Stedelijk Museum *(see chapter* **Museums: The Big Three)** was built exclusively as exhibition space for Amsterdam's artists' guilds and clubs. Sculptors, watercolourists, illustrators, photographers, graphic designers and several mixed-discipline organisations exhibit works of wildly varying content and calibre. This confused anyone associating it with the museum, so in order to

Artoteeks

In Amsterdam you can borrow works of art as you do books from a library – for a week, a month or a year. The *artoteek* (a play on words with *bibliotheek* – the Dutch word for library) and the *kunstuitleen* (*kunst* means 'art', *uit means* 'out', and *leen* means 'lend') work on the same principle as libraries. The main difference between the two is that the *kunstuitleen* is subsidised, rather than run by the city. At both, borrowers can take a work of art home on loan, with the option to buy. Because of the astounding over-supply of artists and the cautious market, *artoteeks* and *kunstuitleens* carry huge numbers of artists. They provide a good cross-section of art – within the restrictions of size, and durability to withstand frequent transport. Artists sometimes sell to these lending libraries, but work is usually rented for a percentage of its value.

The *artoteeks* have proved to be a success, and they provide an excellent means of getting art across to the public. There are five neighbourhood *artoteeks* run by the city. All have exhibition spaces for solo shows and have hundreds of works in stock, but none are in the centre of Amsterdam. As for *kunstuitleens*, only the **SBK** has maintained a semi-independent structure and fairly high standards. It is easily reached, has the large space it requires (there are about 10,000 works by 900 artists), and also represents artists from outside Amsterdam.

SBK Kunstuitleen (Stichting Beeldende Kunst/Fine Arts Foundation)
Nieuwezijds Voorburgwal 325, C (623 9215). Tram 1, 2, 5. **Open** *11am-9pm Tue; noon-5pm Wed-Fri; 9am-5pm Sat.* **Hire cost** *basic* f25 *per month; deposit* f75. When borrowing for the first time, three months hire fee must be paid in advance. Of each hire fee paid, 60% is 'banked' by the SBK, and this money may later be used towards the purchase of a painting.

straighten matters out, responsibility for the new wing was handed over to the museum in January 1993 – it remains to be seen how things will change under its control.

Oude Kerk
Oudekerksplein 23, C (625 8284). Tram 4, 9, 16, 24, 25. **Open** *15 Apr-15 Sept* 11am-5pm Mon-Sat; *16 Sept-14 Apr* 1-5pm Mon-Sat.
Artists are able to rent space for exhibitions in Amsterdam's oldest church. The shows vary enormously. *Wheelchair access with assistance.*

W 139
Warmoesstraat 139, C (622 9434). Tram 4, 9, 16, 24, 25. **Open** noon-6pm Wed-Sun.
This ground-floor space is gigantic by Amsterdam standards. W 139 has close links with the art schools and offers young artists excellent opportunities to produce space-related works and theme shows.
Wheelchair access.

Artists' Books

Few people are aware of the talents put into books made by and for artists – not Rembrandt, Van Gogh or Mondrian, but the folk currently sweating over the work in the galleries, designing, drawing and publishing their own books. There are several small publishers and book designers in Amsterdam producing books by and for artists. Some support their gallery this way, others support their own non-applied arts by making books for their colleagues.

Boekie Woekie
Berenstraat 16, C (639 0507). Tram 1, 2, 5, 13, 14, 17. **Open** noon-6pm Tue-Fri; noon-5pm Sat.

Boekie Woekie exhibits and sells graphics and books by artists. Graphics is a broader term in Dutch than in English – it includes all forms of printmaking – so if Dutch artists say they make graphics (as a huge number will) don't assume they're layout people at an advertising firm.

Events

Art Fairs

Amsterdam's annual art fair is called the **Kunst Rai** (the Rai is Amsterdam's congress centre) and it takes place in late May or early June. So much art in one place at one time can be overwhelming, but everything is there – at least as far as the 'accepted' gallery circuit is concerned. You may buy art at the Kunst Rai or simply go to admire it. *See also chapter* **Amsterdam by Season**.

Open Ateliers

Neighbourhoods with large artist populations and artists' studio complexes hold open days, often in the spring or autumn. Dozens of studios are open to the public for a weekend or more; most present a group show. The events have become popular and have succeeded in reaching a broader spectrum of the public than would normally go to a gallery. If you see 'Open Atelier' banners or posters during your visit, try and go – it may provide a memorable insight into artists' lives and studios, and behind-the-scenes art.

Museums

In the country that has the highest concentration of museums in the world, we discover that there's more to Amsterdam's collection than the Rijksmuseum.

With an average of one per 40 square kilometres (about 15 square miles), The Netherlands has the highest concentration of museums in the world. In Amsterdam the collections are diverse. Some are world-class; others are small gems and a few are unique.

The past few years have been characterised by dramatic cuts in the already ungenerous government funding of the arts. The present funding system for museums is confusing, even for insiders. Three of the Amsterdam museums (the **Rijksmuseum** and the **Van Gogh Museum**, *listed under* The Big Three; and the **Nederlands Scheepvaart Museum**, *under* **Maritime**) are financed by the state, but in order to minimise bureaucracy, the government plans to give them a more independent structure. Another three (the **Stedelijk Museum**, *under* **The Big Three**; the **Amsterdams Historisch Museum**, *under* **Historical**; and the **Willet-Holthuysen Museum**, *under* Golden Age) are

financed by the city of Amsterdam, while the rest are private. The majority of museums house private collections that have been donated to the city or to a specific foundation. Many are also classified as monuments (the Rijksmuseum, the **Theatermuseum**, *under* Theatre, and the **Bijbels Museum**, *under* **Religion**, for instance) and their upkeep is supported by Monumentenzorg, an administrative organisation set up to preserve Amsterdam's architectural heritage.

FUNDING SCHEMES

Commercial sponsorship of museums and exhibitions has become a hot item recently; some observers are predicting that a new Golden Age will descend upon The Netherlands, with generous patrons subsidising the arts. Cuts brought the possibility of closure, but special activities were organised to save threatened museums and focus public attention on their problems. The generosity of a Japanese philanthropist will

Only in Amsterdam...Tour the museums by **Museumboot**. *See* **review** *page 154.*

Home to the city's best modern art collection, the **Stedelijk Museum.** *See* **review** *page 156.*

enable the Van Gogh museum to add a new wing, which is planned to open in 1993.

In the past, Dutch companies have favoured sponsoring sports events rather than the arts, but times are changing and it is now becoming more prestigious for companies to have their name linked to that of an important museum, through the financing of special exhibitions or restoration of specific paintings. And foundations such as the Rembrandt Vereniging (Rembrandt Association), which provides funds for purchases, or the Prins Bernhard Fonds, which subsidises restoration projects, assist several museums including the Rijksmuseum.

Temporary exhibitions, such as the 1992 special exhibition focused on Rembrandt, have proved to be successful both in short-term fund-raising, and more importantly as an easy way of increasing attendance figures to make a museum eligible for subsidies.

Charging for admission is not a recent thing – the Rijksmuseum introduced entrance fees in the thirties. While increases in admission prices provoke no real outcry, there were grumbles about the recent jump in the cost of the Annual Museum Card (*see below* **Tickets and Discounts**), which rose from f25 to f40.

While government funds are drying up for existing museums, the tap has been turned on for a new multi-million guilder project planned for a location near Centraal Station. Some time in early 1995, the present **Technologie Museum NINT** (*under* **Technology**) will be reborn there in the form of a world-class Science Centre. Designed by the architect of the Centre Pompidou in Paris, the 'supermuseum' will be the first technological museum in the world to give chemistry a prominent position.

FURTHER AFIELD
With museums spread throughout the country devoted to the likes of clogs, clocks, salt, skates, wine and cheese, there will be something to tickle the fancy of even the staunchest museum-hater. Below we list a few of the major art collections (*under* **Further Afield**), but for more museums outside Amsterdam, *see chapters* **Excursions in Holland, The Randstad** *and* **The Provinces.** A guide brought out by the Museum Card foundation containing listings (in Dutch) of some 830 museums can be bought from various bookshops. The VVV tourist offices (*see chapter* **Essential Information**) are also helpful.

MUSEUM BOAT
Amsterdam is among the few Dutch cities that offers the possibility of reaching a museum by water (another is Giethoorn; *see chapter* **The Provinces: Overijssel**). The Museumboot is remarkably good value, even for tourists on a tight budget. Tickets entitle holders to get on and off at any of the five stops serving 16 of the capital's 40-odd museums located on or near a canal or by the River IJ near Centraal Station. Tickets also give up to 50 per cent discount on admission prices; *see also below* **Tickets and Discounts**.

Museumboot
Office and main boarding point: Stationplein 8, C (625 6464/622 2181). Tram 1, 2, 4, 5, 9, 13, 16, 17, 24, 25. **Departs** every 30 mins, 10am-4.45pm daily. **Stops at** *Prinsengracht* (for Anne Frankhuis, Theatermuseum); *Singelgracht* (for Museumplein, Rijksmuseum, Van Gogh, Stedelijk, Technologie Museum); *Herengracht/Leidsegracht* (for Bijbels, Amsterdam Historisch, Allard Pierson); *Amstel/Zwanenburgwal* (for Rembrandthuis, Joods Historisch, Hortus Botanicus, Tropenmuseum); *Oosterdok/Kattenburgergracht* (for Scheepvaart Museum, Werf 't Kromhout); *Centraal Station* (for Madam Tussaud, Museum Amstelkring). **Tickets** f15 per day; f12.50 under-13s, CJP card holders; *combination tickets* (boat plus free admission to 3 museums) f25 per day; f22.50 under-13s, CJP card holders. **No credit cards.**

TICKETS AND DISCOUNTS
Most museums are reasonably priced, between around f5 and f10. If you're thinking of taking in more than a few – in Amsterdam or elsewhere in the country – the **Annual Museum Card**

(*Museumjaarkaart*) is a good buy. Costing f40 (f25 for under-18s and pensioners), the ticket offers free or reduced-price admission to almost 400 museums throughout The Netherlands. Special exhibitions are normally not covered by the ticket, but you may be entitled to a reduction. The card can be purchased at one of the participating museums (indicated in the listings below) or at VVV tourist offices. Reductions can often also be obtained with a valid student identity card, or a CJP under-26 card, available at the AUB Uitburo (*see chapter* **Essential Information**).

Top of the list for good value is the **national museum weekend** (17-18 April 1993, 16-17 April 1994) – two days on which some 350 museums throughout the country are open free of charge (*see chapter* **Amsterdam by Season**). But it's only really worthwhile if you're on a shoestring budget, since you'll have to vie with the large number of locals taking advantage of this popular freebie.

This doesn't mean that the Dutch steer clear of museums the rest of the year; temporary exhibitions at the major museums are often popular at weekends for family outings. It's also wise to avoid Wednesday afternoons if you're going to a museum that may be popular with children, as most primary schools have this afternoon off. Also, some museums are closed on Monday. Not all museums have captions and explanations in English, but many sell reasonably-priced English-language guidebooks. Enquire about this when you buy your ticket. Several museums also offer guided tours in English for groups; always phone to enquire or to make a booking.

Many museums are closed on public holidays (*see chapter* **Essential Information**). Always phone to check.

The Big Three

Rijksmuseum

Stadhouderskade 42, OS (673 2121). Tram 2, 5, 6, 7, 10/Bus 63, 170. **Open** 10am-5pm Tue-Sat; 1-5pm Sun, public holidays. **Admission** f10; f5 under-18s, CJP card holders, over-65s; free with Museum Card; group discounts (min 20 people). **No credit cards.**
If you've been to Amsterdam's Centraal Station, you might think you're seeing double when you glimpse The Netherlands' largest national museum, the Rijksmuseum. Both of these splendid neo-Renaissance buildings were designed by PJH Cuypers. Opened in 1885, the Rijksmuseum is backed by a small garden with sculptures, a pleasant end to what could be an exhausting visit. The Museum gets some one million visitors a year – almost twice as many as its closest rivals, the Van Gogh Museum and the Stedelijk (*see below*), which respectively have 600,000 and 500,000 annually. The collection has expanded tremendously since William V first started putting pieces together for his private amusement in the eighteenth-century. A single day won't be enough to view all the treasures, which include a fabulous collection of

The Rijksmuseum

Unless you want to get lost, don't start a tour of the Rijksmuseum (The Netherlands' largest national museum, *see above* **The Big Three**) without a map or a guidebook. The shop on the first floor stocks an English-language guidebook (f7.50) and also provides Viewfinders, fold-out floor plans each devoted to a different, changing theme.

If you only have a limited amount of time, head first for the exhibition on the first floor, which features Holland's claim to artistic fame: the seventeenth-century Dutch masters. Top of the list of the best works in this section would have to be Rembrandt's *Night Watch*. The exhibition in the room next door which explains why the painting was so innovative is also worth a visit.

Rembrandt was indisputably the most prolific of the Dutch masters, but also impressive are the works by his contemporaries. *The Kitchen Maid* and *The Young Woman Reading a Letter* by Johannes Vermeer capture a moment in the lives of two women from totally different backgrounds. Pieter de Hooch was another seventeenth-century painter to excel in scenes of domestic interiors, while Jan Steen focused on life in the lower social classes. Together with the landscapes of Jacob van Ruisdael and Paulus Potter, the winter scenes of Hendrik Avercamp and Jan van de Capelle, and the maritime scenes of Willem van de Velde the Younger, this section of fifteenth- to seventeenth-century Dutch art offers an excellent insight into life in The Netherlands during the Golden Age.

Other attractions include superb examples of Delftware, porcelain, pottery, silverware and oriental art. In the past year the presentation of exhibits on the ground floor, covering Dutch history, has vastly improved, with the addition of many more English explanations. The display of early eighteenth-century dolls' houses is worthy of note, and gives a good insight into the type of establishment where the works of Rembrandt and Vermeer were originally hung.

paintings from the fifteenth century until around 1850 and decorative and oriental arts; *see also p155* **The Rijksmuseum**. Temporary exhibitions are often held in the National Print Room. There's a special exhibition on the Golden Age ('De Dageraad van de Gouden Eeuw'), featuring paintings and *objets d'art* of the sixteenth and seventeenth centuries, which runs from 11 December 1993 until 7 March 1994.

Café. Educational department. Films and slide shows. Guided tours by prior arrangement. Shop. Wheelchair access with assistance.

Stedelijk Museum

Paulus Potterstraat 13, OS (573 2911/Dutch recorded information 573 2737). Tram 2, 3, 5, 12, 16. **Open** 11am-5pm daily; 11am-4pm public holidays. **Admission** f7.50; f3.75 under-17s, CJP card holders; free with Museum Card, under-7s. **No credit cards.**
Picking up where the Rijksmuseum (*above*) leaves off, the Stedelijk (Municipal) Museum houses the best collection of modern art in Amsterdam. After occupying various locations around the city, the Stedelijk finally settled down in its present neo-Renaissance building, designed by AW Weissmann in 1895. The building soon became too small for the ambitions of its directors and an ugly new wing was tacked on in 1954. The Museum focuses on particular trends or the works of specific artists which are exhibited in spacious, well-lit rooms. Highlights include paintings by Monet, Cézanne, Picasso, Matisse, Kirchner and Chagall. In addition, the Museum has a prize collection of paintings and drawings by the Russian artist, Kasimir Malevich. Also well-represented is the Dutch De Stijl group, of which Piet Mondrian is probably the most famous member, as well as other post-1945 artists including De Kooning, Newman, Ryman, Judd, Stella, Lichtenstein, Warhol, Nauman, Middleton, Long, Dibbets, Van Elk, Kiefer, Polke, Merz and Lounellis. Interior design buffs will enjoy the extensive collection of furniture by Gerrit Rietveld. Don't forget to pop into the Appelbar or the restaurant – both have been decorated by another Dutch artist, Karel Appel. The restaurant has a terrace overlooking the sculpture garden, and is a lovely place to sit on a sunny day. Outstanding temporary exhibitions are replaced in the summer by a selection of the permanent collection.

Café and restaurant. Guided tours f65 (book at least two weeks ahead). Occasional lectures with special exhibitions (f7-f10). Library (open to library card holders only, phone for details), closed July, Aug. Art History courses, f100 for 8 sessions, advance booking essential. Shop. Wheelchair access and toilets for the disabled.

Van Gogh Museum

Paulus Potterstraat 7, OS (570 5200). Tram 2, 3, 5, 12, 16. **Open** 10am-5pm Mon-Sat; 1-5pm Sun, public holidays. **Admission** f10; f5 under-18s; f3.50 with Museum Card; free CJP card holders; group discounts (min 20 people). **No credit cards.**
The Van Gogh Museums is one of the few museums in The Netherlands devoted to a single artist. The exterior may be bland, but the collection is remarkably colourful. Apart from the bright colours of his palette, Van Gogh is also known for his productivity, and both are clearly reflected in the 200 paintings and 500 drawings that form part of the permanent exhibition. An exceptionally good selection of works by Van Gogh's contemporaries, such as Toulouse-Lautrec, Bernard and Gauguin, is also on view. Van Gogh was influenced by Japanese prints and a selection of these is housed on the second floor. His development as an artist is further illustrated by changing exhibitions. Every second Sunday of the month a classical concert is held in the museum. Entry is free of charge, for both the concert and the museum, but tickets must be obtained in advance from the museums' ticket office.

Library. Restaurant. Shop. Cassette tours f6.50. Wheelchair access and toilets for the disabled.

The **Nederlands Filmmuseum** *acts as an exhibition space, cinema, and home to 35,000 films. See* **review** *page 157.*

Archaeology

Allard Pierson Museum

Oude Turfmarkt 127, C (525 2556). Tram 1, 4, 9, 16, 24, 25. **Open** 10am-5pm Tue-Fri; 1-5pm Sat, Sun, public holidays. **Admission** f5; f3.50 over-65s, CJP card holders; f2 12-15s; free with Museum Card, under-12s. **No credit cards.**

An extensive collection of archaeological exhibits – the world's richest university collection of its type – from Egypt, Greece, Rome and other ancient civilizations. The mummy coffins are colourful, but the displays of statues, sculptures, clay tablets, ceramics and numerous other items are unimaginative, sometimes even amateurish. Established in 1934, the Museum moved to this building, originally built to house the Netherlands Central Bank, in 1976. It's normally fairly quiet, but the temporary exhibitions draw larger crowds. Texts are sporadically in English, but often in obscure places or in such small print that they are difficult to read. Recent renovation of the Egyptian rooms have proved a great improvement. *Wheelchair access with assistance.*

Art

Rembrandthuis

Jodenbreestraat 4-6, C (624 9486). Tram 9, 14. **Open** 10am-5pm Mon-Sat; 1-5pm Sun, public holidays. **Admission** f5; f3.50 10-15s, over-65s; free with Museum Card, under-9s; group discount (min 15 people). **No credit cards.**

Rembrandt may not have painted everything he signed, but the controversial Dutch master must have had his hands full just working on the large legacy of etchings that he left behind. About 250 of these are on display at the charming three-storey house (built in 1606) in which he lived for over 20 years. The museum has an intimate atmosphere, enhanced by the low-level lighting used to preserve the etchings. The etchings themselves are well-illuminated, however, allowing visitors to trace Rembrandt's development as an etcher and his interest in biblical scenes and human emotions. The only paintings here are by Rembrandt's teacher, Pieter Lastman, and his pupils. Don't miss the amusing drawings (by Rembrandt) indicating the men's and women's toilets in the basement. *Guided tours by prior arrangement.*

Botanical

Bosmuseum

Koenenkade 56, Amsterdamse Bos, OS (643 1414). Bus 70 (Sundays) 146, 147, 170, 171, 172. **Open** 9am-5pm daily. **Admission** free.

This exhibition recounts the history, use and management of the extensive forest – the Amsterdamse Bos – located on the outskirts of the city (*see chapter* **Sightseeing**). Don't interrupt a picnic to see it, but keep it in mind if it starts to rain. *Shop & pancake restaurant. Wheelchair access.*

Hortus Botanicus

Plantage Middenlaan 2, IE (625 8411). Tram 7, 9, 14. **Open** *Oct-March* 9am-4pm Sat, Sun, public holidays; *April-Sept* 9am-5pm Mon-Fri; 11am-5pm Sat, Sun, public holidays. **Admission** f5; f3 under-14s, over-65s, CJP card holders; f3 with Museum Card.

If Amsterdam's other museums have left you exhausted, head for the Hortus Botanicus. You don't need to be a keen gardener to enjoy the greenery of more than 6,000 herbs, shrubs and plants. Established in 1682, when ships from the East Indies Company brought back trop-

ical plants and seeds from distant lands, to create a medicinal garden for doctors and pharmacists, the Hortus is a haven for those wanting respite from the city. *Café. Wheelchair access.*

Hortus Botanicus of the Vrije University

Van der Boechorststraat 8, OS (548 4142). Bus 23, 65, 173. Tram 5. **Open** 8am-4.30pm Mon-Fri. **Admission** free.

As it was only created in 1967, the Hortus of the Vrije University doesn't have the historical charm of its older counterpart in the city centre (*above*), but it's a very pleasant place for a stroll if you happen to be in the neighbourhood – on the outskirts of town near Amstelveen. The fern collection is one of the largest in the world, while the Dutch garden shows the great variety of flora originally found in this country. *Wheelchair access.*

Cinema

Nederlands Filmmuseum

Vondelpark 3, OS (589 1400). Tram 12. **Open** *box office* 8.30am-¼ hour before last film ends Mon-Fri; 3pm-¼ hour before last film ends Sat; 3pm-¼ hour before last film ends Sun; *library* 10am-5pm Tue-Fri. **Tickets** *cinema* f8.50-f12.50; ten-visit cards f50; 25-visit cards f100; 60-visit cards f200; *library* free. **Membership** f25, f12.50 3 months; f75, f50 1 year. **No credit cards.**

A must for film buffs, the Filmmuseum covers the history and development of the cinema. Magic lanterns, zoetropes, old cameras and projectors form the bulk of the small permanent exhibition, alongside a collection of often unique movie posters. Changing temporary exhibitions also take place, but the main business of the museum is screening films from its extensive national and international collections in the two recently-restored cinemas (*see chapter* **Film**). The museum vaults hold some 35,000 films, and in late 1992 hit the world headlines with the discovery of some unique early Disney films among them. The museum's trendy café Vertigo, with its terrace overlooking Vondelpark, is an ideal place for sun-lovers, and on summer evenings occasionally hosts open-air film screenings.

Ethnography

Tropenmuseum (Tropical Museum)

Linnaeusstraat 2, OE (568 8253). Tram 9, 10, 14. **Open** 10am-5pm Mon-Fri; noon-5pm Sat, Sun, public holidays. **Admission** f7.50; f4 under-18s, CJP card holders, students; free with Museum Card. **No credit cards.**

When it was built in the twenties, the Tropenmuseum was designed to justify and glorify the activities of the Dutch in their colonies. However, the permanent exhibitions have changed course dramatically since World War II. Instead of focusing on the noble deeds of the Dutch in their overseas territories, the Museum now takes an honest look at daily life and problems in all tropical and subtropical regions. The well-integrated displays vividly depict the present situation in the Third World, new developments and the responsibility of industrialised countries. The 'bazaars' and other displays (reproductions of an Indian village with taped sounds, an African compound, a nomad tent and so on) are so lifelike that they suspend reality for a moment. Compared to these, the collection of cultural/historical exhibits such as textiles, musical instruments and Oceanic art tends to become a bit dull. Excellent temporary exhibitions are mounted in the large hall on the ground floor. The shop has a good selection of souvenirs and books from or dealing

Museum Willet-Holthuysen

Herengracht 605, IS (523 1870). Tram 4, 9, 14. **Open**
10am-5pm Mon-Fri; 11am-5pm Sat, Sun. **Admission**
f2.50; f1.25 under-12s; group discount (min 15 people).
No credit cards.
Originally built in 1689, the interior of this pleasant patrician's mansion on one of Amsterdam's most elegant canals
is more reminiscent of a French château than a Dutch canal
house. Both the Louis XV and neo-Louis XVI styles are very
much visible. The latter was mainly introduced by the Willet-
Holthuysen couple who acquired the house in 1860 and who
gave the Museum its name. Their passion for over-embell-
ishment is also apparent in their legacy of rare *objets d'art* –
glassware, silver, fine china and paintings. There are no
English texts to accompany the exhibits, but an English-language video on the ground floor gives a comprehensive
review of what visitors can expect. The charming eighteenth-
century garden is unfortunately overshadowed by several
twentieth-century buildings.

Museum Van Loon

Keizersgracht 672, IS (624 5255). Tram 16, 24, 25.
Open 10am-5pm Mon-Fri; 11am-5pm Sat, Sun.
Admission f5; free under-12s. **No credit cards**.
Behind the classical seventeenth-century façade of this
canal house lies a furnished interior, showing how wonderful it was to be a wealthy resident of Amsterdam in
Holland's Golden Age. Built by the architect who
designed the New Lutheran Church on Singel (*see chapter* **Sightseeing**), Adriaan Dortsman, the patrician's
house was home to a former pupil of Rembrandt,
Ferdinand Bol. Apart from the Louis XV décor, the museum has an unusually large collection of family portraits
from the seventeenth and eighteenth centuries, added after
the purchase of the house in 1884 by Hendrik van Loon.
The eighteenth-century garden, laid out in the French
style, contains a coach house from the same period (now
a private home).
Guided tours (min 10 people) by prior arrangement.

*The domestic splendours of the Golden Age
can be seen at* **Museum Van Loon**.
See **review**.

with Third World countries. Attached to the main museum
is the Tropenmuseum Junior, for children aged between
6 and 12, *see chapter* **Children & Parents**.

Golden Age

Amstelkring Museum, 'Our Lord in the Attic'

*Oudezijds Voorburgwal 40, C (624 6604). Tram 1, 2, 4,
5, 9, 13, 16, 17, 24, 25.* **Open** 10am-5pm Mon-Sat; 1-
5pm Sun, public holidays. **Admission** f4.50; f3 CJP
card holders, students; free with Museum Card; group
discount. **No credit cards**.
One of the most surprising of the smaller museums in
Amsterdam, the Amstelkring is undeservedly neglected
by most visitors. Located in the heart of the red light district, this unique building, housing the only remaining attic
church in Amsterdam (*see chapter* **The Golden Age**), was
happily saved from demolition in the late nineteenth century by a group of historians who called themselves the
Amstelkring (Amstel 'circle') and were mainly concerned
with preserving the city's Catholic past. The lower floors
of the house include furnished living rooms that could
have served as the setting for some of the seventeenth-
century Dutch masters. Upstairs, the chaplain's room has
a cupboard bed. The pilgrimage upwards leads visitors to
the highlight of the museum: the beautifully preserved
attic church, the altarpiece of which features a painting by
eighteenth-century artist Jacob de Wit. Built in 1663, the
church is sometimes used for services and a variety of
other meetings.
Guided tours by prior arrangement.

Historical

Amsterdams Historisch Museum

*Kalverstraat 92, C (523 1822). Tram 1, 2, 4, 5, 9, 14,
16, 24, 25.* **Open** 11am-5pm daily. **Admission** f5; f2.50
under-16s; f12.50 family ticket (2 adults, 2 children);
free with Museum Card; group discount (min 20
people). **No credit cards**.
The courtyard of the Amsterdam Historical Museum is an
oasis of peace in the midst of the busy Kalverstraat, one
of Amsterdam's main shopping thoroughfares. The main
entrance is hard to find, though – look out for a tiny alley
and a lopsided arch bearing the three crosses of the city's
coat of arms. The Museum is housed in a former convent
and orphanage dating from the sixteenth century. The
development of the city from the thirteenth century to the
present day is illustrated in a masterful way by various
objets d'art, archaeological finds and interactive displays.
The best view of the Civic Guard Gallery – a covered street
gallery with several massive group portraits commissioned by wealthy burghers in the sixteenth and seventeenth centuries – is from the second floor of the museum.
Another attraction is the adjacent Begijnhof (see chapter
Sightseeing). The 'lifesize model of Goliath in the museum's adjoining restaurant is a favourite with kids, as are
the pancakes. It's a good place to take a well-earned rest
– this is definitely a museum for sensible walking shoes.
Restaurant.

Anne Frankhuis

Prinsengracht 263, IW (626 4533). Tram 13, 14, 17.
Open *Sept-May* 9am-5pm Mon-Sat; 10am-5pm Sun,
public holidays; *June-Aug* 9am-7pm Mon-Sat; 10am-7pm

Sun, public holidays. **Admission** f7; f3.50 10-17s, over-65s, CJP card holders; free under-10s; group discount. **No credit cards**.

The Anne Frank House was opened to the public in 1960 and now attracts more than half a million visitors a year. The building, on the border of the Jordaan, dates from 1635, but the upstairs annex where Anne's family and four other Jews hid before being deported to concentration camps toward the end of World War II was added a century later. A bookcase marks the entrance to the sober, unfurnished rooms which sheltered the eight inhabitants for two long years. Unfortunately, it's hardly ever quiet enough to imagine what their lives must have been like during that time. To avoid the crowds, go early or take advantage of the longer opening hours in summer. The permanent and temporary exhibitions on the fight against anti-semitism and other forms of discrimination are sobering, but enlightening. Translations of Anne's diary can be bought in the bookshop downstairs. *See chapter* **World War II**.

Bookshop. Documentation department (Keizersgracht 192, tel 626 4533). Educational department. Guided tours by prior arrangement. Videos.

Verzetsmuseum Amsterdam (Museum of the Resistance)

Lekstraat 63, OS (644 9797). Tram 4, 25. **Open** 10am-5pm Tue-Fri; 1-5pm Sat, Sun, public holidays. **Admission** f3.50; f1.75 under-17s, CJP card holders; free with Museum Card; group discount (min 15 people). **No credit cards**.

Out of the way, but worth the extra effort, the Verzetsmuseum is located in a former synagogue in the southern part of the city, an area renowned for its early twentieth-century architecture typical of the Amsterdam School. The hardships of World War II and the heroic deeds of the Dutch Resistance fighters are depicted by

photos, tape recordings, newspaper clippings and other objects from the war. *See chapter* **World War II**. *Computer games. Guided tours by prior arrangement, f1. Library and video access by prior arrangement. Wheelchair access and toilets for the disabled.*

Maritime

Nederlands Scheepvaart Museum (Maritime Museum)

Kattenburgerplein 1, IE (523 2222). Bus 22, 28. **Open** 10am-5pm Tue-Sat; noon-5pm Sun, public holidays. **Admission** f10; f7.50 6-18s, over-65s, CJP card holders; free with Museum Card, under-6s. **No credit cards**.

The national maritime museum takes visitors on a voyage as far back as Roman times. It's housed, appropriately, in what was the Sea Arsenal of the United Provinces of The Netherlands, in the heart of Amsterdam's nautical district (*see chapter* **Amsterdam by Area**). Dating from 1656, this monumental building was used as a warehouse for the upkeep of the city's fleet of warships. Exhibitions trace the importance of water to The Netherlands' development as a major trading nation, and the museum contains some spectacular old charts, as well as paintings of famous sea battles. *Café. Shop.*

Werf 't Kromhout

Hoogte Kadijk 147, IE (627 6777). **Bus** 22, 28. **Open** 10am-4pm Mon-Fri; noon-5pm Sat, Sun for group bookings only. **Admission** f3.50; f1.75 over-65s, CJP card holders; f1.50 under-14s. **No credit cards**.

Located diagonally opposite the Maritime Museum (*above*) the Kromhout is one of the few surviving shipyards that were once numerous in the eastern port area of Amsterdam during the seventeenth and eighteenth centuries. Antique vessels being repaired under the cast-

The **Tropenmuseum***: transformed from colonial apologist to cultural showcase.* See **review** *page 157.*

Café. Library (10am-5pm Tue-Fri). Shop. Slide shows every half hour. Walks: July, Aug: Tue 11am and 2pm, f5 (1½ hours); Thur 11am and 2pm, f7.50 (2½ hours).

Joods Historisch Museum (Jewish Historical Museum)

Jonas Daniel Meijerplein 24, C (626 9945). Tram 9, 14. **Open** 11am-5pm daily; *closed* Yom Kippur. **Admission** free (except special exhibitions). **No credit cards.**
Located in a former High German Synagogue in the heart of what used to be a prominent Jewish neighbourhood, the museum is a short walk from Waterlooplein and the nearby Muziektheater (*see chapter* **Music: Classical & Opera**). Until 1987, the museum was housed in the Waag (Weigh House, *see chapter* **Sightseeing**), near the red light district. The new premises are both a suitable and interesting backdrop for an exhibition on the Jewish religion and the history of this minority group in The Netherlands. The permanent display contains some beautiful *objets d'art*, but these are somewhat overshadowed by a gripping exhibition on the persecution of Jews during World War II. The Museum organises walks around the Jewish neighbourhood and group visits to the nearby Portuguese Synagogue. The Jewish character of the coffee shop on the premises is not particularly prominent, but bookings can be made in advance for kosher lunches. The Museum gets particularly crowded on Jewish religious holidays.
Guided tours by prior arrangement.

Technology

Technologie Museum NINT

Tolstraat 129, OS (570 8111). Tram 3, 4. **Open** 10am-5pm Mon-Fri; noon-5pm Sat, Sun. **Admission** f7.50; f5 5-12s; free under-5s. **No credit cards.**
Until its grand transformation into a super Science Centre at the beginning of 1995, NINT will continue to be housed in the former workshop of Asscher, one of Amsterdam's best-known gem companies. Even those who loathe science get a buzz out of the place – it takes the principles of physics out of stuffy textbooks and into the real world. Some of the more popular exhibits deal with automation in shops, car repair, holography and micro-computers. Eight multi-media machines help explain such things as CAD/CAM and fractals. The Museum is popular with kids and teenagers, who love getting their hands on the displays. *See also chapter* **Children & Parents.**
Café (closes at 4pm). Shop (closes at 4pm).

iron roof are photogenic (completed ships are not on show), but the steam engines, tools and instruments on display in the adjoining museum are only interesting for real connoisseurs.
Guided tours. Wheelchair access with assistance.

Religion

Bijbels Museum (Biblical Museum)

Herengracht 366, IW (624 7949). Tram 1, 2, 5. **Open** 10am-5pm Tue-Sat; 1-5pm Sun, public holidays. **Admission** f3; f2 under-16s; free with Museum Card, CJP card holders. **No credit cards.**
Many tourists visit the biblical museum for the two adjoining patrician's houses that accommodate it. Built in 1660-1662 by the renowned Dutch architect Philip Vingboons, the houses feature stunning early-eighteenth century ceiling paintings by Jacob de Wit and a splendid spiral staircase which connects them. The museum itself is also remarkable. You have to look hard to find the fine selection of bibles; the emphasis of the permanent and temporary exhibitions is more on life in Biblical times, vividly illustrated by archaeological finds from Egypt and the Middle East, a reconstruction of a Palestinian house, models of Solomon's temple – including a modern, perspex construction – and various audio-visual displays. Special exhibitions are usually staged during religious holidays, but these are also often the busiest times to visit. In conjunction with the Amstelkring Museum (*see above*) the Biblical Museum organises walks around historical monuments of religious significance in July and August; unfortunately, the commentary is in Dutch only.

Theatre

Theatermuseum

Herengracht 168, IW (623 5104). Tram 13, 14, 17. **Open** 11am-5pm Tue-Sun. **Admission** f5; f3 under-14s, CJP card holders; free with Museum Card. **No credit cards.**
Possessing the first neck gable in Amsterdam (built in 1638 by the architect Philip Vingboons), the Theatermuseum is an architectural gem worth visiting for its interior alone. The eighteenth-century plasterwork, the ceiling paintings by Jacob de Wit and the spiral staircases are simply magnificent. The delightful décor distracts somewhat from the permanent and temporary exhibitions which relate the story of Dutch theatre. Important chapters include stage costumes, models of stage scenery and a selection of related drawings and prints. Children enjoy creating wind and rain with the special machines on display. Tea and cake in the lovely old garden behind the house is a treat in summer. The museum also boasts an extensive library. *See also chapter* **Theatre.**

Café. Guided tours (f4, min. 15 people, by prior arrangement). Library closed Sun.

Town Planning

Informatiecentrum Ruimtelijk Ordening
Zuiderkerkhof, C (622 2962). Metro Nieuwmarkt.
Open noon-5pm Mon-Wed, Fri; noon-8pm Thur.
Admission free.
Unless you're really interested in town planning and housing, the setting of this museum – a beautifully restored seventeenth-century church located near the red light district, run by the Urban Planning Information Centre – is possibly more interesting than the temporary exhibitions. These focus on current housing projects, through photographical and textual displays (English texts are being added but progress is slow). There are also model reproductions and slide shows. The Amsterdams Historisch Museum (*see above* **Historical**) is a better place to trace the development of the city through the ages.
Wheelchair access with assistance.

Transport

Aviodome
Schiphol Centre (604 1521). Train to Schiphol Airport.
Open *Oct-May* 10am-5pm Tue-Fri; noon-5pm Sat, Sun;
May-Sept 10am-5pm daily. **Admission** f6; f4.50 4-12s;
free under-4s. **No credit cards.**
It helps to be mad about aviation to enjoy this place. There are over 30 historic aircraft on display (some suspended from the ceiling), including the first motorised plane – the Wright Flyer from 1903 – and the Spider, designed by Dutch aviation pioneer Anthony Fokker. Kids enjoy clambering into a cockpit and pretending to be Biggles in an exhibit especially reserved for that purpose. Also popular is the Space Department, which contains the American Mercury capsule. The hangar-like aluminium dome also shows films and has a large collection of models, photos and airplane parts. The Dutch-language guidebook has a summary in English. There are special weekend aviation markets and fairs, as well as theme weekends focusing on subjects such as restoration (information is available from VVV tourist offices, the local press or from the museum). An information centre, opened in 1990, houses a permanent exhibition detailing the future and the role of Schiphol Airport, and related environmental issues.
Films and slide shows. Shop. Wheelchair access except to 1st-floor Space Department.

Electrische Museumtralijn (Electric Tram Museum)
Amstelveenseweg 264, OW (673 7538/615 2983).
Tram 6, 16. **Open** *April-Oct* 10.30am-5.30pm Sun.
Trams depart every 20 minutes 10.30am-5.30pm Sun;
July, Aug also at 1pm, 2.15pm, 3.30pm, Tue-Thur, Sat.
Admission f4.50; f2.25 4-11s, over-65s, CJP card holders; free under-4s. **No credit cards.**
When open, the Electric Tram Museum is almost always on the move. Some of the antique trolleys, collected from cities throughout Europe, are still in use. Kids in particular love going for a 30-minute ride in one of the museum's colourful conveyances through the nearby – and surprisingly rural – Amsterdamse Bos; *see chapter* **Children & Parents.**
Café at Haarlemmermeer station.

University History

Universiteitsmuseum De Agnietenkapel
Oudezijds Voorburgwal 231, C (525 3341). Tram 4, 9, 14, 16, 24, 25. **Open** usually 9am-1pm, 2-5pm, Mon-Fri; may open at weekends, phone to check. **Admission** usually free; small charge (max f2.50) for special exhibitions.
The Agnietenkapel (chapel), built in 1470 and part of the University since its foundation in 1632, is one of the few Gothic chapels to have escaped demolition. It has a sober, Calvinistic beauty, with lovely stained glass windows and old wooden beams and benches. The chapel is more stimulating than the collection, which focuses on the history of education, research and student life at the University of Amsterdam. One of the most interesting things in the museum is the Grote Gehoorzaal (Large Auditorium) where seventeenth-century academics Vossius and Barlaeus gave their first lectures. It has a beautiful wooden ceiling, decorated with soberly painted ornamental Renaissance motifs such as angels, masks, flowers and a portrait of Minerva, the Roman goddess of Science and Arts. The Auditorium is now used for symposia, the presentation of certificates and occasional lectures.

Zoological

Artis Zoologisch Museum
Plantage Kerklaan 40, IE (623 1836). Tram 7, 9, 14.
Open 9am-5pm daily; last Planetarium show 4pm.
Admission *Zoo, Planetarium and Zoological Museum* f17.50; f10 under-10s; free under-4s; group discount (min 20 people). **No credit cards.**
This zoo, planetarium and zoological museum makes a great outing for children – although it's a bit pricey. Apart from the usual range of animals, including a section for nocturnal creatures and a fascinating aquarium, the beautiful gardens of the 150 year-old Artis Zoo (*see chapter* **Sightseeing**) contain a small but interesting zoological museum featuring thematic exhibitions and a collection of stuffed animals. A slide show presents scenes of wildlife in the Dutch coastal dunes. The narration in the Planetarium is in Dutch but a short English translation is now available and the spectacular visuals make it well worthwhile. The feeding ground for humans is ideally situated between a pond with pink flamingoes and a popular children's playground. *See also chapter* **Children & Parents.**
Café and restaurant. Guided tours by prior arrangement (free). Schools educational programme. Shop. Wheelchair access and toilets for the disabled.

Miscellaneous

Cannabis Info Museum
Oudezijds Achterburgwal 150, C (624 0386). Tram 4, 9, 16, 24, 25/Metro Nieuwmarkt. **Open** 11am-6pm Mon-Wed; 11am-10pm Thur-Sat; 11am-5pm Sun.
Admission f6. **No credit cards.**
The only one of its kind throughout Europe, the Museum explains the use of marijuana throughout the ages. Various paraphernalia more recently associated with cannabis, such as comics and T-shirts, would be more at home in the shop next door, which sells all the accoutrements for growing the stuff at home. The authorities would like to see both the museum and the shop shut down.
Wheelchair access with assistance.

Don't attempt the **Rijksmuseum** *without a guidebook. See* **review** *page 155.*

The Torture Museum

Leidsestraat 27, C (620 4070). Tram 1, 2, 5, **Open**
10am-7pm daily. **Admission** f7.50; f5.50 over-65s, CJP
card holders, students; f5.50 with museum card; f4
under-12s. **No credit cards.**
Definitely not a museum for the queasy, this museum –
newly and more successfully housed on Leidsestraat –
contains over 60 torture instruments, showing the depths
that man can sink to. The instruments, which come from
all over Europe, are antique (from the Middle Ages to
the nineteenth century). Some of the more gruesome
items include a guillotine and the chair of nails from the
Inquisition. Each device is accompanied by a historical
poster showing how it was used, plus an explanation in
ungrammatical English.

National Spaarpottenmuseum (Piggy Bank Museum)

Raadhuisstraat 12, C (556 7425). Tram 13, 14, 17.
Open 1-4pm Mon-Fri. **Admission** f1; 50c under-13s, CJP
card holders; free with Museum Card. **No credit cards.**
A good place to take kids, the permanent exhibition consists of over 2,000 examples from a vast collection of
12,000 money boxes and piggy banks, brought together
from all over the world by an eccentric former bank
director. Silver savings banks and other antique curiosities are juxtaposed with the more numerous ceramic and
plastic versions in all sorts of shapes and sizes. The presentation is rather unimaginative, but some of the individual pieces are quite extraordinary. The collection is
housed in neon-lit toyshop-like premises near the Dam.
It tends to get busy during school holidays.
Wheelchair access.

Sex Museum

Damrak 18, C (627 7431). Tram 4, 9, 16, 24, 25.
Open 10am-11.30pm daily. **Admission** approx f3.95.
No credit cards.
'Museum' is a pretentious title for this commercial
enterprise behind a fairly respectable-looking façade on
a busy shopping street. The scientific basis of the museum is dubious. The endless display of erotica, including historic objects and images such as lithographs,
etchings, oil paintings, photos, movies and statues, surprises and shocks at first, but becomes somewhat
monotonous after a while. Not for those wanting a
healthy family outing.

Further Afield

Boymans-Van-Beuningen, Rotterdam

Mathenesserlaan 18-20 (010 441 9400). **Open** 10am-
5pm Tue-Sat; 11am-5pm Sun, public holidays.
Admission f3.50; f1.75 CJP card holders; free with
Museum Card, under-16s; group discount (min 15
people)
No credit cards.
The Boymans rivals the Rijksmuseum in the quality of
its canvases and outstrips it in organisation. Much of the
best Dutch art isn't in Holland, but the Boymans has
gems by Van Eijck, Rembrandt, Bosch and the old
masters. A lot of the best French and surrealist art is here
too, along with modernist paintings and sculpture, industrial design and major exhibitions.
Guided tours by prior arrangement. Wheelchair access.

De Lakenhal, Leiden
Oude Singel 28-32 (071 254620). **Open** 10am-5pm
Tue-Sat; 1-5pm Sun, public holidays. **Admission** f2.50;
f1.25 6-16s; free with Museum Card. **No credit cards.**
An awe-inspiring collection of decorative arts and paint-
ings. There's almost too much to see here, but don't
overlook the extraordinary *Last Judgement* by Lucas van
Leyden, Pieter Xavery's charming terracotta court
scene *De Leidsche Vierschaar* or the reconstructed
Guild room upstairs.
*f1.50 for groups of 20 people. Library (10am-12.30pm
Tue, Thur, Fri; 2-5pm Wed).*

Frans Hals Museum, Haarlem
Oudemannenhuis, Groot Heiligland 62 (023 319180).
Open 11am-5pm Tue-Sat; 1-5pm Sun, public holidays.
Admission f4.50; f2 10-18s; free with Museum Card,
under-10s; group discount (min 20 people).
No credit cards.
Some of Hals' finest canvases are here, plus paintings by
his illustrious contemporaries. There are reconstructed
rooms illustrating the building's original use as an
almshouse or *hofje*, the Oudemannenhuis (for elderly
men). Hals is famous for his group portraits of civic
guards and almshouse regents; two of the eight displayed
here depict the regents of the Oudemannenhuis itself.
*Guided tours 1.30pm Sun. Wheelchair access to most of
the museum and toilets for the disabled.*

Mauritshaus, The Hague
Korte Vijverberg 8 (070 365 4779). **Open** 10am-5pm
Tue-Sat; 11am-5pm Sun, public holidays. **Admission**
f6.50; f3.50 under-18s; free with Museum card.
No credit cards.
This museum, in one of the country's finest Golden Age
houses (recently restored), has masterpieces by Rubens,
Van Dyke, the Flemish School and rooms devoted to
Rembrandt, Van Steen, Holbein and Vermeer.

University and Other Collections

Amsterdam has a variety of small, specialised
collections, dealing with subjects ranging from
the life and times of famous Dutch authors
(whose names you might come across on street
signs) to embryological specimens. Museum is
too grand a word for a number of the smaller
collections, which are only really interesting for
connoisseurs. The collections listed can only
be visited by appointment; telephone or write
in advance.

Anatomy

Museum Vrolik
*Entrance on south side of AMC medical faculty,
Meibergdreef 15, 1105 AZ; OE (566 4600). Bus 59, 60,
61, 120, 126.*
The museum (an anatomical embryological laboratory)
contains eighteenth- and nineteenth-century specimens
of human embryos collected by Professor Gerardus
Vrolik and his son Professor Willem Vrolik.

Gas and Electricity

GEB Bedrijfsmuseum
Spaklerweg 20, 1096 BA; OE (597 5226). Bus 46, 169.
Industrial artefacts relating to gas and electricity pro-
duction and distribution.

Literary

Bilderdijkmuseum
*De Boelelaan 1105, 1082 SB; OS (645 4368). Bus 8,
23, 26, 48, 49, 64, 65, 67, 158, 173, 197.*
The life and times of the Dutch writer/academic Willem
Bilderdijk (1756-1831) is illustrated by displays of his
manuscripts, etchings he did himself and personal
belongings.

Frederik van Eedenmuseum
*University Library, Singel 425, 1012 WP; Ç (525
2476). Tram 1, 25.*
The collection includes objects, manuscripts and letters
relating to the Dutch poet, physician and writer Frederik
van Eeden (1860-1932).

Multatuli-Museum
*Korsjespoortsteeg 20, 1015 AR; C (638 1938/624
7427). Tram 1, 2, 5, 13, 17.*
The life of the nineteenth-century writer E Douwes-
Dekker (who wrote under the pseudonym Multatuli) is
illustrated by photographs and other objects. There is
also a library.

Schriftmuseum JA Dortmund
*University Library, Singel 425, 1012 WP; C (525
2476). Tram 1, 25.*
The focus is on the art of writing from approximately
3000BC to the present day.

Railway

Werkspoormuseum
*Oostenburgergracht 77, 1018 NC; IE (625 1035). Bus
22, 28.*
Paintings, prints, models and other objects illustrate the
history of the Dutch railway.

Religious

Historisch Documentatiecentrum Van de Vrije Universiteit
*De Boelelaan 1105, 1082 SB; OS (548 4648). Bus 8,
23, 29, 64, 65, 67, 68, 158, 173, 197.*
The history of the Dutch Protestant University and its
founder Abraham Kuyper is explained with the help of
documents, photos, and artefacts.

Social History

Ferdinand Domela Nieuwenhuis Museum
Herengracht 266, IW (550 1601). Tram 13, 14, 17.
Documents focusing on the life of Ferdinand Domela
Nieuwenhuis (1846-1919, *see chapter* **Between the
Occupations**) and the labour movement.

Instituut voor Sociale Geschiedenis
Cruquiusweg 25, OE (668 5866). Tram 6, 10/Bus 22.
An international library specialising in the social history
of the Western world, run by the Institute for Social
History. The library also contains original writings by
Karl Marx and Friedrich Engels.

Zoology

Instituut voor Taxonomicsch Zoologie
*Entomology Department, Plantage Middenlaan 64, IE
(525 6258). Tram 7, 14.*
Collections of insects from all over the world.

Arts &
Entertainment

The rich mix of entertainment on offer in Amsterdam, much of it accessible to English-speakers, has improved immeasurably in the last decade. We explain how to find out what's on, where the venues are and what they're like, and where to find that late-night bar when it's all over.

Contents

Media

What's in the daily news (and where to buy it), plus the complexities of broadcasting in Europe's most cabled city unravelled.

The Press

For those who can handle the language (and if you know a bit of German you should be able to read some) the Dutch press is extensive – in shades of opinion as well as bulk. One of the most striking aspects of the Dutch press is that several leading papers started life as underground news-sheets during the Nazi occupation. Although today this does not mean these journals fly in the face of injunctions to print investigative truths, it does occasionally give them a mildly anarchic flavour, and a loyal readership.

FOREIGN PRESS

The natural ability and willingness of the locals to pick up foreign languages, and the abundance of tourists, ensure that non-Dutch newspapers and magazines are easily available throughout the city. All the British dailies and Sundays are on sale by mid-morning of the day of publication, as are the US-angled *International Herald Tribune* and *Wall Street Journal Europe*. The press of other major European countries trickles in during the day.

Branches of the AKO and Bruna newsagent chains are located all over town (including Leidsestraat, Centraal Station and Regulierbreestraat in the centre, *see chapter* **Survival** for addresses), and offer a broad range of international publications. But for the best selection head for WH Smith (Kalverstraat 152): its ground floor carries just about every title available in any UK high street branch. The American Discount Book Center (Kalverstraat 185) has the best choice of US periodicals.

Newspapers

De Telegraaf

Politically similar to its British namesake, the conservative *Daily Telegraph*, *De Telegraaf* (f1.35; f1.95 Saturday edition) was the only Dutch paper allowed to publish during the Nazi occupation – not because the people who worked on it were collaborators or even convinced Nazis, but because unlike other papers, it never overtly criticised the occupying government. But any resemblance to the *Telegraph* stops on the front page; it's the closest the Dutch get to a morning tabloid, dressed up as a broadsheet. And like the most notorious of the British tabloids, the *Sun*, it has far and away the biggest circulation, although the titillation is less of the sexual than the pop star/TV personality-scandal variety. Worth buying for the

accommodation ads on a Wednesday (get it early to stand a chance).

Algemeen Dagblad

Milder than *De Telegraaf* (although with headlines still out-screaming the stories), and with a more progressive outlook than most British tabloids, this populist sheet (f1.40; f1.95 Saturday edition) takes the shock-horror approach to more off-beat issues. Its financial pages, like those of *De Telegraaf*, are quite highly regarded.

De Volkskrant

Set up as a Catholic paper in 1922, it shed the religious tag to attract a broadly left-wing audience after the war (during which it was censored). Now the Dutch equivalent of the British *Guardian* or the American *Washington Post*, with occasional eccentric quirks, it's widely read and respected by the professional classes – and very much a paper with which to be seen in cafés. Published by the same company as *Trouw* and *Het Parool* (*see below*), and carrying the same small ads, it's another useful source for local services and accommodation. Price f1.75; f2.15 Saturday edition.

AT5, *a local commercial TV station, was launched in April 1992. See* **review** *page 169.*

NRC Handelsblad

Formed from the merger of two nineteenth-century papers – one from Amsterdam, the other from Rotterdam – this evening daily (f1.60) is one of the few examples of co-operation between the two rival cities. Although sometimes mocked for its intellectual pretensions (some say it thinks it's *Le Monde*) the *NRC* is probably the most respected national, with a well-educated, business-oriented readership. The Thursday *Donderdag Agenda* supplement is an encyclopaedic guide to cultural events nationwide. Price f1.75.

Trouw

Protestant in origin, this national daily (f1.75; f2 Saturday edition) went underground during the war but has been less successful in expanding circulation and moving away from religious identification than *De Volkskrant*: it still publishes a regular church page.

Het Parool

Het Parool ('The Password') was first published in 1941 and rapidly became the main organ of the Resistance *(see chapter* **World War II***)*. Now trying to inch away from strong socialist associations, it has successfully emphasised its role as Amsterdam's local paper – although it is also distributed nationally and covers national and international news (often translating articles from the British *Independent*). At one time seen as the pinnacle of well-written journalism, with novelists such as Simon Carmiggelt providing regular columns, it lost ground during the eighties and is trying to claw back its market share – partly through the 'local' tag. Written in fairly straightforward language, it's a good paper for foreigners to practise Dutch on. It also has some very good examples of the best in Dutch atmospheric news photography, and an excellent example of the best Dutch humour in the regular cartoon 'Het Dagelijkse Leven' (Daily Life). Price f1.50 Mon-Fri; f1.75 Sat.

Het Financieele Dagblad

Strictly for those who need Dutch business/financial news, this paper's international business coverage is thinner that the *Financial Times*, which is easily obtainable on the day of publication. But it is the only Dutch daily with a summary in English, and this gives much more coverage of Dutch affairs that the FT. Price f1.95.

Periodicals

Avenue, Elegance

A monthly upmarket style-bible for glossy living, the large-format *Avenue* (f8.95) appeals to the well-heeled of both sexes as well as wannabes who dream of affording some of its exotic travel recommendations. A similar publication, *Elegance* (f9.95), is directed at wealthy, mature women. Both have beautifully produced photos.

Elsevier, De Tijd, Haagse Post, De Groene Amsterdammer, Forum

Weekly current affairs magazines, these fit into a category known in The Netherlands as *opiniebladen* and as such offer readers a weekly dose of their favourite political medicine.

Nieuwe Revu, Panorama, Privé

Few serious opinions are offered by these high-colour titillators. *Nieuwe Revu* (f3) has youth appeal; *Privé* (f2.55) is famous for its dirt-mongering salaciousness.

Vrij Nederland

Another Resistance baby, this Friday weekly (f5.25) has a strong emphasis on long, mildly investigative stories and culture, particularly literature. Its colour supplement is filled with arty photos.

Listings Magazines

City Life Amsterdam

A monthly listings magazine in English (f4), *City Life* provides comprehensive information on all that's happening in the arts, music, theatre, cinema and the club scene locally, and has interviews and general features. CLA prides itself on being the city's most complete listings publication, not (just) for tourists, with the majority of readers being young Amsterdammers. Available from newsagents, and some shops and hotels.

Uitkrant

Although written in Dutch, this monthly tabloid freesheet offers relatively straightforward, easily decipherable listings, though not much background information. Since it's published by the city council's own cultural service, AUB (which also sells tickets through the Uitburo, *see chapter* **Essential Information**), criticism does not rate as an editorial priority. Available from the Uitburo, central library (*see chapter* **Survival**), and many bookshops.

What's On In Amsterdam

Fortnightly small-format English-language magazine (f2.50), published by the VVV tourist office (*see chapter* **Essential Information**) and aimed squarely at the basic tourist market. Information is limited, and editorial content rarely changes from issue to issue. Again, not noted for its objectivity, and available from newsagents and some hotels.

Radio and TV

Broadcasting in Amsterdam is currently undergoing some major changes. For years protected from commercial pressures, both national and local systems are now being 'liberalised'. The process began in early 1992 with a local re-organisation that brought new, advertising-funded stations on air. National broadcasting looks set to follow the same pattern in the near future.

At the time of writing, Dutch national broadcasting (universally known as 'Hilversum' after the city where it is based) remains one of the few strictly non-commercial systems in Europe. It is also the most complicated. Based on the principle that even the tiniest minority should have its own platform, airtime on all three TV and five radio channels is shared between different organisations, many representing religious and political viewpoints.

The result is a clear distinction between channels and 'stations'. The latter have different names, jingles, announcers and programmes. So, for instance, the Nederland 1 TV channel has four completely different identities depending on who is providing the programmes. On radio, all nine main broadcasters get time on every network. The amount of time, and the proportion of licence and advertising income they get, depends on how many 'members' they have. 'Members' are simply those who subscribe to the organisation's TV and radio guide (on sale at newsagents and supermarkets). So when the Dutch buy a guide, they are effectively making a political

Amsterdam Extra *was the result of a merger between two community radio stations.*
See **review** *page 169.*

statement, although each guide carries details of all programmes.

Regulations ensure that programming is balanced in style, but for years scheduling has been far from user-friendly. Only since mid-1992, in answer to the increasingly competitive broadcasting environment, have Hilversum's broadcasters begun co-operating more closely on programmes and schedules. The Dutch now have a chance to tune in at the same time and on the same frequency each day, and have a reasonable idea of what they'll see or hear.

Commercials are allowed to take up around five per cent of airtime and are scheduled in blocks at regular times: for instance, before and after the news. No programme may be interrupted by an advertisement, and each individual commercial begins and ends with recognisable (and excruciating) jingles to distinguish it from the programme.

CABLE CRAZY

Meanwhile, the audiences have probably voted with their remote controls. Holland is one of the most cabled countries in Europe, with over 80 per cent of homes getting perfect reception of dozens of TV and radio channels from satellite and neighbouring countries. Amsterdam's cable network pipes over 20 channels into virtually every home and hotel in the city.

Although Dutch commercial stations have until now not even been allowed on cable, a few enterprising companies have got round the rules by registering as 'foreign' and beaming their signals via satellite from outside Dutch territory, despite having all their studio facilities inside the country. Consistent and populist, their ratings are steadily increasing.

LOCAL BROADCASTING

Local broadcasting developed in Holland in the eighties, modelled on the national system. Small community radio stations were allowed on air – but with advertising strictly forbidden and transmitter power low, they remained mostly very amateurish. Amsterdam has three local community radio channels (plus three more on cable only) and a cable TV channel. Dozens of organisations share airtime, most representing specialist interest and ethnic groups, and are on air for only an hour or two each day. This system changed in 1992, with the introduction of local commercial radio and TV. Still in their infancy, it remains to be seen how much they will shake up the stuffy face of Dutch broadcasting.

National TV

Nederland 1

Very much the 'establishment' channel, carrying programmes from the Catholic KRO, orthodox Dutch reformed NCRV and independent AVRO. The result is a rather worthy, conservative channel with a bias towards earnest discussion (a Dutch favourite), current affairs, quality drama and documentary, with an appeal to older audiences.

Nederland 2

The home of the two main crypto-commercial stations, Veronica and TROS, and (incongruously) the evangelical EO. The former are younger and more populist than Nederland 1, with more comedy, a lot of popular US programmes (all in English and subtitled), plus talk and game shows. Veronica sometimes airs late-night soft porn. EO, on the other hand, favours 'wholesome' family fare. Nederland 2 is also the home of the Dutch Open University, Teleac.

Nederland 3

Major sporting and cultural/entertainment events, plus general programmes, are broadcast by the NOS, the broadcasters' umbrella organisation, which also provides the news on all three channels. General entertainment comes from the socialist VARA, while on Sundays and Mondays, the radical VPRO offers an intellectual diet of quality documentaries, discussions and comedy, a lot of it culled from Britain's Channel 4.

Cable TV

AT5

Launched in April 1992, the much vaunted local commercial station has got off to a precarious start. A couple of hours-worth of local news, talk and entertainment shows, all made on a very obvious shoestring, are repeated throughout the evening.

Kanaal 5 (SALTO)

A local public access channel, offering time to a variety of community broadcasters, many of them for immigrant communities. Mostly shot on home video equipment, programme quality is usually pretty dodgy, but the highbrow arts shows on Sunday and local news magazine on Wednesdays can be worth catching.

RTL 4

After a shaky start in 1989, when it beat the state in a court battle to be declared 'foreign', this Luxembourg-based channel has proved itself very much to Dutch tastes. It's unashamedly lowbrow, with comedy, soaps, talkshows and lots of ads. But the news service is highly regarded and decent movies turn up pretty regularly (often very late at night). A lot of US, and some British, imports flesh out the schedules, from *The Simpsons* to *Oprah*.

There are also a number of foreign and satellite stations on the cable network: BBC1 and BBC2 (UK); BRT TV1 and TV Twee (Belgium); ARD, ZDF and West 3 (Germany); TV5 (France); RAI Uno (Italy); TRT Int (Turkey); CNN (the US news network); MTV (pop music); Super Channel (music, B-movies and features in English); Eurosport and Sportnet; Lifestyle (soaps and game shows in English); Kindernet (children's cartoons) and Filmnet (pay-TV movies). Several more channels are promised.

Radio

National Stations

Radio 1 (747kHz AM/90.4MHz cable): mostly news, features, debates and sports commentaries; **Radio 2** (92.6MHz FM/90.9MHz cable): MOR and easy listening music, plus chat and some comedy and arts coverage; **Radio 3** (675kHz AM/96.8MHz FM/91.5MHz cable): the national pop station – daytimes are chart/oldies based, the evenings more specialist and adult-oriented;

Radio 4 (98.9MHz FM/92.4MHz cable): classical music; **Radio 5** (1008kHz AM/92.8MHz cable): a kind of dumping ground for everything that doesn't fit anywhere else, particularly minority-interest, educational and ethnic programmes.

Local Stations

Amsterdam Extra/AFM (105.9MHz cable)
Formed in March 1992 from the merger of two community stations, the potential of this radio for 'young Amsterdam' was rather dampened by having its FM frequency taken away, and by constant bickering between the two partners. Daytimes feature upbeat chart sounds, nights include club dance, progressive and specialist music, with some shows in English.
Radio Amsterdam (107.9MHz FM/105.5MHz cable)
Also launched in March 1992, this new commercial station was supposed to provide a full news, information and music service specifically tailored for the city. As it is, it's of real appeal only to diehard Dutch *schlager* (pop) fans.
Radio 100 (100.2MHz FM)
A pirate station that in typical Amsterdam fashion has come to be more-or-less tolerated by the authorities, though occasional raids do close it down briefly. Closely linked to the Tetterode community (*see chapter* **History: Post-war**), it's worth tuning into for a taste of the weird side of local life. In true anarchic fashion, all involved do their own thing: comparatively straightforward dance and world music shows rub shoulders with dub poetry, hardcore punk, political ranting and endless ambient industrial sounds.
Radio Noord Holland (94.3MHz FM/93.3MHz cable)
A regional station within the state system; music is interspersed with reasonably good local news and what's on information. The station to tune to for Amsterdam traffic news, if you speak Dutch.
SALTO Kanaal 3 (106.8MHz FM/103.8MHz cable)
A mishmash of tiny community stations with a mission to 'inform'. Most are ethnic or religious, but of note are MVS (6-9pm), the gay station which features the no-holds-barred English-language talk show *Alien on Sundays*, and MART (10pm-10am) with world music and chat, also sometimes in English.
Other local stations are: SALTO Kanaal 1 (106.1MHz FM/102.4MHz cable), mostly Dutch *schlager* and gospel; SALTO Kanaal 2 (105.2MHz FM/104.6MHz cable), programmes for immigrants; and Concertzender (104.2MHz cable), classical music.

Cable Stations

BBC Radio 4 (106.6MHz; also 198kHz AM): the British national news, talk and drama station. Also clearly audible on long wave in Amsterdam. **BBC World Service** (101.3MHz; also 648kHz AM): international news, plus talks, magazines and some music from London. The AM version also has programmes in French and German. **Concert Radio** (90.0MHz): classical music. **Deutschlandfunk** (97.9MHz): the German national news, talk and music station. **Eurojazz** (99.9MHz): a firm favourite in jazz-crazy Amsterdam. **Hit Radio** (107.9MHz)/Power FM (107.1MHz): soundalike new and old chart hit stations. **Holland FM** (95.5MHz)/RTL 4 Radio (102.9MHz)/Radio Noordzee Nationaal (100.4MHz): MOR music, much of it local, plus chat. **Radio France Internationale** (98.5MHz): the French world service. **Radio 10 Gold** (89.4MHz): oldies. **Sky Radio** (100.9MHz): DJ-free 'soft pop', immensely popular among Dutch thirtysomethings and as aural wallpaper in shops. **VOA Europe** (99.1MHz): the Voice of America's specially tailored service for young Europeans. The accent is on current hit music plus regular news bulletins from the US and around the world, and includes bite-size features on American life and history, all in English.

Children & Parents

As cities go, this is a good place for kids: its size, friendliness and easy-going attitude mean that parents and children should have a hassle-free visit.

Amsterdam wasn't built for kids – which city was? – but its hidden hofjes and beautiful canals with weird and wonderful houseboats (*see chapter* **Sightseeing**) give children the space and the opportunity to explore. In the summer months many activities are organised for school-age children in the city's parks, playgrounds and Buurthuizen (neighbourhood centres, listed as *Buurthuis* in the telephone directory). There's usually an array of reasonably-priced (sometimes free) activities which enable kids to fraternise with their Dutch counterparts.

If the weather drives you indoors, options include one of the many indoor pools (*see chapter* **Sport & Fitness**), a children's theatre performance, or the NINT Museum for a hands-on experience. Check with the VVV (*see chapter* **Essential Information**) about current events, or look in the free monthly events guide *Uitkrant* – listings (under *jeugd*) are mostly in Dutch, but the guide provides telephone numbers, so you can investigate further.

FAMILY LIFE

Dutch families were traditionally quite large until the sixties. By the early seventies, the norm was two kids per family, although three-child families are now more common. In general, women born after World War II have started and completed their families at an older age. The rise of the divorce rate during the eighties means that about one third of children have divorced parents, and there are many one-parent families. That parent is usually the mother, who in some cases has chosen to bring up a child by herself.

The Dutch don't make a great distinction between the worlds of children and adults. Children are often taken along to restaurants, parties and other occasions – usually no one minds their presence.

SCHOOL DAYS

Most children spend between a few months and a couple of years at a pre-school crèche before going to a *basisschool*. At the age of 12, pupils make a choice between different kinds of secondary school, depending on their academic or practical ability and their intentions to work as soon as possible, or take professional training or higher education. Each child is schooled for a minimum of ten years (normally up to the age of 16), and if they start work early, they must complete their studies part-time.

LEGALITIES

About a third of the Dutch population – 5.5 million people – is under the age of 25. Legally, children become adults at the age of 18, when they can vote. However, the age of consent is 12 (though if a child between 12 and 16 is having sex with somebody over 16, the parents can object through the courts); beer may be bought from the age of 16, spirits at 18.

Kinderrechtswinkel (Children's Rights Shop)

Brouwersgracht 44, IW (626 0067). Tram 1, 2, 4, 5, 13, 17. **Open** by appointment (*consultations* 2-5pm Wed, Sat).

This office supplies information about children's legal rights, and the responsibilities of teachers and employers, to children under 18. Kids may phone or visit; staff will answer questions from adults, but prefer dealing with the children involved.

Kindertelefoon (Childline)

(622 4455). **Open** 2-8pm daily.

Young people from 8 to 18 are welcome to phone this line to get an answer to questions on the trivial, like cake recipes, to the important, such as matters concerning parents and teachers (victimisation, child-abuse, running away from home and so on). Staff do not give information on children's entertainment.

Transport

The centre of Amsterdam is small and well laid-out, so almost all the interesting places for youngsters are easy to reach on foot, although navigating a pushchair over the older cobbled sections can be frustrating. The fastest and most convenient way to get around is by tram, bus or metro, although some of the older buses and trams can be hard to get on, and you have to remember that the bottom step on a tram must be pressed down to keep the doors

NINT Museum of Science & Technology.
See **review**.

open (*see chapter* **Essential Information**). For fun, go by water taxi or rent a pedalo (*see chapter* **Sightseeing**). Children can steer and handle a pedalo by themselves from about the age of ten, but remind them to navigate on the right-hand side of the waterway. Pleasant, and free, is a trip on the River IJ ferry to Amsterdam North; boats leave from behind Centraal Station every ten minutes.

Electrische Museumtramlijn
Haarlemmermeerstation, Amstelveenseweg 264 (673 7538). Tram 6, 16. **Departs** *Apr-Jun, Sept-Oct* every 30 mins, 10.30am-5.30pm Sun; *July, Aug* 10am, 2.15pm, 3.30pm Tue, Thur, Sat; every 30 mins, 10.30am-5.30pm Sun. **Admission** f4 adult; f2 4-12s; free under-4s. **No credit cards.**
This is not so much a museum as a pleasure ride. The antique electric tram carriages come from cities throughout Europe and the 30-minute tram ride in one of the colourful old trolleys south through Amsterdamse Bos (*see chapters* **Sightseeing** and **Sport & Fitness**) to Amstelveen is particularly enjoyable.

Attractions

Children's Farms

Artis Zoo Children's Farm
Artis Zoo, Plantage Kerklaan 40, IE (523 3400). Tram 7, 9, 14. **Open** *Zoo* 9am-5pm daily; *Children's farm* 10am-1pm, 2-4.30pm, daily. **Admission** *Zoo & farm* f17.50 adults; f10 under-10s; free under-4s; group discount (min 20 people). **No credit cards.**
The farm animals at Artis Zoo Children's Farm are very used to visitors, so you can get up close and stroke some of them. But they're inquisitive and will nibble your valuables if you don't keep them hidden. The farm is part of Artis Zoo, which also houses Artis Planetarium (for both, *see chapter* **Sightseeing**) and the Zoological Museum (*see chapter* **Museums**), so you can have a full day out for one admission price. Its popularity is a problem, though; the farm gets very busy and the staff aren't able to give the sort of attention you get at the free local *kinderboerderijen* (children's farms) we list below.

De Dierenpijp
Lizzy Ansinghstraat 82, OS (664 8303). Tram 12, 25. **Open** 1-5pm Mon, Wed-Sun. **Admission** free.
Centrally located in the Pijp district, this farm is also a

short walk from NINT (*see below* **Museums**). You can meet all the usual farm beasts here, but without the crowds to be found at Artis Zoo (*above*).

Het Ruige Riet
President Allendelaan 2, OW (611 8851). Bus 19, 68. **Open** 8.30am-5pm Mon-Thur, Sat, Sun. **Admission** free.
This children's farm is situated in Sloterpark (*see chapter* **Sport & Fitness**). There are animal feeding times at 8.30am and 4pm, and children can help. Between May and August you can watch the staff make goat's cheese.

De Uylenburg
Staalmeesterslaan 420, OW (618 5235). Bus 18, 19, 48, 64. **Open** *Sept-Apr* 10am-4pm daily; *May-Aug* 10am-5pm daily. **Admission** free.
A city farm in Rembrandtpark, which also has a playground and a place where children can build simple huts under supervision. Free horse rides are also offered in the park.

Museums

See chapter **Museums** for details of the **Netherlands Maritime Museum**, where children can handle exhibits on the ships docked outside; the **Aviodome**, an aviation museum with an exciting flight simulator; and the **Piggy Bank Museum**, full of unusual money boxes. For **Artis Planetarium** and **Madame Tussaud's** wax museum, *see chapter* **Sightseeing**.

TM Junior
Linnaeusstraat 2, OE (568 8233 Mon-Thur). Tram 9, 10, 14. **Open** entrance by booking only, two weeks in advance. **Admission** f3 6-12s. **No credit cards.**
TM Junior is a branch of the Tropenmuseum designed especially for children aged between 6 and 12 years. Guided tours are the only way to see the museum: they last 75 minutes and start at 12.15pm, 1.30pm and 2.45pm on Sundays and public holidays; and at 11am on weekdays during school holidays. TM Junior's long-running exhibitions introduce young people to the cultures of the developing world in a personal way: staff (who speak English) play with their young visitors, telling stories and answering questions, and children can participate in all sorts of workshop activities. Throughout June 1994 you can see 'Invisible Guest': an exhibition about gods, demons and ancestors in Bali and the role they play in daily life.
Shop. Wheelchair access.

NINT Museum of Science & Technology
Tolstraat 129, OS (570 8110). Tram 4. **Open** 10am-5pm Mon-Fri; noon-5pm Sat, Sun. *Closed* 25 Dec, 1 Jan. **Admission** f7.50 adults; f5 under-13s; free under-6s. **No credit cards.**
Everybody is busy doing something at NINT, one of the few museums in which visitors are allowed to touch and handle objects, and where children's needs are considered in the design: even the holograms are at kids' height. Test your reaction times, or see your shadow frozen on the fluorescent wall. In the main hall upstairs the computers ask you to play with them; they have menus in English and all display texts are in four languages, including English. NINT is particularly stimulating for children over the age of six, but younger kids will have a nice time here too. Staff are very helpful.
Baby-changing facilities. Café (10am-4pm Mon-Fri; noon-4pm Sat, Sun). Shop. Wheelchair access; toilets for the disabled.

Out of Town

Children can enjoy trips to the windmills, castles, bulb fields and traditional towns near Amsterdam (*see chapter* **Excursions in Holland**). The following places are especially suitable for kids.

De Efteling, Kaatsheuvel

Europalaan 1, Kaatsheuvel, Noord Brabant (04167 8811). **Getting there** *car* 110km (68 miles) from Amsterdam, off A261 just north of Tilburg; *rail* NS Day Excursion ticket (includes train, bus and admission). **Open** *Easter-Oct* 10am-6pm daily. **Admission** f28; f25 group discount (min 20 people). **Credit** AmEx, DC, MC, V.
The brainchild of illustrator Anton Pieck, this is the most original theme park in The Netherlands. Pieck designed an enormous fairytale forest in which Sleeping Beauty's bosom rises and falls with each breath, rubbish bins talk and fakirs fly on magic carpets. Inevitably, there are also the usual roller-coasters and fairground rides. There's also a hotel, open all year (04167 8200).
Café and restaurant. Shops. Wheelchair access; toilets for the disabled.

Land van Ooit, Drunen

Parklaan 40 (04163 77775). **Getting there** *car* A2, then take A59 to Drunen before 's Hertogenbosch; *train* to 's Hertogenbosch then bus 137, or NS Day Excursion ticket (includes train, bus and admission). **Open** *Easter-mid Oct* 10am-6pm daily (closed selected Mon, Tue in Sept, Oct; phone to check). **Admission** f18 adult; f14 4-11s; free under-4s. **No credit cards**.
A fantasy park that's particularly good for under-12s and is unusual in having no machine-powered rides. Children themselves operate pedal cars shaped like a shoe or a pie, or a swan-like pedalo on water: so the rides are slower – and safer – than those in other parks. Kids

can climb into the tree-house café or over statues of giants and test their strength against them. Actors dress up as princesses, lords and such like, giving performances around the park (in Dutch, although if crowds are small they may explain in English). More easily understood are the shows in the puppet theatre. There's a brochure in English.
Restaurants. Wheelchair access; wheelchairs available free; toilets for the disabled.

Linnaeushof, Bennebroek

Rijksstraatweg 4, Bennebroek (02502 47624). **Getting there** *car* 20km (13 miles) on A5 to Haarlem, then on N208 south; *rail* NS Day Excursion ticket (includes train, bus and admission). **Open** *Apr-Oct* 10am-6pm daily. **Admission** f10; f8 group discount (min 20 people). **No credit cards**.
Between Haarlem and the Lisse bulb fields is this huge leisure park, formerly the estate of the Swedish Botanist Carl von Linné. The pleasant grounds of woods, gardens and picnic-spots include some 300 attractions designed for children, including a Wild West train, 'moonwalkers', pedalos, mini-golf, trampolines and (for an extra charge) go-karts.
Café and restaurant. Shops. Wheelchair access; toilets for the disabled.

Madurodam, The Hague

Haringkade 175, The Hague (070 355 3900). **Getting there** *car* 57km (35 miles) on A4; *rail* direct to The Hague or NS Day Excursion ticket (train, bus and admission). **Open** *Mar-May* 9am-10.30pm daily; *June-Aug* 9am-11pm daily; *Sept* 9am-9.30pm daily; *Oct-Jan* 9am-6pm daily. **Admission** f12.50 adult; f7.50 4-11s; free under-2s; f10 group discounts (min 20 people). **Credit** AmEx, $£TC.
This miniature village is popular with younger children, less so with taller tourists prone to back-ache when wading through the knee-high buildings. An odd jumble of

Kids can try out their circus skills at the **Kindertheater Elleboog**. *See* **review** *page 173.*

the country's most famous features, it incorporates working models of Rotterdam's port, Schiphol airport and the inevitable windmills. Less predictably, it prides itself on keeping up with the latest architecture. The best time to go is on a summer's evening, when the models are lit from inside. There's another miniature town at Middelburg, Zeeland (*see chapter* **The Provinces**), called Walcheren (Koepoortlaan 1, 01180 12525, open daily Apr-Oct).

Café and restaurant. Shop. Wheelchair access; wheelchairs for hire; toilets for the disabled.

Entertainment

Parks and Playgrounds

Parks (*see chapters* **Sightseeing** *and* **Sport & Fitness**) are the best places for children's entertainment, whether for a puppet show, boating lakes or playgrounds. **Vondelpark** is famous for its summer programme of free afternoon entertainment, which might include musicians, mime artists and acrobats; Amstelpark on Europalaan has train and pony rides. But Amsterdam's larger green areas are on the edge of town: **Amsterdamse Bos**, in the New South, has boating lakes, an open-air theatre, large playgrounds and wild deer; **Gaasperpark**, in Amsterdam South East, has superb sport and playground facilities including a paddling pool; and **Twiske**, north of the IJ River, is a pleasant area of countryside.

During the summer months (and in some school holidays), there are supervised activities such as trampolining, games, face painting and clowning sessions. Phone the Sport and Recreation Department (596 9111) or look under *Buurthuis* in the telephone directory for details. All the parks have playgrounds and most public spaces in local neighbourhoods include the obligatory sand-pit or slide and climbing frame. Many parks now include 'gedoog zones', separated from the main park areas, where dogs can run and waste to their hearts content.

In winter, older children can try the ice-skating rink in Leidseplein – it's not a good option for smaller children though, as they are likely to get run down by fast-moving teenagers.

Theatre and Circus

The children's theatre phoneline (622 2999), has recorded information in Dutch.

Kindertheater Elleboog
Passeerdersgracht 32, IW (626 9370). Tram 5, 7, 10/Bus 67, 171, 172. **Circus sessions** *non-members* alternate weekends 1.30-5pm Sat; 10.30am-4pm Sun; *club* 3.30-5.30pm Mon, Thur; 6.30-8.30pm Tue; 1.15-3pm, 3.30-5.15pm, Wed; 10.30am-12.30pm Sat. **Admission** *non-member sessions* f5 Sat; f7.50 Sun; *club membership* f40 per year, plus f1.50 per visit. **No credit cards.**
At the Elleboog circus, kids aged from 6 to 16 can try out circus skills, learning conjuring tricks, make-up skills, unicycle riding, juggling and tight-rope walking. The non-member sessions are always busy, mostly with

Dutch kids, but the volunteer staff do speak English. The club has about 400 members, who attend once a week for drama sessions and to experiment with theatre and circus equipment. Disabled children are welcome. *Book in advance (10am-noon, by phone). Drinks provided. Wheelchair access.*

De Krakeling
Nieuwe Passeerdersstraat 1, IW (625 3284/624 5123). Tram 7, 10. **Shows** 2pm Wed, Sat, Sun; 8pm Fri. **Admission** f7.50 adults with child, f12.50 unaccompanied; f5 4-17s. **No credit cards.**
De Krakeling has separate productions suitable for over-12s and under-12s – phone to check what's on. For non-Dutch speakers, there are puppet and mime shows. Shows are listed in a programme available from the theatre and in *Uitkrant*. *Wheelchair access.*

Poppentheater Diridas
Hobbemakade 68, OS (662 1588). Tram 16. **Shows** *under-5s* 11am Sun; *over-5s* 3pm Sat, Sun. Closed Aug. **Admission** f3 under-5s show; f4 over-5s show. **No credit cards.**
Shows at Diridas Puppet Theatre feature either marionettes or glove puppets. Every Sunday, there's a new play for the under-5s. The show for older kids is in Dutch, but if you're foreign, tell the puppeteer in advance and you'll be given a short summary of the plot before the play starts. Children celebrating a birthday get special attention. *Book in advance (from 10am Fri-Sun).*

Children's Films

There are a few special children's film shows at the **Kriterion**, **Rialto** and at the **Filmmuseum** (*see chapter* **Film**). Most films for the under-10s are dubbed into Dutch (indicated by the words 'Nederlands gesproken'). However, most family-oriented films are sub-titled.

Babyminders

If there's somewhere you're unable to take your little darling to – or if you need a rest from your *enfant terrible* – contact the service listed below. Unfortunately, babysitters are the only option, since Amsterdam lacks available crèches where children can be left with others their own age. Babysitting in a hotel is usually less comfortable than at a home, so you'll be charged a higher rate, although a number of hotels offer their own babysitting service. After midnight only night-buses operate, so if you're staying in a suburb, you'll be asked to take the babysitter home or pay for a taxi.

Oppascentrale Kriterion
Roetersstraat 170, OS (624 5848). Tram 6, 7, 10. **Open** *booking* 5.30-7pm daily. **Rates** *basic charge* f4, *then 7pm-midnight* f5 per hour; *midnight-3am* f7 per hour; *3am-7am* f10 per hour; *8am-7pm* f6 per hour; f2.50 supplement on total bill for Fri, Sat evenings; f20 minimum charge. **No credit cards.**
Male and female registered students, all of whom are vetted, are employed by this babysitting service. They're particularly busy at weekends, so it's best to book in advance.

Clubs

Small enough to be friendly, but with regular injections of international DJs and sounds, Amsterdam's clubs can tempt the most jaded of revellers.

Amsterdam nightlife has a relaxed and carefree mood that overrides the lack of an individual style. In recent years the post-house music crowd has started something of a club-culture scene in music and fashion, but it's the laid-back attitude of the locals that gives special appeal to a night out.

A great advantage is that nearly all clubs are situated within the relatively small city centre. Distances between venues are walkable, and for many people an evening out means a trek around a few different clubs. Another advantage is that admission prices are extremely low, although they can rise a little at weekends. Bar prices are also very reasonable. However, tipping the doorman when you leave is an established custom – expect to donate at least five guilders.

Most clubs open at 11pm but rarely get going until 1am or 2am. Although there has been a crackdown on late licences, most places stay open until 4am and an hour later at weekends. Watch out for rogue taxi drivers who sometimes wait outside busy clubs (official taxis never do this). They have been known to threaten to drop you off in the middle of nowhere unless you give them all your cash.

The Roxy is the only club with a strict membership policy.

GOING UNDERGROUND

It was once possible to attend what locals would call a 'new-wave' club and hear a mixture of music ranging from punk through to hip hop. These have now been replaced by specialist clubs and one-nighters. Often top guest DJs from the UK or USA are the attraction, although the standards of local DJs are high.

In the Leidseplein and Rembrandtsplein areas you will find a selection of commercial discos playing chart music. Some are quite tacky, attracting an out-of-town crowd known locally as the 'Leidseplein Public', and a Saturday night drunken punch-up may be hard to avoid. One of the better venues is **Bunnies**.

Local club culture has seen many changes in the past few years. With the advent of house music, big underground dance parties started taking place in large warehouses around town, all reflecting a similar atmosphere of drug-induced unity. These days the rave scene is more fragmented. At weekends it will always

be possible to find a house-party, usually with an entrance fee of between about f25 and f50. Mainly illegal, these parties last beyond 6am, sometimes even longer. Most are allowed to go ahead by the authorities, and more and more organisers are trying to obtain licences.

There are also numerous smaller, more intimate all-night parties around – check local record shops and clubwear outlets for details.

Many clubs hold one-night events, with regular DJs and hosts; some promote live acts. For example, at the time of writing, **Mazzo** puts on a jazz dance night (Wednesdays) and a progressive house night (Fridays).

The Clubs

April's Exit
Reguliersdwarsstraat 42, C (625 8788). Tram 1, 2, 4, 5, 9, 14, 16, 24, 25. **Open** 11pm-4am Mon-Thur, Sun; 11pm-5am Fri, Sat. **Admission** free.
The dancefloor is reached through a comfortable bar. This is a male gay club (although women are admitted) that attracts a trendy crowd. Spectacular lights and a good mix of current upbeat dance music make this small club worth checking out.

Bunnies
Korte Leidsedwarsstraat 26, IS (622 6622). Tram 1, 2, 5, 6, 7, 10. **Open** 10pm-4am Mon-Thur, Sun; 10pm-5am Fri, Sat. **Admission** f2.50.
One of the best of the small discos in the Leidseplein area. A good sound system and cosy bar area make this a good place to go if you are looking for an undemanding night out. The dress code is conventional.

Cash
Leidseplein 12, IS (627 6544). Tram 1, 2, 5, 6, 7, 10. **Open** 10pm-4am Thur-Sun. **Admission** f10.
Well at least they're honest! The name says it all. This is a fairly small, unashamedly commercial disco that plays top 40 music, complete with tacky décor, thick-pile carpets and plastic palm trees. Smart attire essential.

Chic
Rozengracht 133, IW (622 1031). Tram 13, 14, 17. **Open** 10pm-4am Thur-Sun. **Admission** f10.
A small club, Caribbean in flavour, playing African, reggae, salsa and soft soul to a mainly Surinam and Turkish crowd. Dress smartly. Look out for posters and leaflets for reggae and salsa events at the Rotaanhuis, a band venue below Chic.

Dansen bij Jansen
Handboogstraat 11, C (620 1779). Tram 1, 2, 5. **Open** 11pm-4am Sun-Thur; 11pm-5.30am Fri, Sat. **Admission** f3.50-f4.
If you want to meet the town's student population, then

STOP
FASCISM!

Subscribe for one year by sending cheque or postal order for £24 (UK), £32 (Europe) or £52 (rest of world) in sterling to Levelprint Ltd., i-D Magazine, 44 Earlham St., London WC2H 9LA, England or tel. 071 240 3282.

Mazzo, *home to various one-nighters. See* **review**.

this is the place. It gets packed on most term-nights although the sound system is weedy and the music selection very safe. Officially this is a student-only club and you need a student card to get in. No dress restrictions.

Escape
Rembrandtsplein 11, IS (622 3542). Tram 4, 9, 14. **Open** 10pm-4am Sun-Thur; 10pm-5am Fri, Sat. **Admission** f10.
A huge cavernous commercial disco. The impressive lighting complete with lasers and giant video screen can't disguise the fact that the place has no real atmosphere. Dress conventionally, but note that no jackets or trainers are allowed.

iT
Amstelstraat 24, IS (625 0111). Tram 4, 9, 14. **Open** 11pm-4am Sun, Wed, Thur; 11pm-5am Fri, Sat. **Admission** about f10.
The largest gay club in town, with a mixed crowd on Thursday and Sunday. It gets packed on a regular basis; hi-NRG and house music are the sounds played.

Korsakoff
Lijnbaansgracht 161, C (625 7854). Tram 10, 13, 14, 17. **Open** 11pm-4am Mon-Thur, Sun; 11pm-5am Fri, Sat. **Admission** usually free.
An alternative grunge club where live bands are featured on Wednesdays. Sounds include hip-hop, metal and even crossover rock. Small but friendly.

Mazzo
Rozengracht 114, IW (626 7500). Tram 13, 14, 17. **Open** 10pm-2am Sun-Thur; 10pm-3am Fri, Sat. **Admission** free.
Plenty of place to sit and talk as well as great visuals and a neat dance area make this one of the most relaxed clubs in town. Jazz dance through to techo is played, and guest international DJs are featured. The sound system lacks bass, but punters don't seem to mind, as the club gets very busy. There are no dress restrictions and the door personnel are friendly.

Melkweg
Lijnbaansgracht 234, IW (624 8492). Tram 1, 2, 5, 6, 7, 10. **Membership** f3.50. **Admission** times and prices vary according to programme.
This multi-media centre functions mainly as a live venue, but at weekends after the bands finish, a varied mix of dance music is played. There are no dress restrictions.

(36 Op De Schaal Van) Richter
Reguliersdwarsstraat 36, IS (626 1573). Tram 1, 2, 5. **Open** 11pm-4am Sun-Thur; 11pm-5am Fri, Sat. **Admission** f7.50-f10.
A small tow-tiered club, which has a good sound system, three bars and plenty of areas to sit and talk. Officially you have to be a member, but if you look smart, you stand a good chance of getting in.

Roxy

Singel 465, C (620 0354). Tram 16, 24, 25. **Open**
11pm-4am Sun, Wed, Thur; 11pm-5am Fri, Sat.
Admission f7.50-f10.
An old converted cinema with a large dancefloor and
upstairs balcony. A loud high-quality sound system just
about combats the acoustic problems of the high ceiling.
Two bars make getting a drink easy, but unfortunately
there are very few places to sit and get away from the
music. The Roxy can be hard to get in, especially at weekends, unless you have a membership card. Wear something trendy.

Soul Kitchen

Amstelstraat 32, C. Tram 4, 9, 14. **Open** 11pm-5am
Fri, Sat.
This spacious club plays a truly varied selection of music,
from sixties soul through seventies disco to the present day.
The age group is slightly older than the usual club crowd,
and there are big queues despite the size of the place.

Out of Town

Distances from Amsterdam are so small that
many people regularly make the effort to travel out to these three clubs. All three frequently provide a free coach service to and from the
centre of Amsterdam for special events.

The Palace

Korte Hogendijk 2, Zaandam (075 700811). **Open**
9pm-4am Thur-Sun. **Admission** f5 Thur, Fri, Sun; f10
Sat. **Credit** AmEx, MC, V.
A huge, purpose-built, glittering discotheque with
expensive lighting effects and a large and loud sound
system. Hip-hop and swing-beat are very popular.
Many local and a few big-name American acts perform
live. Regular after-hour parties take place from
5.30am-noon every first Sunday morning of the
month.

Stalker

Kromme Elleboogsteeg 20, Haarlem (023 314652).
Open 11pm-3am Thur; 11pm-5.30am Fri, Sat; 10pm-
3am Sun. **Admission** free Thur, Sun; f5 Fri, Sat.
No credit cards.
Hidden down a dark alley in this picturesque town
is this small but ambitious club. Lots of guest DJs
and acts from Amsterdam perform here. The club
has an excellent sound system and attracts a lively
crowd.

De Waakzaamheid

Hoogstraat 4, Koog a/d Zaan (075 285829). **Open** *café*
7pm-2am daily; *disco* 7pm-5am Fri, Sat. **Admission**
f7.50. **No credit cards.**
In the middle of a sleepy village just outside
Zaandam, this adventurous venue attracts a mixed
crowd from the surrounding towns. Housed in a
beautiful old wooden building, it claims to have
staged one of the last concerts by Billie Holiday in
the fifties. Nowadays you get a surprisingly upfront
dance mix from a variety of local DJs and the occasional guest from the UK. A good range of different
beers, excellent bar food and a separate salsa/jazz
room are also big attractions.

Dance

In the last decade, dance in The Netherlands has blossomed: Amsterdam is where most of the movement occurs.

The Netherlands has been exposed to a diverse collection of cultures through its pre-eminence as a trading nation, and in recent years this contact has given Dutch dance a refreshing vitality. Up until the seventies, two companies dominated the scene: **Het Nationale Ballet** and the **Nederlands Dans Theater** (*see under* **Companies**), but over the past decade the situation has changed dramatically. Foreign artists have settled in Amsterdam, giving rise to new and diverse modern dance groups. Now you can find post-modern dance New York-style, German expressionistic dance, or dance with its roots in the Orient or in jazz.

Choreography is often more of a strong point than technique, though the quality of dance academies has improved recently. Look out for Truus Bronkhorst, an intense and striking performer. Lisa Marcus is another special talent – originally from America, her work is theatrical and daring. Other names to watch are Angelika Oei, Harijono Roebana and Maria Voortman. Also noteworthy are the innovative choreographer's collective Coup d'Amour, and Dansgroep Charmante Haaien (the Charming Sharks).

Tickets can be purchased from **AUB Uitburo** or the **VVV** offices (for both *see chapter* **Essential Information**). To find out which companies are currently performing in the city, pick up the latest edition of *Uitkrant* magazine, free at every venue.

FESTIVALS AND EVENTS

The **Groningen Festival**, in the north of the country, is a choreographers' competition where prizes are awarded for short ensemble choreographies. It takes place every other year; the next one is in 1993. Also biennial is **Cadans** (next in 1994) in Den Haag, where modern dance is showcased. Information about festivals, competition events, performances, courses and workshops can be obtained from the **Theater Instituut Nederland**, Herengracht 168, IS (623 5104). Open 11am-5pm Mon-Sat.

Venues

Bellevue

Leidsekade 90, IS (624 7248). Tram 1, 2, 5, 6, 7, 10. **Open** *information and bookings* 10am-4pm Mon-Fri; 11am-4pm Sat, Sun; *ticket office* 7.30-8.30pm before performances. **Tickets** f17.50, f15; f12.50 CJP card holders. **Performances** 8.30pm. **No credit cards**.
Modern dance companies such as Dansgroep Krisztina de Châtel (*listed under* **Companies**) and Reflex (*under* **Companies: Out of Town**) often perform at this handsome, small theatre.
Café. Wheelchair access by arrangement.

De Brakke Grond

Nes 45, C (626 6866). Tram 4, 9, 14, 16, 24, 25. **Open** *box office* 10am-1.30pm, 2-4pm, Mon-Sat; also 7pm-start of performance. **Tickets** f17.50; f12.50 CJP cards holders and over 65s. **Performances** 8.30pm. **No credit cards.**
You'll find this place in 'Amsterdam's theatre boulevard' – a small street near the Dam. De Brakke Grond is a Flemish centre for the arts, and it's where to find the best of Belgian dance. *See also chapter* **Theatre.**
Café (open 11am-1am Mon-Thur; 11am-2am Fri, Sat). Wheelchair access to Expozaal and Rodezaal only.

Captain Fiddle

Kloveniersburgwal 86, C (623 0363). Tram 9, 14, 16, 24, 25/Metro Nieuwmarkt. **Open** *information and booking* 10am-5pm Mon-Fri; *box office* 8-8.30pm Wed-Sat. **Tickets** f10. **Performances** 9pm. **No credit cards.**

*The modern **Muziektheater** – home to the Nationale Ballet and Netherlands Opera. See review page 180.*

A fringe theatre, permanently suffering from a lack of money, where young dance and theatre companies stage productions. Four performances are staged every week from October to June.
Bar. Wheelchair access with assistance.

Danswerkplaats Amsterdam
Overamstelstraat 39, OE (694 9466). Tram 8, 15/Metro Wibautstraat. **Open** *box office* one hour before performance. **Tickets** f10; f7.50 CJP card holders. **Performances** usually 8pm. **No credit cards.**
The only venue permanently dedicated to dance. It's a small, informal theatre, situated a little outside the city centre near Wibautstraat. Four or five nights a week it hosts shows by new companies and artists.

Frascati
Nes 63 (box office Nes 45), C (622 7860). Tram 4, 9, 14, 16, 24, 25. **Open** *box office* 10am-4pm, 7-9pm, Mon-Sat. **Tickets** f15;f10 CJP card holders. **Performances** *Frascati 1* 7.30pm; *Frascati 2* 9pm. **No credit cards.**
Two halls that house modern dance companies such as Dansproduktie (*see below* **Companies**).
Café (open 4pm-1am Mon-Thur; 4pm-2am Fri, Sat). Wheelchair access. Toilets for the disabled.

De Meervaart
Osdorpplein 205, OW (610 7498). Tram 19. **Open** *box office* 11am-4pm Mon-Sat; one hour before performance. **Tickets** f15-f25; reductions for CJP card holders, over-65s. **Performances** 8.15pm, 9pm. **No credit cards.**
Keep an eye on the Meervaart, a middle-sized theatre in Osdorp, a suburb in the west of Amsterdam. This unbecoming location sometimes surprises by staging interesting dance performances.
Café (open 10.30am-1 hour after performance Mon-Sat). Wheelchair access. Toilets for the disabled.

Muziektheater
Waterlooplein 22, C (625 5455). Tram 9, 14/Metro Waterlooplein. **Open** *box office* 10am-6pm Mon-Sat; noon-6pm Sun. **Tickets** f20-f45; reductions for CJP card holders, over-65s. **Performances** 8.15pm. **No credit cards.**
The new Muziektheater is Amsterdam at its most ambitious. The plush crescent-shaped building with the Stadhuis (town hall) at the back opened in 1986, seats 1,500 and is the home of both the Nationale Ballet (*see below* **Companies**) and the Nederlands Opera. The big stage is also used by visiting companies such as the Royal Ballet, the Frankfurt Ballet and the Merce Cunningham Company. The panoramic glass walls of the three-level lobbies give an impressive view of the River Amstel by night. *See also chapter* **Post-war** *and chapter* **Music: Classical & Opera.**
Wheelchair access and toilets for the disabled.

Perron 2
Arie Biemondstraat 107, OW (612 4324). Tram 1, 6, 7, 17. **Open** *information and booking* 11am-1pm Mon-Fri; performance weekends 11am-1pm Sat, Sun. **Tickets** f7. **Performances** 8.30pm. **No credit cards.**
The dance studio at Perron 2 stages performance weekends two or three times a month. Modern dancers who studied at one of the Amsterdam dance academies often top the bill.
Bar.

Felix Meritis Theater
Felix Meritis Building, Keizersgracht 324, IW (information 9am-5pm Mon-Fri 626 2321). Tram 1, 2, 5. **Open** *box office* 3pm-start of performance Tue-Sat; *telephone bookings* 3-7.30pm daily. **Tickets** f16.50, f12.50; reductions for CJP holders, over-65s. **Performances** 8pm Tue-Sat. **No credit cards.**

The theatre has a total of three halls, and used to be a centre of communist activity. The Amsterdam Government now wants to close the building and turn it into a centre for new music. However, the theatre seems to be winning the battle. *See also chapter* **Theatre.**

De Stadsschouwburg
Leidseplein 26, IS (624 2311). Tram 1, 2, 5, 7, 10. **Open** *box office* 10am-6pm Mon-Sat; 75 mins before performance. **Tickets** f15-f45; reductions for CJP card holders, over-65s. **Performances** 7.30pm, 8.15pm. **No credit cards.**
Together with the American Hotel, this nineteenth-century building dominates Leidseplein. Performances range from musicals to experimental theatre and modern dance. The smaller Bovenzaal often gives space to small dance companies. *See also chapter* **Theatre.**

Soeterijn
Linnaeusstraat 2 (568 8500). Tram 9, 10, 14. **Open** *telephone bookings* 2-4pm Mon-Fri; *box office* one hour before performance. **Tickets** f12.50-f22.50. **Performances** usually 8pm. **No credit cards.**
Located in the Tropen Instituut, this theatre holds regular non-western dance programmes, as well as musical and theatrical events.

Het Veemtheater
Van Diemenstraat 410, IW (626 0112). Tram 3/Bus 28. **Open** *box office and information* 10am-9pm Mon-Sat. **Tickets** f12.50; f10 CJP card holders. **Performances** 9pm. **No credit cards.**
A former warehouse next to the port, which specialises in mime and movement theatre.
Café (open 8pm-1 hour after performance ends).

Out of Town

AT&T Danstheater
Schedeldoekshaven 60, 2511 EN, Den Haag (070 360 9931). **Open** *box office* 10am-3pm Mon-Sat; one hour before performance. **Tickets** f35; occasional reductions for CJP card holders. **Performances** 8.15pm; *matinées* 2.30pm. **No credit cards.**
Since 1987 this venue in The Hague has been the home of the Nederlands Dans Theater (*see below* **Companies**). The building's design, by leading Dutch architect Rem Koolhaas, is both daring and handsome. It's considered to be a much better venue than Amsterdam's Muziektheater, as it was designed exclusively for dance.
Wheelchair access by arrangement.

Rotterdamse Schouwburg
Schouwburgplein 25, 3012 CL, Rotterdam (010 404 4111). **Open** *box office* 11am-7pm daily; one hour before performance. **Tickets** f30-f45; reductions for CJP card holders, over-65s. **Performances** 8.15pm, 8.30pm. **Credit** Schouwburg credit card.
Designed by Dutch architect Wim Quist, this large theatre first opened its doors in 1988. Because of its square shape it has been nicknamed the '*kist*' (box) of Quist'. It plays host to the bigger national companies as well as dance troupes from abroad.
Bar. Café. Shop. Wheelchair access; toilets for the disabled.

Toneelschuur
Smeedestraat 23, 2011 RE, Haarlem (023 312 439). **Open** *box office* 3-6pm Mon-Sat; also from 7.30pm. **Tickets** f15; CJP card holders f10. **Performances** 8.30pm. **No credit cards.**
Many dance and theatre lovers from Amsterdam go to Haarlem (15 minutes away by train, *see chapter* **The Randstad**) to congregate at the Toneelschuur. This the-

atre has two halls and is nationally renowned for its programmes of theatre and modern dance.
Bar. Café. Wheelchair access.

Companies

Nationale Ballet

Information from Muziektheater (*see above* **Venues**).
When the Dutch National Ballet left the Stadsschouwburg
in 1986 to move to the Muziektheater, its repertoire
changed markedly. Now that 1,500 seats have to be filled
every night, the company tends to lean heavily on classical ballets such as *Swan Lake* and *Sleeping Beauty*, which
are performed with consummate skill. This is the largest company in The Netherlands and it has over 20
Balanchine ballets in its repertoire, the largest collection
outside New York. Toer van Schayk is the main choreographer, and favours expressionistic classical dance.

Nederlands Dans Theater

Information from AT&T Danstheater (*see above*
Venues: Out of Town).
In 1987 the Nederlands Dans Theater left its shabby
housing near Centraal Station in The Hague to settle in
its own theatre. This clever building suits the repertoire
of the company, the black stage walls directing all the
attention towards the quality of the movements. Ballets

from the Czech artistic director Jiri Kylian form the core
of the programming. The company also has a group of
younger dancers named NDT2. In Amsterdam, NDT
stages regular performances in the Muziektheater, and
NDT2 usually performs in the Stadsschouwburg.

Dansgroep Krisztina de Châtel

Plantage Muidergracht 155, 1018 TT; IE (627 3970).
Tram *7, 14.* **Open** *office* 9am-5pm Mon-Fri.
An outstanding modern dance company. Hungarian-born
de Châtel formerly based her choreography on repeated
movements, but in recent years she has taken to a more
theatrical approach. Performances in Amsterdam usually take place in the Bellevue (*see above* **Venues**).

Folkloristisch Danstheater

Kloveniersburgwal 87, C (623 9112). **Tram** *9,
14/Metro Nieuwmarkt.* **Open** *box office* 11am-3pm
Mon-Fri; one hour before performance; *information*
9am-5pm Mon-Fri.
Clog dancing apart, The Netherlands has a dearth of folk
dance. Therefore this Amsterdam-based company performs dance from all over the world, especially eastern
Europe. In summer, special events are staged for
tourists, combined with a boat trip through the canals.
The company regularly tours, so you may not be able to
catch it in Amsterdam. In recent years the theatre has
been used as a venue for Nationale Ballet workshops.

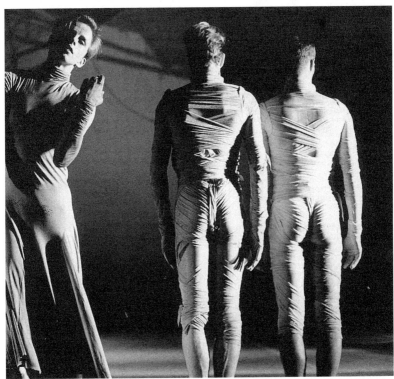

'*Weep, Cry and Tangle*'. **Dansgroep Krisztina de Châtel** *in a 1992 production. See* **review**.

Out of Town

The Amsterdam performances of these companies usually take place in the Stadsschouwburg (*see above* **Venues**). Unless otherwise specified, further information on the companies can be had from the Theater Instituut Nederland (*see above* **Festivals and Events**).

Djazzex
In 1983 Djazzex started in The Hague as a middle-of-the-road, jazz-cum-showdance company, but it soon developed its own style – a mixture of jazz and modern dance. The company has been a pioneer of jazz dance in The Netherlands.

Introdans
Introdans is a touring company, based in Arnhem, that tries not to be too highbrow. Productions vary from easy-going dramatic ballet to innovative work by Dutch choreographers. In keeping with the increasing internationalisation of dance, the company has recently collaborated with choreographers from abroad.

Raz
A new, large modern company, based in the southern city of Tilburg, has recently been making waves under the artistic leadership of Hans Tuerlings.

Reflex
Reflex, based in Groningen in the far north, has in a few years built up a repertoire that is both varied and tasteful. Since the artistic leadership was taken over in 1990 by Patricia Tuerlings, an air of the absurd punctuates their work.

Rotterdamse Dansgroep
Information from Rotterdamse Schouwburg (*see above* **Venues: Out of Town**).
One of the most vigorous exponents of New York dance in The Netherlands. Imported dance routines are mixed with work by young Dutch choreographers.

Scapino Ballet
Information from Rotterdamse Schouwburg (*see above* **Venues: Out of Town**).
The Scapino Ballet has its home in the newly built Rotterdamse Schouwburg. It is the oldest company in the country and until recently put emphasis on youth dance and 'family' programmes. But under the leadership of Ed Wubbe the company's image is more in line with current trends.

Theatre and Dance

Cloud Chamber: As is typical of Amsterdam dance companies, many nationalities are represented in Cloud Chamber. It provides the truest representation of the so-called post-modern multi-media spectacle, often convincing while you are watching, but which leaves you with many questions afterwards.

Het Concern: Het concern can mean either 'the company' or 'caring'. This collective of modern dancers in their late thirties often collaborates with stage directors to fuse the best of theatre and dance. A fine example of the genre.

Onafhankelijk Toneel (Independent Theatre): A pioneer in mixing dance and theatre. Its trademark is a very precise style, combining movement and speech. The results are either highly sophisticated or utterly boring. **The Shusaku and Dormu Dance Theatre**: After experimenting with the amalgamation of oriental and surreal influences, the work of this company (led by the Japanese Shusaku Takeuchi) is now heading in a western direction.

Events

Spring Dance
Information and bookings (030 332032).
Spring Dance, held in Utrecht in late April-early May, attempts to give an overview of recent developments in modern dance all over the world, including work from Dutch artists.

Holland Festival
Bookings (from February) *Nederlands Reserverings Centrum, Postbus 404, 2260 AK Leidschendam (070 320 2500)*. **Tickets** f20-f100. **Credit card bookings** *621 1211*. **Direct sales** (from May) from AUB Uitburo and VVV tourist offices and individual theatres.
Premières by large and small Dutch dance companies are held at this annual festival of performing arts (in June). Major companies from abroad also appear. *See also chapters* **Amsterdam by Season** *and* **Theatre**.

Uitmarkt
Museumplein, OS. Tram 2, 3, 5, 12, 16.
Dance, music, theatre and cabaret are performed *al fresco* in the last weekend of August every year.

Holland Dance Festival
Information and bookings *AT&T Danstheater (070 360 9931)*.
Every other September (1993, 1995), the Holland Dance Festival takes place in The Hague's Danstheater. Many of the world's larger companies are attracted to the event, and the Nederlands Dans Theater usually performs.

Dansfestival Breda
Information and bookings *Breda VVV (076 222 444)*.
In Breda (one and a half hours away by train) in the south of the country, a dance festival takes place every October. Programming varies greatly, so check before you go.

Courses and Workshops

Artemis Kunstcentrum
Keizersgracht 676, IS (623 2655). Tram 4, 16, 24, 25. **Open** 10am-3.30pm Mon-Sat. **Classes** 12.30pm-2pm, 1-2.30pm, Mon-Fri; 11am-12.30pm Sat. **Cost** f12. **No credit cards.**
A former church, which has been turned into a handsome centre for the arts. Courses and workshops in both modern and classical dance are run, often by dancers from the Nationale Ballet or other modern dance companies. Because of this activity, Artemis is turning into a meeting place for those involved in dance.
Coffee shop (open 10.30am-when they feel like closing).

Danswerkplaats Amsterdam
Arie Biemondstraat 107, OW (612 4324). Tram 1, 6, 7, 17. **Classes** 10.15am-11.45am, noon-1.45pm Mon-Sat. **Cost** f11 per class; weekly workshops approx f350. **No credit cards.**
Daily classes include t'ai chi, yoga, improvisation and the Alexander technique. Modern dance classes are run for experienced dancers. Visiting teachers come from all over Europe and the USA, and workshops are run during summer and at weekends.

Film

Whether you're a tourist looking for a rainy day matinée or a two-film-a-day buff, Amsterdam's cinemas can provide the answer.

Amsterdam's internationalism is perfectly reflected by its cinema; and though, as yet, it has nowhere near as many screens as Paris or London, there are plans to build additional multi-screen complexes in both northern and southern suburbs of the city. But the city can still offer just as much variety as anywhere else in Europe; and on occasions, is even a step ahead (Eddie Murphy's *Boomerang* opened in Amsterdam at least two months ahead of London).

The current city centre complexes, all owned by MGM Cannon, are the massive City and Tuschinski and the medium-sized Alfa, Alhambra, Bellevue Cinerama, Calypso and Riks Bioscoop. Just out of town in the west is the imaginatively named Cinema. There are also a number of smaller independent houses within easy reach of the city centre; typically De Uitkijk, Cinecentre, Movies, NFM, Rialto, Desmet and Kriterion. Together with MGM

Cannon, they offer a cosmopolitan mix of Hollywood blockbusters, world cinema, documentaries, re-runs and retrospectives.

Almost all films are shown in their original language (predominantly English) with Dutch subtitles etched by laser along the bottom. Occasionally, films such as the Disney's *Belle En Het Beest* (*Beauty and the Beast*) have been dubbed – watch for the words 'Nederlands Gesproken' by the title.

Amsterdam is unquestionably the country's film capital, and since 1988 has played host each December to the International Documentary Film festival. In recent years, competition has come from Rotterdam, where an internationally respected film festival runs in January, and from nearby Utrecht, where the 'Dutch Film Days' festival takes place in September. The only other film city of note is The Hague.

*The seven-screen **City** is Amsterdam's largest cinema. See **review** page 185.*

HOME-GROWN TALENT

Until recently, Dutch movies generally got a low billing, both at home and abroad. In the domestic market at least, this is no longer the case. The comedy *Flodder In Amerika* played to packed houses. With its Carry On-style jokes and New York backdrop, the film occupied the number one spot for months. Curiously, it vied for top position with the thriller *Basic Instinct*, by Dutch director Paul Verhoeven. Indeed, a whole host of home-produced films have laid almost permanent siege to screens, as film houses discover a ready and seemingly inexhaustible domestic audience.

Dutch cameramen are particularly successful. Robby Muller is the regular choice of German director Wim Wenders, Jordan Cronenwerth is a Hollywood regular, and then there's Jan De Bont (*Basic Instinct, The Jewel Of The Nile, Ruthless People*), plus a small army of editors and technicians in Hollywood. The director Peter Greenaway shoots many of his films in Holland using local crews, most recently *The Baby of Macon* (its backdrop was the Oude Kerk in the heart of the red light district).

Dutch film industry budgets are small, with a total annual government subsidy of around f18 million available through two funds: The Netherlands Film Fund (documentaries and art house); and the Production Fund (features).

Despite their limited opportunities, Dutch directors excel. Paul Verhoeven (*Basic Instinct, Robocop, Total Recall, Turkish Delight*) is almost a national hero. Dick Maas is riding on the recent success of *Flodder* and will be remembered for *Amsterdamned*; also notable are Fons Rademaker (*The Assault*) and George Sluizer (*The Vanishing*).

In front of the camera, Rutger Hauer (*Wedlock, Blade Runner, The Hitcher* and star of Guiness advertisements) is slogging it out with Jeroen Krabbé (*Kafka, The Living Daylights, Crossing Delancy*, plus the US television soap *Dynasty*) for the title of most visible Dutch actor world-wide. Derek de Lint (*The Unbearable Lightness of Being, Stealing Heaven*) is one to watch, as is Thom Hoffman (*De Avonden*). Of the talented female actresses around, only Renee Soutendijk and Monique van de Ven have really become better known, by moving into American TV drama. Otherwise, as with anywhere else, Holland has its share of unemployed actors and actresses.

STUDENT WORK

Like Verhoeven and Jan de Bont, many Dutch film-makers begin their careers at the Nederlandse Film en Televisie Academie (Ite Boeremastraat 1, tel 683 0206), a faculty of the Amsterdam Hogeschool Voor De Kunsten, the city's school of arts. Around 250 students attend the four-year course with 75 per cent of graduates finding work, such is the college's high international reputation.

There are two other film courses, both at the University of Amsterdam (Nieuwe Doelenstraat 16, tel 525 2980/fax 525 2938). The first offers an MA course in Film and Television studies. A research-only programme, it leads to a PhD for which the thesis can be written in English. Enrolment is from September each year, but no later than 1 July for that autumn's term. The second course is a recent addition (it began in 1990) and offers a BA degree in *Film en Televisie Wetenschap* (film and television studies). Unlike the Film Academie, the course does not directly lead to film-making, concentrating instead on theoretical analysis. Though some guest lectures are in English, the course and exams are entirely in Dutch.

The Cinemas

There's really no excuse for being ignorant of Amsterdam's film programme. In virtually every café and bar there's a seven-day listing of films and venues. Other reliable sources include comprehensive monthly listings in *City Life Amsterdam*, the *Uitkrant's* 'Filmagenda' section (though the paper's early deadline prevents it listing anything showing at MGM Cannon) and the Wednesday edition of *Het Parool*. There is also a general overview in the free monthly Dutch film mag, *De Filmkrant*, though it contains very little listings information. Although most of these listings are in Dutch, they can be easily understood by the non-native.

Programmes change each Wednesday. In the multi-screens prices range between f11.25 and f15.50 (there are usually discounts for children), while in the MGM Cannon theatres on Wednesdays most evening shows are reduced to f10. First shows are generally around 2pm, the evening programmes begin around 7pm and 9.30pm, with the film itself starting some 15 minutes later. Late shows are generally confined to Friday and Saturday nights and start at around midnight. In the art houses (*filmhuizen*) times vary greatly and prices tend to be a little lower. At most venues a ticket can be reserved in advance for a nominal charge of 50c.

A few negative points. Be prepared for an obligatory 15-minute *pauze* (interval), slapped into every main picture regardless of length, and usually at a crucial moment. From fringe to mainstream, nearly all cinemas operate this dreaded *pauze*. Also (a common European problem) some of Amsterdam's out-of-centre multi-screens are hastily designed and have bad acoustics. Smoking is banned everywhere.

First-run and Mainstream

Alhambra

Weteringschans 134, IS (623 3192). Tram 6, 7, 10, 16, 24. **Open** *box office* 1-3pm, 6-10pm, Mon-Fri; 12.30-10pm Sat, Sun. **Tickets** f12.50; f10 Wed. **No credit cards.**
A small and rather drab Cannon house on a busy road, whose bold metallic exterior suggests more glorious days long past. The films are usually transfers from the City or Tuschinski (*below*) and tend to run and run until well and truly exhausted.
Wheelchair access with assistance to Screen 2.

Calypso/Bellevue Cinerama

Marnixstraat 400, IW (623 4876). Tram 1, 2, 5, 6, 7, 10. **Open** *box office* 1-11pm Mon-Fri; noon-11pm Sat, Sun. **Tickets** f12.50, f13; f10 Wed. **No credit cards.**
Two separate and glitzy cinema complexes, next to each other and sharing a common box office. The titles tend to lack the weight of those at the Tuschinski and City (*below*), though the more highbrow and wonderfully comfortable Bellevue is always worth a visit. Also home to the occasional first-run or European première.
Wheelchair access to all screens with assistance.

Cinema

August Allebèplein 4, OW (615 1243). Tram 1. **Open** *box office* 1-3pm, 6-9pm, Mon-Fri; 12.30-9pm Sat, Sun. **Tickets** f13; f10 Wed. **No credit cards.**
A plush, modern and very comfortable two-screen complex in a drab part of western Amsterdam. It typically shows blockbusters running simultaneously at either the City or Tuschinski (*below*). It's also the home of almost all press and special invitation screenings.

City

Leidseplein, IS (623 4579). Tram 1, 2, 5, 6, 7, 10. **Open** *box office* 12.15-10pm daily. **Late shows** midnight Fri, Sat. **Tickets** f11.25, f13; f10 Wed. **No credit cards.**
Where the Tuschinski (*below*) has charm, its Cannon cousin the City has hard sell. The large frontage and huge electronic advertisement hoarding dominate the Kleine Gartman Plantsoen, a small road leading to the Leidseplein, and a bank of TV sets in the foyer runs a constant diet of trailers. Much frequented by tourists, the City is Amsterdam's largest cinema with a total seven-screen audience capacity of some 2,094. The fare is family-oriented mainstream, and non-English-language films are pretty rare; trade is heavy all week, with long queues at weekends. There are occasional premières. For special screenings the City 1 and City 7 theatres are combined into one enormous whole, and City 1 is also available for hire for conferences and parties.
Wheelchair access with assistance to Screens 1-4.

Tuschinski

Reguliersbreestraat 26, IS (626 2633). Tram 9, 14. **Open** *box office* 12.15-10pm daily. **Tickets** f11.50, f15.50; f10, f12.50, Wed; deluxe and selected balcony seats, eight person box (with glass of champagne), phone for details. **No credit cards.**
One of Europe's most beautiful and unusual cinemas (built in 1922 as a variety theatre for rich merchant families), the Tuschinski is Amsterdam's most prestigious cinema, which inevitably means long box office queues spilling out into the street at evenings and weekends. For a mainstream venue, the film choice is lively and occasionally inspired. As well as the seven-screen programme, the building's stunning art deco design attracts many visitors, so much so that tours of the cinema are organised each July and August. These are at 10.30am on Mondays and Sundays; tickets (f7.50) are available from the box office.
Wheelchair access with assistance to all screens except Screen 5.

Revival and Art Houses

Alfa

Hirschgebouw, Leidseplein, IS (627 8806). Tram 1, 2, 5, 6, 7, 10. **Open** *box office* 1-3pm, 6-11pm, Mon-Thur; noon-midnight Fri-Sun. **Late shows** midnight Fri, Sat. **Tickets** *Screen 1 & 2* f13; *Screen 3 & 4* f12; f10 Wed. **No credit cards.**
An MGM Cannon art house, the Alfa is a former dancehall whose entrance is tucked down a little sidestreet. The décor is austere but the film choice reliably intelligent, if a little too predominantly English-language. There are also kids' matinées on most afternoons and a documentary festival each summer. Packed houses at the City (*see above* **First-run and Mainstream**), which is just across the road, usually means the overspill will find its way here, so expect a crush at weekends.
Wheelchair access to all screens with assistance.

Cinecenter

Lijnbaansgracht 236, IS (623 6615). Tram 1, 2, 5, 6, 7, 10. **Open** *box office* 2.15-10.30pm daily. **Tickets** f13; f10 Wed, matinées; no charge for ticket reservations. **No credit cards.**
The Cinecenter, on a Leidseplein sidestreet cluttered with Indian and Indonesian restaurants, requires some seeking out, but it's worth the effort. It's a novel and welcoming place, with *commedia* prints adorning the walls and stairways; the four screens each have their own name and décor – Coraline, Peppe Nappa, Pierrot and the tiny 52-seat Jean Vigo. The movies are about 60% French to 40% English-language, with Spanish and Russian screenings as well. A pleasant café adjoining the theatres sells toasties and apple pie.
Wheelchair access to all screens with assistance.

Desmet

Plantage Middenlaan 4A, IE (627 3434). Tram 7, 9, 14/Metro Waterlooplein. **Open** *box office* 6.30pm-½ hour before last film ends, daily. **Late shows** 11pm daily. **Tickets** f10, f13.50; f10 Wed; f80 ten-visit cards. **No credit cards.**
The art house answer to the Tuschinski (*see above* **First-run and Mainstream**), the Desmet is far smaller but of similarly striking art deco design. Its ornate downstairs café area usually houses an exhibition of paintings or photographs. The film choice is steadily imaginative and wholly international, with regular festivals and Dutch or even European premières common, and documentaries shown every Sunday at 2pm. The weekend gay screenings are well attended, while the lates are far more Hollywood than the usual Desmet fare.
Wheelchair access with assistance by prior arrangement.

Kriterion

Roetersstraat 170, IE (623 1708). Tram 6, 7, 10/Metro Weesperplein. **Open** *box office* 1-10.30pm Mon-Thur, Sun; 1pm-midnight Fri, Sat. **Late shows** 12.15am Fri, Sat. **Tickets** f11.50. **No credit cards.**
An exuberant and slickly designed venue run entirely by volunteer students, with a broad film choice which includes children's matinées on Wednesday, Saturday and Sunday. Festivals are a speciality but the late-night screenings centre on cult American or erotic French movies. The downstairs bar, lively in the evenings and at weekends, has recently had a face-lift, and is open all day to non-filmgoers.
Wheelchair access to Screen 1.

The Movies

Haarlemmerdijk 161, IW (638 6016). Tram 3. **Open** *box office* 2pm-½ hour before last film ends, Mon-Sat; noon-½ hour before last film ends, Sun. **Late shows**

The café at **The Movies**.

midnight Sat, Sun. **Tickets** *Screen 1* f13.50, *Screen 2 &
3* f12.50; f10 Wed. **No credit cards.**
The most aesthetically pleasing of the city's art houses,
The Movies dates from 1928, when it was a prominent
feature of what was then a bustling main street. The spirit of Haarlemmerdijk may have faded because of tram re-
routing after World War II, but the cinema, complete
with a beautiful café, recaptures its former glory thanks
to renovations which began in the early seventies. The
small theatres have an intimacy which is enhanced by a
busy collection of posters on the interior walls. The café,
which is worth a visit in itself, has been restored to its
full thirties' charm. There's regular live jazz and folk
music to while away the time before a late screening, plus
a jukebox crammed with hits from the sixties and seventies. The films themselves are international, ranging
from obscure to near-mainstream, but almost always
worth seeing. Children's films are shown at 2.30pm on
Wednesday and Saturday, and 12.30pm on Sunday.
Wheelchair access with assistance.

Rialto

Ceintuurbaan 338, OS (662 3488). Tram 3, 12, 25.
Open *box office* 5.30-10pm daily. **Tickets** f11, f15; f8.50
under-14s; f7.50 members; f40 five-visit cards.
Membership f20, f50. **No credit cards.**
A stylish alternative cinema just a short journey from the
centre of town. Recently refurbished, and run mostly by
volunteers, it offers a mixed diet of new and old international flicks, children's matinées on Wednesday and
Sunday plus regular tributes to directors. The children's
matinées often feature excellent little-seen animation
from around the world. The membership packages entail
ticket discounts and permanent seat reservations.
Wheelchair access to Rialto 2.

Riks Bioscoop

Reguliersbreestraat 31, C (626 2633). Tram 4, 9, 14.
Open *box office* 11am-9pm daily. **Tickets** f2.50. **No
credit cards.**
Formerly the Cineac, this cinema has changed from a
mainstream house to what the Americans call a Dollar
Cinema (in Holland's case this is a f2.50 coin called a
rijksdaalder). The idea is to take last year's top films and
put them on a constant loop. Films change every
Wednesday, and it's proving a massive success.

De Uitkijk

Prinsengracht 452, IS (623 7460). Tram 1, 2, 5. **Open**
box office ½ hour before film starts. **Tickets** f13.50; no
charge for ticket reservations. **No credit cards.**
Amsterdam's oldest cinema, the staunchly independent
De Uitkijk dates from 1913 and is a charming, 158-seat
converted canal house. It boasts a grand piano which
was installed shortly after the cinema was built and
which, though no longer playable, is too big to be
removed. Films that prove popular tend to stay put. The
owner's 'movies over ice-cream' policy means there are
no refreshments, though we suspect lack of space may
have something to do with this. Best of all, De Uitkijk
refuses to use the dreaded *pauze*.
Wheelchair access with assistance.

Multi-media Centres

De Melkweg

*Lijnbaansgracht 234A, IW (624 1777). Tram 1, 2, 3, 5,
6, 7, 10.* **Open** *box office* noon-1am daily. **Late shows**
12.30am Fri, Sat. **Tickets** f10.50. **Membership** f3.50
monthly, f5 quarterly, f15 annually (included in
admission price). **No credit cards.**
Though better known as a rock venue and theatre, De
Melkweg runs a consistently imaginative film programme
in its cosy first-floor cinema, running from mainstream
action/adventure through cult films to art house movies. *See
also chapter* **Music: Rock, Folk & Jazz.**

Soeterijn

Linnaeusstraat 2, OE (568 8500). Tram 9, 10, 14.
Open *box office* 10am-4pm Mon-Fri; 10am-8pm Sat,
Sun. **Tickets** f7.50, f11. **No credit cards.**
Situated right next to the Tropenmuseum (*see chapter*
Museums), the Soeterijn stages regular ethnic music
events, theatre and, occasionally, documentaries and fea-
ture films from the developing countries. Film night is
Monday, with one show at 8.30pm. During occasional
festivals celebrating the Third World, films are shown
throughout the week.

Film Museum

Nederlands Filmmuseum

Vondelpark 3, OS (589 1400). Tram 12. **Open** *box
office* 8.30am-¼ hour before last film ends Mon-Fri;
3pm-¼ hour before last film ends Sat; 3pm-¼ hour
before last film ends Sun; *library* 10am-5pm Tue-Fri.
Tickets *cinema* f8.50-f12.50; f50 ten-visit cards; f100
25-visit cards; f200 60-visit cards; *library* free.
Membership f75; f50 students. **No credit cards.**
Idyllically housed in a former nineteenth-century tearoom in the Vondelpark, the Government-subsidised
(and recently extensively modernised) Filmmuseum
was established in the forties and boasts a strong three-
films-a-day programme aimed at pleasing all tastes.
Most of the titles at the 5pm screenings are drawn from
the museum's own 60,000-plus collection of Dutch and
European movies dating back a century, while the later

shows cover various genres, from Egyptian documentaries to Ealing comedies. Silent movies get live piano accompaniment. In the ground-floor Café Vertigo there are Sunday afternoon film seminars and discussions, of which about half are in English, and in the summer occasional screenings are held outdoors on the first-floor terrace. Also worth seeing is the well-constructed exhibition on the development of European cinema. The library (Vondelstraat 69-71) houses the country's largest collection of film books and periodicals, but sadly, because of theft, books can no longer be borrowed. The museum also holds an excellent hoard of more than 30,000 posters and stills.

Film Festivals

Dutch Film Days

Festival office, Hoogt 4, 3512 GW, Utrecht (030 322 684). **Open** 10am-6pm Mon-Fri. **Tickets** phone for details. **No credit cards.**
An all-Dutch affair aimed at the Dutch public and film industry, running for a week in the third week of September, and celebrating its twelfth anniversary in 1993. The festival shows around 100 feature films in a variety of venues, plus shorts and a selection of TV programmes. All new Dutch productions are shown here, along with a selection of students' efforts from the Amsterdam Film Academie. As in Rotterdam (*see below*), there are also lectures from guest

speakers and workshops on technique aimed at students. The festival presents its own awards to those films judged the year's best.

Rotterdam Film Festival

PO Box 21696, 3001 AR, Rotterdam (010 411 8080). **Tickets** phone for details. **Credit** AmEx, MC, V.
The Rotterdam Film Festival, which has been going for nearly 25 years, is the biggest film festival in The Netherlands and is international in scope, with around 90 films in its main programme, and up to a hundred others shown in retrospectives. There's also an accompanying series of lectures and seminars by guest directors, actors, producers and others involved in the industry. Each afternoon there are workshops on film technique. The festival is non-competitive (there are no awards), and has an emphasis on 'art' movies. The festival runs from the end of January to the beginning of February – exact dates to be announced.

International Documentary Film Festival

(020 627 3329). **Tickets** phone for details. **Credit** AmEx, MC, V.
As the name suggests, documentaries are the staple diet of this annual festival (in keeping with the Dutch appetite for discussion). The sixth festival is to be held in December 1993, and boasts a f10,000 prize in the name of the late documentary film maker Jori Ivens.

Riks Bioscoop *is Amsterdam's successful version of a Dollar Cinema. See* **review** *page 186.*

Music: Classical & Opera

From the Concertgebouw to carillon concerts, classical music in the capital embraces international stars as well as local idiosyncrasies.

Until 1988, Amsterdam wasn't really a touring stop for top-rank classical performers. The only exceptions were specialists in baroque, which is extremely popular in The Netherlands, and most of those were Dutch. It was a received wisdom in the concert management business that audiences would never fork out more than f50 for a ticket, and the resulting scene was unexciting, average in quality, and not very international.

Then in 1988 came Vladimir Horowitz and the subsequent renovation of the **Concertgebouw** (*listed under* **Venues**). The concert pianist easily sold out the hall at an unheard of f200 per seat. Encouraged by this success, the Concertgebouw arranged a series of benefit concerts by major international orchestras to help raise money to rebuild the foundations of the 100 year-old monument. Since then, Amsterdammers have discovered a whole new world of music.

The eighties was a very controversial decade for The Netherlands, as the government decided it would no longer support the arts from cradle to grave. Many of the cuts were dramatic and ill-considered, have enforced poor standards and wiped out entire sectors of the musical establishment. At the top, the number of major orchestras has been reduced from 13 to 8; at grass roots level, the organisation that arranged about 80 per cent of concerts by young musicians in The Netherlands has been guillotined. On the other hand, there is suddenly a lot of room for the really enterprising artist to seek unusual venues and business sponsorship, and experience the freedom (and often heartache) of the marketplace.

Competition is keener and the atmosphere is livelier than would have been imaginable a few years ago. Amsterdam now enjoys something of the best of both worlds: enough international stars to spark a high level of interest and quality; and a stronger, tighter local scene that still has plenty of Dutch flavour and idiosyncrasy. The cuts proved to be the breath of fresh air that The Netherlands was gasping for, although the revitalisation has been achieved at a terrible price in lost jobs and wrecked careers.

WHAT'S ON

To find out what's on where, get a copy of the free Dutch listings paper *Uitkrant*. The VVV (*see chapter* **Essential Information**) will give details of forthcoming concerts. Small recitals are often advertised on lamp-post posters.

Although ticket prices are still relatively low, you won't find any bargains: the only discounts are for students, over-65s (and some venues only accept Dutch ID) and CJP card holders (*see chapter* **Essential Information**).

Venues

AGA Zaal and Wang Zaal

Damrak 213, 1012 ZH, C (627 0466). Tram 4, 9, 16, 24, 25. **Open** *box office* 12.30-6pm Tue-Fri; 12.30-5pm Sat; 75 mins before performance for ticket sales and collection. **Tickets** f10-f40; reductions for CJP card holders. **No credit cards.**
Nobody was ever very happy in the old stock exchange, whose tenants included various branches of the city government, until the merging of the Amsterdam Philharmonic with the Netherlands Chamber Orchestra and Netherlands Opera Orchestra made a home for the new conglomerate an urgent matter. The new ensemble (the Netherlands Philharmonic) was offered the building (designed by Amsterdam School architect HP Berlage) but not the money for the necessary alterations. Thus began one of the most innovative funding partnerships in the history of corporate arts sponsorship. Finally it was agreed that the major sponsor of each part (Wang Computers for the large hall, AGA Gas for the recital hall and Arke Travel for the foyer) would have its name used for a renewable 10-year period, in return for a grant. The necessary architectural changes were carried out sensitively and the overall result has been pleasing to all concerned, financially and artistically.
Wheelchair access and toilets for the disabled.

Concertgebouw

Concertgebouwplein 2-6, OS (ticket reservations 10am-7pm daily 671 8345/recorded information in Dutch 675 4411). Tram 3, 5, 12, 16. **Open** *box office* 10am-7pm Mon-Sat; 40 mins before performance for ticket sales and collection. **Tickets** f30-f175; reductions for CJP card holders. **Performances** 8.15pm. **Credit** AmEx, DC, MC.

Opposite: *The* **Engelsekerk**. *See* **review** *page 190.*

Both the Concertgebouw's hall and its world-renowned orchestra (see p191 **Ensembles**) celebrated their hundredth birthday in 1988 with films, concerts and a renovation of the building. The controversy surrounding the aesthetics of the new glass wing has died down; as the coffee is hot and the views inside and out provide plenty of entertainment, there's less criticism and more enjoyment of the 'improvements' (coffee in the interval is a sacred Dutch tradition, and it is a poor performance indeed that cannot provide it). The Grote Zaal (Large Hall) hosts orchestral performances and recitals by major artists who can generate the necessary ticket sales. The world-famous acoustics are among the planet's most divine for both players and listeners throughout the hall. The Kleine Zaal (Small Hall) is a home from home for dozens of recitalists and chamber ensembles throughout the season. Acoustically and visually it is a small replica of the Grote Zaal. Here is where young Dutch and visiting soloists make their débuts, and there are also a number of lunch-time and chamber music series.
Wheelchair access by arrangement.

Engelsekerk

Begijnhof 48, C (624 9665). Tram 1, 2, 4, 5, 9, 14, 16, 24, 25.
This lovely English Reformed Church (Presbyterian) has up to four concerts a week; monthly programmes are available from the church. The series of free lunch-time concerts in July and August (phone for details) generally feature young players and new ensembles. Evening concerts may include well-known Dutch musicians, visiting artists and groups, choirs and chamber music. The acoustics are very live, the audiences informal and tickets are reasonably priced.
Wheelchair access.

IJsbreker

Weesperzijde 23 , C (668 1805/recorded information in Dutch 693 9093/fax 694 6607). Tram 3, 6, 7, 10/Metro Weesperplein. **Open** *box office* 9am-8.30pm Mon-Sat; 9am-5.30pm Sun; *café* 10am-1am Mon-Thur, Sun; 10am-2am Fri, Sat. **Tickets** f15-f20; CJP card holders f12.50-f17.50. **Performances** 9pm. **No credit cards.**
The famous Dutch centre for contemporary music, run by director Jan Wolff. Because of his years of determined subsidy-hunting and publicity, the vast majority of the artists get paid for their performances – something of a record in the twentieth-century music business. Many of the concerts feature Dutch works and musicians. One of the most interesting features of the IJsbreker are the 'Weeks' dedicated to specific instruments or composers. The foundation also hosts weekly concerts broadcast live by the Concertzender cable radio station.
Café. Wheelchair access with assistance.

Muziektheater

Waterlooplein 22, C (625 5455). Tram 9, 14/Metro Waterlooplein. **Open** *box office* 10am-8pm Mon-Sat; 11.30am-8pm Sun. **Tickets** *opera* f17.50-f100; reductions for CJP card holders, over-65s. **Performances** *opera* 8pm. **Credit** AmEx, CB, DC, MC.
The result of a building project that has provoked controversy for the best part of the twentieth century (see chapter **Post-war**), this is internationally renowned as the lemon to top (bottom?) them all. One of the architects defended it by claiming that there were so many zoning and building restrictions for the site that it couldn't have been designed a centimetre differently. Acousticians were called in, at an ever-mounting cost, to come up with solutions. At last the top expert arrived. He opened the door, glanced around the theatre, shrugged his shoulders expressively, said mournfully, 'I'm sorry, it's hopeless,' and flew home with a suitable five-figure fee in hand. Every musician in Amsterdam could have offered the

The **IJsbreker,** *the Dutch centre for contemporary music. See* **review.**

same advice for nothing, and did. Acoustics are not the only problem. The ballet rehearsal rooms have low ceilings, making it impossible to practice lifts. Although the orchestra was provided with a spacious pit and sumptuous dressing rooms, there is no purpose-built rehearsal room. Now they have a heated basement storage area. The ground and stage level loading entrances are at opposite ends of the building from the scenery lifts, which are too small to accommodate harps in cases or tall props. The list goes on. In fact the only success of the structure is the public area, which is strongly reminiscent of New York's Lincoln Center and commands a breathtaking view of the Amstel River. This is the only venue in Amsterdam where you can see grand opera performed, and if you can get a seat in the centre of the first row of the first balcony it may be possible to hear the orchestra and singers in reasonable balance. Otherwise, you may be disappointed. Several conductors and visiting companies have taken to using microphones and the management is also experimenting with surtitles – translations of the libretti projected above the stage (in Dutch, of course). The Muziektheater is home to the National Ballet and the Netherlands Ballet Orchestra (see chapter **Dance**) as well as the Netherlands Opera Foundation and Opera Orchestra (which draws its members from the Netherlands Philharmonic Orchestra conglomerate). Tours of the building are given on Wednesdays and Saturdays at 4pm, costing f8.50. If you book in advance, the guide will be prepared with English translations.
Wheelchair access and toilets for the disabled.

Nieuwe Kerk

Dam, C (Nieuwekerk foundation 626 8168). Tram 1, 2, 4, 5, 9, 13, 14, 16, 17, 24, 25. **Open** 11am-5pm daily. **Tickets** f7.50; f5 CJP card holders, students. **Performances** 8pm Thur, Sun. **No credit cards.**
Hosts primarily organ concerts of the top Dutch and visiting international players. Gustav Leonhardt (see p191 **Ensembles**) is the resident organist, and frequently plays on the magnificent sixteenth-century organ. There's no regular programme, but it's a popular venue for organ series. *See also chapter* **Sightseeing.**
Wheelchair access with assistance.

Oude Kerk

Oudekerksplein 23, C (625 8284). Tram 4, 9, 16, 24, 25. **Open** 11am-5pm Mon-Sat. **Tickets** f6.50-f15; f5-f12.50 CJP card holders, over-65s. **Performances** 8.15pm. **No credit cards.**
Jan Sweelinck, The Netherlands' famous seventeenth-century composer, was organist here, and a host of other important musicians have been associated with the Oude Kerk over the centuries. Concerts include organ

and carillon recitals and chamber music concerts. *See also chapter* Sightseeing. *Wheelchair access with assistance.*

Sweelinck Conservatorium

Van Baerlestraat 27, OS (664 7641). Tram 2, 3, 5, 12. **Performances** *Oct-June* 12.30pm Thur. Students at this conservatory give free lunch-time recitals.

Waalsekerk

Oudezijds Achterburgwal 157, C (625 0078). Tram 4, 9, 16, 24, 25. Small, elegant, and intimate, the Waalse church was the French Huguenot church for Amsterdam. It is now a very popular location for chamber music, early music and choral concerts. Musica Antiqua Köln from Germany, The Netherlands Chamber Choir and Gustav Leonhardt are frequent performers here.

Out of Town

Anton Philipszaal

Houtmarkt 17, 2511 DM, Den Haag (box office 070 360 9810/information 070 360 7927). **Open** *box office* 10am-3pm; 75 mins before performance. **Tickets** f20-f80; reductions for CJP card holders; over-65s. **Performances** usually 8.15pm. **Credit** AmEx, DC, MC. The home of The Hague's Residentie Orchestra since 1987. The old concert hall burned down in 1964 and the Orchestra was buried in a conference hall at the great Congressgebouw (congress building) for over two decades. The horrendous non-acoustics nearly destroyed morale and did nothing for the sound either. You couldn't find a happier bunch now as the Orchestra grows into its new quarters. It's an odd-looking structure from the outside, resembling a crashed UFO, but inside it's a soundly designed rectangular hall with excellent acoustics. *Wheelchair access and toilets for the disabled.*

Doelen

Kruisstraat 2, 3012 CT, Rotterdam (010 217 1717). **Open** *box office* 10am-6pm Mon-Thur, Sat, Sun; 10am-9pm Fri. **Tickets** f16-f150; reductions for CJP card holders, students. **Performances** 8.15pm. **Credit** MC. The Doelen is a large, modern, black edifice housing large and small concert halls and the Rotterdam Philharmonic Orchestra. The sound in the large hall is one of the reasons why the Rotterdam Phil sounds so wonderful on tour: it has to really work for a warm, expressive sound at home. The Doelen hosts about two dozen series a year, ranging from orchestral contemporary to jazz and just about everything in between, in addition to the RPO's schedule, which runs from September to June. The ticket office is one of the most efficient in the country and the audience is chic. Standing ovations are the rule at every concert regardless of quality, but if the audience really likes it, there will be plenty of stamping, cheering and vocal appreciation as well. Another eccentricity: the management lengthened the interval rather than making the coffee service more efficient. *Wheelchair access and toilets for the disabled.*

Vredenburg Music Centre

Vredenburgpassage 77, post box 550, 3500 Utrecht (box office 030 31 45 44; 24-hour concert information 030 31 31 44). **Open** *box office* noon-6pm Mon; 10.30am-6pm Tue-Sat; 45 minutes before performances. **Admission** f12.50-f45; reductions for CJP card holders, over 65s. **Credit** AmEx, CB, DC, MC. Worth the half-hour train ride from Amsterdam, as many performers make their only appearances in Holland at this venue. Though the concrete hall is an example of the least inspiring seventies' institutional

architecture (and it's attached to a shopping mall), acoustically it's a favourite among musicians. Frans Bruggen and the Orchestra of the Eighteenth Century regularly make recordings here, and it's a prime venue for the Holland Festival of Early Music. Ticket prices tend to be below those charged in Amsterdam. The Vredenburg also features pop, rock and jazz concerts.

Ensembles

Amsterdam Baroque Orchestra

Postal and telephone enquiries: Meerweg 23, 1405 BC, Bussum (02159 36050). Artistic director and harpsichordist Ton Koopman's authentic tempi are as wild as his frizzy grey hair and beard. A pupil of Gustav Leonhardt, Koopman helped build the hardcore early music scene that began in Holland. His orchestra is a model of the partnership between government funding and corporate sponsorship. The orchestra's many major label recordings and worldwide tours make this one of The Netherlands' premier musical exports. The ABO covers the full baroque territory from Bach to Biber to Dutch composer Pieter Hellendaal.

ASKO Ensemble

Postal and telephone enquiries: Keizersgracht 261, 1062 EC (622 3476). In a city where the contemporary music scene is varied and competitive, the ASKO Ensemble stands out through its work with renowned conductors such as Reinbert de Leeuw and Oliver Knussen. Ligeti, Stockhausen, Xenakis and Varese are the stock names of this ensemble specialising in twentieth-century chamber music. It forges into innovative opera productions as well. Recent productions with the Netherlands Opera at film studios at the city's outskirts were accessible only by boat, and were memorable evenings of contemporary cacophony.

Koninklijk Concertgebouworkest

Postal and telephone enquiries: Jacob Obrechtstraat 51, 1071 KY (679 2211). The one and only resident in the Concertgebouw turned 100 in 1988. Conductor Ricardo Chailly has changed a lot of things since he was appointed two years ago – including getting the players to look up from the music now and again. It's not every conductor's favourite orchestra and became rather sluggish and set in its ways under Bernard Haitink's somewhat lop-sided programming: Brahms, Mahler, Bruckner and more of the same. Chailly has introduced the orchestra to a more twentieth-century repertoire: Berio, Hindemith, Varese. Even fiery Verdi is finally getting a fair shake, ignored for years by cold and blasé Amsterdam audiences. Haitink comes back for the occasional Mahler symphony for which he and the orchestra are famous. They've still got that lush sound, but the relatively average quality of the individual players (notably in the brass section) does show, and often appallingly. If Chailly replaces retiring members with top-ranking players, he might have himself a truly great orchestra.

Gustav Leonhardt

The grandfather of modern baroque keyboard practice still gives plenty of concerts in Amsterdam. He is the resident organist at Nieuwe Kerk (*see p190* Venues), and also gives harpsichord recitals and continuo contributions in other venues.

Nederlands Kamerkoor (Chamber Choir)

Postal and telephone enquiries to Paulus Potterstraat 16, 1071 CZ (662 5199).
World-renowned and for good reason. That this group manages to stay in voice with such an exhausting schedule is a miracle in itself. Its concerts are varied and highly polished. This is without doubt one of the world's finest vocal ensembles. It has no base of its own: catch it at venues across the city.

Nederlands Kamerorkest (Chamber Orchestra)

Postal and telephone enquiries to Beurs van Berlage, Damrak 213 , 1012 ZH (627 1161).
Now under the wing of the Netherlands Philharmonic (*below*), the Kamerorkest draws its players from the larger orchestra, and is struggling to maintain its identity and quality. In spite of the complaints, it remains one of the world's finest chamber orchestras, and gets top-rate soloists and conductors reasonably often as well. Based at the AGA Zaal (*see p188* **Venues**).

Nederlands Opera

Postal and telephone enquiries to Waterlooplein 22 , 1011 NV (551 8922).
Since Pierre Audi left London's Almeida Theatre in 1988 to take over as Artistic Director, the Netherlands Opera has begun to forge an international reputation for daring and innovative productions of the standard operatic repertoire as well as world premières. The company is beginning to attract big names as well. Alfred Schnittke's *Life with an Idiot* was highly-acclaimed in 1992, and brought Mstislav Rostropovitch to the podium. Nikolaus Harnoncourt's Mozart productions have by now become legendary and are the only productions to bring in major vocal talents usually seen in bigger opera houses. More recently, Simon Rattle and Peter Sellars have brought their respective musical and theatrical talents to the Muziektheater's stage. Ticket prices never top f100, making Amsterdam one of the cheapest cities in which to see opera. The beautifully produced librettos are, alas, only in Dutch as are the surtitles above the stage, so opera fans should brush up on their plot summaries.

Nederlands Philharmonisch Orkest

Postal and telephone enquiries to Beurs van Berlage, Damrak 213, 1012 ZH (627 1161).
Still suffering from all the upheavals caused by the cutbacks and mergers, this orchestra used to be three different ensembles, and must still form and reform constantly to meet the schedules of a chamber orchestra, symphony orchestra and opera orchestra. The quality of all three have definitely suffered, and difficulties with conductors don't improve matters. A good bet if you're interested in the up-and-coming young soloists from The Netherlands and the rest of Europe.

Niew Sinfonietta Amsterdam

Post and telephone enquiries: Keizersgracht 261, 1016 EC (620 4909).
Founded in 1988, the Niew Sinfonietta has managed to distinguish itself in the Chamber Music field both in its home city and abroad. Under the direction of Lev Markiz, founder of the Moscow Soloists, the ensemble is best known for its interpretations of works by Tchaikovsky and twentieth-century Russians from Shostakovitch to Schnittke. Despite this reputation, the ensemble plays the classical and romantic standards as extensively and has premièred several commissioned Dutch compositions. In addition to touring around the world, the Nieuw Sinfonietta has its own series at the Concertgebouw, plays every year in the Holland Festival, and boasts an award-winning roster of recordings. How the ensemble manages to stay so good when its members have to rehearse without pay is one of the great mysteries of Amsterdam musical life.

Orchestra of the 18th Century

Postal and telephone enquiries to Oudezijds Voorburgwal 225-227, 1012 EX (626 8236).
Flautist and recorder player Frans Brüggen wanted an orchestra, and what Frans wants he gets. You could do a lot worse than a band made up of the *crème de la crème* of baroque and classical players from around the globe. They play in Amsterdam on their thrice-yearly whirlwind tours. Daring tempos, brilliant string passages, and wild exploits from natural horns (with no valves) make for some of the most exciting performances available anywhere. Not for the faint of heart or the closed of mind.

Residentie Orchestra

Postal enquiries to Stichting het Residentie Orkest, PO Box 11543, 2502 AM, Den Haag.
The Hague's resident orchestra suffered for years in a wretched hall, which was finally replaced with palatial new quarters in the Anton Philipszaal (*see p191* **Venues: Out of Town**). Conductor Hans Vonk is not noted for charisma or daring interpretations, and this very good band frequently produces better results under guest batons. The company does more contemporary work than many orchestras, but its Dvorak tells its story best. The Residentie plays occasionally in Amsterdam – most often as an opera orchestra.

Rotterdam Philharmonic Orchestra

Postal and telephone enquiries to De Doelen, Kruisstraat 2, 3012 CT, Rotterdam (010 217 1700).
The Netherlands' best-kept orchestral secret. Youthful, energetic, and full of the cream of Dutch players, the ensemble is also very liberally salted with top-quality foreigners. This organisation has vigorously bucked the political system at every possible turn in order to get the best players available, and the results have been well worth the trouble. Under James Conlon, Rotterdam developed into the kind of orchestra that young conductors like to challenge and old conductors like to make music with. They work hard to sound good in the Doelen (*see p191* **Venues: Out of Town**), and given a kinder hall sound full and lush.

Schoenberg Ensemble

Postal and telephone enquiries to Keizersgracht 261, 1016 EC (620 2849).
Reinbert de Leeuw's band of intrepid performers of contemporary chamber music is often on tour so it's hard to catch in Amsterdam. Well-presented programmes, although sometimes on the conservative side, have a depth and subtlety that can be missing from American and British performances. De Leeuw's tempos, gruellingly slow at times, may not be to your taste but the standard is high. The Ensemble plays all over town, most frequently at the Concertgebouw and the IJsbreker.

Willem Breuker Kollektief

Postal and telephone enquiries: Prinseneiland 99, 1013 LN (623 9799).
The Kollektief is never easily placed in a specific musical or theatrical category. For most of the 18 years since its foundation, the Kollektief has been famous on the improvisory jazz circuit. Recent forays into the music of Kurt Weill, Satie, Gershwin, Ravel and Prokofiev, much of it in conjunction with the eight-piece Mondriaan Strings, further confuse the catalogists and record store owners. Composing much of the music himself, Willem Breuker doesn't care what category the Kollektief fits

into. The ensemble still functions as a collective: its 11 members are responsible for everything from publicity to setting up chairs, to the death-defying solos improvised at every concert. Their annual St Matthew Passion is one of the silliest events of the year and not to be missed. The Kollektief also organises its own festival, the 'Klap op de vuurpijl' every year between Christmas and New Year.

Events

As well as the annual events listed below, look out for the occasional 'Grand Piano Festival', a series of piano recitals sponsored by Cristofori, which also arranges the Prinsengracht classical concert (*see chapter* **Amsterdam by Season**). The heats of the Gaudeamus Concours, an international competition for contemporary music held every spring in Rotterdam, are not open to the public, but for details of tickets for the final, contact the venue, the Doelen (*listed under* **Venues: Out of Town**). The AUB Uitburo and the VVV can give further details on all the events listed below.

Holland Festival
Dates 1-30 June 1993, 1994. **Admission** f12.50-f110.
Highlights of this internationally famous annual festival are plenty of Dutch contemporary music, performances by the best of Dutch theatre, musical and dance ensembles, and reasonable ticket prices. *See also chapter* **Amsterdam by Season**.

Lunch-time concerts
Whether you're low on cash or time, Amsterdam's free lunch-time concerts will take care of the longing for musical stimulation. Most concerts are abbreviated versions of a particular evening's programme. The Concertgebouw features its own orchestra at lunch-time several times a year. Most of the major Dutch musical ensembles and soloists put in an appearance as well as a few international performers. Conservatory students and ensembles fill the gaps in between. On Tuesdays concerts are held in the Muziektheater and on Wednesdays in the Concertgebouw at 12.30pm. The IJsbreker has concerts once a month at lunch-time. In Rotterdam, try de Doelen and in the Hague, the Anton Phillipszaal. The concerts are open to all and seating is on a first come, first served basis. For information contact each venue or look for schedules at box offices around town.

Uitmarkt
Dates 27-29 August 1993, 1994 to be announced. **Admission** free.
Held on and around Museumplein, this annual event is a hugely popular open-air 'music-market'. Musicians and ensembles play on temporary stages, previewing concerts scheduled for the coming season. *See also chapter* **Amsterdam by Season**.

Utrecht Festival for Early Music
Postal and telephone enquiries: Postbox 734, 3500 AS Utrecht (030 340 921). **Dates** 27 Aug-5 Sept 1993.
Admission f10-f40.
Baroque and classical artists and ensembles from around the world appear here. There is also a book, recordings and sheet music market, midnight concerts and nicely-priced tickets. Visiting musicians can go to classes and join in workshops.

Musical Asides

Carillons

Amsterdam's seemingly perpetual jingle of pint-sized bells clattering out intricate tunes on the quarter-hour has been happening for about four centuries. Amsterdam has five regular carillons: at **Oude Kerk, Zuiderkerk, Westerkerk, Koninklijk Paleis** and **Munttoren**. Played as an instrument since 1510, the carillon can (and does) render anything from Bach to the Beatles. Carillon concerts are a feature of many churches' calendars: in Amsterdam these are held at the Westerkerk most Wednesdays at noon, and at the Oude Kerk most Saturdays at 4pm. They are best heard from the street.

The Carillon School
Grote Spui 11, 3811 GA Amersfoort (033 752638).
Admission free.
For enthusiasts, there is a splendid specimen in the civic tower here. This is played at 10am on Fridays and 10am, noon and 5pm on Saturdays. The School has a small collection of campanological exhibits, but no formal opening hours; phone in advance or try ringing the doorbell.
Wheelchair access.

National Beiaardmuseum (Bell Museum)
Ostaderstraat 23, Asten (04936 91865). **Open** 1-5pm Mon, Sat, Sun; 9.30am-5pm Tue-Fri. **Admission** f4.50; f2.50 under-15s; group reductions. **No credit cards.**
A collection of clocks and bells from around the world, including a carillon that chimes every half-hour.
Coffee bar. Wheelchair access and toilets for the disabled.

Shops

Donemus
Paulus Potterstraat 16, OS (676 4436). Tram 2, 3, 5, 12. **Open** 9am-5pm Mon-Fri. **No credit cards.**
The Dutch contemporary music publisher. This office promotes contemporary Dutch music and is not a shop as such, but the friendly staff will bring out reasonably priced music by Dutch and Netherlands-resident composers. There's also a large library of compositions from decades back.

G N Landré b.v. Muziekantiquariaat
1e Anjeliersdwarsstraat 36, IW (624 7056). Tram 3.
Open 11am-5pm Wed-Sat. **No credit cards.**
Georges Landré comes from a long line of musical families who have had their fingers in every sort of melodious pie, from composing to criticising. His musicological and performing background and his wife Angela's energy and organising ability come together in a collection of about 20,000 books and pieces of sheet music, plus musical postcards, fine music boxes, posters, etchings and book plates.

Muziekmagazijn Opus 391
Rustenburgerstraat 391, OS (676 6415). Tram 12, 25.
Open 10am-6pm Tue-Sat. **No credit cards.**
If it was popular in the sidewalk cafés of Europe in the twenties and thirties, then here's your shop: sheet music for tea dance, early jazz and salon ensembles; there's even a service to locate a fox-trot trio for parties. Owner Anke Kuiper is herself a member of the Max Tak Film Orchestra, and really knows her stuff.

Music: Rock, Folk & Jazz

Amsterdam's eclectic music scene thrives in small-scale clubs, backstreet bars and cafés.

Amsterdam is a great city for live music. There is a good selection of medium-sized venues, plus numerous small bars and clubs. In summer, the parks and the squares are turned into impromptu free festival grounds. The city lacks a large music venue – although one with a capacity of more than 3,000 is planned as part of the IJ-Oevers development (*see chapter* **Amsterdam Today**) – which means that big names tend to skip Amsterdam, heading instead for Rotterdam's Ahoy or Utrecht's Vredenburg. Both are easily accessible by train.

The eclecticism of the city's permanent and transient population is one of the reasons the music scene thrives. Busking is legal and encouraged, and you're as likely to witness a technically brilliant Russian jazz quartet as you are a troupe of travelling hippy musicians. Furthermore, the major venues are non-profit making *stichtings*, and receive generous subsidies from the council (although these are becoming less and less generous). As usual, the roots of this subsidy system go back to the radical sixties and seventies. The result is that multi-media centres such as the Paradiso and the Melkweg (*both listed under* **Venues**) can take the risk of putting on little-known and underground artists without worrying about whether they sell out or not. Local artists and bands are particularly encouraged, with organisations such as the GRAP and Stichting Pop Nederland giving specific help to struggling musicians. The subsidies also benefit concert-goers, as tickets are among the cheapest in Europe.

THE LOCAL SCENE

Amsterdam has few internationally famous artists, but bands such as Soft Parade (signed to Dave Stewart's Anxious label) and Urban Dance Squad are beginning to gain at least some of the international recognition they deserve. There has also been a recent upsurge in locally-produced dance acts, with artists such as Fierce Ruling Diva, Human Resource and Quazar entering the American Billboard charts and putting Amsterdam firmly on the dance music map.

Visitors into the 'oom-pah-pah' variety of traditional Dutch music should head to the Jordaan area. To find out what's going on, pick up a free *pop lijst* at the AUB on Leidseplein (*see chapter* **Essential Information**). This list provides details of events a month at a time, from small club gigs to big festivals. For national events, the (rock) music magazine *Oor* contains a pull-out music listings section covering the whole country.

Venues

The venues listed below range from large multi-media centres to small squat venues and backstreet bars where you can hear live music every night of the week. Many of the late-night clubs also regularly feature live bands (*see chapter* **Clubs**), and the RAI Congresgebouw (*see chapter* **Business**) is increasingly being used as a pop venue.

For smaller venues, opening times and admission prices vary – phone to check.

Akhnaton
Nieuwezijds Kolk 25, C (624 3396). Tram 1, 2, 5, 13, 17.
The original policy of this venue was as a forum for the city's ethnic community to meet and perform. These days the programme includes events ranging from jazz dance afternoons and hip-hop jams to native American

There's folk music at the weekends at the **Blarney Stone**. *See* **review** *page 195.*

The **Melkweg**: *once a dairy, now a multi-media centre. See* **review** *page 197.*

poetry reading sessions. All events have a local atmosphere to them.

Blarney Stone
Nieuwendijk 29, C (623 3830). Tram 1, 2, 5. **Open**
10am-1am Mon-Thur, Sun; 10am-2am Fri, Sat.
An Irish pub close to Centraal Station that attracts a regular crowd of Irish builders, ex-pats and drinkers. The pool table at the back is old and wobbles, but that doesn't stop people queuing up to use it. At weekends live music is provided by mainly locally-based folk acts.

Café Haasjes
Hazenstraat 19, OW (639 1094). Tram 13, 14, 17.
Open 8pm-2am daily.
A blues bar situated close to the Jordaan and probably at its best on Sunday nights. Regulars include former Jimi Hendrix side-kick Curtis Knight (now living in Amsterdam) and other local luminaries. There's always someone playing, and the atmosphere can get really hot and sweaty.

Canecao
Lange Leidsedwarsstraat 68, IS (638 0611). Tram 1, 2, 5, 6, 7, 10. **Open** 8pm-1am Mon-Thur, Sun; 8pm-2am Fri, Sat.* **Admission** free.
A centrally-located bar that throbs to the sound of live samba and salsa every weekend. The bar attracts a mixture of South Americans, tourists and locals who tend to get exceedingly drunk on the selection of strong cocktails. During the week the place is emptier but no less atmospheric.

CMA
Beijersweg 28, OE (668 3800). Tram 9.
A small venue with a capacity of around 200. On Saturday nights rock bands take to the stage.

Cruise Inn
Zeeburgerdijk 272, OE (692 7188). Tram 6, 10. **Open**
8pm-2am Fri, Sat. **Admission** usually free.
The stronghold of the few rock 'n' roll enthusiasts – complete with motor bikes, quiffs and brothel-creepers – left in Amsterdam, who hang out at this wooden club house. DJs and visiting bands often appear on Saturday nights, and there's a 'Rock 'n' Roll Jamboree' open-air event every summer in the middle of June (phone for details).

Iboya
Korte Leidsedwarsstraat 29, IS (623 7859). Tram 1, 2, 5, 6, 7, 10.
A small theatre, restaurant and live music venue catering for South American music lovers. There are live bands at weekends unless a theatre production is taking place; phone for details. Regular customers are a friendly and enthusiastic Dutch and Surinam crowd.

Korsakoff
Lijnbaansgracht 161, OW (625 7854). Tram 10. **Open**
11pm-1am Mon-Thur, Sun; 11pm-2am Fri, Sat.
A hang-out for the rock and metal crowd. The music varies from heavy metal to indie dance and hip-hop, but the general sound is hard. Live bands feature on Wednesdays, when a nominal entry fee is usually demanded.

De Kroeg
Lijnbaansgracht 163, OW (420 0232). Tram 10. **Open**
10pm-3am Tue-Thur; 10pm-4am Fri, Sat.
This bar features mainly local bands, usually playing rock and blues. Recently refurbished, no doubt to offer more competition to the always crowded Korsakoff next door. A promising venue.

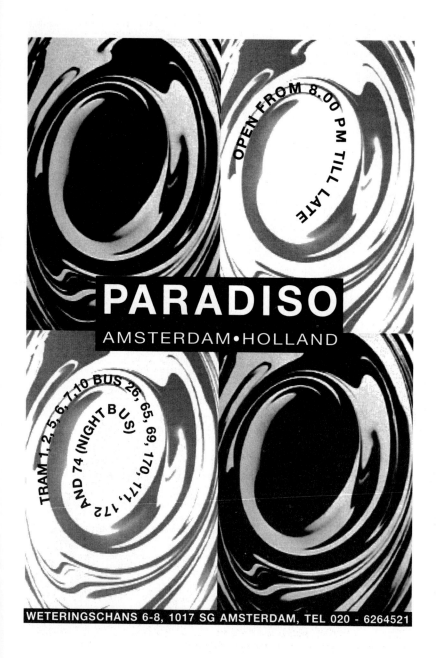

OPEN FROM 8.00 PM TILL LATE

PARADISO
AMSTERDAM•HOLLAND

TRAM 1, 2, 5, 6, 7, 10 BUS 26, 65, 69, 170, 171, 172 AND 74 (NIGHT BUS)

WETERINGSCHANS 6-8, 1017 SG AMSTERDAM, TEL 020 - 6264521

Melkweg

Lijnbaansgracht 234, IW (624 8492). Tram 1, 2, 5, 6, 7, 10. **Open** 7.30pm-late Tue-Sun; *disco* 1am-4 or 5am Fri, Sat. **Admission** f10-f20. **Membership** f3.50 per month.
Housed in a wonderful old wooden building that was once a dairy (hence the name – the 'Milky Way'), the Melkweg opened in the sixties, and is still run on a co-operative basis. The multi-media centre hosts bands, theatre, dance and film events. If the main hall gets too crowded, there's a separate bar where you can relax and get something to eat. Friday night is the Roots Rhythm Club, with live African or South American musicians; live bands, usually of the British or American indie rock variety, play on Saturdays. Look out for posters or pick up one of the monthly information sheets from the foyer. *See also chapters* **Film** *and* **Clubs.**

Mulligans

Amstel 100, IS (622 1330). Tram 4, 6, 7, 10. **Open** 4pm-1am Mon-Thur; 4pm-2am Fri; 2pm-2am Sat; 2pm-1am Sun. **Music** Fri, Sat. **Admission** free.
Home-from-home Irish bar with a great atmosphere and live music provided on Friday and Saturday evenings by the resident crew and visiting folk musicians. Weekends are always busy and the Guinness may take a long time to pour. Centrally situated on the Amstel in an otherwise mainly gay area.

Paradiso

Weteringschans 6-8, IS (623 7348). Tram 6, 7, 10. **Open** 8pm-1am (approx) various days, phone for details. **Admission** f7.50-f17.50. **Membership** f3 per month.
From the outside, the Paradiso is dark and forbidding – it's a blackened old church that looks like a goth's paradise. But the interior is light and airy and this is an excellent place to see bands. The weekly programme caters for a wide range of musical tastes, from local band nights to bigger names on tour. There's also a strong emphasis on reggae, African and Latin music. Tickets can be bought at the door, but are also available from the AUB ticket office, VVV tourist offices (for both *see chapter* **Essential Information**) and major record shops.

PH 31

Prins Hendriklaan 31, OS (673 6850). Tram 2. **Open** 8pm-2am daily; closed July, Aug. **Music** Thur. **Admission** free.
This ex-squat bar, now a one-room venue with a small stage and a separate theatre room, is situated in an unlikely residential area of town, beyond Vondelpark. Local residents seem to tolerate noisy comings and goings, which is lucky as the sound system is powerful. Politically motivated local bands are regular performers.

Rembrandt Bar

Rembrandtsplein 3, IS (623 0688). Tram 4, 9, 14. **Open** 4pm-1am Mon-Thur, Sun; 4pm-2am Fri, Sat. **Admission** free.
One of the best of the several brown bars around Rembrandtsplein which have live Dutch folk music. The beer flows and the music gets louder as the night wears on.

Rodos Bar

St Jacobsstraat 40, C (622 0168). Tram 1, 2, 5, 13, 17. **Open** noon-1am Mon-Thur, Sun; noon-2am Fri, Sat. **Admission** free.

One of the city's best venues, the **Paradiso**. *See* **review**.

High-quality jazz musicians can be heard at **Alto Jazz Café***. See* **review***.*

A dingy hang-out for street musicians and old hippies who occasionally get up and pay off their drink tabs with a performance. It can get rowdy as the night goes on and the *jenever* takes effect.

Rootaanhuis
Rozengracht 133, IW (623 5969). Tram 13, 14, 17. **Admission** f5-f10.
A basement dive, popular with a Turkish and Surinam crowd, that can get heavy at times. Reggae sound systems and Surinam bands make regular appearances at weekends.

Sleep-in
's-Gravensandestraat 51, OE (694 7444). Tram 6, 10/Metro Weesperplein. **Open** 10pm-3am Wed, Thur; 10.30pm-3am Fri.
Part of one of the main budget hostels in Amsterdam (*see chapter* **Accommodation**). The admirable agenda consists of local bands, student discos and a good selection of international musicians.

Soeterijn Theatre
Linnaeusstraat 2, OE (568 8200). Tram 9, 14. **Open** *information and reservations* noon-4pm Mon-Fri; *box office* one hour before performance. **Admission** f12.50-f22.50.
The Soeterijn is a small theatre attached to the Tropenmuseum and is closely connected with the Tropeninstitut (Mauritzkade 63, OE/568 8500) next door. Both venues provide global entertainment and education. The world music is worth checking out.

String
Nes 98, C (625 9015). Tram 4, 9, 14, 16, 24, 25. **Open** 8pm-2am Mon-Thur, Sun; 8pm-3am Fri, Sat. **Admission** free.
This bar used to be home the city's buskers when the sun went down. These days the booking is more organised, with mainly folk and blues acts taking to the tiny stage.

Vondelpark
OS. Tram 1, 2, 3, 5, 6, 12. **Open** dawn-dusk daily.
During the summer months the open-air theatre is the focal point of activities in the park. On Sunday afternoons it seems that the whole town turns up to wander around and watch buskers, jugglers and African drummers in a scene that hasn't changed much since the sixties. The main podium stages a programme of local musicians and singers. Look out for some of the more famous Dutch names such as Mathilde Santing and The Nits, who always get an enthusiastic reception for their brand of folk-influenced indie pop.

Jazz

Alto Jazz Café
Korte Leidsedwarsstraat 115, IS (626 3249). Tram 1, 2, 5, 6, 7, 10. **Open** 9pm-3am Mon-Thur, Sun; 9pm-4am Fri, Sat. **Admission** free.
One of the best and most famous jazz pubs in town, and although situated in the commercial Leidseplein area is surprisingly relaxed. The club puts on excellent bands every evening, with saxophonist Hans Dulfer hosting Wednesday evenings. Booze prices are slightly steep (a small beer costs f4), but the atmosphere is good.

Bimhuis
Oudeschans 73, C (623 1361). Tram 9, 14/Metro Nieuwmarkt. **Open** *box office* 8-9pm Thur-Sat. **Tickets** f9.50-f20.
The city's main avant garde and experimental jazz venue, which regularly manages to book big acts from overseas. Because of the entry fee (high by Amsterdam standards),

the audience is made up of serious, even élitist, jazz fans. The club also offers free sessions on Mondays and Wednesdays in the early evening when (in theory) anyone can join in the jam sessions.

Bamboo Bar

Lange Leidsedwarsstraat 115, IS (624 3993). Tram 1, 2, 5. **Open** *8pm-2am Mon-Thur; 8pm-3am Fri, Sat.* **Admission** free.
A late-night jazz and blues bar with live music every night. It's hard to get close to the stage, but the drinks are reasonably priced and some of the jam sessions are pretty groovy. The place gets very busy at weekends, and the music is very loud.

De Engelbewaarder

Kloveniersburgwal 59, C (625 3772). Metro Nieuwmarkt. **Open** *noon-1am Mon-Thur, Sun; noon-2am Fri, Sat.* **Admission** free.
A scruffy, relaxed and student-filled jazz bar. On Sunday evenings the place comes to life with impromptu jam sessions.

Gambrinus

Ferdinand Bolstraat 180, OS (671 7389). Tram 3, 12, 24, 25. **Open** *11am-1am Mon-Thur, Sun; 11am-2am Fri, Sat.* **Admission** free.
A small bar in the *Oude Zuid* (Old South) area of Amsterdam, beyond the Heineken brewery. A good place for an early evening meal (the kitchen is open from 6-10pm daily), with local jazz musicians providing the background music on Sunday afternoons from 4pm onwards.

Het Heerenhuys

Herengracht 114, C (622 7685). Tram 1, 2, 5. **Open** *9pm-1am Mon-Thur; 9pm-2am Fri, Sat.* **Admission** free.
A beautiful club where jam sessions are regularly held and local artists hold court. It's not that near other jazz clubs, but worth the walk.

De Heeren Van Aemstel

Thorbeckeplein 5, C (620 2173). Metro Rembrandtsplein. **Open** *4pm-1am Mon-Thur, Sun; noon-2am Fri, Sat.* **Admission** free.
Situated just off Rembrandtsplein, this is a large venue/restaurant where saxophonist Candy Dulfer currently hosts Sunday evening funk jazz sessions. Prior to events such as the North Sea Jazz Festival, it's possible to see jazz greats on stage here. The food is pretty good too, in a carnivorous Dutch way (meals cost from f15). The music kicks off at 9pm.

Joseph Lam Jazz Club

Van Diemenstraat 8, IW (622 8086). Tram 3. **Open** *9pm-3am Sat; 9pm-2am Sun.* **Admission** f6 *Sat;* free *Sun.*
This venue is a little off the beaten track, in an old harbour area to the west of Centraal Station. It attracts an older group of jazz enthusiasts who come to hear traditional and Dixieland jazz.

Odeon Jazz Kelder

Singel 460, C (624 9711). Tram 1, 2, 4, 5, 9, 14, 16, 24, 25. **Open** *10pm-3.30am Mon-Thur, Sun; 10pm-4.30am Fri, Sat.* **Admission** f5-f10.
A cellar venue where occasional live jazz nights are held. Otherwise recorded jazz dance keeps students happy and the dance floor busy.

Rum Runners

Prinsengracht 277, IW (627 4079). Tram 13, 14, 17. **Open** *4pm-1am Mon-Thur; 4pm-2am Fri; noon-2am Sat; noon-1am Sun.* **Admission** free. **Credit** (bar and restaurant) *AmEx, DC, MC, V.*
A cool and relaxing Caribbean bar/restaurant most of the

week, at weekends Rum Runners gets very crowded. Jazz combos and Latin bands provide the entertainment once a week, from 4pm to 9pm on Sunday. The place is easy to find, sandwiched between the Westerkerk and Anne Frankhuis. *See also chapter* **Restaurants**.

Festivals

Koninginnedag

Date 30 April.
This Dutch national holiday is the best day of the year to be in Amsterdam. In honour of the former Queen's birthday, all laws concerning sales taxes and licensing are suspended and a massive jumble sale engulfs the city. The trading is accompanied by music, which blasts out from every street corner. Stages are erected in every available space and bands of all kinds play from midday to midnight, by which time everybody is too drunk to go on. In recent years more sound systems with DJs have sprung up to challenge the traditional domain of the bands, and outdoor 'raves' are much more frequent. *See also chapter* **Amsterdam by Season**.

Pink Pop & Park Pop Festivals

Dates *Pink Pop* 1 day in mid to late May (31 May 1993); *Park Pop* 1 day in late June (27 June 1993).
Information and tickets available in Amsterdam from VVV tourist offices *(see chapter* **Essential Information***)*, from December; tickets for Pink Pop approx f15; admission to Park Pop free.
Taking place in The Hague (Park Pop), and in a small village outside Rotterdam (Pink Pop) these major outdoor pop festivals have impressive line-ups of famous Dutch and international stars. But be warned, it always seems to rain on the day.

Mundial World Music

Date 13 June 1993. **Information** Amsterdam's Uitburo and VVV tourist offices. **Tickets** about f15.
The first Mundial World Music festival takes place in 1993. Situated outdoors at Tilburg, it looks likely to be worth the travelling time from Amsterdam. Artists are expected to reflect cultures from all around the world.

North Sea Jazz Festival

Dates 3 days in mid-July (9-11 July 1993).
Information *Festival organisers* PO Box 87840, 2508 DE Den Haag. **Tickets** from f30 per day, available in Amsterdam from Uitburo and VVV tourist offices.
Founded in the early seventies, the North Sea Jazz Festival (in The Hague's Congresgebouw) plays host to an astonishing list of international performers.

Jazz Mecca Maastricht

Dates three days at the end of October. **Information** Amsterdam's Uitburo and VVV tourist offices. **Tickets** from f30 a day.
A three-day event that promises an eclectic mix of jazz. The 1992 event featured a blues room, a funk room and a room for bebop.

Amsterdam Festivals

Several less well-known festivals take place in Amsterdam during the summer. From the end of April, there are numerous small and large festivals catering for all musical tastes, especially jazz and blues. Some of these events take place in the Vondelpark, the Museumplein (behind the Rijksmuseum) and on the Dam. Stages are erected for the few days these events take place and beer and food stalls appear in the area around them. The best way to find out about these festivals, many of which are publicised by posters and fliers, is to check with the Uitburo or VVV offices *(see chapter* **Essential Information***)*.

Sport & Fitness

For fitness fanatics or keen spectators, Amsterdam has plenty to offer those who lead the sporting life.

Although Amsterdam's status as the cultural capital of The Netherlands is rarely disputed, few people are aware that the city is also a major centre for sports. The health craze has hit the city hard, with health and fitness clubs rapidly increasing in number, and more and more joggers pounding the parks and streets. Most parks have recreational facilities, but the best are Vondelpark, with its tennis courts and amateur footballers, and Amsterdamse Bos, which has a training circuit marked out and facilities for rowing, canoeing, fishing (carp, pike and perch) and even swimming, although the water's rather dirty. For both, *see chapter* **Sightseeing**.

The most popular sports in The Netherlands are soccer, skating, cycling and tennis. In winter skating comes to the fore – even when it doesn't freeze. The World and European Skating Championships become the main topic of conversation in bars, and the events are broadcast live on television. When it freezes, almost all the Dutch put their skates on.

For therapy centres, *see chapter* **Services**. For further information on sports and leisure facilities and events in Amsterdam, phone the city's Sport & Recreation Department on 552 2490.

Spectator Sports

Baseball

Pirates
Jan van Galenstraat Sportpark, Jan van Galenstraat, OW (616 2151). Tram 13/Bus 19, 47. **Season** Apr-Oct. **Admission** f6.50. **No credit cards.**
The team to see if you want to catch a competition match in Amsterdam, the Pirates are the city's best club, attracting up to 2,500 spectators.

Basketball

Canadians Amsterdam
Apollohal, Stadionweg, OS (671 3910). Tram 5, 24/Bus 15. **Matches** *end Sept-mid June* 8pm Sat. **Admission** f10. **No credit cards.**
This is the best team in Amsterdam and one of the top five in The Netherlands. Both the men's and women's teams play in the first division.

Cricket

KNCB (Dutch Cricket Board)
Nieuwe Kalfjeslaan 21B, PO Box 898, 1182 AA, Amstelveen (645 1756/fax 645 1715). Bus 8, 26, 65, 146, 147, 170, 171, 172, 173. **Open** 10am-5pm Mon-Thur.
Cricket is still a minority sport in The Netherlands. In 1992 the Dutch Cricket Federation had just over 5,900 members, 75 clubs and 250 teams, whereas the Dutch Skate Federation had more than 200,000 members. However, the national cricket team is improving all the time. During the 1991 Haarlem Cricket Festival, they beat an A team from the West Indies, and in 1992 they lost to Pakistan only in the last over. The ground is also home to several local sides: from May to August 40-over games are played on Saturdays from noon; 60-over games from 11am on Sundays. Admission is free.

Cycling

Cycling is a Dutch passion. The country has two great cycling advantages: it's flat (though windy) and it has the the best facilities in the world. Despite the flat terrain, The Netherlands has reared professional cyclists who have excelled in the French Alps during the Tour de France, in which the legendary Joop Zoetemelk came second six times before winning in 1980; in 1985, at the age of 38, he also became world champion in Italy.

Most Dutch avidly follow the Tour de France on TV and afterwards watch the spate of criteriums (road races) around The Netherlands, in which Tour de France heroes ride round a village about 70 times and receive a lot of money for it. Although on the decrease, these criteriums sometimes attract crowds of over 50,000. For further information, contact the **Koninklijke Nederlandsche Wielren Unie** (Dutch Cycle Federation), PO Box 136, Polanerbaan 15, 3447 GN, Worden (03480 11544).

If you want to cycle in The Netherlands, contact the **Nederlandse Toer Fiets Unie** (Netherlands Cycletouring Union), Landjuweel 11, 3905 DE Veenendaal (08385 21421). For both cycle hire and for cycle touring, *see chapter* **Getting Around**.

8 van Chaam

Chaam, Noord Brabant (Mr Coenraadf 01619 1503; private number, please ring at reasonable times). **Date** first Wed after Tour de France. **Admission** f15. **No credit cards.**
The biggest and oldest criterium in The Netherlands (first run in 1933), attracting thousands of spectators. A hundred professional riders and twice as many amateurs cycle 12 times around the 8km (5 mile) circuit of this village in the south of the country.

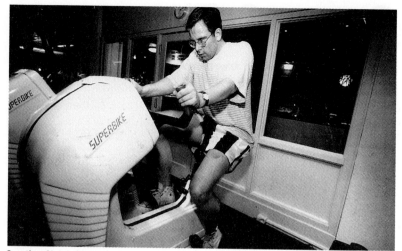

Sporting Club Leidseplein, *a unisex heath and fitness centre. See* **review** *page 203.*

Football

Soccer has long been the number one sport in The Netherlands and there are now almost a million registered members of the KNVB, the national football federation. The Dutch national team has had mixed fortunes recently – winning the European Championships in 1988, giving a disappointing performance in the 1990 World Cup, but winning the European Cup again in 1992. Amsterdam's major club is the world-famous Ajax.

If you want to play soccer yourself, we recommend a trip to Vondelpark (*see chapter* **Sightseeing**).

Ajax

Middenweg 401, OE (694 6515). Tram 9/Bus 138, 150, 152, 154, 158. **Admission** *standing* f12.50; *seated* family f17.50 per person, f22.50, f30, f32, f37. **Matches** *Sept-June* 2.30pm Sun. **No credit cards.**
Under coach Louis van Gaal, Ajax reached second place in the 1992 league table (their great rival RSV Eindhoven came top). But the city's première club made up for this by winning the UEFA Cup in 1992, having just emerged from a one-year ban from European competition. As we went to press, the club was involved in a court case following allegedly unauthorised transfer payments. Going to an Ajax match is reasonably safe, although there are some dodgy matches, which are heavily policed. These are usually against Feyenoord, FC Den Haag, FC Utrecht and PSV Eindhoven. We advise you to buy seat tickets. Following lengthy delays, work is just about to begin on a new stadium just outside the city.

Feyenoord

Olympiaweg 50, Rotterdam (010 492 9499). **Admission** *matches against Ajax* f27 standing, f42, f62, f72, seated; *all other teams* f15 standing, f20, f30, f40, seated. **Matches** *Sept-June* 2.30pm Sun. **No credit cards.**

Although Feyenoord is no longer as strong as it was in the seventies it remains in the first division and still has the biggest stadium in the country. Almost all The Netherlands' internationals are played here.

PSV

Fredericklaan 10/A, Eindhoven (040 501 609). **Admission** *standing* f15-f20; *seated* f22.50-f50. **Matches** *Sept-June* 7.30pm Sat; 2.30pm Sun. **Credit** AmEx, DC, MC, V.
Though Bobby Robson was briefly manager of PSV, the current manager is Kees Ploegsma. It is sponsored by the Philips company and is the wealthiest club in The Netherlands, with a blissfully comfortable stadium.

Hockey

Amsterdam

Wagener Stadium, Nieuwe Kalfjeslaan, OS (640 1141). Bus 125, 170, 171, 172, 173, 194. **Admission** *league games* free; *internationals* f22. **Matches** *Sept-Pentecost* 12.45pm Sun (women); 2.30pm Sun (men). **No credit cards.**
This is the strongest club in the region. The team's ground also hosts most of the home matches of the national teams. To see The Netherlands play costs about f22, while all league matches are free. The stadium has a capacity of 7,000.

Korfball

A hybrid of netball and volleyball, korfball has caught on swiftly and now the national federation has 90,000 members. It can be played indoors and out; the rules are the same but the size of the teams varies. The sexes compete on equal terms as players are only allowed to mark opponents of the same sex. The season has three stages: from September to mid-November and from April to June matches are played outdoors; from mid-November to mid-April the game goes indoors. There are about 20 teams in Amsterdam; the two best are **Blauw Wit**, which has its own hall and fields, and **Rohda**, the national outdoor champions in 1990-1991.

Blauw Wit
Joos Banckersweg, OW (Barbara Geeredzen 020 614 1614; private number, please ring at reasonable times). Tram 12, 14/Bus 15, 21. **Admission** free. **Matches** 2pm Sun.

Rohda
Sportpark Ookmeer, Willinklaan, Osdorp, OW (611 0416). Bus 19, 68. **Admission** usually free; *finals* f5; free under-16s, over-65s. **Matches** 2pm Sun; occasionally 2pm Sat. **No credit cards.**

Motor Sports

TT Races
De Haar Circuit, Assen (05920 55000/fax 05920 56911/race day information 05920 13800). Exit Assen South off motorway A28, then follow signs. **Dates** 21-26 June 1993. **Admission** *grandstand* f85; *other stands* f65; *circuit* f50. **No credit cards.**
More than 100,000 people come to see this spectacular event, lasting for a week, and culminating in the Grand Prix races for sidecars and 125, 250 and 500cc bikes on the final Saturday. On Tuesday the European championships are run for all classes of bike, and Thursday sees the TT Formula One and historic TT races. Real fanatics go along on the intervening days to watch the practice laps. Tickets can be booked in advance from TT Assen, PO Box 150, 9400 AD, Assen.

Zandvoort
Stichting Exploitatie Circuit Park, Burgemeester Van Alphenstraat (02507 18284). Train to Zandvoort from Centraal Station. **Admission** *paddock* f35; *grandstand* f17.50. **No credit cards.**
The car-racing track at the resort of Zandvoort, about 30km (19 miles) from Amsterdam (*see chapter* **The Randstad**), was once a venue for Formula One racing and the Director's plan is to bring it back for 1994. Meanwhile a programme of international races, including some nostalgic events, is in operation roughly every other weekend between March and October. Tickets are available at the door from 8am on the day.

Activities

Basketball & Skateboards

Basketball and skateboard fiends can play or skate for free on Museumplein, near the Rijksmuseum. There are several courts and two ramps where you can usually join in, but you have to be good.

Fishing

Amsterdamse Hengelsport Vereniging (Dutch Fishing Federation)
Nicolaas Witsenstraat 10, IS (626 4988). Tram 6, 7, 10. **Open** 10am-3pm Tue-Fri. **No credit cards.**
For a f35 annual fee and a five-minute wait, you can get the permit you need to fish legally in The Netherlands, plus a book (in Dutch) telling you where to do it. Staff will need to see your passport. The Amsterdamse Bos is

a convenient place to fish (*see chapter* **Sightseeing**); a local fishing permit can be obtained from any post office, or from tackle shops, and costs f13. *See also* **The Provinces: Overijssel**.

Golf

Because major events are shown on BBC and Eurosport television, golf has become quite popular, but is still considered to be élitist by most Dutch people. If you're a member of a British club, you are allowed to play on any Dutch course. Otherwise, you can only play on public courses.

Further information can be obtained from **De Nederlandse Golf Federatie** (Dutch Golf Federation), Soestdijkerstraatweg 172, 1213 XJ, Hilversum (035 857 060).

Sloten
Sloterweg 1045, OSW (614 2402). Bus 176, 179. **Open** *golf course* 8.30am-dusk Mon-Fri; *driving range* 8.30am-5.30pm Mon-Fri. **Cost** *golf course* f13.50 per day; *driving range including hire of 60 balls* f6.50. **No credit cards.**
A public course with nine holes and friendly staff. A half-set of golf clubs can be hired for f10.

Spaarnwoude
Het Hogaland 2, Spaarnwoude (023 385599). **Open** *summer* 7am-9pm daily; *winter* 8.30am-4pm daily. **Cost** *18-hole course* f32 per round; *12-hole course* f8 per round; *9-hole course* f16 per round. **No credit cards.**
A par 70 18-hole public course with water and wind hazards to trap the unwary or unskilled. There are also 12- and 9-hole courses. No advance reservations are taken but you can book by phone for the same day from 8.30am.

Health and Fitness

For women-only saunas *see chapter* **Women's Amsterdam**; for saunas for gay men *see chapter* **Gay Amsterdam**.

Splash
Looiersgracht 26, IW (624 8404). Tram 7, 10. **Open** 10am-10pm Mon-Fri; 11am-6pm Sat, Sun. **Admission** *1-day pass* f25; *1-week pass* f50; *2-week pass* f75; *1-month pass* f105. **Credit** AmEx, V.
Facilities here include a weights room with room for up to 50 people, a Turkish bath, a massage service and a sauna. There are eight aerobics classes daily. Everything is free once you have paid to get in.

Sporting Club Leidseplein
Korte Leidsedwarsstraat 18, IS (620 6631). Tram 1, 2, 5, 6, 7, 10. **Open** 9am-midnight Mon-Fri; 10am-6pm Sat, Sun. **Admission** *1-day pass* f25. **No credit cards.**
A central health club with a weights room and a sauna.

Skating

When temperatures drop to freezing, many Dutch put on a Walkman and go skating over the iced-over polders, keeping warm by drinking hot chocolate and alcoholic drinks bought from stalls on the banks. When the ice gets very thick, Dutch people start talking about the *elfstedentocht*, an 11-city marathon in the province of

Friesland (*see chapter* **The Provinces**) last held in 1986. If your visit coincides with the event, go to Friesland immediately; you'll never forget it. Though Amsterdammers skating on their own canals make a great spectacle, bear in mind that the canal water is dirty and the waterways hardly ever freeze completely in winter.

During the winter you can skate for free at Leidseplein (*see chapter* **Amsterdam by Area**), but the rink is very small. There are also many places close to Amsterdam (such as Loosdrecht, Vinkeveen, Muiden, Edam, Volendam or Broek-in-Waterland) also good for skating. If the winter is mild, visit an indoor ice rink, but don't expect to be able to skate in the summer – all the rinks close and even professionals are reduced to practising on roller skates.

Jaap Edenhal
Radioweg 64, OW (694 9652). Tram 9/Bus 8, 69, 120, 169. **Open** *Mid-Oct-Early Mar* 8.30am-5pm, 7.30-9.30pm, Mon, Wed; 8.30am-5pm Thur; 8.30am-4.30pm, 8-10pm Tue, Fri; 2-4pm Sat; 10.30am-4.30pm Sun. **Admission** f6; f4 under-15s and OAPs. **Skate hire** f6.50. **No credit cards**.
You can hire skates here for a mere f6.50, but the staff will ask for a deposit of a passport, a driver's licence or f100. The rink is open from the middle of October until the end of March.

Snooker and Carambole

Potting the black has become popular, thanks to the BBC, Eurosport and Sportnet's snooker coverage, and there are several halls where you can play fairly cheaply, although there are no tables in bars. When it comes to *biljart* (billiards),

carambole, played on a table without pockets, is still the major variation. Listed below are some snooker and carambole centres where drinks are also sold.

Biljartcentrum Bavaria
Van Ostadestraat 97, OS (676 4059). Tram 3, 12, 16, 24, 25. **Open** 11am-1am Mon-Thur, Sun; 11am-2am Fri, Sat. **Cost** *snooker* f13.50 per hour; *carambole* f9 per hour. **No credit cards**.
Famous in Amsterdam for its billiards team, which plays in the first division of the league. There are four floors here, the third and fourth devoted to carambole and billiards, the second floor to snooker and the first to pool. The use of cues is included in the table hire. Phone before turning up, as some evenings are for members only.

Snookercentrum de Keizer
Keizersgracht 256, IW (623 1586). Tram 13, 14, 17. **Open** 1pm-1am Mon-Thur, Sun; 1pm-2am Fri, Sat. **Cost** f12 per hour before 3pm; f17 per hour after 3pm; half price if playing alone. **No credit cards**.
This place has eight snooker tables each in its own room. There are telephones in all the rooms so players can phone orders down to the bar and have drinks sent up. Members pay a reduced rate but anyone is welcome to play here.

Snookerclub Overtoom
Overtoom 209, OW (618 8019). Tram 1, 6/Bus 171, 172. **Open** 10am-1am Mon-Thur, Sun; 10am-2am Fri, Sat. **Cost** f10 per hour before 2pm; f15 per hour after 2pm. **Membership** f25 per year. **No credit cards**.
The atmosphere in this ex-church is quiet, making it a club for the serious snooker player. While anyone can play here, members pay f2.50 less per hour.

Sports Centre

Dorchland
Borchlandweg 8-12, OSE (696 1441/1444). Metro Stranduliet. **Open** 7.30am-midnight Mon-Sat; 8.30am-

*Enjoy a swim in sub-tropical temperatures at **Mirandabad**. See **review** page 205.*

midnight Sun. **Credit** AmEx, DC, MC, V.

The only big *omni-sportcentrum* (sports centre) in Amsterdam, offering squash, outdoor and indoor tennis, ten-pin bowling, badminton and a restaurant. Rates are higher in the evening and at weekends.

Squash

Dickysquash
Karel Lotsylaan 16, OS (646 2266). Metro Zuid/Bus 48, 63. **Open** 9am-midnight Mon-Sat; 9am-11pm Sun. **Cost** *½ hour* f17.50; *1 hour* f32.50. **No credit cards.**
Dickysquash caters for the more experienced player.

Squash City
Ketelmakerstraat 6, IW (626 7883). Bus 18, 22. **Open** 8.45am-11.15pm Mon-Fri; 8.45am-9pm Sat, Sun. **Cost** *during the day and Sat* f13.50 per player; *evenings and Sun* f26.25 per player. **Credit** AmEx, MC, V.
This is the place to head for if you see squash as more of a hobby than a battle. You can use the sauna and weights room at no extra charge.

Swimming Pools

For **Sloterparkbad** open-air pool, *see below* **Watersports.**

Marnixbad
Marnixplein 9, OW (625 4843). Tram 3, 7, 10. **Open** 7-9am, noon-1pm, 3-5pm, Mon; 7am-5.30pm, 8-10.45pm, Tue; 7am-1pm, 4-5.30pm, 9.30-10.45pm, Wed; 7-10am, 11am-5pm, Thur; 7-10am, 11am-5.30pm, Fri; 10am-noon Sat; 10am-noon, 3.30-5.30pm, Sun. **Admission** f4; f3.50 under-18s. **No credit cards.**
As well as a 25m (82ft) indoor pool, with water slides and a whirlpool, Marnixbad also boasts a sauna.

Mirandabad
De Mirandalaan, OSE (644 6637). Tram 15, 69, 169. **Open** *indoor pool* 7am-10.15pm Mon, Fri; 7-8.45am, noon-1.30pm, 3-10.15pm, Tue; 7-9.45am, 12.15-10.15pm, Wed; 7-10am, 11am-5.30pm, 7-10.15pm Thur; 10am-5.30pm Sat, Sun; *outdoor pool May-Aug* 10am-6pm daily, depending on the weather. **Admission** f5.25; 4-17s f4.25; over-65s f3.25. **No credit cards.**
The only sub-tropical pool in Amsterdam, Mirandabad is very clean, with a stone beach and a wave machine that's switched on every half hour. There's also a water slide, a whirlpool and an outdoor pool.

Zuiderbad
Hobbemastraat 26, OS (679 2217). Tram 1, 2, 5/Bus 26, 66, 67, 170, 179. **Open** 7am-6pm, 7-10.30pm Mon; 7-9am, noon-5pm, 6-9.30pm, Tue; 7-10am, noon-10.30pm, Wed; 7-9am, 11.30-6pm, Thur; 7am-10.30pm Fri; 8am-2.30pm Sat; 10am-3.30pm Sun. **Admission** f3.80; f3.30 under-18s; f2.55 over-65s.
No credit cards.
The Zuiderbad was built in 1912, making it one of the country's oldest pools. Recently extensively renovated, it still retains its original, picturesque detail. There's nude swimming between 4pm and 5.15pm on Sundays.

Tennis

There are four busy open-air courts at Vondelpark (*see chapter* **Sightseeing**).

Amstelpark
Karel Lotsylaan 8, OS (644 5436). Metro Zuid/Bus 26, 48, 63, 158. **Open** 8am-midnight daily. **Hire costs**

indoor courts f30 per hour; *outdoor courts* f25 per hour. **Racket hire** free. **No credit cards.**
The Amstelpark has 36 courts in all. During the summer there are ten indoor courts, and in the winter six of the outdoor courts are covered over, giving a total of sixteen indoor courts. Reservations may be made by phone.

Buitenveldert
Van der Boechorststraat 38, OS (642 9641). Metro Buitenveldert/Bus 69, 169. **Open** 8am-midnight daily. **Hire costs** *outdoor courts* f25 per hour; *indoor courts* f27.50-f47.50 per hour depending on date and time. **Racket hire** free. **No credit cards.**
There are 4 indoor and 20 outdoor courts. The outdoor courts are often booked in the evenings by clubs, so phone first to check.

Kadoelen
Kadoelenweg, N (631 3194). Bus 92. **Open** 9am-midnight daily. **Hire costs** *mid Apr-mid Sept* f20 per hour; *mid Sept-mid Apr* f40 per hour. **Racket hire** f5. **No credit cards.**
Kadoelen is subsidised by the local council, so the nine indoor courts cost less to hire than elsewhere. Tennis lessons can be arranged in advance. Outdoor Badminton courts are due to open in 1993.

Watersports

As The Netherlands is a land of water, watersports are very popular. Sailboards are normal holiday luggage for the Dutch, despite the wet climate. If you want to go sailing, visit Loosdrecht (25 kilometres/15 miles south-east of Amsterdam) or go to the IJsselmeer; in Muiden (20 kilometres/12 miles east of Amsterdam) catamarans can be rented. For information about canoeing phone the **Dutch Canoe-Federation** on 033 62 2341, and *see chapter* **The Provinces: Overijssel**. Most water-sports schools ask for a deposit when you rent a boat; in most cases a passport will suffice. The Dutch often take their sailboards out to the North Sea resorts (such as Zandvoort, *see chapter* **The Randstad**), where boards can also be hired.

Duikelaar, Sloterpark
Noordzijde 41, OW (613 8855). Tram 13, 14/Bus 19. **Open** 9am-6pm Mon-Fri; 11am-5pm Sat, Sun. **Hire costs** *sailing boat* f15 per hour; *one and two person canoes* f7.50 per person per hour; *three person canoe* f10 per person per hour; *sailboard and wetsuit* f15 per hour. **Deposit** f100 plus passport.
No credit cards.
At this water-sports centre on the banks of the Sloterplas lake (in the western suburbs), you can rent small sailing boats, canoes and sailboards. The season runs from May to October; from November to April only canoes are available for hire. The **Sloterparkbad** indoor and open-air (summer) swimming pools are here, too (611 4565).

Park Gaasperplas
OSE. Metro Gaasperplas/Bus 59, 60, 158, 174. **Open** 24 hours daily.
Tucked away behind the Bijlmemeer in Amsterdam South-East, this park was laid out for 'Floriade 1982' (*see chapters* **Excursions in Holland: Flowers**). Its large lake has become a centre for watersports and windsurfing. There's also a campsite.

Theatre

Since the 'tomato action' of 1968, experimental drama and fringe productions have dominated the capital's theatre scene.

Theatre in The Netherlands is characterised by its wide variety. Musicals, revues and cabaret are surprisingly popular in a country that has a reputation for sobriety and seriousness.

The Dutch theatrical tradition dates back to medieval times. Seventeenth-century Dutch theatre companies used to perform all over Europe, as far afield as the Baltic. In the Golden Age, Dutch was the international language of trade. The Dutch playwrights of that period – Hooft, Bredero and Vondel – are still occasionally performed, both in classic rendition as well as modern.

'They don't think the profession of an actor the only trade a man ought to have, so they won't allow anybody to grow rich on a profession that so little conduces to the good of the commonwealth', wrote Joseph Addison after seeing a play in Amsterdam in 1703, performed by 'tradesmen that after their day's work is over earn about a guilder a night by personating kings and generals'. Throughout the eighteenth and nineteenth centuries, theatre was still by and for the people. It was not until the end of the nineteenth century that it became an élitist affair, something for those with an 'education' – actors and public alike. This attitude is still fairly entrenched.

FROM REVOLT TO RESPECTABILITY

In 1968 a group of young actors and drama students started the 'tomato action' by throwing tomatoes during performances by their older, established colleagues. At the time, Dutch theatre was more-or-less controlled by a small, exclusive group of actors and directors. The aim of the tomato-throwing was to provoke discussion between those on the stage and those who wanted to be there and who wanted to introduce new ideas and forms. The rebels were so successful that – ironically – they themselves now form the 'establishment' in the theatre world.

They have begun to perform classic works and employ traditional styles of acting from other parts of the world, a process that has been greatly influenced by the influx of information and talent from eastern Europe, and there have been an increasing number of co-productions and exchanges. Indeed, it's striking how few original Dutch-language productions are currently being staged. There is also a healthy

avant-garde movement, although for the most part un-subsidised. The most innovative fringe groups are Nieuw West, Orkater, De Trust, and the Mexicaanse Hond (Mexican Dog). The forte of Dutch theatre is design; sets, lighting and costumes are often striking and innovative, while the acting itself tends towards the declamatory.

There is no national theatre company; the best of the mainstream Dutch groups are Toneelgroep Amsterdam, resident at the Stadsschouwburg (*listed under* **Venues**), whose interpretations are solid if not inspiring; and Theatre van het Oosten, De Appel and RoTheater, all based outside Amsterdam but frequent visitors to the capital's larger venues.

CUT-BACKS AND MERGERS

The view held by the present Dutch government is not so different from that described by Addison in the early eighteenth-century. Dutch theatre only enjoyed the luxury of subsidies after World War II, and in the mid-eighties the government started a programme of drastic cut-backs in arts support. Like some of the major orchestras, several companies have been forced to merge, and a few have disappeared altogether. And, as so often happens in these situations, 'serious' theatre loses out to more popular forms of entertainment, such as cabaret and musicals, which attract more sponsors and investors as well as larger audiences.

LOCATION THEATRE AND FESTIVALS

Festivals and location theatre are the latest trends in The Netherlands. Every self-respecting city in the country has its own theatre festival. During the summer these are held not only in Amsterdam (*see below* **Festivals and Events**), but also in most of the major cities in the Randstad. For those prepared to travel further out, try the Oerol Festival in June, on the northern island of Terschelling (*see chapter* **The Provinces: Friesland**). Location theatre is another new development: venues such as warehouses, factories, stables and fortresses form an integral part of performances. One of the highlights of the Oerol Festival is a bicycle tour with theatrical interruptions, encouragement and rest-stops.

English-Language Theatre

English theatre companies visited The Netherlands as early as 1590, playing the theatres of The Hague, Leiden, Utrecht and Amsterdam, and – if they could get the permission of the city authorities – at fairs outside the towns. In the middle of the seventeenth century, Utrecht could even boast a resident company of 'comedians'. Their Dutch colleagues were thus familiar with the English repertoire, which enabled them to write Dutch adaptations of works by Shakespeare, Kyd and Marlowe. Sometimes, when the Dutch playwrights have stolen a little here and borrowed a little there, the original English material is difficult to spot. Other plays are clearly Dutch versions of popular English works: *The Taming of the Shrew, The Spanish Tragedy* and *Doctor Faustus* were reworked and staged in Amsterdam and elsewhere in Holland.

Seventeenth- and eighteenth-century Holland had a considerable English-speaking community. Audiences would include English politicians and soldiers in The Hague, medical students in Leiden, merchants and bankers in Amsterdam and Scottish law students in Utrecht. There were plenty of theatre-loving tourists: Holland was the starting or finishing point for many a well-heeled young gentleman on his Grand Tour. There were English churches, English taverns and English booksellers in Amsterdam and The Hague. In 1710 one book-

seller, Thomas Johnson, whose shop was next to The Hague's theatre, started publishing a collection of English plays – 70 in all – which included works by Shakespeare, Dryden and Vanbrugh.

By the end of the eighteenth century, however, Holland had fallen under the spell of French language and culture. A contest in Paris even established that the best actress in the French Empire (which Holland was a part of at that time) was Dutch. It was not until the end of the nineteenth century that there was a resurgence of interest in English plays. Works by Oscar Wilde and later Bernard Shaw were staged in Dutch translations. But it was quite a long time – the 1960s in fact – before English theatre companies were treading the boards again in The Netherlands. The occasional production by the Royal Shakespeare Company paved the way for other, less established groups. Amsterdam proved fertile ground for English-language theatre, both mainstream and fringe. It is not surprising that this resurgence coincided with a growing population of English and American expatriates. But the audience at English-language productions is still largely made up of natives, some of them seeing Shakespeare for the first time and finding out that they can get the gist without recourse to subtitles.

ENGLISH-LANGUAGE THEATRE

Because virtually everyone in Amsterdam speaks English there is a potentially large audience for English-language theatre in the capital. However, there is quite a fast turnover of English-language companies, which come and go in Amsterdam. In addition to the Stalhouderij, which has its own playing space (*see below* **Venues**), and Theatre de Bochel (the Hunchback) which have converted a bathhouse into a playing space, there are several other companies working in English, which play venues like the Bovenzaal (Stadsschouwburg), and the Rob van Reijn Theatre. Panache, for example, typically puts on two or three productions a season, usually in the summer. Their work generally concentrates on popular pieces from England and the US. The Euro-American Theater, on the other hand, focuses more on a classical repertory, often touring schools. There is also a handful of groups – The Alliance, Bits and Pieces, The American Actor's Theater –

who, though they produce plays less frequently, help keep the flow of English-language theatre constant.

There are also quite a few touring companies which pass through Amsterdam and perform in English. Impresarios such as Jaap van Baasbank and Wim Visser are doing a great job getting top-quality productions from Britain (sometimes with backing from the British Council), the United States and South Africa.

INFORMATION AND BOOKINGS

Uitkrant is a monthly freesheet, published by the AUB Uitburo cultural office (*see chapter* **Essential Information**), with listings for almost every venue in Amsterdam. It's available in most theatres, bookshops and tourist information centres. For information (not reservations) on performances and concerts, phone 621 1211 (10am-6pm Mon-Wed, Fri, Sat; 10am-9pm Thur; English is usually spoken). The *Amsterdam Times* (free from most hotels) and

What's On in Amsterdam (f2.50 from VVV tourist offices) both give details of selected events in English.

Tickets can be bought or reserved direct from theatre box offices, or from the Uitburo, from 10am to 6pm Monday to Saturday (until 9pm on Thursday). There is a f2 booking charge, f5 for telecredit booking. You can also book or purchase tickets from the VVV tourist offices, or through their telephone reservation service (626 6444); there is a f3 surcharge.

Venues

Amphi Theater
WG Terrein, opposite 1e Helmerstraat 115, OW (616 8942). Tram 1, 6. **Open** *box office* noon-5pm Mon-Fri. **Tickets** f10, f12.50; f10, f7.50 CJP card holders, over-65s. **No credit cards.**
The complex in which this alternative theatre is housed used to be a hospital. It presents smaller productions, often of an experimental nature.

De Brakke Grond
Nes 45, C (626 6866). Tram 4, 9, 16, 24, 25. **Open** *box office* 10am-1.30pm, 2-4pm; 7pm-start of performance. **Tickets** *Grote Zaal* f17.50; f12.50 CJP cards holders and over 65s. **Performances** 8.30pm. **No credit cards.**
Operating on a similar artistic basis to its neighbour, the Frascati (*below*), De Brakke Grond places more emphasis on Flemish productions. The building also houses regular exhibitions.

DNA
Spuistraat 2, C (627 8672/8699). Tram 1, 2, 5, 14, 17. **Open** *box office* 10am-5pm Mon-Fri; also 7.30pm-start of performance. **Tickets** f15; f12.50 CJP card holders, over-65s. **No credit cards.**
Amsterdam's only subsidised theatre to produce multi-cultural work. De Nieuw Amsterdam (DNA) is a whole network of artists; at any one time there might be a reading (every third Sunday in the month, often in English), story-telling from around the world, major productions either in their own space or on tour, experimental studio productions, school programmes, and even the company's own radio talk show (Radio 100, every third Wednesday of the month at 6pm). DNA is the brainchild of renowned director Rufus Collins.

Engelenbak
Nes 71, C (626 6866/3644). Tram 4, 9, 16, 24, 25. **Open** *box office* 10am-1.30pm, 2-4pm, Mon-Sat; also 7pm-start of performance. **Tickets** *Grote Zaal* f12.50; f10 CJP cards holders and over 65s. **Performances** 8.30pm. **No credit cards.**
A nice venue, mainly used by amateurs trying out their stuff on the capital.

't Fijnhout Theater
Jacob van Lennepkade 334, OW (618 4768). Tram 3, 7, 12, 17. **Open** 10am-4pm Mon-Fri. **Tickets** f7.50; reductions for CJP card holders, over-65s. **Performances** 9pm Fri, Sat. **No credit cards.**

Opposite: Koninklijk Theater Carré *(top);*
AUB Uitburo ticket shop *(bottom).*

This small theatre, housed in a converted factory, sometimes has English-language shows by various international companies.

Frascati
Nes 63, C (626 6866/623 5723). Tram 4, 9, 16, 24, 25. **Open** *box office* 10am-1.30pm, 2-4pm, Mon-Sat; also 7pm-start of performance. **Tickets** *Grote Zaal* f17.50; *Kleine Zaal* f15; reductions for CJP card holders and over 65s. **Performances** *Grote Zaal* 9pm; *Kleine Zaal* 8.30pm. **No credit cards.**
One of Amsterdam's better venues for interesting new work, including one large auditorium and two smaller ones.

Koninklijk Theater Carré
Amstel 115-125, OS (622 5225). Tram 6, 7, 10. **Open** *box office* 10am-7pm daily. **Tickets** f25-f100; reductions for CJP card holders, over-65s. **Performance** 8.15pm. **Credit** DC.
A former circus, home to some of the best Dutch comedians and solo performers. You may catch Jango Edwards, an Amsterdam-based American whose shows are a wild mixture of stand-up comedy and rock 'n' roll; Rudi van Dantzig's dance-music-theatre spectacle 'Live Life' was staged here to international acclaim. The traditional venue for musicals, recent productions have included *Cats* and *Les Misérables*. Other offerings include folk dance, cabaret and revues. The theatre is being largely refurbished: backstage tours are due to resume in 1994.

De Melkweg
Lijnbaansgracht 234A, IS (624 1777/624 8492). Tram 1, 2, 5, 7, 10. **Open** *box office* noon-4.30pm Mon-Fri. **Tickets** *theatre tickets* f10 plus membership. **Membership** f4 monthly; f6 3 months; f20 yearly. **No credit cards.**
This multi-media centre behind the Stadsschouwburg (*see below*) opened its doors in 1970 on the site of a former milk factory. The symbol of Amsterdam liberalism and tolerance in the seventies, the Melkweg has managed to survive its own legend and retain its worldwide reputation as a cultural meeting-place. In 1983 it became a founder member of Transeuropehalles, an international network of multi-media cultural groups. The theatre provides an important stage for new international groups and solo performers, and offers space to young directors and groups to develop ideas. The Melkweg's director, Cornelius Schlösser, and theatre programmer Suzanne Dechert keep coming up with new acts – whether ethnic, gay, lesbian, stand-up comedy, improvisation or gestural theatre. *See also chapters* **Film, Music: Rock, Folk & Jazz,** *and* **Clubs.**

Felix Meritis Theater
Felix Meritis Building, Keizersgracht 324, IW (information 9am-5pm Mon-Fri 626 2321). Tram 1, 2, 5. **Open** *box office* 3pm-start of performance Tue-Sat; *telephone bookings* 3-7.30pm daily. **Tickets** f16.50, f12.50; reductions for CJP holders, over-65s. **Performances** 8pm Tue-Sat. **No credit cards.**
Occasionally you can catch English-language theatre groups in this beautiful, early nineteenth-century building, which was the centre of fringe theatre in the early seventies. During July and August the Amsterdam Summer University (*see chapter* **Students**) runs an extensive daytime programme of courses, workshops and seminars in the arts and sciences (all in English). In the evenings a multi-cultural programme covers theatrical performances, dance, music, video and seminars.

Rob van Reijn
Haarlemmerdijk 31, C (627 9988). Bus 18, 22, 44. **Open** *box office* 7.15pm-start of performance. **Tickets** f17.50; f12.50 CJP card holders, over-65s. **Performances** 8.15pm. **No credit cards.**

Until recently the sole domain of its namesake, pantomime artist Rob van Reijn, this intimate theatre now hosts a wide variety of productions, from transvestite spectacle to English-language contemporary plays.

De Stadsschouwburg

Leidseplein 26, IS (624 2311). Tram 1, 2, 5, 6,7, 10. **Open** *box office* 10am-7pm Mon-Sat; 1½ before performance Sun and holidays. **Tickets** f13-f45; reductions for CJP card holders, over-65s. **Performances** 8.15pm. **No credit cards.**
The Stadsschouwburg (municipal theatre) is into its third incarnation: the first two buildings were destroyed by fire in the seventeenth and eighteenth centuries. The present theatre, opened in 1894, is a beautiful and impressive baroque building built in the traditional horseshoe shape, and seats about 950. Director Cox Habbema is responsible for a policy which not only nurtures traditional Dutch theatre, but also a wide variety of national and international productions. Perhaps the best-known of the Dutch classics, *Gijsbrecht van Aemstel*, written in 1638 by Joost van den Vondel, is performed every January at the Stadsschouwburg. The story is based loosely on the life of the feudal lord of Amsterdam, during the siege of Amsterdam in the fourteenth century. The play was written to celebrate the opening of the first Stadsschouwburg. There's also a space for small-scale productions here, called the **Bovenzaal** – originally the prop room and situated right underneath the roof.

De Stalhouderij

1e Bloemdwarsstraat 4, IW (bookings 1-6pm Mon-Sat 626 2282). Tram 13, 14, 17. **Open** *box office* 8pm-start of performance; reserved tickets to be collected before 8.15pm. **Tickets** f15; CJP card holders, over-65s, students f12.50. **Performances** 8.30pm. **No credit cards.**
For a number of years this former stable (*stalhouderij* means livery-stable) has been the home of the Stalhouderij Theatre Company, an international collective of artists. In addition to performing contemporary English-language plays, the company runs a workshop studio, where teachers from English-speaking countries and The Netherlands offer a broad variety of courses, ranging from scene study to technical movement. It's the smallest theatre in Amsterdam – the size of an average living-room – and is unusually intimate. The friendly bar upstairs is often manned by actors not involved in the current production. Booking in advance is imperative, as productions tend to sell out.
Wheelchair access with help.

Vondelpark Theater

Vondelpark, OS (523 7700). Tram 1, 2, 3, 5, 6, 12. **Performances** *Early June-early Sept* Thur-Sun. **Free.**
Throughout the summer months, Vondelpark hosts a wide variety of theatre and music. The open-air theatre is situated in the middle of the park by the fountain. Cabaret, drama, concerts, kids' programmes or dance all feature. The atmosphere alone is worth the trip. *See also chapter* **Music: Rock, Folk & Jazz.**

Festivals and Events

Holland Festival

Bookings (from February) *Nederlands Reserverings Centrum, Postbus 404, 2260 AK Leidschendam (070 320 2500).* **Tickets** f20-f100. **Credit card bookings** *621 1211.* **Direct sales** (from May) from AUB Uitburo and VVV tourist offices and individual theatres.
Amsterdam's most prestigious entertainment festival takes place throughout June every year, and presents not only theatre, but also music and dance in major venues. Director Jan van Vlijmen has a reputation for spectacle and extravagance, which is good for the Festival's pub-

licity, but not so good for fiscal continuity. Advance programme information is available from Holland Festival, Kleine Gartmanplantsoen 21, 1017 RP, Amsterdam (627 6566). Its office is open 9am-6pm Mon-Fri.

Off Holland Festival

The official 'fringe' of the Holland Festival *(above)*, and certainly no less interesting than the real thing. Lots of activity takes place in the smaller theatres: one-man shows, mime, music, dance and combinations by Dutch and international performers. The Off Holland schedule is available in the *Holland Festival Daily* (from participating theatres and the usual ticket outlets). At the time of writing, the future of the festival is in the balance because of lack of sponsorship, but it will probably continue in one form or another.

International Theatre School Festival

Tickets *De Brakke Grond, Nes 45, C (information/reservations phone 626 6866 10am-5pm, 7-9pm daily). Tram 4, 9, 14, 16, 24, 25.* **Open** *box office* 10am-9pm Mon-Sat. **Tickets** f10; reduction card f15 (tickets f2.50 with card). **No credit cards.**
A festival of theatre school productions from all over the world takes place at the end of June in the so-called Nes theatres: De Brakke Grond (Nes 45), De Engelenbak (Nes 71), Frascati (Nes 63), and at the Stadsschouwburg *(above)*. The programme is gradually becoming more international, with groups from the US and Germany appearing.

Uitmarkt

Museumplein, OS. Tram 2, 3, 5, 12, 16. **Dates** 27-29 August 1993.
A cultural market rather than a festival. In the last weekend of August every year, theatres, performing artists and companies preview and sell their programmes for the coming season. From Friday to Sunday Museumplein turns into a lively marketplace, with free music, dance, theatre and cabaret performances on several outdoor stages.

Theatre Museum

Nederlands Theater Museum

Herengracht 168-170, IW (623 5104). Tram 13, 14, 17. **Open** 11am-5pm Tue-Sun. **Admission** f5; f3 students, CJP card holders; free under-4s. **No credit cards.**
The museum forms part of the Netherlands Theatre Institute, which also houses an excellent library and a theatre bookshop. The building itself is an example of seventeenth-century splendour, with beautifully decorated walls and ceilings. The collection includes a fine eighteenth-century miniature theatre, modelled after the second Stadsschouwburg, working rain, thunder and wind machines and other old-fashioned stage machinery. In various regularly-changing exhibitions you can admire a wonderful collection of costumes, masks, posters and anything relating to Dutch theatre. *See chapter* **Museums.** *Guided tours (min. 15 people).*

Bookshop

International Theatre & Film Books

Leidseplein 26 (in the Stadsschouwburg building, to the right of the main entrance), IS (622 6489). Tram 1, 2, 5, 6, 7, 10. **Open** 10am-6pm Mon-Sat. **Credit** AmEx, MC.
This bookshop offers a wide variety of international magazines and books on the stage and screen. There are books on everything from history to theatre management, often in English, as well as texts of current productions. Fancy starting your own theatre or theatre company? There are books that tell you how to do that too.

Early Hours

Amsterdam for night-owls: all your post-midnight whims and needs answered.

To the outsider it may seem that Amsterdam closes down at 1am, but if you know where to look, there are still places open to assuage hunger and slake thirst before setting off home as the sun rises.

But first, if something disastrous should happen, ring 0611 for **police**, **fire** or **ambulance** and ask for the relevant emergency service. For less major **medical emergencies** *see chapter* **Survival** for a list of 24-hour casualty departments.

If you need a **chemist** or **pharmacist** late at night, phone the **Central Medical Service** (Centraal Dokters Dienst) on 664 2111 or 679 1821 (24 hours daily), or consult the daily newspaper *Het Parool*, which publishes details of which *apotheek* are open late that week. Details are also posted in the local *apotheek*.

If you need to change some money, the GWK **bureau de change** in Centraal Station stays open 24 hours a day, as does the branch in Schiphol airport.

The tram and Metro systems stop running after midnight and don't start again until 6am. **Night buses** are numbered from 71 to 77, and numbers 73 to 76 run through the city centre. Night bus stops have a black square with the bus number printed on it. However, even the night buses stop running between 2am and 4am Monday to Friday and 2.30am to 3.30am on Saturday and Sunday, so between these hours the only alternatives are walking or taking a taxi. Since Amsterdam is a small city, walking may well be the best choice, but for those whose feet refuse to carry them any further **taxis** can usually be found at the ranks at Centraal Station, Rembrandtplein, Leidseplein and the junction of Kinkerstraat and Marnixstraat. Taxis can be ordered by phoning the 24-hour central taxi control on 677 7777. For car drivers, the following are the main 24-hour **petrol stations** (*benzinestation*) within Amsterdam: Gooiseweg 10-11, OE; Sarphatistraat 225, IE; Marnixstraat 250, IW; Spaarndammerdijk 218, OW.

Shops

Scattered throughout the city are 'nightshops' (*avondwinkel*), usually open until 1am. Although the goods are overpriced, they are the only places open for those late-night necessities: coffee, tea, milk and cigarettes.

Avondmarkt
De Wittenkade 90-96, OW (686 4919). Tram 10. **Open** 6pm-1am Mon-Fri; 5.30pm-1am Sat, Sun. **No credit cards.** Recommended – well worth a tram ride.

Baltus Sterk
Vijzelstraat 127, IS (626 9069). Tram 16, 24, 25. **Open** 4pm-1am Mon-Fri; 1pm-1am Sat; 6pm-1am Sun. **No credit cards.**

Dolf's Avondverkoop
Willemsstraat 79, OW (625 9503). Tram 3. **Open** noon-1am daily. **No credit cards.**

Doorneveld
De Clercqstraat 3-7, OW (618 1727). Tram 12, 13, 14. **Open** 6pm-1am daily. **No credit cards.**

Heuft's First Class Night Shop
Rijnstraat 62, OS (642 4048). Tram 4, 25. **Open** 4pm-1am daily. **Credit** AmEx, DC.
Go in person, or phone and ask for a delivery of anything from champagne and oysters to full meals.

Bars

Bars in Amsterdam are usually open until 1am from Monday to Thursday and Sunday, and 2am on Fridays and Saturdays. For the dedicated barfly, we list below three very late night bars.

Barbarella
Van Woustraat 36, OS (679 0867). Tram 4. **Open** 8am-6am daily. **No credit cards.**
Snacks are served later than anywhere else here. The choice ranges from chips to cigarettes.

Koophandel
Bloemgracht 49, IW (623 9843). Tram 10, 13, 14, 17. **Open** 4pm-very late daily. **No credit cards.**
A bar for the dedicated drinker. Don't bother turning up before midnight, when the bar is virtually empty, and be prepared not to leave before dawn.

De Pieter
St Pieterspoortsteeg 29, C (623 6007). Tram 4, 9, 14, 16, 24, 25. **Open** 11pm-3am Mon-Thur, Sun; 11pm-4am Fri, Sat. **No credit cards.**
Something of a student hang-out, this is a small, dark and noisy bar that gets even smaller and noisier when the owner squeezes in a live band.

Restaurants

Most of the so-called night restaurants are located around Leidseplein and vary from okay to awful. They can get crowded after 1am. An alternative for hungry homeward-bound clubbers is the **Febo** chain, which does a virtually round-the-clock service of food from slot machines. Heated dishes, plus good chips and sauces from mayonnaise to piccalilli, are available. There are branches throughout the city, but there are particularly popular ones on Leidsestraat and Kalverstraat.

Bojo
Lange Leidsedwarsstraat 51, IS (622 7434). Tram 1, 2, 5, 6, 7, 10. **Open** 5pm-2am Mon-Thur, Sun; 5pm-6am Fri, Sat. **No credit cards.**
An Indonesian restaurant of variable quality in the middle of Amsterdam's late-night district. It's often crowded and noisy, with a long wait to be served. You'll see all kinds of crazy types here, so it makes for good entertainment at a reasonable price.

Mama's Shoarma
Between Sedap and Christine LeDuc Sex Shop, Korte Leidsedwarsstraat, IS (no phone). Tram 1, 2, 5, 6, 7, 10. **Open** 5pm-5am daily. **No credit cards.**
Mama's serves the best (and one of the cheapest) shoarma (or kebab) in Amsterdam. This Middle Eastern speciality is perfect for late-night appetites, and the Egyptian staff are friendly and not into the drug dealing that goes on in some of the other grill-bars.

Sedap
Korte Leidsedwarsstraat 60, IS (627 4743). Tram 1, 2, 5, 6, 7, 10. **Open** 4pm-6am daily. **Credit** AmEx.
A relatively quiet place serving Indonesian food of acceptable quality. Most dishes cost less than f15.

In Focus

Some groups of visitors have very specific requirements of a city. Here we concentrate on their disparate needs, listing solutions and ideas for all situations: whether it's a computer hire firm, a gay sauna, a women-friendly bar, or a student information line.

Contents

Business

A run-down of Amsterdam's role in the Dutch economy, plus essential information for the business traveller.

Given its history as a trading nation, it's not surprising that the Dutch economy today is dominated by international trade. Some 65 per cent of gross domestic product (GDP) is exported, and it was the ever-increasing sales abroad that paid for the country's rapid industrialisation after 1945. Dutch agriculture, now highly mechanised and with one of the world's highest yields per hectare, accounts for around a quarter of total exports. The Netherlands is thought to be the world's largest exporter of dairy products, poultry and seed potatoes, and its outright earnings from agricultural exports rank second only to the USA. Horticulture makes up 20 per cent of total agrarian exports – the famous tulip bulbs (*see chapter* **Excursions in Holland**) account for only a fraction of this. Recent figures indicate that over half the world's cut flowers and pot plants originate in Dutch soil.

Dutch industry was developed largely during this century and is based around mostly small and medium-sized companies. However there are three notable exceptions to this trend – Royal Dutch/Shell, Unilever and Philips are Dutch-based companies and are among the 25 largest industrial concerns in the world.

The most important industrial sector is food, drink and tobacco manufacturing, which accounts for 18 per cent of industrial turnover. The chemicals and petroleum sector contributes 17 per cent and electrical engineering 14 per cent; printing and mechanical engineering follow. Then come vehicle manufacture, shipbuilding materials and rubber products.

SERVICE ECONOMY

The service sector – banking, insurance, transport, communications and tourism – is where the Dutch make much of their money. It now generates 50 per cent of net national income and employs half of the workforce. The ABN AMRO bank is one of the world's top 30 banks. The country is a net exporter of capital, and investment abroad by companies based in The Netherlands is still on the rise. The largest Dutch insurance company, Nationale-Nederlanden, ranks fifteenth in the world.

Transport and distribution account for eight per cent of The Netherlands' GDP. The Dutch play a vital role in the European Community (EC) in these sectors. Rotterdam is now easily the world's biggest port in terms of volume handled. With around 292 million tonnes/287 million tons passing through each year, it's twice as big as its nearest rival, New York. The Netherlands today generates six per cent of total EC gross national product, but it handles 37 per cent of EC transport. Schiphol, Amsterdam's airport, carries much EC freight. It also handled 17 million passengers in 1991. The country's system of bonded warehouses and customs depots is designed to encourage the free movement of commodities. Goods in transit can be sorted, assembled and repacked or stored indefinitely without incurring duties or value added tax (BTW in Dutch).

FREE TRADE

The liberal and non-discriminatory attitude the Dutch have developed over centuries of trade has prompted some 3,500 foreign firms to set up Dutch offices. Companies such as Fuji, ITT, Nissan, IBM, EMI, Polaroid, Rank Xerox, Sony and Canon have established their European distribution centres in the country. There are very few restrictions on the repatriation or transfer abroad of profits, capital repayments, dividends or earnings. Free trade is enshrined in trading law, with no licence required for either importing or exporting in the majority of cases. Major corporations benefit from the free-enterprise economy – any company physically or statutorily based in The Netherlands is exempt from tax on the earnings of foreign subsidiaries in which they have at least a five per cent stake. Foreign international corporations, in other words, can set up a Dutch BV (private limited company) or NV (public company) and save on tax bills. This device has helped Dutch-registered companies become leading foreign investors in the USA.

But while the Dutch economy remains one of the most open and well-managed in Europe – and the Dutch guilder, linked to the Deutschmark, is traditionally strong – business predictions are not entirely optimistic. Export growth is projected to fall over the next few years and the country's exceptionally low inflation is set to rise. Wage costs are likely to climb, and the national debt ratio – 79 per cent of GNP in 1992 – is worryingly high. Against a background of declining world trade, the task of reducing this will not be eased by the combined facts that the Dutch run the second most expensive welfare state in Europe (after the Scandinavian countries); long-term unemployment persists; and income on exports of natural gas can be expected to wane during the next century (The Netherlands is the fourth largest gas producer in the world). The massive costs of cleaning up the environment (*see chapter* **Green Issues**) could brake economic growth further.

AMSTERDAM TODAY

So where does Amsterdam fit into today's Dutch business scene? The city's port is fighting back, but has a long way to go: throughput in 1991 was about one-tenth of Rotterdam's and it is currently the fourteenth largest in Europe. Around the port are petrochemical and petroleum-blending installations, distribution centres (Japanese car manufacturer Nissan is the latest) and ship repair yards. Hi-tech and light manufacturing – for example, the fashion industry – are in good health. The traditional diamond industry, now recovered from the decimation of its workforce during World War II (it was, and still is, largely run by Jewish people), numbers some 20 diamond workshops; the majority of

production is geared to industrial use. Tours are run around several of these workshops (*see chapter* **Sightseeing**).

The city is home to the headquarters of the Nederlandsche Bank (the Dutch National Bank), the ING Postbank and ABN AMRO banks, the European head offices of companies including IBM, and to countless trading houses and brokers. Tourism is a substantial earner, and nearly eight and a half million people visited Amsterdam in 1992.

Financial services are the city's biggest invisible money-spinner: Amsterdam contains over 400 stockbroking firms and 500 domestic and foreign bank branches. The Effectenbeurs lists some 250 Dutch companies and 315 foreign firms. It also trades around 1,500 bond issues. A system known as ASAS allows players to trade shares in a number of US stock issues directly from Amsterdam in dollars rather than guilders. Along with the Effectenbeurs, the **Optiebeurs** (the European Options Exchange, or EOE, *see below* **Exchanges**) and the major banks are part of a drive to make Amsterdam home of the Central European Bank.

The Dutch capital may not be the commercial hub it was in the Golden Age, but behind the doors of the old merchants' canal houses and in the gleaming new office blocks of Amsterdam's *Zuid-Oost* business park, a lot of money is still changing hands.

Information

Many of the agencies listed below are in The Hague (Den Haag). For details of embassies and consulates, and libraries in Amsterdam, *see chapter* **Survival**.

American-Netherlands Chamber of Commerce

Carnegieplein 5, 2517 KJ, Den Haag (070 347 8292). **Open** 9am-4pm Mon-Fri.

British Embassy, Commercial Department
Lange Voorhout 10, 2514 ED, Den Haag (070 364 5800). **Open** 9am-1pm, 2.15-5.30pm, Mon-Fri.
Based in The Hague, this office co-operates with the British Department of Trade and Industry to assist British companies operating in The Netherlands.

British-Netherlands Chamber of Commerce
Bezuidenhoutseweg 181, 2594 AH, Den Haag (070 347 8881). **Open** 9am-4pm (trade enquiries 10am-noon, 2-4pm) Mon-Fri.

Centraal Bureau voor Statistiek (CBS)
Prinses Beatrixlaan 428, 2273 XZ, Voorburg (070 337 3800). **Open** 9am-noon, 2-5pm, Mon-Fri.
The Central Bureau for Statistics provides statistics on every aspect of Dutch business, society and the economy.

Commissariaat voor Buitenlandse Investeringen Nederland (Netherlands Foreign Investment Agency)
Bezuidenhoutseweg 91, 2500 EC, Den Haag (070 379 72333/fax 070 379 6322). **Open** 8am-6pm Mon-Fri.
Probably the most useful first port of call for business people wishing to relocate to The Netherlands.

Douane Amsterdam (Customs)
Leeuwendalersweg 21, OW (586 7511). Tram 12, 14/Bus 21, 68, 80. **Open** 7.30am-5.30pm Mon-Fri.

Douane Rotterdam (Customs)
West Zeedijk 387, Rotterdam (010 478 6528). **Open** 8am-5pm Mon-Fri.

Economische Voorlichtingdienst, EVD (The Netherlands Foreign Trade Agency)
Bezuidenhoutseweg 151, 2594 AG, Den Haag (070 379 7883). **Open** 9am-4pm Mon-Fri.
A very useful library and information centre for business people. It incorporates the Netherlands Council for Trade Promotion (NCH), another handy source of information.

Kamer van Koophandel (Chamber of Commerce)
De Ruijterkade 5, C (523 6600). Tram 1, 2, 4, 5, 9, 13, 16, 17, 24, 25. **Open** 9am-4pm Mon-Fri.
Amsterdam's Chamber of Commerce is a spanking new building on the harbour front. A sign of renewed confidence in Amsterdam, or just bluff? Staff have lists of import/export agencies, companies by sector and government trade representatives. They will also advise on legal procedure, finding an office and hiring local staff. The bureaucracy can be baffling, but persevere: once you've found the right person, you can get all the information you need.

Ministerie voor Economische Zaken (Ministry of Economic Affairs)
Bezuidenhoutseweg 30, 2594 AV, Den Haag (070 379 8911). **Open** 9am-4pm Mon-Fri.
The information department of this ministry will provide answers to general queries concerning the Dutch economy. Detailed enquiries will probably be referred to the EVD (Netherlands Foreign Investment Agency, *see above*).

Ministerie voor Buitenlandse Zaken (Ministry of Foreign Affairs)
Bezuidenhoutseweg 67, 2594 AC, Den Haag (070 348 6486). **Open** 9am-4pm Mon-Fri.
Staff at the Ministry's information department will answer general queries only. Detailed enquiries will probably be referred to the EVD (Netherlands Foreign Investment Agency, *see above*).

Banking

The branches listed below are head offices. Most do not have general banking facilities, but staff will be able to provide a list of branches that do. For information about foreign exchange, *see chapter* **Essential Information**.

ABN AMRO
Vijzelgracht 32, IS (629 9111). Tram 6, 7, 10, 16, 24, 25. **Open** 9am-5pm Mon-Fri.
ABN and AMRO were The Netherlands' two biggest banks. They merged at the end of 1990 and this is their main office. Before the merger, there were about 80 branches of both banks in Amsterdam.

Barclays Bank
Weteringschans 109, IS (626 8630). Tram 6, 7, 10. **Open** 9am-5pm Mon-Fri.
Deals with business transactions only.

Citibank NA
Herengracht 545-549, IS (551 5911). Tram 16, 24, 25. **Open** 9.30am-3pm Mon-Fri.
This company is affiliated to the US Citibank.

Credit Lyonnais Bank Nederland NV
Keizersgracht 515, IS (556 9111). Tram 1, 2, 5. **Open** 9am-4pm Mon-Fri.

Lloyds Bank
Leidseplein 29, IS (524 9300). Tram 1, 2, 5, 6, 7, 10. **Open** 9am-5pm Mon-Fri.
Only business transactions can be carried out here.

London Amsterdam Merchant Bank NV
Paleisstraat 1, C (550 2602). Tram 1, 2, 5, 14. **Open** 8.30am-5pm Mon-Fri.

ING Postbank Group
Bijlmerplein 888, OE (563 9111). Metro Bijlmer/Bus 59, 60, 62, 137. **Open** 9am-4pm Mon-Fri.
This recently merged group now incorporates the 50 Amsterdam branches of the post office bank offering full banking and exchange services.

Rabobank
Wilhelminaplantsoen 124, OS (569 0569). Bus 136. **Open** 9am-4pm Mon-Fri.
Rabobank has 39 Amsterdam branches, some of which are closed on Monday mornings.

Société Générale
Museumplein 17, OS (571 1500). Tram 3, 5, 12, 16. **Open** 9am-5pm Mon-Fri.
Only commercial transactions are undertaken by this bank.

Swiss Bank Corporation
Hoogoorddreef 5, OE (651 0510). Metro Bijlmer. **Open** 8.30am-5.30pm Mon-Fri.
Commercial transactions only are offered by this investment bank.

Verenigde Spaarbank
Singel 548, C (520 5911). Tram 4, 9, 14, 16, 24, 25. **Open** 9am-5pm Mon-Wed, Fri; 9am-5pm, 6.30-8pm, Thur.
Full banking facilities are offered. There are 41 branches in Amsterdam.

Exchanges

Effectenbeurs (Stock Exchange)
Damrak 62A, C (523 4567). Tram 4, 9, 16, 24, 25.
Open 10am-4.30pm Mon-Fri.
Stock for officially-listed Dutch companies is traded here.
Phone for an appointment to view proceedings from the
visitors' gallery.

Nederlandse Termijnhandel
(Dutch Association of Futures and
Options Traders)
Damrak 261, C (638 2239). Tram 4, 9, 16, 24, 25.
Open 10.45am-4pm Mon-Fri.
This commodity exchange is where futures contracts are
traded in potatoes and pigs.

Optiebeurs (European Options Exchange)
Rokin 65, IW (550 4550). Tram 4, 9, 14. **Open** 10am-
4.30pm Mon-Fri.
The new EOE opened in 1987 and is now the largest
options exchange in Europe. Trading share, gold and silver options as well as bond and currency options, it
books about 55,000 transactions daily: way ahead of the
City of London. Tours around this impressive building
run every weekday morning at 10.30am and 11.30am.
You can watch trading on the floor from a visitors' balcony. Phone to reserve a place.

Conferences

Amsterdam has established itself as an important
congress and conference venue. Most major
hotels offer full conference facilities and the city's
main congress centre, the **RAI** (*listed below*)
hosts some 65 international events a year. A number of specialist conference organisers have
sprung up to arrange these events.

Grand Hotel Krasnapolsky
*Dam 9, C (554 9111/fax 622 8607/telex 12262 KRAS
NL). Tram 1, 2, 5, 13, 14, 16, 17, 24, 25, 49.*
Bang in the centre of the city, the recently refurbished
Krasnapolsky now has the most comprehensive in-hotel
meeting facilities, including a convention centre for up
to 2,000 people. The largest meeting room is suitable for
conferences of up to 700. *See chapter* **Accommodation.**

RAI Congresgebouw
*Europaplein, OS (549 1212; exhibition centre and
restaurant: fax 646 4469/telex 1601). Tram 4, 25/NS
railway from Schiphol Airport to RAI Station.*
Open *office and enquiries* 9am-5pm Mon-Fri.
A self-contained congress and trade fair centre in the south
of the city. The building contains 10 halls totalling 63,000sq
m/56,000sq yds of covered exhibition space and 18 conference rooms which can seat between 40 and 1,750 people. Full translation and business services are available.

Stichting de Beurs van Berlage (Berlage
Exchange Foundation)
*Damrak 277, C (626 5257/fax 620 4701). Tram 4, 9,
16, 24, 25.* **Open** *office and enquiries* 9am-5pm Mon-Fri.
This stunning building was completed in 1903, to be used
as a commodity exchange. Later (1978-1987) it was the
venue for the European Options Exchange. It is now
used for cultural events and smaller trade fairs (up to
2,500 visitors can be provided with buffet dinners).
Berlage Hall, within the building, provides a stylish conference venue for between 50 and 200 people.

RAI Congresgebouw: *a congress and trade
fair centre. See* **review.**

World Trade Center
*Strawinskylaan 1, OS (575 9111/fax 662 7255/telex
12808). Tram 5/NS railway from Schiphol Airport to RAI
Station.* **Open** *office and enquiries* 9am-5pm Mon-Fri.
Just about anything you might need to run a conference
can be provided here. Facilities include an international
press centre, small studios for top-level meetings and 14
business-class rooms seating from 4 to 40 people. A conference room seating up to 250 costs fl,625 per full day
from 8am-11pm (excluding VAT and services).
Worldwide conference facilities and secretarial, translating and legal services can be supplied. *See also below*
Office Services: Office Hire.

Conference Organisers

NOVEP (Netherlands Organization
Bureau for Events and Projects)
*Paulus Potterstraat 40, OS (662 1922/fax 662 8136).
Tram 2, 3, 5, 12.* **Open** 9am-5pm Mon-Fri. **Credit**
AmEx, DC, MC, V.
NOVEP will organise congresses or conferences to your
specifications.

QTL Convention Services
*Keizersgracht 782, IS (626 1372/fax 625 9574/telex
14527). Tram 4.* **Open** 9am-5pm Mon-Fri.
Credit AmEx, MC, V.
These specialists in teleconferencing will organise and
supply the equipment for congresses and seminars.

Business Services

You can send faxes from Telehouse and some
district post offices 24 hours a day, but some
commercial locations, such as Teletalk Centre,
are less expensive. For details of these, *see chapter* **Survival.** Major hotels have fax services for
guests (and sometimes non-guests, if the hotel
is not too busy), but prices are high. The **World
Trade Center** (*listed under* **Office Hire**) also
has full reception and transmission facilities.

Couriers and Shippers

Bluesprint
JJ Viottastraat 37, OS (664 4311). Tram 16. **Open** 24
hours daily. **No credit cards.**
Bluesprint transports documents across the world. Rates

to London start at f90 for a 0.5kg/1.1lb delivery in 24 hours. Motorcycle delivery in Amsterdam within an hour costs from f20.50.

Intercontinental Couriers
Vrachtegebouw 1, Kamer 211, Schiphol (648 1636).
Train to Schiphol Airport from Centraal Station. **Open** 24 hours daily. **No credit cards.**
Next-day delivery is guaranteed for many destinations, including London and Paris at a cost of f45 for documents (f80 for non-documents) for the first 0.5kg/1.1lb and then f5 for each additional 0.5kg plus f35 if the package is subject to duty. All packages received before 4pm are delivered before noon the next day.

International Couriers Amsterdam
Coenhavenweg Loods 610, Pier Europa, N (686 7808/7805). Bus 40. **Open** 24 hours daily.
No credit cards.
A worldwide courier service that will transport packages across Amsterdam within an hour for f18.50. Rates for London (up to 0.5kg/1.1lb, arriving before noon the following day) start at f85.

XP Express Parcel Systems
Hessenbergweg 8-10, OSE (06 099 1234/fax 020 912 050). Metro Bullewijk/Bus 48, 62, 158. **Open** 7am-7pm Mon-Fri. **No credit cards.**
Documents of up to 250g/9oz can be delivered to London within 24 hours for f100 (f134 for parcels up to 1kg/2.2lb). Overnight delivery to destinations throughout The Netherlands costs f32 plus f1 per kilogram.

Forwarding Agent

Geytenbeek BV
Kernweg 1, 3542 AE, Utrecht (030 489 212/fax 030 48 9316/telex 76438). **Open** 9am-5pm Mon-Fri.
No credit cards.
A business removals, and exhibition delivery service, Geytenbeek deals with all customs formalities.
Branch: RAI Congresgebouw, Europaplein 8, OS (644 8551/fax 644 0603).

Printing and Duplicating

Grand Prix Copyrette
Weteringschans 84A, IS (627 2703). Tram 16, 24, 25. **Open** 9am-pm Mon-Fri.
No credit cards.
Branches of this firm offer both monochrome and colour copying, ring binding and fax services. The Parnassusweg branch has a laser printer; the Amsteldijk branch is open on Saturday (11am-4pm).
Branches: Parnassusweg 212-218, OS (664 5909); Amsteldijk 47, C (671 4455).

Multicopy
Weesperstraat 65, IE (624 6208/620 4922). Bus 31. **Open** 9am-5.30pm Mon-Fri.
No credit cards.
Typical of Amsterdam's slickly run photocopy shops, the machines here are metered, so rather than annoying staff by asking for change, you pay a total on your way out. You can make colour and black and white copies in A4, A3 and A2 sizes, on white or coloured paper.
Branch: Zeilstraat 30, OS (662 0154/675 1650).

Print & Co.
Utrechtsestraat 138, IS (627 7116/fax 620 4163). Tram 4. **Open** 9am-5pm Mon-Fri. **Credit** AmEx, MC, V.
Both colour and black and white photocopying is undertaken, plus laser printing, offset printing and binding.

Translations (Vertaling)

Berlitz Language Center
Rokin 87, C (622 1375/fax 620 3959). Tram 4, 9, 14, 16, 24, 25. **Open** 8.15am-9pm Mon-Fri. **No credit cards.**
Specialists in commercial, technical, legal and scientific documents. All European languages are translated, as well as Japanese and Arabic. English/Dutch translation costs from f30 per 100 words.

Mac Bay Consultants
PC Hooftstraat 15, OS (662 0501/fax 662 6299). Tram 2, 3, 5, 12. **Open** 9am-5pm Mon-Fri. **No credit cards.**
Specialists in translating financial documents. Dutch/English translations cost f172.50 an hour. Other languages are also translated and there is a copywriting service.

Interpreters (Tolken)

Congrestolken – Secretariaat
Prinsengracht 993, IS (625 2535/fax 626 5642). Tram 4, 16, 24, 25. **Open** 9am-5.30pm Mon-Fri.
No credit cards.
Highly specialised staff are supplied for conference interpreting. Languages offered include Arabic, Japanese, Cantonese and all the European languages. Members of the Association Internationale D'Interprètes de Conference (AIIC).

Randstad Uitzendburo
Strawinskylaan 501, World Trade Center, OS (662 8011). Tram 5. **Open** 8.30am-5.30pm Mon-Fri.
No credit cards.
This branch of the employment agency (*see below* **Office Services: Employment Agencies**) has a number of freelance interpreters and translators on its books. Costs for services vary widely.

Office Services
Equipment Hire

Avisco
Stadhouderskade 156, OS (671 9909). Tram 6, 7, 10. **Open** 7am-6pm Mon-Fri. **No credit cards.**
Slide projectors, video equipment, screens, cameras, overhead projectors, microphones and tape decks are hired out or sold.

Capi-lux
Basisweg 42, OW (586 6333). Bus 42, 44, 82. **Open** 8.30am-5.30pm Mon-Fri. **Credit** AmEx, DC, MC, V.
These audio-visual equipment suppliers specialise in photographic goods: Hasselblad cameras, lights and projectors.

Decorum Verhuur
Jarmuiden 21, OW (611 7905). Bus 44, 82. **Open** 8am-5pm Mon-Fri. **No credit cards.**
Office furniture can be hired from this firm.

Ruad Computer Hire
Kuiperbergweg 33, OSE (697 8191). Metro Bullewijk/Bus 62. **Open** 8am-5pm Mon-Fri.
Credit AmEx, DC, MC, V.
IBM PS machines can be hired for around f300 a month, cheaper than some of the compatibles: a 386/40 Mhz Compaq PC costs f1,619 per month (you might as well buy one). There's a f300 deposit per device (computer, monitor, printer, etc). Fax machines cost from f450 a month, with a f300 deposit. Ruad also hires car phones (f669 a month, f300 deposit) and copiers (f1,540 a month, f600 deposit).

Computer Repairs

De Vakman

Nieuwe Hemweg 6N, NW (684 2425/697 2511). Bus 41. **Open** 24-hour emergency repair service. **No credit cards.**

The staff at De Vakman will attempt to repair all models of computers. A 'diagnosis' costs f65, which is payable whether a client accepts the proposed repair price or not.

Office Hire

Euro Business Center

Keizersgracht 62, IW (626 5749/623 1433/fax 623 1506/telex 16183 EUROCNL). Tram 13, 14, 17. **Open** 8.30am-5.30pm Mon-Fri. **Credit** AmEx, DC, MC, V.

The fully-equipped offices for hire (long or short term) include the use of telex, fax, photocopier, phone and mailbox services and multilingual secretaries. Switchboard operators are also provided. For a minimum of three months, fully-equipped offices cost between f1,500 and f4,500 per month. Private offices cost between f125 and f200 per working day. Personal cheques are not accepted.

Jan Luyken Residence

Jan Luijkenstraat 58, OS (205 730 730/fax 676 3841/telex 16254 HTLIJNL). Tram 2, 3, 5, 12. **Open** *office* 9am-5pm Mon-Fri. **Credit** AmEx, MC, V.

Three fully-equipped offices are for hire, long or short term. Projectors, videos, phones, telex, fax and mailbox are among the many services that can be provided. Small temporary offices cost f350 per day. Conference rooms with capacities of up to 55 people cost f500 to f600 per day.

World Trade Center

Strawinskylaan 1, OS (575 9111/fax 662 7255/telex 12808). Tram 5/NS railway from Schiphol Airport to RAI Station. **Open** *office and enquiries* 9am-5pm Mon-Fri.

Over 200 companies work in the rather soulless, air-conditioned luxury of the trade centre. Offices can be hired long or short term from f155 for one day segment, f235 for two and f375 for three; a day segment is either a morning, an afternoon or an evening. Audio and projection equipment is also for hire. Secretarial services cost f75 per hour, and telex, fax and photocopying facilities are offered. *See also above* **Conferences.**

Employment Agencies (Uitzendbureau)

Content Uitzendbureau

Nieuwezijds Voorburgwal 156, C (625 1061). Tram 1, 2, 5, 13, 17. **Open** 8.30am-5.30pm Mon-Fri. **No credit cards.**

Office, secretarial, medical and technical staff are on this firm's books. There are seven branches in Amsterdam; this is the head office.

Manpower

Van Baerlestraat 16, OS (664 4180). Tram 3, 5, 12. **Open** 8.30am-5.30pm Mon-Thur; 8.30am-6.30pm Fri. **No credit cards.**

A large employment agency with five branches in Amsterdam. Staff can be provided for general office, secretarial, computer and other work.

Randstad

AJ Ernststraat 735A, OS (644 6855). Bus 8, 48, 49, 67. **Open** 8.30am-5.30pm Mon-Fri. **No credit cards.**

There are 13 branches of Randstad in Amsterdam supplying office and secretarial staff, translators and data-entry staff.

Tempo Team

Rokin 118, C (523 6110). Tram 4, 9, 14, 16, 24, 25. **Open** 8.30am-5.15pm Mon-Fri. **No credit cards.**

Secretarial, hotel and catering, medical, technical and academic staff are on Tempo's books.

The **World Trade Center** *offers conference facilities in air-conditioned luxury. See* **review.**

Gay Amsterdam

Nichtenbars, nudist beaches and pressure groups: we survey the scene in the gay capital of Europe.

Amsterdam's gay scene rivals that of Berlin, Paris and London, and for many tourists is the main reason for visiting the city. Although the gay organisation, COC (*listed under* **Help and Information**) has branches throughout The Netherlands, openly gay life is found more in the big cities, to which many young homosexuals migrate from the less tolerant countryside.

ARTICLE 248 TO SECTION 28

The Netherlands originally decriminalised homosexuality in 1811. But in 1911, pressure from moralising Catholics and Calvinists led to Article 248-bis, which made the age of consent 16 for heterosexuals, but 21 for homosexuals. The first wave of protest, led by the newly-founded NWHK (Dutch Scientific Humanity Committee), furthered public understanding and increased gay self-confidence. After World War II, the Shakespeare Club was established, the forerunner of the NVIH-COC, now known as COC. COC gained status as a pressure group, but was not recognised in law until it was granted Royal Assent in 1973.

The high-profile gay rights movement of the sixties and seventies outraged moralists, but generally won tolerance. Traditional sexual roles were being undermined by the new welfare state and the student and feminist movements (*see chapters* **Students** *and* **Women's Amsterdam**). These social movements fortified each other and benefited from overlapping memberships and unity between gays and lesbians, who, unlike in other countries, were covered by the same law.

Gay and lesbian groups were formed in political parties, labour unions, educational institutions and churches – understanding for the 'homophile fellow-man' was even advocated in ecclesiastical circles, both Protestant and Catholic. The Dutch Reformed Church is allowed to bless gay relationships (*see below* **Remonstantse Broederschap**). Proud of their sexuality, influential groups of radical homosexuals – mostly students – adopted the old nicknames *flikker* (gay) and *poot* (lesbian), criticising COC for concentrating on integration

Justus, the creative director of Hard, the gay night at **Roxy**. *For details, see chapter* **Clubs** *page 175.*

with heterosexual lifestyles. Article 248-bis was finally abolished in 1971. Groups such as *Roze Front* (Pink Front, *see below* **Roze Zaterdag**), which raised public awareness by organising publicity stunts and demonstrations, redirected their energies towards other issues such as gay marriage and Section 28, Britain's anti-gay law. The Dutch branch of the AIDS activist group ACT UP! (Amsterdam branch tel 639 2522) was founded in 1990 and has already secured the availability of the AIDS medicine DDI in The Netherlands.

Homo-monument
Westermarkt, IW. Tram 13, 14, 17.
The Homo-monument is the world's first memorial to persecuted gays and lesbians. Designed by Karin Daan, its three triangles of pink granite form a larger triangle that juts out into Keizersgracht. You can read about its history in a book by Pieter Koenders, *The Monument*. Those victimised in World War II are commemorated here every 4 May, but flowers are frequently laid in memory of more private grief, particularly on World AIDS Day (scheduled for 1 December in 1993 and 1994). The monument is also a positive symbol for the homosexual community and a focus for demonstrations. The date of the monument's unveiling in 1987, 5 September, is celebrated as 'Coming Out Day' and parties are held here on occasions such as Queen's Day (*see chapter* **Amsterdam by Season**).

Remonstantse Broederschap
Nieuwegracht 27, 3512 LC, Utrecht (030 316 970).
If you want your relationship blessed, whether or not you are Dutch or belong to the Dutch Reformed Church, write to this church giving your name, address and phone number. You'll receive English-language information and then, if you wish to proceed, the address of the minister to contact. The whole process takes from three to six months. At the time of writing, such blessings do not carry legal status in The Netherlands.

Roze Zaterdag (Pink Saturday)
Information on location and events from **Gay & Lesbian Switchboard** *(623 6565).* **Dates** 26 June 1993; 25 June 1994.
The Roze Front (Pink Front) is a co-operative organisation embracing a number of gay and lesbian groups. It organises the national gay pride demonstration, Roze Zaterdag (Pink Saturday), which is held in a different town every year (Maastricht in 1993, Amsterdam in 1994). The day begins with the *roze kerkdienst* (pink divine service – there are a lot of gay church groups). Then between 5,000 and 10,000 people take part in a march followed by a festival.

POLITICS OF CRUISING
The term 'cruising' is derived from *kruysen*, the old Dutch word for seeking sexual contacts. In the seventies, there were protests against municipal laws that enabled police to arrest cruising gays as prostitutes and outlawed the 'alternative use' of public urinals as gay meeting places. With general support among councillors, gay activists opposed the replacement of old two-man urinals with one-man urinals and demanded that the police should catch *potenrammers* (gay-bashers) instead of harassing those being victimised. After Amsterdam's Court of Justice adjudged in

1985 that cruising was not prostitution, the by-laws were abolished.

Council policy is now more tolerant than ever before. Public expressions of affection, cruising, and even discreet sex in open spaces (*see below* **Nudist areas**), are all allowed, within reasonable limits in places where offence is unlikely to be taken. The liberal prostitution laws also apply to gays, and the bordellos and 'rent boy bars' in the gay areas (*see below* **Clubs and Bars**) are legal, if not all reputable. Bars and discos that refuse admission to gays or lesbians can lose their night licence, and institutions that discriminate against homosexuals risk losing municipal co-operation and subsidy, although this doesn't always happen in practice.

As cruising areas (*kruisenbaan*), urinals have lost popularity and cruisers now head for Vondelpark (*see chapter* **Sightseeing**); Julianapark, OE; Oosterpark, OE; the Weteringscircuit (1e and 2e Weteringsplantsoen), IS; and local nudist areas.

Nudist areas
Nieuwemeer *on north bank, OW. Bus 43, then along Jaagpad, then 10 mins past Oeverland sign turn right down a short path.*
Spaarnwoude *north of Haarlem, near Spaarndam; nudist area is Westhofbos. Bus 82 from Marnixstraat bus station/car via N5 (A5), then A9.*
Het Twiske *between Oostzaan and Landsmeer, N; nudist areas are Wezenlanden and Geldeveen. Bus 92.*
Zandvoort *gay beach train direct to Zandvoort/car via A5 to Haarlem, then follow signs.*
These legal nudist areas are visited by many gays and don't get raided by police. They are cruisey – in some areas people have outdoor sex. **Spaarnwoude** open area has an official nudist section, Westhofbos (behind a farm called Zorgerij), free for anyone, straight or gay. At the resort of **Zandvoort**, head south to the gay restaurant Zeezicht at the end of the promenade; the Zuidstrand (south beach) is nudist thereafter, but the gay area is a long walk further south (30 mins walk from station in total). The nudist area on the small islands at **Sloterparkbad** (*see chapter* **Sport & Fitness: Water Sports**) is popular with gay men.

GAY CULTURE
The Dutch have come to recognise the cultural and historical significance of homosexuality through both gay and lesbian studies and homosexual literature, whose readership extends beyond the gay community. Early this century there were notable books published by Jacob Israël de Haan and Wilma Vermaat. The principal modern gay writers are Gerrit Komrij and Gerard Reve (*see under* **Vrolijk**). Reve has, like the lesbian writer Andreas Burnier (*see chapter* **Women's Amsterdam**), been active in the gay movement. Translated Dutch literature and other gay books and publications in English can be found at the American Discount Book Center and W H Smith (*see chapters* **Students** *and* **Shopping**) and at the shops listed below. For the lesbian and gay radio station MVS Radio, *see chapter* **Media: Radio/Local Stations**.

COC (Amsterdam) *is a source of information and friendship. See* **review**.

houses an extensive range of literature (books, journals, magazines, newspaper articles, theses and so on). Visitors should write at least one month in advance, giving details of their intended area of study. Homodok will then send a list of material available on that subject, with information of study times.

Help and Information

For sexual health matters, including AIDS, *see* chapter **Survival**.

COC (National)
Rozenstraat 8, IW (623 1192). Tram 13, 14, 17. **Open** 9am-5pm Mon-Fri.
Thankfully, COC doesn't use its snappy full title: *Nederlandse Vereniging tot Integratie van Homoseksualiteit – Cultuur en Ontspannigs Centrum* (the Dutch Union for Integration of Homosexuality – Centre for Culture and Relaxation). With about 6,000 members, and branches throughout the country, it's one of the world's biggest homosexual organisations.

COC (Amsterdam)
Rozenstraat 14, IW (information 1-5pm Wed-Sat 623 4079/office 626 3087). Tram 13, 14, 17. **Open** *office* 9am-5pm Mon-Thur; *information/coffee shop* 1-5pm Wed-Sat; *café* 8pm-midnight Wed; 10pm-3am Fri. **No credit cards**.
COC can help with all matters relating to gays and lesbians, particularly if they're just coming out. Many come here to read magazines or to meet like-minded people in the recently-renovated coffee shop. Staff are well-informed and helpful. COC discos are attended by people from all scenes and age groups, attracted by the friendly atmosphere, cheap drinks and varied music. Discos are mixed (but with a male bias) on Fridays (10pm-3am) and lesbians-only on Saturday (10pm-3am), with admission at f3.50 and a token system for buying drinks (a *strippenkart* costs either f4 or f12).

Gay and Lesbian Switchboard
(623 6565). **Open** 10am-10pm daily.
The English-speaking male and female employees of this phoneline are specially trained in giving information and advice on all gay and lesbian matters, from scene news to safe sex.

Schorer Stichting
PC Hooftstraat 5, OS (662 4206). Tram 2, 3, 5, 12. **Open** 9am-5.30pm Mon-Fri.
This state-funded social agency offers information, support and counselling for gay men and lesbians. Most calls are from people who can't handle their sexuality, but staff can advise on coming out, gay lifestyles and help for older homosexuals, although they can't give legal advice. One department is solely concerned with AIDS and related matters. Phone for an appointment – the staff speak English. Also at this address is *HIV Vereniging* (The Netherlands HIV Association, tel 664 2466), which supports the individual and collective interests of all those who are HIV positive, and produces a fortnightly magazine *HIV Nieuws* (f7).

Sjalhomo
PO Box 2536, 1000 CM Amsterdam (evenings only, 023 312318).
This national organisation (the office is in Haarlem) for Jewish gays and lesbians organises cultural, social and political activities on Jewish feast days. It has contacts with other Jewish organisations and with gay Jewish groups abroad, and welcomes visitors.

Gay and lesbian publications
Top Guide is a regularly updated English-language manual covering Amsterdam's gay scene in great detail. The annual *Best Guide* reviews (in English) gay places in Benelux (Belgium, Netherlands, Luxembourg), in which Amsterdam is prominent. Britain's monthly magazine *Gay Times* carries listings in English on Amsterdam for gays and lesbians. The following are in Dutch: *Gay Krant*, the country's most important gay newspaper; *Homologie*, a cultural and intellectual bi-monthly magazine; *Man-to-Man*, carrying listings of gay places throughout the country; *Sekstant*, magazine of the Netherlands Society for Sexual Reform, which has a list of organisations and information for special interest groups; and *XL*, the COC's monthly.

Intermale
Spuistraat 251, C (625 0009). Tram 1, 2, 5, 13, 14, 17. **Open** noon-6pm Mon; 10am-6pm Tue, Wed, Fri, Sat; 10am-9pm Thur. **Credit** AmEx, MC, V.
A gay bookshop which stocks a large number of titles (many in English) on literature, social science and art, plus a range of magazines and 'what's on' information.

Vrolijk
Paleisstraat 135, C (623 5142). Tram 1, 2, 5, 13, 14, 17. **Open** 11am-6pm Mon; 10am-6pm Tue, Wed, Fri; 10am-9pm Thur; 10am-5pm Sat. **Credit** MC.
Vrolijk has an exhaustive range of new and second-hand gay and lesbian books, many in English, plus a huge stock of international magazines and details of events. Literature is the speciality, so look out for works by Gerard Reve, one of the most popular and controversial Dutch authors. In the sixties, he was prosecuted and only partially acquitted of blasphemy for describing God as an incarnated donkey. Supported by the Attorney General, Reve appealed and was fully acquitted. A year later (1968) he received the PC Hooftprijs, the most important state award for literature.

Gay and lesbian studies
University of Amsterdam *Oude Hoogstraat 24, C (525 2217). Tram 4, 9, 14, 16, 24, 25/Metro Nieuwmarkt.*
University of Utrecht *Haedelbarglaan 8, Utrecht (030 539 111).*
Courses on gay and lesbian topics can be taken by students on most degree courses. From 1-28 June 1993 the University of Amsterdam is holding an international seminar on Lesbian and Gay Studies.
Homodok *Oudezijds Achterburgwal 185, C (525 2601). Tram 4, 9, 14, 16, 24, 25.*
The Documentation Centre for Lesbian and Gay Studies

Clubs and Bars

Amsterdam's gay men have a great choice of bars and discos, but there are far fewer for lesbians (*see chapter* **Women's Amsterdam**). The different gay scenes – **nichten, macho** and **trendy** – have distinct locations and types of bar, but, of course, the boundaries between them aren't rigid. We've selected some of the best, but the scene does change rapidly as venues open or close; comprehensive listings can be found in *Top Guide*. The following have a general, mixed appeal to gays of all ages and persuasions, as does the café and disco at **COC** (*see above* **Help and Information**).

Popular across the board, **The C'ring** *boasts queues at weekends. See* **review.**

The C'ring (Cockring)

Warmoesstraat 96, C (623 9604). Tram 4, 9, 16, 24, 25. **Open** 10pm-4am Mon-Thur, Sun; 10pm-5am Fri, Sat. **Admission** free.

The C'ring night-club has been such a success that it's one of the few gay venues for which you need to queue to get in at weekends. It attracts all types of gays under about 40, although it's located in the leather-and-denim district. The dancefloor sounds are house and pop, with quieter music in the upstairs video bar. Despite the air-conditioning the pulsating mass of people raises the temperature. The C'ring's a cruisey place, with a back room reached through the toilets.

iT

Amstelstraat 24, C (625 0111). Tram 4, 9, 14. **Open** 11pm-4am Thur, Sun; 11pm-5am Fri, Sat. **Admission** f10 Thur-Sun; free before midnight, after 3.30am, Fri; free after 3.30am Sat; free to members.

iT is a big disco with a *nichten* atmosphere (*see below* **Nichtenbars**) that's also popular with all kinds of young gays, lesbians and straights between 20 and 35, particularly students. The disco throbs to acid and house music and sometimes has drag or strip shows. The VIP room is a low-lit bar with quieter music.

Nichtenbars

Nichten is a broad term identified with camp, effeminate gays, who heavily influenced the public image of homosexuals in the sixties, when most gay places were *nichtenbars*. Now concentrated in the Amstel-Rembrandtplein area, *nichtenbars* are cosy and women-friendly, with an animated clientele always willing to sing along with the music. Some of these venues are home to the drag scene.

Amstel Taveerne

Amstel 54, C (623 4254). Tram 4, 9, 14. **Open** 4pm-1am Mon-Thur, Sun; 3pm-2am Fri, Sat. **Admission** free.

The long-established Amstel Taveerne is about the best example of a Dutch neighbourhood bar you could find. As with other *nichtenbars*, it's gay in both senses of the word. The regulars are very exuberant and liable to join in with the Dutch songs spun by the DJ, generating a fun, party-like atmosphere that's very welcoming to foreigners and women. In fine weather, the crowd – and it does get busy, particularly during the 6-7pm happy hour – spills out onto the pavement; on occasions such as Queen's Day, a bar is set up outside to cope with the demand for Amstel beer.

Chez Manfred

Halvemaansteeg 10, C (626 4510). Tram 4, 9, 14. **Open** 4pm-1am Mon-Thur, Sun; 3pm-2am Fri, Sat. **Admission** free.

This cosy neighbourhood bar attracts the exuberant local *nichten* who sing along to the Dutch songs. As the name suggests, the camp bar is owned by singer-entertainer Manfred. Generally packed, it gets particularly busy during happy hour (5.30-7pm, two drinks for the price of one) and on public holidays the crowd overflows into the alley. There are frequent shows and people also get up and sing.

Le Montmartre

Halvemaansteeg 17, C (620 7622). Tram 4, 9, 14. **Open** 4pm-1am Mon-Thur, Sun; 4pm-2am Fri, Sat. **Admission** free.

A cosy bar with original turn-of-the-century murals by Epoe Doeve. As at the Amstel Taveerne (*see above*), the fun-loving regulars can't resist partying on public holidays and other occasions. There are frequent Dutch cabaret, and sometimes drag, acts.

Macho Scene

The cruisey, denim-and-leather scene is concentrated mainly around Warmoesstraat.

Argos

Warmoesstraat 95, C (622 6595). Tram 4, 9, 16, 24, 25. **Open** 9pm-3am Mon-Thur, Sun; 9pm-4am Fri, Sat. **Admission** free.

One of the oldest, most famous leather-and-denim bars in town, and certainly the cruisiest. Although a dress code isn't enforced, the macho atmosphere in the very dark front and back bars is uncompromising – the wall decorations are chains. There's a back room with cabins and videos in the basement.

Club Jaecquess

Warmoesstraat 93, C (622 0323). Tram 4, 9, 16, 24, 25. **Open** 8pm-2am Mon-Thur, Sun; 8pm-3am Fri, Sat. **Admission** free.

A neighbourhood leather-and-jeans bar. It has a back room, but is really more sociable than cruisey.

The Eagle

Warmoesstraat 86, C (627 8634). Tram 4, 9, 16, 24, 25. **Open** 9pm-3am Mon-Thur; 9pm-4am Fri, Sat. **Admission** free.

Gays of all ages into leather and jeans pack this bar with a dancefloor after midnight. Before then it's not too crowded and the whole place is air-conditioned. There are two back rooms, but it's not heavily cruisey.

De Spijker

Kerkstraat 4, IS (620 5919). Tram 1, 2, 5. **Open** 1pm-1am Mon-Thur; 1pm-2am Fri, Sat. **Admission** free.
Spijker means 'nail' or 'tack', and there's a huge nail impaled into the counter of this American-style bar. It has recently become less leather-oriented, but is still very cruisey, with porno videos and regular 'jack-off parties', the f10 entry fees to which are donated to AIDS charities.

The Web

St Jacobsstraat 6, C (623 6758). Tram 1, 2, 3, 5. **Open** 2pm-2am Mon, Thur, Sun; 2pm-3am Fri, Sat. **Admission** free.
Close to Centraal Station, this is an ideal place to start a leather crawl. The dress code is most definitely leather; otherwise the club boasts a pool table, a roof garden, an upstairs bar, two dark rooms and porn videos. The Web has a reputation for throwing wild parties and for having the cleanest toilets of any leather bar in town.

Trendy Scene

See also chapter **Clubs**.

April

Café April *Reguliersdwarsstraat 37, IS (625 9572).*
April's Exit (bar/disco) *Reguliersdwarsstraat 42, IS (625 8788). Tram 1, 2, 4, 5, 9, 14, 16, 24, 25.* **Open** *Café April* 2pm-1am Mon-Thur, Sun; 2pm-2am Fri, Sat; *April's Exit* 11pm-4am Mon-Thur, Sun; 11pm-5am Fri, Sat. **Admission** free.
April café-bar is large and relaxed, with friendly staff serving good light meals. The décor is modern, with photos on display; there's also a notice-board. It quickly fills up with men after work for the happy hour (times vary); drinks are also cheaper in the late evening: at midnight until 1am beer is sold for f1 a glass, and the place gets very busy. April's Exit is a smart disco for trendy young gays. Reached via a separate, comfortable bar, the disco room was once a hay loft; the dancefoor is cruisey and overlooked by a balcony. State-of-the-art equipment pumps out the lights and latest music.

Havana

Reguliersdwarsstraat 17, IS (620 6788). Tram 1, 2, 5, 16, 24, 25. **Open** *bar* 4pm-1am Mon-Thur, Sun; 4pm-2am Fri; 2pm-2am Sat; *disco* 10pm-3am Mon-Thur, Sun; 10pm-4am Fri, Sat. **Admission** free.
An early-closing free-entry bar with a separate dance area upstairs, Havana has become one of the most popular trendy gay bars. A people-watcher's paradise, it gets very busy from around 10pm onwards, especially at weekends. The first-floor dancefloor is often more mixed than the bar itself, and a good place to get into the mood for a late night out in the city.

De Trut

Bilderdijkstraat 165E, OW (612 3524). Tram 3, 7, 12, 17. **Open** 10pm-4am Sun. **Admission** f1.
The Trut disco is in the cellar of the Tetterode squat (*see chapter* **Post-war**), and attracts young, trendy gays and lesbians, as well as squatters and students. Drinks are very cheap and the music's right up-to-date.

Eating

For the gay disco-restaurant Homolulu and women's eating places welcoming gay men, *see* chapter **Women's Amsterdam**. Mandate

Coffeebar (*listed under* **Around Town: Fitness Centre**) and the café at COC (*under* **Help and Information**) have wide gay appeal.

Adrian

Reguliersdwarsstraat 21, IS (623 9582). Tram 1, 2, 4, 5, 9, 14, 16, 24, 25. **Open** noon-3pm, 6pm-midnight, daily. **Credit** AmEx, MC, TC, V.
A high-quality restaurant that is welcoming to gays. French dishes are the speciality; the daily-changing set menus cost f45 (three courses) and f75 (five courses). Dimly lit, Adrian is perfect for a romantic treat.

Downtown

Reguliersdwarsstraat 31, IS (622 9958). Tram 1, 2, 4, 5, 9, 14, 16, 24, 25. **Open** 10am-8pm daily. **No credit cards.**
Evidently successful with gays who know they look good, this modern, white café is still hospitable to individuals, since it's so small you have to share tables. You can people-watch through the large windows or from pavement tables in summer. Good-value light snacks, salads and cakes are served by pleasant, efficient staff. To a background of mellow music, you can peruse the art exhibitions and selection of magazines and newspapers (many in English).

The Eighties

Brouwersgracht 139, IW (626 9874). Tram 1, 2, 4, 5, 9, 13, 16, 17, 24, 25. **Open** *April-Sept* 10am-8pm daily; *Oct-Mar* 10am-6pm daily. **No credit cards.**
The hi-tech design of this new café couldn't contrast more with the surrounding old warehouses (now up-market apartments). There are photographic exhibitions, and plenty of magazines to read, plus an outside terrace.

Leto

Haarlemmerdijk 114-116, IW (626 5695). Tram 3/Bus 18, 22, 44. **Open** 5-11pm Tue-Fri, Sun; 6-11pm Sat. **No credit cards.**
This cheap, intimate restaurant is famous for its camp, impertinent waiters, whose jokes are hilarious on occasional visits, but could prove tiresome if you go often.

Le Monde

Rembrandtplein 6, IS (626 9922). Tram 4, 9, 14. **Open** 9am-midnight daily. **No credit cards.**
The reasonably priced snacks and hot meals served here are popular with both local and visiting gays. A terrace faces the street entertainers on Rembrandtplein and the staff are happy to give information on the gay scene. The branch specialises in Dutch pancakes.
Branch: Rembrandtplein 6, IS (626 9922).

Hotels

It's illegal for 'straight' hotels (*see chapter* **Accommodation**) to refuse accommodation to gays, and it's rare to encounter excuses such as 'all rooms are engaged'. At the following gay hotels, no questions are asked if you take a guest to your room, but you'd be expected to pay for an extra breakfast. The same applies to the Granada Hotel and Quentin Hotel (*see chapter* **Women's Amsterdam**). For a comprehensive list, consult *Top Guide*.

Greenwich Village Hotel

Kerkstraat 25, 1017 GA; IS (626 9746). Tram 1, 2, 5. **Rates** *single* f100-f125; *double* f125. **No credit cards.**
Hotel services Bar. **Room services** Minibar. Phone. TV.

International Travel Club (ITC)
Prinsengracht 1051, 1017 JE; IS (623 0230). Tram 4.
Rates *single* f75-f90; *double* f130-f160; *twin* f130; *triple*
f215-f220. **Credit** AmEx, MC, V.
Hotel services *Bar.*

Hotel New York
*Herengracht 13, 1015 BA; IW (624 3066/fax 620
3230). Tram 1, 2, 3, 5, 13, 14.* **Rates** *single* f80-f140;
double f130-f145; *luxury double* f235; *triple* f275. **Credit**
AmEx, DC, MC, V.
Hotel services *Bar. Coffee shop. Laundry. Room service.*

Orfeo Hotel
*Leidsekruisstraat 14, 1017 RH; IS (623 1347/fax 620
2348). Tram 1, 2, 5, 6, 7, 10.* **Rates** *single* f65-f72.50;
double f75-87.50; *twin* f97.50-f105; *studio apartment*
f120-f150 (one person), f130-f165 (two person), f150-
f180 (three person). **Credit** AmEx, MC, V.
Hotel services *Bar. Laundry. Sauna.*

Unique Hotel
Kerkstraat 37, 1017 GB; IS (624 4785). Tram 1, 2, 5.
Rates *single* f75; *double* f95-f100; *twin* f115-f130. **No
credit cards.**
Hotel services *TV lounge bar.*

Apartments

Gay Interhome Services
*Keizersgracht 33, 1015 CD; IW (625 0071/638
0955/fax 638 0475). Tram 1, 2, 5, 13, 14, 17.* **Cost**
one-bedroom apartment from f500 per week; *two-
bedroom apartment* from f800 per week. **Deposit** one
month's rent. **No credit cards.**
Gay Interhome Services lets out furnished flats for
between one week and three months. The flats, mostly
one-bed and central, are owned by people away for an
extended period. This agency has a good reputation and
a big deposit is required. Lesbians are welcomed.

Around Town

Cinema

Gay & Lesbian Switchboard (*see above* **Help
and Information**) has a list of cinemas and
theatres with shows on homosexual themes,
such as the movies at Desmet (*see chapter
Film*) every Saturday at midnight and Sunday
at 4pm.

Shops

The Condomerie (*see chapter* **Shopping**)
stocks a great variety of condoms. For bookshops, *see above* **Gay Culture**.

The Bronx
*Kerkstraat 53-55, IS (623 1548). Tram 1, 2, 5, 16, 24,
25.* **Open** noon-midnight daily. **Credit** AmEx, MC, V.
A large selection of magazines, books, cards and toys (not
Monopoly) is stocked alongside videos for hire or sale
(plus viewing cabins). A cinema is attached to the shop.

Expectations...
*Warmoesstraat 32, C (624 5573). Tram 1, 2, 4, 5, 9,
13, 16, 17, 24, 25.* **Open** noon-6pm Mon-Fri; noon-5pm
Sat. **Credit** AmEx, MC, V.
If the off-the-peg leather and rubber gear doesn't fit, you

*For a list of cinemas showing films with gay
themes, ring* **Gay & Lesbian Switchboard**.
See page 225.

can have the item you want made to measure. Whatever
your taste in adult toys and bondage equipment they've
probably got it in stock.

RoB Gallery
Weteringschans 253, IS (625 4686). Tram 6, 7, 10.
Open 10am-6pm Mon-Fri; 11am-5pm Sat. **Credit**
AmEx, MC, V.
Leather and rubber clothing and accoutrements can be
bought direct or by mail order, either from stock or made
to measure. The shop has a gallery showing regular exhibitions, on which RoB's series of 'Amsterdam Cards' are
based. Posters, cards, videos and magazines are on sale
and there's also an S&M cellar.

Fitness Centre

Mandate
Prinsengracht 715, IS (625 4100). Tram 1, 2, 5. **Open**
11am-10pm Mon-Fri; noon-6pm Sat; 2-6pm Sun.
Membership daily f21; weekly f62.50; monthly f89. **No
credit cards.**
Mandate is a men-only fitness centre for gays. The well-
equipped gym has a trained instructor. Sauna (no hanky-
panky allowed), shower and towels are included in the
membership fee; the sunbed is extra. **Mandate Coffeebar**
is a good meeting place, whether or not you're a member
or have just used the gym. Many well-priced videos are for
hire or sale.

Saunas

Modern Sauna
Jacob van Lennepstraat 331, OW (612 1712). **Open**
noon-6pm daily. **Admission** f20. **No credit cards.**
A small, intimate sauna, attracting older customers,
many of whom are visitors to the city. In the lounge bar
snacks and drinks can be had, and porn videos are
screened.

Thermos
Thermos Day *Raamstraat 33, IW (623 9158). Tram
1, 2, 5, 7, 10.* **Open** noon-11pm Mon-Fri; noon-6pm
Sat, Sun. **Admission** f21. **No credit cards.**
Thermos Night *Kerkstraat 58-60, IS (623 4936).
Tram 1, 2, 5.* **Open** 11pm-8am daily. **Admission**
f22.50. **No credit cards.**
Both of these clean saunas have a steam room, a dry-heat
room, a bar, videos, private cubicles and a snack bar.
Both are very popular with an uninhibited clientele.
Thermos Night is an alternative to spending money on
a hotel room – although you wouldn't get much sleep.

Students

A run-down of university life in the city of radical protest: where to study, where to stay, and where to hang out.

Amsterdam's 65,000 students constitute almost eight per cent of the city's population. Most are highly integrated with the rest of Amsterdam's inhabitants, as few join the student societies and clubs. Instead, they meet up in favoured bars and discos in the city centre – at least when they're not protesting. Amsterdam's student movement has made headlines ever since the radical heyday of the sixties (*see below* **Union Protest**).

Students in The Netherlands join student unions individually, and foreign students can also use the clubs' and unions' facilities if they become members. The **Foreign Student Service** and the **Student Information** phoneline (*both listed under* **Study**) can help with any queries.

DUTCH DEGREES

There are two sectors of Dutch higher education: **Universities** and **Institutes of Higher Vocational Education (HBO)**. The differences between them are similar to those between British universities and polytechnics, but (as in Britain) are becoming less defined. Universities prepare undergraduates for independent research and work in an academic or professional setting. The minimum duration of study is four years, and the maximum six; students may continue their studies for longer, but will have to pay their own way.

HBOs provide the knowledge and skills necessary for specific professions, such as teaching, social work, drama, accounting and journalism, with work experience an integral part of the course. No academic research is conducted at HBOs.

There are 13 universities in The Netherlands; the oldest was founded in 1575 in Leiden; the youngest, the University of Limburg in Maastricht, opened its first department in 1976. With two universities, and three large and 17 small HBOs, Amsterdam is the educational and scientific centre of the country.

UVA (University of Amsterdam)
Maagdenhuis (administration), Spui, C (525 9111). Tram 1, 2, 5.
The Universiteit van Amsterdam was founded in 1877, but its roots go back to 1632 with the founding of the Atheneum Illustre, which prepared students for one of the existing universities. The University is open to the public. In St Agatha's chapel (Agnietenkapel), which now houses the University Museum (*see chapter* **Museums**), the first two professors, Gerardus Vossius

and Caspar Barlaeus, lectured in history and philosophy respectively. Within 33 years the curriculum had expanded to include mathematics, law, medicine and theology. The UVA is now the largest university in the country. Its (approximately) 30,000 students are educated in a number of buildings in the city centre. The Lutheran Church (Singel 411), is now used as the university's auditorium.

Vrije Universiteit (VU, Free University)
De Boelelaan 1105, OS (548 9222/hospital 548 9111). Bus 8, 23, 26, 48, 49, 64, 65, 67, 173.
In 1878 a group of orthodox Protestants, led by the theologian and politician Abraham Kuyper, formed a society to establish a 'free' Christian university – free of church and state, committed only to the Word of God – which they founded two years later. The VU is no longer orthodox Protestant but Christian generally and, like all Dutch universities, almost fully financed by the state. It's mostly housed in a modern complex in Amsterdam-Buitenveldert, which includes a *mensa* (student restaurant) and an academic bookshop (*see below* **City Life**). The Historical Documentation Centre for Dutch Protestantism (1800-the present) organises temporary exhibitions on the first floor of the main building. The original Vrije Universiteit site is Keizersgracht 162-164, but the buildings are no longer VU property.

UNION PROTEST

The student movement campaigned vigorously during the sixties and seventies, particularly for the democratisation of the universities and for peace in Vietnam. The most dramatic action was the occupation of the Maagdenhuis, the administrative centre of the University of Amsterdam. As a result of the struggle, students gained a lot more influence in university matters, and are now represented on the University Board by student unions such as **ASVA** (left wing) and **OBAS** (liberal).

The current system of funding for students consists of a basic grant, and additional top-up loans that have to be paid back with interest after graduation. Students from low-income families get an additional payment on top of their grant. A fresh wave of protest erupted in the eighties against government proposals to economise in the education sector. These plans included shortening the duration of funded study; re-organising the system of student grants and loans; and increasing tuition fees. Massive student protests, co-ordinated by LSVB, a federal organisation of local university and HBO student unions, resulted in the delay and somewhat less rigorous realisation of these plans.

One of the little streets in the student quarter near **Oudezijds Achterburgwal**.

ASVA

Spinhuissteeg 1, C (union 622 5771/accommodation agency 623 8052). Tram 4, 9, 14, 16, 24, 25. **Open** *union* noon-5pm Mon-Fri. *accommodation agency: July, Aug* 10.30am-4.30pm Mon-Fri; *Sept-June* 12.30-4.30pm Mon-Fri. **No credit cards.**

As the University of Amsterdam's main student union, ASVA can provide assistance for foreign students on all kinds of matters. The union bar and building are occasionally open during the evening, and evening meals are sometimes available. The ASVA Kamerbureau (accommodation agency) can find you a room between f300 and f400 per month, charging a fee of f12.50. Arrive early and wait for rooms to become available. Be prepared for numerous visits before something turns up.

OBAS

Voetboogstraat 2, C (525 2833). Tram 4, 9, 14, 16, 24, 25. **Open** 11am-12.30pm, 2.30-4.30pm, Tue-Fri.

This UVA union is most concerned with law students, but has general members, too. There are no facilities here, but foreign students can contact OBAS for help and information.

SRVU

De Boelelaan 1115B, OS (548 3600). Bus 8, 13, 26, 48, 49, 64, 65, 67, 173. **Open** *July-mid Aug* irregular hours, message in English on answerphone; *mid Aug-June* 12.30-3.30pm Mon-Fri; closed Christmas and Easter holidays.

The union for students at the Free University. SRVU's accommodation service also helps foreign students find a place to stay, as well as providing them with general advice and help.

City Life

It's not easy to find a house or a room in Amsterdam. Foreign students can apply to the **Foreign Student Service** (*listed under* **Study**) or to the *kamerbureau* of **ASVA** (*under* **Union Protest**). If they are studying at UVA, they can apply through the university's housing depart-

ment. Another possibility for those seeking temporary accommodation is to advertise in the university papers *Ad Valvas* (548 4330) and *Folia Civitates* (525 3981). *See also chapter* **Accommodation**.

Students are often entitled to discounts on admission at museums, attractions and places of entertainment; details are given in the relevant chapters of this guide. Presenting an ISIC card is often sufficient, but you can also buy a CJP card (discounts for under-26s) from **Uitburo** (*see chapter* **Essential Information**). Theatres popular with students include the Shaffy and the Stalhouderij, which often stage performances in English (*see chapter* **Theatre**). Night-clubs frequented by students include Dansen bij Jansen, Roxy, Escape (*see chapter* **Night-clubs**) and iT (*see chapter* **Gay Amsterdam**). For discount travel agencies, and advice on hitch-hiking, *see chapter* **Survival**.

Cafés and Bars

You're likely to find students congregating at the following: Aas van Bokalen, De Balie, Frascati, Hoppe and De Reiger; for details, *see chapter* **Cafés & Bars**.

De Blincker

St Barberenstraat 7-9, C (627 1938). Tram 4, 9, 14, 16, 24, 25. **Open** 4pm-1am Mon-Thur; 4pm-2am Fri, Sat. **No credit cards.**

The bar of the Frascati Theatre (*see chapter* **Theatre**). This is a popular student pub with its modern interior of granite and iron.

The Schutter Café

Voetboogstraat 13-15, C (622 4608). Tram 1, 2, 5. **Open** *bar* 11am-1am Mon-Thur, Sun; 11am-2am Fri, Sat; *kitchen* 5.45-10pm daily. **No credit cards.**

A café frequented by students and tourists. There are 40 types of beer, including English varieties, and snacks; drinks prices are average, snacks are cheap. Meals are also available; there are two *dagschotels* (dishes of the day) for f15, as well as vegetarian dishes. Lunch is served between noon and 2.45pm.

Mensae (Student Restaurants)

There are several large *mensae* (student restaurants) in Amsterdam where the food is good and the prices rather low. The mensae are subsidised, and are open to the public, but generally only students and a few budget-conscious people use them. *Trefcentrum* means meeting place.

Het Trefcentrum Atrium

Oudezijds Achterburgwal 237, C (525 3999). Tram 4, 9, 14, 16, 24, 25/Metro Nieuwmarkt. **Open** 9am-7pm Mon-Fri. **Lunch served** noon-2pm, **dinner served** 5-7pm, Mon-Fri. **Average** f10. **No credit cards.**
Het Trefcentrum Atrium is a buffet/self-service restaurant where a meal of soup and a daily choice of meat, fish and vegetarian dishes can be had from as little as f8.25. The restaurant's architecture is an interesting blend of old and new: a former inner court of the building of political science, it now has a pyramid of white glass for a roof. The building once housed the university hospital, and the original separate entrances for men and women can still be seen.

Joodse Studenten Mensa

de Lairessestraat 13 (676 7622) Tram 3, 5, 12, 16. **Open** 5.45-7.15pm. **Average** f13. **No credit cards.**
The Jewish students' mensa has a kosher menu, and while the food is more expensive than in the other mensae, it's still reasonable.

Mensa VU

De Boelelaan 1105, OS (548 9222). Bus 8, 23, 26, 48, 49, 64, 65, 67, 173. **Open** 10am-7pm Mon-Fri. **Dinner served** 5-7pm Mon-Fri. **Average** f7.25. **No credit cards.**
Mensa VU is large, modern and spacious. Visitors get their meals in the cellar, but can eat it at a table on any of the three floors.

Student Shopping

Fortunately for impecunious students, Amsterdam has plenty of outlets selling cheap clothes, food, records and books. For **markets**, cheap and **second-hand shops**, head for the Jordaan, Damstraat, Kalverstraat and Nieuwendijk.

For cheap, second-hand scientific and academic books, often in English, peruse the stalls in **Oudemanhuispoort**. A principal outlet for new academic volumes is the **Athenaeum Nieuwscentrum**. For all of these, *see chapter* **Shopping**. The following bookshops are also worth a visit:

Allert de Lange

Damrak 62, C (624 6744). Tram 4, 9, 16, 24, 25. **Open** 10am-6pm Mon; 9am-6pm Tue-Fri; 9am-5pm Sat. **Credit** MC, V.
Books on the language, literature and culture of France, Germany and England are the speciality of Allert de Lange. You'll also find sections on philosophy, history, history of art, film and photography.

American Discount Book Center

Kalverstraat 185, C (625 5537). Tram 4, 9, 16, 24, 25. **Open** 10am-10pm Mon-Sat; 11am-7pm Sun. **Credit** AmEx, DC, V.
Specialising in American literature, the American Discount Center has an excellent book-ordering department. Students receive a 10% discount on all book and study purchases.

Pegasus

Leidsestraat 25, IS (623 1138). Tram 1, 2, 5. **Open** 1-6pm Mon; 9am-6pm Tue, Wed, Fri; 9am-9pm Thur; 9am-5pm Sat. **Credit** AmEx, MC, V.
A small shop, specialising in political science, politics, social economics, and the culture and art of Russia, Eastern Europe, Asia and South America.

Scheltema, Holkema en Vermeulen

Koningsplein 20, IS (523 1411). Tram 1, 12. **Open** 1-6pm Mon; 9am-6pm Tue, Wed, Fri; 9am-9pm Thur; 10am-5pm Sat. **Credit** (minimum f100) AmEx, MC, V.
Specialists in books on medicine, law, economics and science.

VU Academic Bookshop

De Boelelaan 1105, OS (548 9111). Bus 8, 23, 26, 48, 49, 64, 65, 67, 173. **Open** 9am-5.30pm Mon-Fri. **Credit** AmEx, DC, MC, V.
The VU Bookshop (VU Boekhandel) has a large selection of books relating to all sciences, and a good collection of novels, tourist guides and children's books.

Study

For people wishing to study in Amsterdam, a number of UVA departments offer international English-language courses and programmes for postgraduates, graduates and undergraduates. Details are available from the Foreign Relations Office (Spui 25, 1012 SR, Amsterdam). Most postgraduate institutes of the UVA also take in foreign students. A relatively new initiative is the Erasmus Programme, developed by the European Community to encourage co-operation and exchange between a number of universities throughout Europe, including UVA and VU. The programme allows students from EEC universities to study in equivalent faculties of other European universities; to find out more enquire at your local college.

Amsterdam Summer University

Felix Meritis Building, Keizersgracht 324, IW (620 0225). Tram 1, 2, 5. **Courses** last week of July-end of first week of Sept.
Housed, together with the Shaffy Theatre (*see chapter* **Theatre**), in the Felix Meritis Building, ASU offers an extensive, annual summer programme of courses, workshops, training and seminars in the arts and sciences to international classes. All classes are in English. Courses last between three days and six weeks and are for postgraduates, graduates and undergraduates. During the summer courses a cultural programme, including dance, theatre and music, is held in the theatre. The courses are not part of the regular UVA curriculum.

Foreign Student Service

Oranje Nassaulaan 5, 1075 AH; OS (671 5915). Tram 2. **Open** 9am-5pm Mon-Fri.

The Foreign Student Service (FSS) promotes the well-being of foreigners who come to The Netherlands for study or training. FSS provides personal assistance and general information on studying in The Netherlands and runs the International Student Insurance Service (ISIS), in addition to organising a number of social and cultural activities. It also publishes a catalogue listing the most important institutions offering Dutch language training in Holland.

Student Information

(525 4307).
An information line for Dutch and foreign students. Callers are referred to relevant organisations if Student Information can't help.

UVA Main Library

Singel 425, C (525 2301). Tram 1, 2, 5. **Open** *for study* 9.30am-midnight Mon-Fri; *for book lending* 10.30am-5pm Mon-Fri.
Anyone can use this library for study. For reference you need a consulting card (obtainable free of charge on production of a passport). To get a book you must phone in advance with details of the volume you require, since you can't look for books yourself. Only students of Dutch universities and holders of Dutch degrees can borrow books. No charges are made for study, reference or the borrowing of books. For details of the British Council and American Institute libraries, *see chapter* **Survival**.

VU Main Library

De Boelelaan 1105, OS (548 2613). Bus 8, 23, 26, 48, 49, 64, 65, 67, 173. **Open** 10am-4pm Mon-Fri. **Membership** f30 per year. **No credit cards.**
Anyone can apply for membership, which entitles you to study, borrow and use books for reference.

Dutch Language Courses

If you're feeling guilty about the superb English spoken by Amsterdammers, you can tackle the Dutch language at several institutions. Below we've listed a reputable selection.

VU Department of Applied Linguistics

De Boelelaan 1105, Room 9A21, 1081 HV; OS (548 4968). Bus 8, 23, 26, 48, 49, 64, 65, 67, 173. **Open** *information* 10am-4pm Mon-Fri. **Credit** AmEx, MC, V.
Anyone can enrol on the VU self-study programme Nederlands Tweede Taal (Dutch Second Language) and use the language laboratory facilities. The fee is from f175 for 12 hours of instruction. Beginner's Dutch, a three week intensive course in September and October, runs for five hours a day, five days a week and costs from f225. Levels II, III and IV are eight-week courses with three-hour lessons three times a week and cost from f225 for each course. Level II and III courses start in October, November and December; Level III in February; and Level IV in February and April.

British Language Training Centre

Keizersgracht 389, 1016 EJ; IW (622 3634). Tram 1, 2, 5. **Open** *information* 9am-5pm Mon-Fri.
The British Language Training Centre runs various courses in the Dutch language. The intensive course, Nederlands 1, runs from 9.30am to 3.30pm Monday to Friday for two weeks and costs f925. The Nederlands 2 course runs for one week from 9.30am to 4.30pm and costs from f600. There are five levels of evening courses running for approximately three months. The foundation course starts at f825 and there are two-hour lessons twice weekly. Higher level courses have two hours of lessons per week and cost f510. There are a maximum of 12 students per class. The centre can arrange tailor-made courses at an approximate group rate starting at f200 per hour.

Volksuniversiteit Amsterdam

Herenmarkt 93, 1013 EC; IW (626 1626). Tram 1, 2, 4, 5, 9, 13, 16, 17, 24, 25. **Open** *information* 10am-4pm Mon-Fri. **No credit cards.**
There are three levels of day and evening courses at the Volksuniversiteit. Twelve weekly lessons of 2½ hours each cost from f175, with a maximum of 15 students in a class. The price for an intensive course of 24 lessons starts at f325.

Anyone can use the **UVA main library** *for study. See* **review**.

Women's Amsterdam

Help and information, clubs, hotels and history in a city with impressive feminist credentials.

Amsterdam women are internationally famous for their campaigns to gain equal treatment for women. The protests, Dutch tolerance and progressive legislation have combined to make the city's feminist credentials impressive by the standards of most countries.

SUFFRAGETTE CITY

Like suffragettes in other western countries, Dutch women struggled for the right to vote during several decades around the turn of the century. In addition, they campaigned for better health care and education for women. In 1871 a Dutch university admitted a woman student for the first time. This pioneer, Aletta Jacobs, became the first Dutch woman doctor and fought throughout her lifetime for the improvement of conditions for women.

When the right to vote was granted to women in 1919, the movement lost its strength and did not fully recover until the sixties. Feminist pioneers remained little known until the introduction of women's history to the curriculum in Dutch schools. But in Amsterdam, several streets were named in tribute, including Aletta Jacobslaan and Wilhelmina Druckerstraat.

THE SECOND WAVE

The origins of the 'second wave' of the women's movement lie in the changing cultural climate of the fifties and sixties. The first wave had struggled for *equal rights* for men and women; now women campaigned for *equal treatment* of both sexes.

In 1967 Joke Kool-Smit articulated all the feminist arguments in her book *Het Onbehagen van de Vrouw* ('the discomfort of women'), which became the definitive reference on the subject. Smit was a founder member in 1968 of the radical group **MVM**, *Man-vrouw-maatschappij* (man-woman-society), which aimed at breaking down traditional sexual stereotypes. Another of MVM's founders, Hedy d'Ancona, became Minister for Welfare, Public Health and Culture in 1989, and has since campaigned on such issues as provision of child-care facilities for working women.

Another remarkable group, **Dolle Mina** ('Rebellious Mina', named after Wilhelmina Drucker) was founded in 1969 as a left-wing alternative to the MVM. It became famous for street actions, which included singing 'Faith forever, but who will clean the sink?' to newlyweds outside City Hall. Later, when all feminists groups were united on the abortion issue, it was Dolle Mina which successfully occupied a clinic threatened with closure.

The seventies brought consciousness-raising groups, the recognition of 'body' politics and Women's Studies. An abortion law was finally passed in 1981: after 50 days and before 22 weeks, a woman wanting an abortion must wait five days after discussing the matter with a doctor. In 1985, abortions became available through the national health service, and the Morning After Pill is now also available.

A NEW GENERATION

During the eighties, the public diverted its protesting energies into anti-nuclear and environmental campaigns, and by the late eighties, feminism had became institutionalised and absorbed within the Government. Each city within The Netherlands now has a person in charge of Women's Emancipation who participates in policy making. However, the hard economic realities of the nineties mean that many of the pioneering women's health organisations have been forced to close due to lack of funding.

If you want to relax in female-only company, get sympathetic help or find out more about the women's movement, we've listed where to go. For advice, information and general questions try one of the groups below.

Unless otherwise stated, the clubs, bars, shops and organisations listed below do not accept credit cards.

IIAV

Keizersgracht 10, IW (624 2143/4268). Tram 1, 2, 5, 13, 17. **Open** 10am-4pm Mon, Wed-Fri; 10am-9pm Tue. The International Archives of the Women's & Lesbian Movement (IIAV) relate the history of the movement through international books, documents, press clippings and photographs. Among the many memorable images are some of Dolle Mina activists entering a meeting of

All you need to know about feminist theory, history and literature can be found at **Vrouwen in Druk**. *See* **review** *page 238.*

gynaecologists displaying their bellies, labelled: '*Baas in eigen buik*' – 'Control over our own bellies'. Around 1970 the group claimed back the streets in other creative ways, wolf-whistling at men and pinching their buttocks. And, in protest at the lack of women's public toilets, they tied up urinals with pink ribbons bearing the motto: 'Women too have the right to pee.'

Further archives: **Lesbian Archives**, *see p236* **Lesbian Liberation**; **Centraal Bibliotheek**, *see* chapter **Survival**.

Het Vrouwenhuis (The Women's House)

Nieuwe Herengracht 95, IE (625 2066). Tram 7, 9, 14. **Open** *information* 11am-4pm Mon-Fri; *bar* 7pm-midnight after classes. **Closed** July and Aug.

There's a network of Women's Houses throughout The Netherlands. They organise events for all kinds of women, such as festivities on International Women's Day (8 March), and activities, including workshops, courses and classes on things like massage, dance, and improvisation. Non-lesbian women will appreciate the fact that the bar, which opens after evening classes have finished, is not part of the 'scene'; it also has frequent exhibitions by women artists. Vrouwenhuis also run a women-only disco every second Friday of the month.

Vrouwen Bellen Vrouwen (Women Call Women)

(625 0150). **Open** 9.30am-12.30pm, 7.30-10.30pm, Tue, Thur; 7.30-10.30pm Wed; 9am-noon Fri.

Women can get advice and support by ringing this phoneline.

Zwarte Vrouwentelefoon (Black Women's Telephone)

(085 42 4713). **Open** 9am-noon Mon; 1-4pm Tue; 7-10pm Wed.

This helpline for black women offers support and information.

LESBIAN LIBERATION

The lesbian movement has had a big influence on the changing views on sexuality. For a history of the movement for homosexual rights, *see chapter* **Gay Amsterdam**. It is particularly in the fields of theatre, dance, music and literature that lesbian lifestyles and culture are most visible and accepted. Unlike the more coherent male gay community, Amsterdam lesbians have a low profile. But they do campaign with gay men for the freedom to adopt children and with feminist activists for the right of artificial insemination for single women and lesbians.

The lesbian scene is constantly changing; it overlaps with the gay scene, and women (not only lesbians) are accepted at many gay clubs, bars and cafés. The lesbian and gay centre, COC, in Rozenstraat (*see chapter* **Gay Amsterdam**), has a notice board, a women's café for under-26s

(Saturdays from 8-10pm), a women's-only disco on Saturday nights and ballroom dancing for women on the second Saturday of each month.

The Wildside Group (a lesbian SM group) also meets here (8-10pm, first Saturday of each month) and there's an SM café (8pm-midnight, third Saturday of each month).

The staff of the COC Vrouwensecretariat (Lesbian Women's Secretariat) offer information and advice, and the CO2 Information Coffeeshop is a good source of information for what's on (1-5pm Wed-Sat). You can also try the English-speaking help and information line **Gay & Lesbian Switchboard** on 623 6565. For all the above, *see chapter* **Gay Amsterdam**.

Groep 7152
Crea Café, Turfdraagsterpad 17, C (626 2412). Tram 9, 14, 16, 24, 25. **Meetings** (phone to check) *Sept-June* 6-9pm 3rd Sun of month. **Admission** f5; f3.50 members.
A social support group for lesbians and bi-sexual women, which meets to talk and dance at the Crea Café. For information on this countrywide organisation phone 662 0866, although little English is spoken there.

Lesbian Archives
1e Helmersstraat 17, OW (618 5879). Tram 1, 2, 3, 5, 6, 12. **Open** 6.30-10.30pm Tue; 9.30am-1.30pm Thur; 1-5pm Fri.
These archives are mainly audio-visual. Home-made videos of festivals and events, recordings of speeches and television or radio programmes can be found, including ones in English, French and German.

Publications
For women: *Opzijds* (f7.50) is the leading feminist monthly magazine, and has comprehensive listings of what's on for women; *Savante* is a new Women's Studies magazine (f5.75, quarterly). **For lesbians**: *Wildside* is produced by COC, by and for SM dykes (f6, quarterly); *Ma'dam* is also produced by COC (f2.95, monthly). For details of further lesbian publications, *see chapter* **Gay Amsterdam**.

Going Out

The women's 'scene' is far smaller than it was in the seventies. Amsterdam women now seem to feel less of a need for female-only venues, many of which are run by volunteers and are struggling financially. The Melkweg (*see chapter* **Music: Rock, Folk & Jazz**) has occasional exhibitions for and about women.

Cafés and Bars

Café Vive-la-Vie
Amstelstraat 7, C (624 0114). Tram 4, 9, 14. **Open** 3pm-1am Mon-Thur; 3pm-2am Fri, Sat.
Mainly lesbian women go to this café for a drink and to meet others. The art deco-style interior is perfect for conversation, although the music can get a little too loud in the evening.

Françoise
Kerkstraat 176, IS (624 0145). Tram 16, 24, 25. **Open** 9am-6pm Mon-Sat.
At this mixed, lesbian-owned café and gallery you can

get tea, coffee, home-made pastries and full meals (including vegetarian) and see exhibitions of work by female artists, which change every month. The décor is traditional and the music classical.

De Hemelse Modder
Oude Waal 9, C (624 3203). Metro Nieuwmarkt. **Open** 6pm-midnight Tue-Sun; *kitchen* 6-10pm Tue-Sun.
Situated on the edge of the red light district, by one of its more scenic canals, this mixed restaurant is highly recommended for its candle-lit meals, aesthetic interior and friendly, mostly lesbian and gay, staff. The food is Mediterranean, and there are always vegetarian options available.

Homolulu
Kerkstraat 23, IS (624 6387). Tram 16, 24, 25. **Open** *restaurant & disco* 10pm-4am Tue-Thur, Sun; 10pm-5am Fri, Sat; *women-only evening* 1st Sun of month and 3rd Fri, 8pm-1am; then mixed lesbians and gay men 1am-4am. **Admission** free Mon-Thur, Sun; f5 Fri, Sat; *women-only evening* free. **Average meal** f40.
Owned and run by lesbians, this smart private restaurant/club is frequented by lesbians, gays and a sprinkling of straights. There's a women-only night which gets very crowded after 1am. You can have a reasonably priced, candle-lit meal in the superb restaurant overlooking the mirrored dance-floor, where the music is mainly from the pop charts. The door policy can be selective, so dress up!

De Huyschkamer
Utrechtsestraat 137, C (627 0575). Tram 4, 6, 7, 10. **Open** 3.30pm-1am Mon-Thur, Sun; 3.30pm-2am Fri, Sat.
This pleasant bar-restaurant attracts a mixed, mainly young and artistic lesbian and gay crowd. It's particularly light, airy and spacious, with huge shop windows and a pastel décor, plus the odd neo-classical and wrought-iron touch. The young staff are friendly and seem to know the city's event calendar off by heart. Food prices start from f10.

Café Saarein
Elandsstraat 119, IW (623 4901). Tram 7, 10. **Open** 8pm-1am Mon; 3pm-1am Tue-Thur, Sun; 3pm-2am Fri, Sat.

The hub of the women's scene in Amsterdam is this snug 'brown bar' in the centre of the Jordaan. The staff have a list in English of women's activities in the city and are happy to give help and information over the phone. Though many bars are frequented by women who all know each other, so that foreigners often end up talking to other visitors rather than locals, at Saarein you can always find female company to chat to or play darts or billiards with. There's even a friendly cat called Saartia.

La Strada
Nieuwezijds Voorburgwal 93-95, C (625 0276). Tram 1, 2, 5, 13, 17. **Open** *bar* winter 4pm-1am Mon-Thur, Sun; 4pm-2am Fri, Sat; summer 3pm-1am Mon-Thur, Sun; 3pm-2am Fri, Sat; *kitchen* 5.30-10pm daily.
A spacious café-culinaire, bang in the centre of Amsterdam. The clientele is mainly lesbian, with a sprinkling of gay men. Dinner is served between 5.30pm and 10pm; main courses cost between f15 and f25 and vegetarian meals are available. Each month La Strada displays the work of a different artist.

Van den Berg
Lindengracht 95, IW (622 2716). Tram 3. **Open** 5pm-1am Mon-Fri, Sun; 5pm-2am Fri, Sat.
A cosy place in the Jordaan to have a good dinner or just a cup of coffee on the terrace. Vegetarian meals are available – for between f11 and f22, but the kitchen is shut on Saturdays. It's mainly frequented by women, but men are welcome too.

Cultural Centre

Amazone
Singel 72, C (627 9000/fax 638 6281). Tram 1, 2, 5, 13, 17. **Open** 10am-5pm Tue-Fri; 1-5pm Sat, Sun. **Admission** free.
This foundation promotes artistic and cultural work by (mostly Dutch) women. Recent exhibitions in the gallery have included 'Women in Architecture' and 'Aletta Jacobs' (on the first woman doctor). The bar is open during the regular lectures and the free poetry evenings.

Clubs

Amsterdam tends not to have women-only clubs, but there are regular women's 'one-nighter' discos organised at the following clubs and by **Het Vrouwenhuis** (*see p235*), **Vive-la-Vie** (*see p236* **Cafés and Bars**) and **COC** (for this and **gay clubs** that accept women, *see chapter* **Gay Amsterdam**). Phone before setting out.

De Brug
Kuipersstraat 151 (postal enquiries to PO Box 6189, 1005 ED, Amsterdam), OS. Tram 3, 4. **Open** 8.30pm-2am 1st Sat of month. **Admission** f5.
On the first Saturday of every month there's a disco-evening here for lesbians over 35 (ID required). Younger women are welcome as guests.

Clit Club
Information from Gay & Lesbian Switchboard (623 6565).
A relatively new, and enormously successful, club held weekly on Fridays, which attracts a large international crowd of women, where leather rubs shoulders with lace. There are regular live performances, go-go girls and fierce music. The location varies, so check with the Gay & Lesbian Switchboard for details.

*The **Amazone** foundation promotes artistic and cultural work by women.*

Mona Lisa
Nieuwe Herengracht 95, IE (625 2066). Tram 7, 9, 14. **Open** 10pm-2am 2nd Fri of month. **Admission** free before 11pm, f6 after.
A very popular monthly party organised by Het Vrouwenhuis (*see p235*), and held all year round. The surroundings are freshly and imaginatively themed each month, and the atmosphere is that of a private party. Jazz and blues is played from 10pm to midnight; after that time it's mainly house music. Mona Lisa attracts a mixed crowd of women.

Saunas and Sports

Almost every sports centre, swimming pool and sauna in Amsterdam has women-only sessions; *see chapter* **Sport & Fitness**. We list two women's saunas.

Sauna Kylpy
Mercatorplein 23-27, OW (612 3496). Tram 7, 13. **Open** 10am-11pm Mon-Fri. **Admission** f17.50. **Sunbeds** f17.50 for 20 mins.

Sauna Aquafit
Van 't Hofflaan 4, OE (694 5211). Tram 9. **Open** 7-11pm Tue-Fri. **Closed** during school holidays; phone to check. **Admission** f17.

Shops and Businesses

STEW
Weesperzijde 4, OE (665 5016). Tram 3, 6, 7, 10.
Open 9am-5pm Mon-Thur.
The association has information on women-run businesses and companies throughout The Netherlands.

Women's International Network
PO Box 15692, 1001 ND, Amsterdam (co-founder Agnes Benjamin 679 9951). **Membership** Sept-June fl50.
The professional women members of this network are supportive of each other and have a wealth of contacts and advice for like-minded career women, particularly useful for those who have just moved to Amsterdam. To join you should be of managerial status, be over 25 and have been employed for a minimum of five years. Associate members are women with these qualifications who are temporarily out of work. There's an international mix of women, but given that all communications and meetings are in English, American and English women predominate. They hold monthly meetings, invite guest speakers and organise lectures, workshops and visits, usually with career themes.

Bookshops

For **Vrolijk** bookshop, *see chapter* **Gay Amsterdam**.

Antiquariaat Lorelei
Prinsengracht 495, IW (623 4308). Tram 1, 2, 5, 7, 10.
Open noon-6pm Tue-Fri; noon-5pm Sat. **Credit** V.
Antiquariaat Lorelei stocks a huge selection of second-hand books by and about women. Titles in English cover all subjects from biography and feminist theory to travel and sociology. Lorelei also has a notice-board giving information on events and activities of interest to women.

Vrouwen in Druk
Westermarkt 5, IW (624 5003). Tram 1, 2, 5, 7, 10, 13, 14, 17. **Open** 11am-6pm Mon-Sat.
Situated close to the Homo-monument, this shop stocks second-hand books (with dozens of shelves of English titles) by female authors, covering feminist theory, history and literature.

Xantippe
Prinsengracht 290, IW (623 5854). Tram 1, 2, 5. **Open** 1-6pm Mon; 10am-6pm Tue-Sat. **Credit** MC, V.
The main women's bookstore, stocking new titles, many of them in English. Up-to-date information on what's on for women in Amsterdam is provided.

Specialist shops

Bel Ami
Elandsgracht 51, IW (627 3432). Tram 7, 10, 17.
Open 1-6pm Mon; 10am-6pm Tue-Fri; 10am-5pm Sat.
This shop sells cards, frames and specialist paper.

Ellen Schippers
3rd floor, Eerste Jan Steenstraat 112, OS (662 3883). Tram 3, 12, 16, 24, 25. **Open** noon-5pm Wed-Sat.
Stockists of leather and latex clothing for women.

NVSH
Blauwburgwal 7-9, IW (623 9359). Tram 1, 2, 5, 13, 17.
Open 11am-6pm Mon-Fri; noon-5pm Sat.
The Netherlands' Association for Sexual Reform (NVSH) sells rubber and leather items, books, sex toys and safe sex supplies.

Hotels

There are no women-only hotels, but the following are 'friendly'. Among the other gay hotels, **ITC Hotel** is the most popular with women (*see chapter* **Gay Amsterdam**).

Granada Hotel
Leidsekruisstraat 13, IS (623 6711). Tram 1, 2, 5, 6, 7, 10. **Rates** *single* f75; *double* f120. **Credit** (minimum f100) AmEx, DC, MC, V.
A relaxed, mixed hotel, much frequented by women and gays on a tight budget. Many of the rooms have shared facilities. There's a returnable deposit for keys and you won't be surcharged for overnight company.
Hotel services *Bar. Car park (enclosed) nearby. Laundry. Sitting room.*

Quentin Hotel
Leidsekade 89, IS (626 2187). Tram 1, 2, 5, 6, 7, 10. **Rates** *single* f57.50; *double* f85-f110. **Credit** AmEx, DC, MC, V.
A gay-owned hotel particularly welcoming to lesbians, though not to small children. The English-speaking staff are friendly and have a useful knowledge of the cultural scene in Amsterdam. The hotel is closed in December and January, but you can still make bookings for later.
Hotel services *Car park (guarded) nearby. Snacks and drinks available 24 hours daily.*

Health and Safety

Amsterdam is a relatively unthreatening city for women, although it has places to avoid, particularly after dark. If you've been raped or sexually abused, you can contact **TOSG** on 612 7576 (10.30am-11.30pm seven days a week) or **Blijf-van-m'n-lijf-huis** ('don't touch my body' refuge) on 620 1261 (9am-5pm) or 638 7636 (5pm-9am). For advice on all aspects of HIV and AIDS, phone the **AIDS-infolijn** on 06 022 2220 (2-10pm Mon-Fri). For other health establishments and counselling services, *see chapter* **Survival**.

MR '70
Sarphatistraat 620-626, IS (624 5426). **Open** 9am-4pm Mon-Thur; 9am-1pm Fri.
An abortion clinic which offers help and advice. Phone for an appointment.

Stichting Vrouwen 40-60
Nicolaas Witsenkade 27, OS (626 8080). **Open** 10am-5pm Mon-Fri.
A special centre for women in crisis situations, particularly for women between the ages of 40 and 60.

Women's Healthcentre
Obiplein 4, OE (693 4358). Tram 3, 6, 14. **Open** 9am-noon Tue; 7-10pm Thur; 1-4pm Fri.
Women working at the *Vrouwen-gezondsheidscentrum* give information and advice on all health matters. They refer patients to *vrouwvriendlijke arts* (doctors, clinics and therapists sympathetic to women's specific needs) and run self-help groups on such issues as pregnancy, over-eating and the menopause. Phone to check opening times before setting out.

Trips Out of Town

Amsterdam is not at all representative of The Netherlands, so it's worth trying to see life beyond the city. Easily accessible, the provinces offer culture and countryside, Dutch produce and customs, and a slower pace of life.

Contents

NOORD - HOLLAND
Everything for which the Netherlands is famous

THE NOORD - HOLLAND

VVV CAN TELL YOU MORE

The brochure will tell you about everything that is pleasant, beautiful and exciting in Noord-Holland. But we can well imagine that you would like to know more about certain aspects. Just step inside a VVV <tourist information centre>. You will not only find informative folders but also friendly, expert staff who will be pleased to answer your questions. The VVV's in Noord-Holland are open every day.

WINDMILLS POLDERS FARMSTEADS

WHY ARE THERE AMSTERDAM-STYLE GABLES ON NOORD-HOLLAND FARMHOUSES?

A great deal of money was needed to drain all that land. Money paid by the rich citizens of Amsterdam, in exchange for these lots of land. This explains why the typical Noord-Holland farmhouses have Amsterdam-style gables.

FLOWERS

A FEAST FOR THE EYE ALL THE YEAR ROUND

If you think that there are only a few weeks in which to enjoy the flowers in

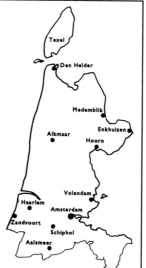

Noord-Holland, we have a pleasant surprise for you: Noord-Holland is in bloom all the year round! Somewhere, there is always something to enjoy in the flower and plant worlds.

FOLKLORE

GET TO KNOW NOORD-HOLLAND THROUGH ITS PEOPLE

The inhabitants of Noord-Holland have customs all of their own. The local costumes of Volendam and Marken, the cheese-market rituals in Alkmaar, the age-old traditions of the cattle markets, all make Noord-Holland a typical part of the Netherlands, continually arousing amazement.

WALKING AND CYCLING

YOU SEE MORE IF YOU DON'T GO FAST...

All things considered, you could spend your holidays for years in cycling and walking through Noord-Holland before exhausting its beauties.

More information =

VVV NOORD - HOLLAND
Florapark 6. 2012 HK Haarlem, Holland.
Tel: 31. 23. 319413.
Fax:31. 23. 340093.

Beyond Amsterdam

Exploring The Netherlands and bordering countries by road, rail and bicycle.

Amsterdam is not typical of The Netherlands. The essence of the country and its people lies in its 12 distinctive provinces. The national borders enclose just 41,864 square kilometres (16,000 square miles), so all but the remotest corners are within a day's drive or train ride; many attractions are less than an hour from Amsterdam. Cycling across the flat landscape or cruising the many waterways by boat are just two ways of enjoying the countryside.

COMMON GROUND

This country, more than almost any other, has been shaped by its inhabitants. Over half the land is below sea level, much of it laboriously reclaimed from the sea (*see chapter* **The Provinces: Fighting the Sea**). In turn, the often hostile elements have moulded the attitudes and lifestyles of the 14.9 million inhabitants, contributing to their stoicism and pragmatism.

The vulnerability of their land explains the Dutch sympathy for the environment and has forced them to work together for the common good (*see chapter* **Green Issues**). One person's failure to maintain his part of a dike could imperil an entire town. This obligation was enforced by medieval polder boards and may explain the early arrival of democracy in the country. A sense of community has become ingrained in the Dutch nature. In the eighties, workers agreed to forego pay rises for five years until the economy could be revived. Social provision has also been generous, from medieval *hofjes* (almshouses) to today's welfare state.

Other Dutch traits can be traced to religion. The humanism of Erasmus has combined with Calvinist beliefs in social responsibility and the liberty of conscience to produce a singular mixture of tolerance and conformity. Generally, it's considered good to be *gewoon* (plain and ordinary); ostentation is shunned. The former Queen (now Princess) Juliana was admired for travelling by bicycle and Prime Minister Ruud Lubbers is respected for taking sandwiches to work. Living at close quarters has resulted in formalities which create distance.

WHERE IS HOLLAND?

The region of Holland has been so dominant in Dutch history that the entire country has confusingly become widely known by that name. In fact, the region accounts for just two of the 12

Centraal Station: *the Netherlands Railway (NS) is efficient, clean and quite cheap.*

provinces: Noord (North) and Zuid (South) Holland. Amsterdam lies in the south of Noord Holland, and is thus an easy day trip away from most of the classic Dutch attractions: windmills, cheese-making towns, national costumes, tulips and clogs. However, many of these traditional sights (*see chapter* Excursions in Holland) have only been preserved for tourists.

The contemporary face of Holland is represented by its ring of major cities called the The Randstad (*see chapter* The Randstad), which also encompasses the province of Utrecht, focus of the transport network and home of the stockbroker belt. Provincial Dutch sometimes see the cosmopolitan Randstad as a rather self-obsessed state-within-a-state, yet it's not homogeneous. People from The Hague are popularly portrayed as gracious; those in Utrecht as proper; and citizens of Rotterdam as industrious. Amsterdammers are considered to be an anarchic, permissive lot, and their city to be a magnet for those who don't grow up *gewoon*. It's been like that since before 1608, when the Pilgrim Fathers fled that 'sinful city' for the calm of Leiden (*see chapter* The Randstad).

The Netherlands, particularly Holland, has for centuries been a hub of transport and maritime trade. Now high-speed road and rail links are unifying the country ever more tightly and binding it into Europe. Regional customs and accents are being eroded in the process, but the provinces are fighting to preserve their identity.

PROVINCIAL CHARM

The people of the predominantly Protestant northern provinces – Friesland, Groningen and Drenthe – are renowned for loyalty and hard work. Friesland was once an independent tribal nation that reached along the coast from North Holland to eastern Germany, and whose people were called 'unconquerable' by the Roman writer Pliny the Elder. Theirs is still the most individualistic province. Famous for their costumes (now seldom worn) and breeds of cattle and dog, they still stick to their own distinct language and literature; even the road signs are bi-lingual. Popular myth attributes the Frisians' greater than average height to constant flooding, which only the tall survived.

Neighbouring Groningen, a staid, rural and conservative area, has a surprisingly liberal university, although graduates don't usually stay around long. Despite state efforts to attract people there, it's the only province with net outward migration. The fens, moors and forests of Drenthe are a world apart, inhabited (sparsely) since the Palaeolithic age. Saxons initially occupied the slightly hillier Overijssel, due east of Amsterdam. Many traditions in this ultra-conservative area have survived tourism and the arrival of new industries.

The largest province, Gelderland, borders Germany and is sandwiched between north and south. Its terrain of wild countryside, orchards and commercial rivers has been continually fought over. Gelderland's coastline became land-locked when part of the Zuider Zee was drained to form Flevoland. That flat, agricultural province is so new that its chief characteristic is its very existence.

Another victory over the sea was the building of the Delta Works flood barrier to protect the islands of Zeeland, once isolated in the river delta bordering Belgium. Increased tourism and industry is transforming this province's traditional way of life.

Caricatures of the Dutch come unstuck in the Catholic south, where there are even a few hills. Relaxed and light-hearted, the people of Noord Brabant and Limburg celebrate carnivals in the streets. The entire Noord Brabant village of Eersel sometimes gathers for weddings in a large tent at the market-place, savouring milk and brandy with sugar. Wedged between Belgium and Germany, the rolling landscape of Limburg is also home to bon vivants, who thrive on its famous cuisine. Ultimately, though, all Dutch provinces share *gezelligheid* – cosiness, friendliness and conviviality.

Travel Information

The Netherlands Board of Tourism (Vlietweg 15, 2266 KA, Leidschendam, tel 070 3705 705) and branches abroad, can help with general information. For each centre of interest, we've listed the VVV tourist office, which will also suggest and reserve accommodation, as will National Reservings Centrum (*see chapter* Accommodation).

Roads

The Netherlands' extensive network of motorways and roads is well-maintained, and clearly signposted. *See chapter* Survival for advice on driving and for the motoring organisation ANWB, which offers a broad selection of maps and suggested excursions.

Buses and Coaches

The national bus service is reasonably priced, but arguably not as punctual, comprehensive or easy to negotiate as the railway (*see below*). For bus information and timetables, contact the GVB (*see chapter* Essential Information). Private coach companies offering good value half- and full-day excursions (from f30 per person for local trips to f60 per person to Belgium) are listed in Sightseeing.

Cycling

The Netherlands is flat (but windy) and cycle paths are plentiful; the VVV and ANWB sell cycle tour maps. Most major railway stations have bike hire depots. You'll need proof of identity and a deposit; rail ticket holders get a discount of 33% and you can reserve a cycle until 11am. Bikes can only be taken on Dutch trains outside peak periods (6.30-9am, 4.30-6pm, Mon-Fri), and cost extra.

Crossing the Border

Because The Netherlands is so small and its transport links so good, the Dutch have become a nation of border-hoppers. Relations with their neighbours, Germany to the east and Belgium to the south, eased by almost non-existent border formalities, have always been close. The Low Countries had a common history until Belgian independence in 1830 and Northern Belgium still shares the Dutch language, although they call it 'Flemish' and speak it, claim the Dutch, with a French accent.

Germany is the main hinterland of Rotterdam's port. Beside the commercial barges, pleasure boats cruise up the Rhine, passing **Köln** (Cologne), then the former West German capital of **Bonn**, and meander on through the **Rhineland** rift valley, lined with vineyards, castles and towns straight out of *Grimm's Fairy Tales*.

Hugging the border with Limburg is the German city of **Aachen**, former capital of Charlemagne, whose bones are contained in the crown-shaped Palatine Chapel, dating from 796. Aachen is also known as Aix-la-Chapelle in this linguistically mixed region, which is bounded on the west by the valleys of the Geul and Gulpen, on the south by the Belgian Ardennes' rocky outcrops and on the east by the volcanic Eifel hills.

The Dutch habitually visit Germany for shopping sprees, particularly at Christmas, to buy goods such as high-quality clothes. Dutch relations with **Belgium** are more complex. Age-old rivalries are epitomised by the con-

tinued existence of **Baarle-Nassau-Hertog**, a Belgian enclave just inside Dutch Noord Brabant, within which there are Dutch areas. Unsurprisingly, administration of the municipality is absurd, with two town halls, two police forces, and a house which has two addresses – 2 and 19 Loveren – because its front door straddles the border.

The Dutch descend on Belgium in droves mainly to shop and eat out. The European Community capital of **Bruxelles** (Brussels), with its English shops, handmade chocolates and superior cuisine is different enough to be exotic (they speak French there), but is only three hours by car or train from Amsterdam. Belgium's main gastronomic region is around **Antwerp**, a city full of tiny shopping streets, small museums and pavement cafés. **Gent** and canal-lined **Brugge** (Bruges) are two of the most important centres of medieval Flemish art and architecture.

Belgium

Belgium Tourist Bureau, Amsterdam *Herengracht 435-437, IS (624 5953). Tram 1, 2, 5.* **Open** 9am-6pm Mon-Fri, 10am-1pm Sat. **Antwerp tourist office** *Grote Markt 15, 2000 (32 3 232 0103).* **Brugge tourist office** *Grasmarkt 63, 1000 (32 2 504 0390).* **Gent tourist office** *Belfortstraat 9, 9000 (32 91 241 555).*

Germany

German Tourist Bureau, Amsterdam *Hoogoorddreef 76, 1101 BG, OE (697 8066). Bijlmer train station/bus 62, 137.* **Open** 10am-4.45pm Mon-Fri. **Aachen tourist office** *Haus Löwenstein, Markt 39, 5100 (49 241 180 2960).* **Köln tourist office** *Unter Fettenhennen 19, 5000 (49 221 221 3345).*

Netherlands Railway (NS)

The prices listed below are a rough guide: fares are updated in January each year.

The extensive NS rail network is efficient, clean, punctual and quite cheap. Services are frequent, so reservations are unnecessary, unless you are heading abroad. Departure times are displayed on yellow station posters; a national timetable can be bought at stations and most newsagents.

As a rule, national tickets are valid for one day only; if you make a return journey over more than one day you must buy two single tickets. The exception is the Weekend Return ticket, which allows outward travel on Saturday, the return journey on Sunday. Children under 4 years travel free; 4 to 11 year-olds pay 60% of the full fare if accompanied by an adult paying full fare, or a flat rate of f1 per journey if on a Railrunner ticket or with an adult holding a Holland Rail Pass (*see below*). Passes offering unlimited rail travel cost f54 (one day) or f129 (one week) second class, f81 and f194 first class; a supplement to include trams, metros and buses costs

f6.15 (one day) or f23 (one week). InterRail tickets are valid in The Netherlands, but a supplement is payable on Eurocity trains; holders of Rail Europe Senior Cards are eligible for discounts of 30%.

The Holland Rail Pass is valid for travel on any three days within a ten-day period. Cost per person is f79 (second class) or f99 (first class). For group travel, the Meermanskaart offers unlimited travel on one day (not before 9am Mon-Fri) for six people; second class prices range from f82 for two people to f138 for six.

Another option, ideal for longer stays, is the Rail-Actief Kaart. Costing f108 and valid for one year, it offers 40% discount on all travel (except before 9am Mon-Fri).

Day Excursions

NS offers 75 all-inclusive excursions (discount rail and other travel, admission to sights and occasional extras) to destinations all over The Netherlands and also to Brugge (Bruges) and Antwerp in Belgium.

Excursions in Holland

Holland may have more than its share of clichés, but there are many splendid monuments, markets and museums worth leaving Amsterdam for.

Most of The Netherlands' stereotypical sights are concentrated in the area around Amsterdam: Noord and Zuid Holland. Both these provinces are small, and many of the places we've reviewed by theme are close to each other and well linked by public transport or special tours (*see chapter* **Beyond Amsterdam**). As well as Amsterdam, Haarlem, Leiden and Utrecht (*see chapter* **The Randstad**) are excellent bases from which to make excursions.

Cheese

The Dutch eat cheese (*kaas*) for breakfast, lunch, dinner and snacks – and still have enough to export around 420,000 tonnes per year. For the types of cheese, *see chapter* **Shopping: Food and Drink**. The summer cheese markets, museums and traditional farms capture the flavour of how this commodity used to be made and sold. The most famous – and the best – is at **Alkmaar**. Little-known but authentic farmers' cheese markets are held all year round in the villages of Bodegraven (Tuesdays) and Woerden (Wednesdays), both between Gouda and Utrecht.

There are many thatched-roof **cheese farms** (*kaasboderijen*) near Gouda, several of which are by the picturesque Vlist River. Look out for the sign '*kaas te koop*' (cheese for sale), indicating a farm shop where you can buy freshly-made Gouda, often laced with herbs, and perhaps look behind the scenes. De Driesprong, at Bergambacht near Schoonhoven (*listed under* **Traditions**), offers a tour (Monday to Saturday from mid-March to 1 December). Tickets cost f2.50; if you make an appointment, another f12 buys a typical Dutch *koffietafel* lunch. Phone 01826 2314 for details.

Alkmaar

Getting there 37km (22 miles) north-west; *by train* direct from Centraal Station.
VVV *Waagplein 2 (072 114 284)*. **Open** *Apr-Sept* 9am-5.30pm Mon-Wed; 9am-7pm Thur; 9am-6pm Fri; 9am-5pm Sat; *Oct-Apr* 9am-5.30pm Mon-Wed; 9am-6pm Thur, Fri; 9am-5pm Sat.

Alkmaar cheese market (mid April-mid Sept, 10am-noon Fri) is as much a ritual for tourists as for members of the cheese porters' guild. Garbed in pristine white uniforms and straw hats with coloured ribbons denoting the competing guild companies, they weigh the cheeses and carry them in wooden barrows hung from their shoulders. Arrive by 9.30am to see the buyers smelling, tasting and testing a core of cheese from each lot. The ceremony, explained in English in a VVV brochure, takes place at the Weigh House, converted in 1582 from a fifteenth-century chapel. There's a *Kaasmuseum* (Cheese Museum) upstairs, and craft stalls outside. The VVV runs a walking tour of the medieval centre, dating from AD 935, which often resounds to the sound of a carillon concert. Then head for the **Hans Brinker Museum**, dedicated to the fictitious boy who stuck his finger in the dike to save Haarlem; the **Biermuseum**, which has a beer-tasting cellar; or to the art and toy collection at the **Stedelijk Museum**. There are boat tours through the drawbridged canals.

Edam

Getting there 10km (5 miles) north; *by bus* 110, 112, 114 from Centraal Station.
VVV *Stadhuis, Damplein (02993 71727)*. **Open** *Nov-March* 10am-noon, 2-4pm, Mon-Sat; *Apr-Oct* 10am-5pm Mon-Sat.

This tiny town was a prosperous port during the Golden Age and has some exquisite façades and bridges. It suffers fewer tourist hordes than Volendam (*see under* **Traditions: Waterland**), which is a 101 bus-ride away. At the **cheese market** (July-Aug, 9.30am-1.30pm Wed), the famous red-skinned cheese arrives by boat. **Grote Kerk**, rebuilt in 1602, has remarkable stained glass, and the *speeltoren* of **Kleine Kerk** has one of the country's oldest carillons (1561). The 1737 **Raadhuis** (town hall) has an elaborate stucco interior. The town has two oddities: the municipal **museum** on Damplein has a floating cellar and in a former **Captain's House** are portraits of a 202kg (445lb) man and 2.75m (9ft) tall woman.

Gouda

Getting there 29km (18 miles) south-west; *by train* direct from Centraal Station.
VVV *Markt 27 (01820 13666)*. **Open** 9am-5pm Mon-Fri; 10am-4pm Sat.

Golden wheels of *kaas* are traded at the Thursday **cheese market** (July-Aug, 9am-1pm) in front of the 1668 Weigh House – which has a gablestone depicting cheese-weighing – and the Gothic City Hall of 1450. Handicrafts, such as wooden shoes, are also sold then; a **general market** (9am-1pm Thur; 9am-5pm Sat) runs all year. Gouda's other famous products include clay pipes and pottery, which are displayed in the De Moriaan Museum, and candles, some 20,000 of which illuminate the square during the Christmas tree ceremony. Adrie Moerings gives ceramic and pipe-making demonstrations at Peperstraat 76 (9am-5pm Mon-Fri). **St Janskerk** (entrance f2.50) boasts over half of Holland's antique stained-glass windows, 70 in all, and holds carillon concerts (*May-mid Sept* 8pm Wed, f10; *Jul-Aug* 11.30am Thur, free). **Caterina Gasthuis Museum**, a hospice and hospital from 1320 to 1910, has Golden Age silver and modern art. You can also see a corn grinding windmill, **Molen de Roode Leeuw**. The VVV runs special group tours (phone for an appointment), or take a cruise on the Reeuwijk lakes. And do sample the local *stroopwafels* – two thin waffles glued together with syrup.

Purmerend

Getting there 26km (15 miles) north-east; *by train* direct from Centraal Station; *by bus* 100 from Centraal Station.
VVV *Kaasmarkt 20 (02990 52525)*. **Open** 1-5pm Mon; 9am-5pm Tue-Fri; 9am-3pm Sat.
Purmerend has become an Amsterdam dormitory town. Its population explosion – from 10,000 to 56,000 since 1960 – has changed its character, but not the Thursday cheese market outside the Renaissance Town Hall (July-Aug, 11am-1pm). The costumed women and dancers, although strictly for tourists, are a colourful sight. More authentic is the Tuesday morning cattle and general market, where deals are sealed by a handclap. There are art exhibitions in **Museum Waterland** and local history in **Purmerends Museum**. The most rewarding return route to Amsterdam is via the country roads through Den Ilp and Landsmeer.

Flowers

The tulip is Holland's hallmark, and when it blooms (March to May) thousands of tourists make for the **Keukenhof Bulb Gardens** in Lisse, on the Noord/Zuid Holland border. But all year round Dutch blooms can be seen in markets, botanical gardens, auctions and flower parades. For export rules on bulbs and flowers, *see chapter* **Shopping: Flowers**.

Floral calendar

Spring: The flower trade's year kicks off in mid to late February with the indoor **Westfriese Flora** *(02285 11644)* at Bovenkarspel, near Enkhuizen (*see below* **Traditions: West Friesland**). From late March to late May, the **bulb district** (*bloembollenstreek*), from Den Helder to The Hague, is carpeted with blooms of the principal crops: daffodils, crocuses, gladioli, hyacinths, narcissi – and tulips. Between late April and early May, residents of Lisse and the Noord Holland towns of Anna Paulowna and Limmen vie to create the season's best **flower mosaics** on their front lawns.
Summer: In mid to late May, golden fields of rapeseed brighten Flevoland, Friesland and Groningen (*see chapter* **The Provinces**). In The Hague (*see chapter* **The Randstad**), the Japanese Garden at **Clingendael Gardens** is in flower from early May to mid June, and in **Westbroek Park** the rose garden (which contains 350 varieties) flowers in July and August. In late June there's the **Floralia** exhibition at the Zuider Zee Museum, Enkhuizen (*see below* **Traditions: West Friesland**). The **Deltaflora** show is held in early August (3-7 Aug 1993) at Stellendam (01870 83002), part of the giant Delta Works (*see chapter* **The Provinces: Zeeland**).
Autumn: Heather purples the landscape (especially in Gelderland's Veluwe, *see chapter* **The Provinces**) during August and September, when greenhouse flowers also emerge. This is the season of most flower parades (*see*

Aalsmeer flower auction. See **review** page 246.

below). The autumn colours are captured at **Herstflora**, held in October (around 24 Oct 1993) at the Singer Museum in Laren, Noord Holland (02153 15656).
Winter: In November, the public and florists from all over the world view new varieties at the **Professional Flower Exhibition** at Aalsmeer Flower Auction (*listed under* **Flower Auctions**). At Christmas time there's the **Kerstflora** show at Hillegom, near Lisse in Noord Holland.

Flower parades

Haarlem-Noordwijk Parade *Via Bennebroek, Hillegom and Lisse*. **Date** last Sat in April (24 Apr 1993). Floats on show at Lisse and Hobahohallen (Fri, Sat evenings).
Rijnsburg Parade *Rijnsburg (11am) via Leiden (1pm) to Noordwijk (4pm)*. **Date** first Sat in Aug (7 Aug 1993). Floats on show at Flora Auction Hall, Rijnsburg (Fri evening) and Boulevard, Noordwijk (Sat evening).
Aalsmeer-Amsterdam Parade *Aalsmeer (9.30am) to Amsterdam (4pm)*. **Date** first Sat in Sept (4 Sept 1993). The Aalsmeer-Amsterdam Parade is Europe's largest flower procession and floats can be viewed (3-10pm Fri; 11am-6pm Sun) in Aalsmeer Auction Hall (*see below* **Flower Auctions**). Highlights are the parade down Amstelveenseweg before lunch, the 4pm reception at Dam Square, Amsterdam (*see chapter* **Amsterdam by Season**), and the illuminated cavalcade through Aalsmeer (9-10pm). Be on site early.

Keukenhof Bulb Gardens

Keukenhof, near Lisse. **Getting there** 27km (17 miles) south-west; *by train* discount train-bus-admission packages for Keukenhof and surroundings from rail stations. **Open** *25 Mar-23 May 1993* 8am-6pm daily; similar in 1993/94. **Admission** f14; f6.50 under-12s, over-65s.
Keukenhof Bulb Gardens contains over 500 varieties of tulip, a plant first imported from Turkey during the Golden Age amid a wave of 'tulipmania' speculation. Altogether over seven million bulbs bloom in the 28 hectares (70 acres) of this former royal 'kitchen garden', some under glass. The gardens and café get overrun, so arrive early with a picnic lunch. With the help of a VVV map, you can tour the bulb district (in bloom from March to late May), from which over half of the world's cut flowers and pot plants originate. The bulb district's history is covered at the Museum voor de Bloembollenstreek (02521 17900), also in Lisse; and at the Bloembollen Museum (02205 1950) in Limmen.
Café. Wheelchairs and pushchairs for hire.

Flower Auctions

Aalsmeer Flower Auction

Legmeerdijk 313 (02977 32185/34567). **Getting there** 15km (9 miles) south-west; *by bus* 172 from Centraal Station to Aalsmeer, then bus 140. **Open** 7.30-11am Mon-Fri. **Admission** f4; under-12s free.

More than 3.5 billion cut flowers and 400 million pot plants are handled annually, mostly for export, at the Verenigde Bloemenveilingen Aalsmeer, the world's biggest flower auction. Try to arrive at the visitors' gallery, which overlooks an auction floor the size of 100 football fields, before 9am. To bid, dealers push a button to stop a 'clock' which counts from 100 down to 1 – bidders risk either overpaying or not getting the goods. This procedure, explained in an English-language brochure, gave rise to the English phrase 'Dutch auction'. Of growing importance is the **Westland Flower Auction** at Naaldwijk, south of The Hague; phone 01740 32158 for details. It stands amid the world's greatest concentration of glass houses (open by appointment, phone 01740 27101).

Broeker Veiling Auction

Voorburggracht 1, Broek-op-Langerdijk (02260 13807). **Getting there** 36km (22 miles) north; *by train* to Alkmaar, then bus 155. **Open** *Apr-1 Oct 1993 (similar in 1994)* 10am-5pm Mon-Fri. **Admission** *auction and museum* f5; f2.50 under-12s; *incl boat trip* f10; f5 under-12s.

This market is now strictly for tourists, who can buy small lots of flowers, fruit and vegetables. Bidding is done as at a professional auction, by pressing a button to stop a 'clock' that is reducing the price. Admission includes a museum of old farming artefacts and (for a small amount extra) a boat trip around the area. A visit is easily combined with a trip to Alkmaar (*see above* **Cheese**).

Nurseries and Gardens

Over a hundred botanical gardens serve as research centres for the industry, notably Hortus Botanicus, Leiden (*see chapter* **The Randstad**) and Hortus Bulborum, Heiloo (02205 1214), which from 15 April to 15 May displays offshoots of the original tulips introduced from Turkey. For Flevohof farm, *see chapter* **The Provinces: Flevoland**.

Frans Rozen Nursery

Vogelenzangseweg 49, Vogelenzang (02502 47245). **Getting there** 25km (16 miles) west; *by train* to Heemstede, then bus 90 to Café Rusthoek, opposite nursery. **Open** *late Mar-May* 8am-6pm Mon-Fri; *July-Sept* 9am-5pm daily. **Admission** f2; under-14s free.

The huge greenhouse and extensive fields of this 200 year-old nursery are open to the public. Here you can gain an insight into commercial cultivation and the meticulous development of new hybrids – and also purchase bulbs for export. There's a tulip show (Apr-May) and summer show (July-Sept).

Traditions

A few Dutch diehards still wear local costume or keep to their old ways. Some make a genuine effort to preserve traditions, as at Staphorst (*see chapter* **The Provinces: Overijssel**), while others entertain tourists looking for authentic

Holland by hauling out their lace caps and turning on windmills (*windmolens*) for special days.

Kinderdijk windmills

Molenkade, Alblasserdam. **Getting there** 60km (37 miles) south-west; *by train* from Centraal Station via Rotterdam to Dordrecht, then bus 152 from station to Alblasserdam, then bus 154. **Open** *Apr-Aug* 9.30am-5.30pm Mon-Sat. **Admission** f2.50; f1.50 6-16s; under-6s free.

The sight of these 19 windmills under sail is spectacular, particularly when they're illuminated in the second week of September. To drain water from reclaimed land, windmills were usually clustered in a co-ordinated group called a *gang* (a term adopted in English). This *gang* now operates just for tourists (July-Aug, 2.30-5.30pm Sat); you can look around inside Nederwaarde mill. The name Kinderdijk (child's dike) comes from an event during the the St Elizabeth Flood of 1421 when a baby in a cradle was placed here.

Schoonhoven

Getting there 48km (30 miles) south; *by train* from Centraal Station to Gouda, then bus 197 from station. **VVV** *Stadhuisstraat 1, (01823 85009)*. **Open** *May-Sept* 10am-noon, 1.30-4pm, Tue-Fri; 11am-3pm Sat.

Schoonhoven has been famous since the Middle Ages for its silversmiths, who crafted such items as filigree jewellery, miniatures and ornaments for traditional costume. You can see antique pieces in **The Netherlands Goud-Zilver-en Klokkenmuseum** (Gold, Silver and Clock Museum) and the **Edelambachthuis** (Museum of Antique Silverware). Since 1900, students of many countries have trained at the special school to be gold- and silversmiths and engravers. There's an annual **silver market** (30 May 1993, 22 May 1994), but silver shops are open all year. Starting at *Silverhuys* (Silver House), Haven 1-3, is a row of buildings full of silver and pewter collectables, many of traditional design. *Klokkenhuys* (Clock House), Haven 9, stocks barometers and 500 timepieces including Frisian clocks. At *Edelambachthuis*, Haven 13, a working silversmith gives demonstrations (Tue-Fri). This attractive town (close to Oudewater, *see below*) retains large sections of its ramparts. Olivier van Noort, the first Dutchman to sail around the world (1598-1601), and Claes Louwerensz Blom, who in 1549 first introduced the windmill to Spain, are buried in **St Bartolomaeus Kerk** (1354); there are great views from its tower, which leans 1.56m (5ft) off centre. The carillon of the 1452 **Stadhuis** has 50 bells made from the guns of Van Noort's ship.

Traditional costume

Bunschoten-Spakenburg 40km (25 miles) south-east; *by train* from Centraal Station to Amersfoort, then bus 116 from station. **Dates** last two Wed of July, first two Wed of Aug.
Schagen 48km (30 miles) north; *by train* direct from Centraal Station. **VVV** *Markt 22 (02240 98311)*. **Dates** *July, Aug* Thur.

About a fifth of Bunschoten-Spakenburg residents still wear traditional dress on special market days. At Schagen, which has two medieval castle towers, costumed dancers entertain tourists (not too many), who also enjoy the cattle and craft markets and parades of horse-drawn carriages. Costumes are also worn at the markets in Hoorn and Medemblik (for both *see below* **West Friesland**), and sometimes on Sundays in Urk, Flevoland and on market day (July-Aug 10am-4pm Thur) in Middelburg, Zeeland (for both, *see chapter* **The Provinces**). The **National Costume Museum** is in The Hague (*see chapter* **The Randstad**).

Witches' Weigh House, Oudewater

Getting there 29km (18 miles) south; *by train* from Centraal Station to Gouda, then bus 180 from station.

Broek-in-Waterland.

VVV *Markt 8 (03486 4636)*. **Open** *Apr-Oct* 10.30am-4pm Tue-Sat; 1-4pm Sun; *Nov-Mar* 10.30am-12.30pm Tue; 1.30-3.30pm Thur; 10.30am-4pm Sat.
Witches' Weigh House *Leeuweringerstraat 2 (03486 3400)*. **Open** *Apr-Oct* 10am-5pm Tue-Sat; noon-5pm Sun, public holidays; *Nov-Mar* closed. **Admission** f2; f1.50 under-12s.
Dating from AD 1000, Oudewater (just north of Schoonhoven, *see above*) was known for cheese, rope-making and its particularly honest merchants. Then in 1487 an epidemic of witch hunting broke out. Oudewater achieved fame for weighing suspected witches and warlocks in the *Hexenwaag* (Witches' Weigh House). Each of the accused received a document, recognised throughout Europe, verifying that he or (usually) she was too heavy to travel by broom. Thus thousands were saved from being burnt at the stake. Today's (free) certificate comes in six languages for the myriad tourists who step on the scales. The Weigh House also has a museum of witchcraft.

Waterland

Until the IJ tunnel was built in 1956, the Waterland district north of Amsterdam was accessible mainly by ferry and steam tram to Volendam. That isolation preserved much of the area's heritage. For nearby Edam and the Museum Waterland in Purmerend, *see above* **Cheese**.

Broek-in-Waterland
Getting there 10km (6 miles) north-east; *by bus* 111 from Centraal Station.
For VVV, *see under* **Monnickendam**.
Full of eighteenth-century charm, this town has Waterland's greatest collection of old wooden buildings. Even rich Amsterdam merchants declined to build their country homes here in stone, for fear of them sinking.

Marken
Getting there 15km (9 miles) north-east; *by train* NS Excursion ticket (including Edam and Volendam); *by bus* 110 from Centraal Station to Volendam and then boat to Marken; or bus 111 from Centraal Station to Marken.
For VVV, *see under* **Monnickendam** or **Volendam**.
Now reached by a causeway, this island was once full of fishermen, but is now bursting with costumes, souvenir shops and tourists. However, it's bearable out of season and is far more attractive and authentic than Volendam (*see below*), a boat ride away. The pristine wooden houses are painted green with white stripes and stand on stone piles to escape flooding. The **Marker Museum** explains the island's history. You can still see a wooden shoe-maker carving *klompen* (clogs), at Kast 52, 9am-5pm daily, and buy a souvenir pair.

Monnickendam
Getting there 12km (7½ miles) north-east; *by bus* 111 from Centraal Station.
VVV *De Zarken 2 (02995 1998)*. **Open** *Sept-June* 10am-noon, 2-5pm, Mon-Sat; *July-Aug* 10am-6pm daily.
A remarkable proportion of Monnickendam's ancient buildings have been preserved, from the homes of its wealthy Golden Age merchants to herring smokehouses by the harbour. The good harbour fish restaurant, Stuttenburgh (Haringburgwal 2-5, 02995 1869), displays a collection of music boxes. On the *speeltoren* of the old town hall, now a museum, there's a delightful antique carillon, with two mechanical white knights parading as it plays.

Volendam
Getting there 18km (11 miles) north-east; *by train* NS Excursion ticket 56; *by bus* 110 from Centraal Station.
VVV *Zeestraat 21 (02993 63747)*. **Open** 10am-1pm Mon, Tue, Thur, Fri; 10am-3pm Wed; 9am-1pm Sat.
Volendam was such a successful fishing village that its flag flew at half-mast when the Zuider Zee was enclosed

in 1932, cutting off access to the sea. Their enterprise was soon applied to creating a theme park out of their historic features, which are modest compared to Marken (*above*) and Edam (*see under* **Cheese**). The gaily garbed locals can barely be seen for the crowds of tourists and the coaches that dump them there. Avoid it – unless you want to be photographed in a cardboard costume.

De Zaanse Schans

*near Zaandijk (information **Zaandam VVV** Gedempte Gracht 76 (075 162221)*. **Open** 9am-5.30pm Mon-Fri; 9am-1pm Sat.

Getting there 14km (9 miles) north; *by train* NS Excursion ticket 56 (includes cruise on River Zaan, admission to windmill museum and a pancake); *by bus* 89 from Marnixstraat.

De Zaanse Schans is a reconstructed museum village with a difference – people actually live in it. It's done well, but is becoming more commercialised, and now sees around 800,000 visitors a year. The Zaan district was noted for industrial windmills (making paint, flour and lumber), and you can buy mustard produced in one of the five working mills here. Amid the gabled homes, green with white trim, are an old-fashioned Albert Heijn grocery store (forerunner of Holland's biggest supermarket chain), a former merchant's home and a cheese house that's more commercial than authentic. Boat trips on the adjacent Zaan River provide another perspective.

West Friesland

Facing Friesland across the northern IJsselmeer is **West Friesland**. Although part of Noord Holland for centuries, it has its own customs and slightly fewer visitors. One way to visit is to take a train via **Hoorn** to **Enkhuizen**, then a boat to **Medemblik**, returning to Hoorn via the **Museum Stoomstram** (steam railway); there's an all-inclusive NS Excursion ticket for this route.

Enkhuizen

Getting there 45km (28 miles) north-east; *by train* direct from Centraal Station, NS Excursion ticket 9 (includes admission to Zuider Zee Museum).

VVV *Tussen Twee Havens 1 (02280 13164)*. **Open** *May-mid Sept* 8am-5pm daily; *mid Sept-Apr* 10am-5pm Tue-Sat.

Zuider Zee Museum *Wierdijk 18 (02280 10122)*. **Open** Binnenmuseum 10am-5pm daily; Buitenmuseum *Apr-Oct* 10am-5pm daily. **Admission** fl2.50; fl7.50 under-18s, over-65s.

This once-powerful fishing and whaling port has many relics of its past, but most people come to visit the remarkable **Zuider Zee Museum** (opened 1983). It comprises two separate sites: the indoor Binnenmuseum with its section on seafaring life and crafts, and an open-air reconstructed village, the Buitenmuseum. To make good use of the one-way crowd control system, start with the Buitenmuseum; it's reached by boat from the main jetty or the station jetty. Take a guided tour, or just wander around the hundred or so homes, shops, and other buildings transplanted from towns around the Zuider Zee and authentically arranged.

Hoorn

Getting there 33km (20 miles) north-east; *by train* direct from Centraal Station.

VVV *Nieuwstraat 23 (02290 18342)*. **Open** *Sept-June* 1.30-5pm Mon; 10am-5pm Tue, Wed, Fri; 10am-5pm, 7-9pm, Thur; 10am-2pm Sat; *Jul-Aug* 1.30-6pm Mon; 10am-6pm Tue, Wed, Fri, Sat; 10am-6pm, 7-9pm, Thur.

Museum Stoomstram Hoorn-Medemblik Tickets from Postbus 137, 1620 AC Hoorn (02290 14862), or any rail station; NS Excursion ticket 340. **Trains run** *mid Apr-mid Oct* 11.15am daily.

One of Holland's prettiest towns, this port dates from 1311 and grew rich on the Dutch East Indies trade; its success is reflected in grand architecture. Local costume and crafts can be seen in the weekly folklore celebrations called *Haartje Hoorn* (Jul-Aug 10am-5pm Wed). The baroque former Staten-College (council building) of 1632 now houses the **Westfries Museum**, which is better on art and décor than explanation of the region's past. The **Bossuhuizen** buildings are noted for Frisian sculptures and the visit by Spanish Admiral Bossy after his 1573 defeat in the harbour. Even older are the **hoofdtoren** (harbour towers) and **St Jansgasthuis**, a hospital between 1563 and 1922, and now an exhibition centre.

Medemblik

Getting there 45km (28 miles) north; *by train* from Centraal Station to Hoorn, then steam train (*see above* **Hoorn**) to Medemblik.

VVV *Dam 2 (02274 2852)*. **Open** *Nov-mid Apr* 10am-noon, 2-4pm, daily; *mid Apr-Oct* 10am-5pm daily.

An ancient port dating from AD 334 and dominated by the Gothic St Bonifacius Kerk and **Radboud Kasteel**. Built in 1289, the castle is smaller than when it defended Floris V's realm, but retains its knights' hall, towers and prison, and has a cellar tavern. Costume is worn at the Saturday market (July-Aug), when goods are brought in by barges. Nearby is the circular village of **Opperdoes**, built on a *terp* mound (*see chapter* **The Provinces: Fighting the Sea**), and the 'long-village' of **Twisk**, with pyramid-roofed farm buildings.

Castles

The Netherlands is studded with 400 castles (*kastelen*), and many fortress (*vesting*) towns retain large parts of their defences. Some of the best examples are within half an hour from Amsterdam; for those further afield, *see chapter* **The Provinces**. Eighty of the castles are open for tourists, business conferences or hotel guests; the late fifteenth-century Kasteel Assumberg at Heemskerk, between Haarlem and Alkmaar, is now a youth hostel (02510 32288). Alternatively, you can indulge in the ultimate power lunch by flying from Schiphol to Maastricht, by Air Excel (043 650700), and booking a four-course lunch at either Château Neercanne in Maastricht (043 251359) or Kasteel Erenstein in Kerkrade (045 461333). Far closer and cheaper is the castle tour you can do simply by driving, cycling or boating down the River Vecht.

De Haar

Kasteellaan 1, Haarzuilens, Utrecht (03407 1275). **Getting there** 30km (19 miles) south; *by train* NS Excursion ticket 60 (includes admission, coffee and apple pie). **Open** *Mar-2nd Sun in Aug, and 2nd Sun in Oct-mid Nov* (tours every hour: bookings 03407 3804) 11am-4pm Mon-Fri; 1-4pm Sat, Sun. **Admission** *castle and grounds* fl10 adults (no children under-5); *grounds only* fl1.

De Haar looks just like a medieval castle should. However, its romantic embellishments are a relatively recent neo-Gothic re-creation. In 1887, the baron who inherited the ruin of De Haar married a Rothschild and

together they recreated it on a majestic scale, commissioning the Rijksmuseum's architect, PJH Cuypers and moving the entire village of Haarzuilens 2km (¾ mile) to make room for the outstanding formal grounds. The whole process took over 20 years. The castle (the largest in The Netherlands) had previously been completed in 1391, destroyed in 1482, rebuilt in 1505 and damaged again, by the French, in 1672-73. The lavish interior boasts tapestries, Louis XIV-XVI furniture and Far Eastern art, with spectacular stone carvings and stained glass in the hall.
Car park (f1).

Muiden (Rijksmuseum Muiderslot)

Herengracht 1, Muiden (02942 61325). **Getting there** 12km (7½ miles) south-east; *by bus* 136 from Amstel Station. **Open** *Apr-Sept* 10am-5pm Mon-Fri; 1-5pm Sat, Sun (tours hourly 10am-4pm); *Oct-Mar* 10am-4pm Mon-Fri; 1-4pm Sun (tours hourly 10am-3pm).
Admission f5 adults; f3.50 under-12s, CJP holders, over-65s; free Museum Card holders; group discounts by arrangement. **No credit cards.**
Muiden is a moated rectangular castle strategically situated at the mouth of the the River Vecht to repel attacks from land or water. It was originally built in 1280 for Count Floris V, who was murdered here in 1296 (*see chapter* **Early History**). Devastated and rebuilt in the fourteenth century, the fortress has been through many sieges and frequent renovations. It now contains seventeenth-century furnishings from the period of its most illustrious occupant, the Dutch poet and historian P C Hooft, who entertained the Muiden Circle of writers, musicians and scholars in the splendid halls. You can look round only on a guided tour (in English by arrangement). The grounds include a herb garden.
Café (Apr-Oct).

Naarden

Getting there 20km (12 miles) south-east; *by train* direct from Centraal Station; *by bus* 136 from Centraal Station.
Naarden VVV *Adriaan Dortsmanplein 1B (02159 42836).* **Open** *May-Sept* 9.15am-12.45pm, 1.30-5pm, Mon-Fri; 10am-4pm Sat; noon-4pm Sun; *Oct-Apr* 10.30am-2pm Mon-Fri; 10am-2pm Sat; *Easter and autumn holidays* 10am-12.45pm, 1.30-5pm, Mon-Fri; 10am-3pm Sun.
Vestingmuseum *Turfpoortbastion, Vestvalstraat 6 (02159 45459).* **Open** *Easter-Oct* 10am-4.30pm Mon-Fri; noon-5pm Sat, Sun, public holidays. **Admission** f3.50; f3 over-65s; f2.50 5-12s; free under-5s, Museum Card holders.
A double-moated, star-shaped stronghold with arrowhead-shaped bastions – one of Europe's most perfectly preserved fortified towns. It was in active service until 1926 and is still being reconstructed. The defences are explained in the **Vestingmuseum**, located partly underground in the Turfpoort (Peat Gateway) bastion; admission includes a boat trip around the *vesting* (fortress). Cannons are fired by men in sixteenth-century soldiers' uniforms (2-4pm third Sun of month, May-Sept). The fortifications date from 1675, after the inhabitants were massacred by the Duke of Alva's son in 1572. The slaughter is depicted on the wall of **Spaansehuis** (Spanish House), now a museum. Bach's St Matthew Passion is presented in the **Grote Kerk**, noted for its fine acoustics, on the Thursday (7pm), Friday and Saturday (both 11.30am) before Easter.

River Vecht tour

Getting there 12-35km (7½-22 miles) south-east; *by train* NS Excursion ticket 64 (includes train to Utrecht, return cruise to Loenen, admission to Terra Nova gardens and refreshment – must be booked at least one day in advance).
Cruise Utrecht Canal Touring Co *(030 319 377/03402 41376).* **Times** *mid Apr-mid Oct* leaves Utrecht 9.30am to Loenen for lunch, returns to Utrecht 6pm. **Tickets** (including lunch) f40 adults, f25 under-13s.
Meandering upstream from Muiden (*see above*) into Utrecht province (*see chapter* **The Provinces**), you reach **Loenen**, a charming town of cobbled streets, with a leaning church spire and the restored castle of **Loenersloot**, with a thirteenth-century keep. Gracing the river banks are seventeenth- and eighteenth-century mansions, built as retreats by Amsterdam merchants. At Breukelen, which gave its name to Brooklyn, New York, is the elegant, classical house of **Gunterstein** (rebuilt in 1681). Beyond it on the other bank is **Nijenrode**, a medieval castle destroyed in 1672 and rebuilt, which fell into disrepair and was restored in 1907 in seventeenth-century style. It's now a business school. Across the river is **Oudaen**, a country house partly dating from 1303. A detour east around Loosdrechtse Plassen lake leads to **Sypesteyn**. Built on the foundations of a manor house destroyed in about 1580, this castle was rebuilt at the turn of the century in medieval style; its art and museum collection includes Loosdrechtse porcelain. Phone 02158 23208 for tours (*Easter-mid Sept* Tue-Sun; f6 adults, f3 5-14s). Back on the Vecht, between De Haar castle (*see above*) and the city of Utrecht (*see chapter* **The Randstad**) is **Slot Zuylen** at Maarsen; phone 030 440 255 for tours (*mid Mar-mid May, mid Sept-mid Nov,* Sat, Sun; *mid May-mid Sept* Tue-Sun; f5 adults, f3 3-15s, f3.75 over-65s). Surrounded by woods and a moat, it dates from about 1300, but has an eighteenth-century façade.

Naarden: *one of E...*
preserved fortifie...

The Randstad

The Hague, Rotterdam, Utrecht and Amsterdam form The Randstad – the powerhouse of The Netherlands.

You'll never see a signpost to it, but the Randstad is the cultural, political and economic powerhouse of The Netherlands. It's the vast, almost circular conurbation bounded (in anti-clockwise order) by Amsterdam, Haarlem, Leiden, The Hague, Delft, Rotterdam and Utrecht. The town of Gouda (*see chapter* **Excursions in Holland: Cheese**) and increasingly the city of Dordrecht (*see below*) could also be counted in the clique. Regarded by many as a masterpiece of planning, the Randstad manages to house 6 million of The Netherlands' 15 million population in under 20 per cent of the country's land area, as well as enclosing a sanctuary of green space and lakes the size of Greater London. The towns are separately administered and fiercely independent, yet they work together by choice for their common good.

The Randstad's influence on Dutch life is huge: it has an impressive road, rail and waterway system and a strong economy accounting for half of the national turnover. It contains the world's largest port (Rotterdam), a major international airport (Schiphol, Amsterdam), a huge agricultural belt (*see chapter* **Excursions in Holland: Flowers**), a major European banking and finance centre (Amsterdam, the country's capital) and the seats of government and royalty (The Hague).

Regarded with awe and sometimes resentment by the outlying provinces, the Randstad is often accused of monopolising government attention and funds, although it has no formally defined status and is still prone to bitter rivalries between cities and municipalities.

PROMOTING DORDRECHT

'One ought to stay in Dordrecht', wrote Marcel Proust, and the oldest of Dutch cities (given city rights in 1220) has now been targeted for development to make it the southern outpost of the Randstad. The aim is to attract people to live in converted warehouse apartments and new housing estates. Known locally as 'Dort', the city still has an active waterfront at the confluence of three rivers, the sunsets over which have inspired painters from the Cuyps to Van Gogh, who worked here as a bookseller. The centre, dominated by the distinctive slanting tower of the enormous **Grote Kerk**, is full of character, and there's a great art collection in **Dordrechts Museum**. As is the fashion in

The market square and De Keyser's Town Hall in **Delft**.

nearby Rotterdam, dilapidated buildings are to be refurbished, not demolished.

Dordrecht's VVV office is at Stationsweg 1 (078 132800).

Delft

The best thing about Delft is its compactness. Almost everything you need to see is located along the Oude Delft, as are the best views of the old city. Position yourself in the middle of the canal, either on the Boterbrug bridge or on one of the floating cafés, for a spectacular view of one of Holland's most photogenic waterways. Delft was built largely from trade generated through a fourteenth-century canal link to the Maas at Delfshaven (now swallowed up by Rotterdam). The decline in trade has enabled the city's centuries-old gables, hump-backed bridges and shady canals to remain unchanged.

To get an idea of how little it has altered, stand on the Hooikade, where Vermeer, whose home town this was, painted the *View of Delft* now hanging in Mauritshuis (*see below* **The Hague**).

Delft invariably means blue and white Delftware pottery. The **Lambert van Meerten Museum**, Oude Delft 199 (10am-5pm Tue-Sat; 1-5pm Sun), is a nineteenth-century mansion housing fine pieces of tin-glazed earthenware from the city's Golden Age pottery boom, and a vast collection of magnificent ebony-veneered furniture. The enormous range of tiles – depicting everything from battling warships to copulating hares – compares startlingly with today's mass-produced 'New Delft' (post-1876) trinkets. If you must buy, avoid tourist shops around the Markt and head for a pottery like De Porceleyne Fles (*see chapter* **Shopping: Pottery**).

Museums in Delft have the air of private residences, and perhaps for this reason are happily devoid of crowds, even in high summer. **Het Prinsenhof** on Sint Agathaplein (10am-5pm Tue-Sat; 1-5pm Sun) has permanent exhibitions on William the Silent, who was assassinated here in 1584, and on the building's role until 1572 as the convent of St Agatha. Opposite, another wing of the convent houses the ethnographic collection and exhibitions of the **Nusantara Museum** (10am-5pm Tue-Sat; 1-5pm Sun).

The city also has two spectacular churches, whose soaring spires can be seen for miles across the Schieland polders. The **Nieuwe Kerk**, in the Markt opposite De Keyser's 1618 Town Hall, contains the mausoleums of William the Silent and lawyer-philosopher Hugo de Groot. Not to be outdone, the Gothic **Oude Kerk**, with its picturesque tilting tower, is the last resting place of Vermeer (1632-75). A delightful contrast is the tiny, late-Gothic **Hippolytus Chapel** nearby, a vestige of one of Delft's many vanished convents.

Transport and Information

Getting there 60km (37 miles) south-west on A4, then A13; *train* 53 mins direct; 1 hour change at The Hague. **VVV Office** *Markt 85 (015 126 100)*. **Open** 9am-6pm Mon-Fri, 9am-5pm Sat; *Apr-Sept* also 11am-3pm Sun.

Eating and Sleeping

Restaurants Just out of Delft in the village of De Zweth on the River Vecht is Zwethheul *Rotterdamweg 480 (010 470 4166)*; quiet and expensive, it's in a former farmhouse. In summer, delicious sandwiches are served on a canal barge at Klijwegs Koffiehuis *Oude Delft 133 (015 124 625)*.
Hotels De Ark *Koommarkt 59-65 (015 140552/157999)* is up-market with single rooms at f140-f175 and doubles at f175-f235; Dish *Kanaalweg 3 (015 569358)* is reasonably priced with singles at f125 and doubles f170; the cheapest is De Kok *Houttuinen 15 (015 122125)* where singles cost f95-f125 and doubles f125-f150.

The Hague

The quiet boulevards and patrician houses of The Hague (Den Haag in Dutch, or 's-Gravenhage, to use its correct name) have always been dismissed by Amsterdammers (whose city is the capital) as stuffy, particularly as it's the seat of government, the royal residence and the diplomatic centre all in one. But the air of restrained *hauteur* which pervades its public buildings and old shops is precisely what gives the city its charm (try the area around Noordeinde for a taster).

The Hague, once the centre of a vast forest, was founded in 1250 by Count William II of Holland, who started a palace craze by building a castle – Die Haghe – on the site of the present **Binnenhof** parliament buildings. These retain a bastion-like appearance, complete with water lily-filled moat and medieval Ridderzaal (Knights' Hall). This is where, every third Tuesday in September, the Queen arrives in a golden coach for the State Opening of Parliament. You can see proceedings in the First and Second Chambers, although because Dutch politicians are often willing to compromise, debates are less than dynamic. For a hint of more visceral politics, pop across Hofweg to the Gevangenpoort (prison gate), once used as a gaol for political prisoners, outside which the brothers De Witt were lynched.

The Dutch respect rather than revere their monarchs, and expect them, if not to live, then at least to work like ordinary citizens. Sadly, today you cannot visit the palaces: Voorhout Paleis and Paleis Noordeinde at each end of the fashionable Lange Voorhout avenue, and Queen Beatrix's residence, Huis ten Bosch, at the far end of Haagse Bos. One former regal home which can and must be seen, however, is Mauritshuis (*see chapter* **Museums: Further Afield**). Located in the Binnenhof, it houses a breathtaking art collection.

The Hague is one of the greenest cities in Europe, and is peppered with parks and woods: Clingendael has a Japanese garden and Meijendel, out of town, is part of the ancient forest. The Scheveningse Bosjes, big enough to get lost in, is flanked by the Madurodam miniature city (*see chapter* **Children & Parents**), and by the **Haags Gemeentemuseum**, Stadhouderslaan 41 (closed Mon). Notable for housing works by Mondrian and other modern masters, the museum incorporates the Dutch costumes, clogs and caps of the **Kostuum Museum**, and is linked to the **Museon**, a hi-tech ethnological display, and the **Omniversum**, a planetarium with state-of-the-art projections. Between the Scheveningse Bosjes and the city is **Vredes Paleis**, the Peace Palace, built in 1907 to

The Hague - *much more than just the seat of government.*

host peace conferences, a role it still has as the UN's Court of International Justice. More cultural diversions are the Anton Philipszaal concert hall (*see chapter* **Music: Classical & Opera**) and the North Sea Jazz Festival in early July (*see chapter* **Music: Rock, Folk & Jazz**).

Just beyond the parks is **Scheveningen**, a former fishing village once linked to The Hague only by canal, but now a huge resort with high-rise hotels and, in summer, an impossible choice of beach cafés where topless sunbathing is *de rigueur*. Presiding over the beach is the 1887 Kurhaus (spa hotel), a legacy of Scheveningen's days as a bathing place for Europe's high society. The main salon, with its monstrous chandeliers and awesome glass cupola, is a wonderfully intimidating place to take tea. To stand any chance of recapturing the past, avoid the pier, which is over-priced, and head back towards The Hague to visit **Mesdag Museum**, Laan van Meerdervoort (closed Mon), which contains paintings by members of the Hague School. Displayed round the corner at Zeestraat 65 is the remarkable 360-degree painting, **H W Mesdag's Panorama** (open daily), depicting Scheveningen village in 1880. You can still visit the dune-top from which it was painted.

Transport and Information

Getting there 50km (31 miles) south-west on A4, then A44; *train* 50 mins direct.

VVV Office *Koningin Julianaplein, at Centraal Station (070 354 6200)*. **Open** *mid Apr-Sept* 9am-9pm Mon-Sat; 10am-5pm Sun; *Oct-mid Apr* 9am-6pm Mon-Sat; 10am-5pm Sun.

Eating and Sleeping

Restaurants So popular with locals that you must book, Luden *Frederikstraat 36 (070 360 1733)* serves expensive Dutch food with a French gloss. Schlemmer *Lange Houtstraat 17 (070 360 8580)* has a medium-priced restaurant frequented by politicians and a trendy upstairs café. At Salvatore *Deltaplein 605-606 (070 325 9635)* an Italian meal costs around f30.

Hotels Des Indes Intercontinental *Voorhout 54 (070 363 2932)* is the most luxurious hotel in town, with a restaurant – and prices – to match. City Hotel *Renbaanstraat 1-3 (070 355 7966)* has singles for f65 and doubles at f145; the youth hostel, NJHC Hostel Ockenburg, is at *Monstersweg 4 (070 397 0011)*; *see chapter* **Accommodation** for rates.

Haarlem

All trace of Haarlem's origins as a tenth-century settlement on a choppy inland sea disappeared with the draining in the mid-nineteenth century of the Haarlemmermeer, a massive lake which is now the site of Schiphol airport. Today the city somehow lacks a sense of purpose and has spilled indiscriminately over its outer canal, as more people abandon Amsterdam to set up home in the increasingly bustling provincial capital of Noord Holland. However, it isn't difficult to locate the **Church of St Bavo**, rising majestically at the confluence of eight roads. St Bavo's, featured countless times in Dutch paintings, is among the loveliest of Dutch churches, with cavernous, whitewashed transepts as high as nave and choir. At its foot lies the Grote Markt, with the Vleeshal, a former meat market built in 1602, now full of tiny gift shops.

The Netherlands' highest concentration of **almshouses** or *hofjes* (*see chapter* **Sightseeing: Hofjes**) is in Haarlem. Prime examples are: the town's largest, Proveniershuis, reached by a portal on Grote Houtstraat; Brouwershofje, on Tuchthuisstraat, one of the oldest (1472); and Hofje van Loo, Barrevoetestraat. Frans Hals is famous for his group portraits of almshouse regents, including those of the **Oudemannenhuis**, a former shelter for elderly men at the foot of Groot Heiligland which now houses the **Frans Hals Museum** (*see chapter* **Museums**). Haarlem produced almost all of the major Golden Age landscape painters, and was a favourite subject for Jacob van Ruisdael, perhaps because its main industry, linen, offered the sight of people bleaching huge lengths of the cloth in the fields.

At Sparne 16 is Holland's oldest museum (1778), the **Teylers Museum**, (10am-5pm Tue-Sat, 1-5pm Sun), where fossils and minerals sit uncomfortably alongside antique scientific instruments in a passable imitation of an alchemist's workshop. Unexpectedly, it also has a superb collection of 4,000 drawings dating from the sixteenth to the nineteenth centuries.

Although polders have distanced the sea, it's still only 11km (7 miles) from the town centre. Nearby **Zandvoort**, one of the busiest Dutch resorts, has been transformed from a sleepy village by Amsterdammers who flock there whenever the sun comes out. For watersports and the Zandvoort motor-racing circuit, *see chapter* **Sport & Fitness**. Just to the north are the rugged dunes and woods of the Kennemer Duinen National Park; take the 81 bus from Haarlem's Stationsplein.

Transport and Information

Getting there 20km (12 miles) west on A5; *train* 17 mins direct to Haarlem, continuing to Zandvoort.
VVV Office *Stationsplein 1 (023 319 059)*. **Open** *Apr-Oct* 9am-5.30pm Mon-Sat; *Nov-Mar* 9am-5.30pm Mon-Fri; 9am-4pm Sat.

Eating and Sleeping

Restaurants Mooi Java *Kruisweg 32 (023 323121)* serves Indonesian meals from f27.50; French food at Jack House *Gen Cronjéstraat 14 (023 276476)* is mid-priced, dinner costs from f35; Coach House Inn, *Oude Gracht 34 (023 312760)* has basic snacks and grills from f5.
Hotels Carlton Square Hotel *Baan 7 (023 319091)* is as pricey as it sounds (single f225, double f260); Waldor *Jansweg 40 (023 312622)* is reasonably priced at f85 for singles and f110 for a double; NJHC Hostel Jan Gijzen *Jan Gijzenpad 3 (023 373 793)* is a youth hostel; *see chapter* **Accommodation** for rates.

Leiden

Leiden bravely stood up to the Spanish during the Dutch Revolt in 1574 (*see chapter* **War & Reformation**), and was almost starved out under siege. The city was rescued when William of Orange had dikes opened to flood central Holland, enabling his ships to sail up to the town walls. *Leidens Ontzet* (The Relief of Leiden) is still an excuse for a carnival-like binge every 3 October, when stew, herring and white bread are consumed in vast quantities (and museums are closed). Festivities centre on the ninth-century Burcht, a fortress built on an artificial mound. Its walls command a good view of the city.

William rewarded Leiden's courage in 1581 by founding its famous university, the residents having declined the alternative – exemption from taxes. The oldest university in The Netherlands, it attracted Descartes and American president John Quincy Adams. The university itself isn't easy to spot; much of it is hidden behind former merchants' houses and a nunnery. Better than the buildings, though, is the university's Hortus Botanicus (*see chapter* **Excursions in Holland: Flowers**). The main student quarter is around Pieterskerk. The Pilgrim Fathers fled England to Amsterdam in 1608 and then to Leiden, where they held services in the home of their leader John Robinson on the site of Jean Pesijnhofje. In 1620, 30 pilgrims left for Delfshaven (*see under* **Rotterdam**) without Robinson, who is buried in Pieterskerk. They later sailed on the *Mayflower* to America from Plymouth. The **Pilgrims' Documentation Centre**, is at Vliet 45.

Leiden is rich in museums, the most comprehensive being the former cloth hall, De Lakenhal (*see chapter* **Museums**). It includes paintings by Jan Steen, who's buried in Pieterskerk, and Rembrandt, who was born in Weddesteeg, a site since lost under a housing development. Nearby on Binnenvestgracht are both the superb

ethnographic collection of the **Rijksmuseum voor Volkenkunde** (closed Mon) and **Molenmuseum Valk** (closed Mon), a restored corn-ginding, stage windmill of 1743. On the Rapenburg, the **Museum van Oudheden** (Antiquities Museum; closed Mon) is huge, and is especially strong on grisly Egyptian mummies and local archaeological finds.

Transport and Information

Getting there 40km (24 miles) south-west on A4; *train* 30 min direct.
VVV Office *Stationsplein 210 (071 146 846)*. **Open** 9am-5.30pm Mon-Fri; 9am-4pm Sat.

Eating and Sleeping

Restaurants Try the café De Oude Harmonie *Breestraat 16 (071 122153)*.
Hotels Mayflower *Beestenmarkt 2 (071 142641)* has singles at f125-f150 and doubles at f170-f200; Nieuw Minerva *Bookmarkt 23 (071 126358)* has singles at f80-f110 and doubles at f100-f160; Bik Hotel *Witte Singel 92 (071 122602*; closed Oct) is cheaper at f40 for singles and f100-f160 for a double.

Rotterdam

Practically the whole of Rotterdam's old city centre was destroyed by bombs in May 1940 and, with commendable daring, the authorities decided to start afresh rather than try to reconstruct its former maze of old canals. Modern boulevards such as Coolsingel and Meent were once navigable waterways, and the sites of once-great buildings and squares are remem-

bered in name only. Perch on the busy Willemsbrug bridge for a magnificent view of the futuristic skyline, or, if you can stomach the expense and the height, go up the **Euromast** at Het Park for an overview of the immense Rhine-Maas delta.

Not every bomb-site was developed immediately, because the city first wanted to plan its future function. One success of this policy is the redeveloped **Old Harbour**. It's a lesson in imaginative modernism and has given the world Piet Blom's witty *Kijk-Kubus*. These tilted, cubic houses on stilts are nicknamed 'the bleak woods', but are popular with tourists, who can visit number 70 *(010 4142285)*.

The few surviving original buildings have become icons. **St Lawrence Church**, built in 1646, has been heavily restored; a solitary row of merchants' houses survives on Wijnhaven; but best of all is **Schielandshuis**, Korte Hoogstraat, off Beursplein (closed Mon), a seventeenth-century mansion which doubles as an excellent city museum. Its displays recreate life in Rotterdam from late medieval times – when it was the village where Erasmus was born in the fifteenth century – to the construction of the Nieuwe Waterweg.

This deep-water channel to the sea facilitated the creation of the world's biggest harbour, **Europoort**. Go and see it if you can; take one of the various SPIDO boat tours from Willemsplein (010 413 5400 – boats leave Apr-

Sept, 9.30am-5pm, every 45 minutes; Oct and Mar 10am-2.30pm, every 90 minutes; Nov-Feb, 11am and 2pm daily). Or follow the *Havenroute* map (from the ANWB motoring organisation; *see chapter* **Survival**). Just downstream is **Delfshaven**, where genuinely old buildings are being restored. These include the former warehouses containing the **Museum de Dubbelde Palmboom** (closed Mon), which covers working life in the Meuse estuary. A plaque on the quay marks where, in 1620, the Pilgrim Fathers left for America, via Plymouth, having held a final service at the nearby **Oude Kerk**, where they are also commemorated.

Unsurprisingly, the best shops in Rotterdam are major, modern stores, although Europe's first pedestrian precinct, the Lijnbaan, isn't one of the city's better constructions.

Without doubt the best museum in Rotterdam is the Boymans-Van Beuningen (*see chapter* **Museums**), but look out for the **Prins Hendrik Maritime Museum**, Leuvehaven 1 (closed Mon). A startling piece of architecture with stunning river views, it has comprehensive if slightly exhausting displays on seafaring, plus interesting ships docked outside.

Transport and Information

Getting there 73km (45 miles) south on A4, then A13; *train* 1 hour direct.
VVV Offices: Coolsingel 67 *(010 402 3200)*. **Open** 9am-6.30pm Mon-Thur; 9am-9pm Fri; 9am-5pm Sat; *Easter-Sept* also 9am-5pm Sun. **Centraal Station** *(06 9292)*. **Open** 9am-10pm daily.

Eating and Sleeping

Restaurants Tropicana *Maasboulevard 100 (010 402 0720)*, is an expensive revolving restaurant with great river views. The fine food at Zocher's *Baden Powellaan 12 (010 436 4249)* averages f50 a head. Café de Unie *Mauritsweg 34 (010 411 7394)* is a reconstruction of a famous pre-war café; the well-presented (usually fish) dishes are medium-priced.
Hotels King's Garden *Westersnglaan 1 (010 4366633)* has singles for f85 and doubles for f150; the NJHC youth hostel is at *Rochussenstraat 107-109 (010 436 5763)*; *see chapter* **Accommodation** for rates.

Utrecht

St Willibrord, patron saint of The Netherlands, chose Utrecht as a base from which to convert the country to Christianity in about AD700. It obviously worked, because eight centuries later the city produced Adrian VI, the only Dutch pope, who, if he'd lived longer, would have inhabited the **Paushuize** on the peaceful Pausdam square. Yet the city was firmly committed to the Dutch Revolt; indeed the Union of Utrecht in 1579 authorised Protestantism as the United Provinces' official religion.

Taking its name from *oude trecht* (old ford), Utrecht was founded by the Romans in AD47 as a strategic ford over the Rhine. Still The Netherlands' transport focus, it's the appropriate site of the **National Railway (Spoorweg) Museum**, at Maliebaan Station (closed Mon). But it's the medieval past that dominates the city, in the shape of the Domtoren (cathedral tower) looming over **Oudegracht**. It's the highest steeple in the country – and it's possible to climb it. Only on closer inspection do you realise there's no nave connecting the beautifully proportioned Gothic spire to the dignified but rather forlorn-looking chancel.

Utrecht is a mecca for music lovers. All year round choirs give free concerts in the cathedral, usually at lunch-time, and the city hosts classical events such as the Festival of Early Music in early September (27 Aug-5 Sept 1993), and (during May 1994), the Liszt Piano Competition at Vredenburg Muziek Centrum. For both, *see chapter* **Music: Classical & Opera**. Whether or not you're with children, you should see the **Rijksmuseum van Speelklok tot Pierement** ('from music box to street organ'), where the guides will gladly demonstrate the exhibits.

Among the many museums, try **Centraal Museum**, Agnietenstraat 1 (closed Mon), although it takes some getting round because of its sheer diversity. Exhibits cover decorative arts, paintings and archaeological finds, and the complex also incorporates a school for orphans and two almshouses. By contrast, the **Catharijneconvent**, Nieuwegracht 63 (closed Mon), has won awards for presentation of its important medieval art collection. Alternatively, join the trail of architecture pilgrims for a guided tour of the **Rietveld-Schröder House**, Prins Hendriklaan 50A (tours Tue-Sun; book at least a day ahead on 030 517926). Designed in 1924 by Gerrit Rietveld, whose famous red-blue chair is displayed inside, it looks like a three-dimensional projection of a Mondrian painting. As a masterpiece of the De Stijl movement (*see chapter* **Between the Occupations**), the house is on the World List of Protected Buildings.

Transport and Information

Getting there 40km (25 miles) south-east on A5; *train* 28 mins direct.
VVV Office *Vredenburg 90 (06 34034085)*. **Open** 9am-6pm Mon-Fri; 9am-4pm Sat.

Eating and Sleeping

Restaurants De Oude Muntkelder *Oudegracht a/d Werf, 112 (030 316773)* is a pancake house, with meals from f6; Auberge Het Oude Tolhuis *Weg naar Rhijnauwen 13-15 (030 511215)* has food from f21; Pomo *Wittevrouwenstraat 22 (030 319272)* has food from Surinam and Indonesia, starting at f14.
Hotels Hotel Ouwi FC *Donderstraat 12 (030 716303)* charges f56-f77 for singles, f76-f97 for doubles; Hotel Ibis *Bizetlaan 1 (030 910366)* has singles at f125 and doubles at f135; the Park Hotel *Tolsteegsingel 34 (030 516712)*, is a budget hotel with a swimming pool: singles f50, doubles f75-f87.

The Provinces

There's more to The Netherlands than Holland: we take you on a tour of the other ten Dutch provinces.

Many visitors to The Netherlands see only North and South Holland, and miss out the other ten provinces. But if you take the trouble to explore further, you'll find that not all of the country is one big urban sprawl and that each region has its own subtly distinctive character. We have listed the VVV tourist offices for each province (most accept only postal and phone enquiries), and for important regional centres; unless otherwise stated, they're open from 9am to 6pm Monday to Saturday. We've also stated if there's an appropriate NS rail excursion ticket (*see chapter* **Beyond Amsterdam**). There's a sketch map of The Netherlands at the back of this book; for a scale map, the *Falk Plan* tourist map has a useful place index.

Drenthe

Drenthe's affectionate nickname – *De Olde Landschap* (the old landscape) – goes back centuries, but human habitation dates back even further – about 50,000 years. Located in the north-east of the country, the province has tended to be neglected by the more vibrant west, which could explain why it has the reputation of being a dark, mysterious landscape haunted by its pagan past. It's certainly why the population took so long to abandon Catholicism and also partly why the area was, until recently, relatively backward economically. Even today, Drenthe is very rural. The best place to appreciate what much of the countryside looked like as little as 20 years ago is in **Orvelte** at the Oud Saksisch Kijkdorp (Old Saxon Village).

To find out more about the province's prehistoric, Roman and Merovingian past, start at the magnificent Drents Museum (open Tue-Sun) in **Assen**. The area is full of ancient sites. The most impressive monuments are the **hunebedden**, towards the German border. Burials took place between 3400BC and 2300BC in this string of megalithic burial sites, constructed from boulders shed by the nearby *Hondsrug* (Dog's Back), a glacial moraine on which most of Drenthe is built. The history of the monuments is explained at the **National Hunebedden Information Centre** in Borger.

The Drenthe countryside is the perfect backdrop to the hunebed tombs. Rivulets run

through peat cuttings (look out for villages ending in *veen*, meaning 'peat bog') on huge silent heaths such as the Fochtelooer Veen near Assen and the Dwingeloose Heide and Uffelter Veen, either side of Uffelte. There's also a great forest near Uffelte, the Drentse Wold, and another, Ellertsveld, west of the hunebedden. Near Ellertsveld is a more chilling reminder of the past, the Nazi transit camp at Westerbork (*see chapter* **World War II**).

Further Information

Drenthe province VVV *PO Box 10012, 9400 CA Assen (05920 51777)*. **Open** 9am-5pm Mon-Fri.
Assen VVV *Brink 42, 9401 HV (05920 14324)*. **Open** 9am-5.30pm Mon-Fri; *Sept-Apr* 9am-1pm Sat; *May-Aug* 9am-3pm Sat.
Emmen VVV *Raadhuisplein 2, 7811 AP (05910 13000)*. **Open** *mid May-mid Sept* 9am-5pm Mon-Fri; 9am-4pm Sat; *mid Sept-mid May* 9am-5pm Mon-Fri; 9am-1pm Sat.
Nationaal Hunebedden Informatie Centrum *Bronnegerstraat 12, Borger (05998 36374)*. **Open** Feb-Dec 10am-5pm Mon-Fri; 1-5pm Sat, Sun.
Orvelte Saxon Village *Dorpstraat 3 (05934 2335)*. **Open** *Apr-Oct* 9.30am-5pm Mon-Fri; 11am-5pm Sat, Sun, public holidays. **Admission** f8.50; f6.50 5-12s; f7.50 over-65s; free under-4s. **No credit cards**.

Flevoland

Just north-east of Amsterdam, Flevoland only became a province in its own right in 1986, when the polders of South Flevoland and East Flevoland were combined with the North-east Polder (formerly in Overijssel, *see below*). It's the most recent stage in The Netherlands' massive, historic land reclamation process. Drained between 1950 and 1957 to create more room for the burgeoning population, Flevoland, when finished, offered little to entice new residents. The authorities are still worrying about how to create new jobs and attractions.

Flevoland's capital, **Lelystad**, named after Dr C Lely who championed the Zuider Zee Reclamation Act of 1918, should have been a planner's dream. Development there is refreshingly low-level and it has an interesting community centre, the Agora, but it's tiresome to get to and sits symbolically hunched on the windy outer edge of the province. By contrast, the beautiful space-age city of **Almere**, intended as a satellite to Lelystad, is almost embarrassingly successful. Now an outpost of Amsterdam, with

*The old Saxon village at **Orvelte** is a reminder of Drenthe's rural past. See page 256.*

low-cost, low-energy housing, it attracts thousands of the capital's commuters.

There's a large bird sanctuary at the **Oostvaardersplassen** lake, south-west of Lelystad, and an enormous working farm museum at **Flevohof**.

Reminders of Flevoland's recent past as a sea bed are periodically unearthed by archaeologists. Centuries-old remains, some Roman, of vessels, anchors and cannon balls are now displayed in the Schokland Museum (open Apr-Sept daily, Oct-Mar Tue-Sun) and Scheepsarcheologiemuseum (Museum of Maritime Archaeology) in **Ketelhaven**.

Further Information

Provincial VVV *Postbus 548, 8200 AM Lelystad (03200 30500).* **Open** 9am-5pm Mon-Fri.
Almere-Stad VVV *Spoordreef 20, 1315 GP (03653 34600).* **Open** 9am-5pm Mon-Fri; 9am-1pm Sat.
Lelystad VVV *Agorahof 4, 8224 BZ (03200 43444).* **Open** 9am-5pm Mon-Fri; 9am-1pm Sat.
Urk VVV *Postbus 9, 8321 AA (05277 4040).* **Open** *Apr-mid Oct* 10am-1pm, 2-5pm, Mon-Fri; *mid Oct-Mar* 10am-1pm Mon-Fri. *NS rail excursion.* **Open** 10am-5pm Mon-Fri; 10am-1pm Sat.
Flevohof *Spijkweg 30, Biddinghuizen (03211 1514).* **Open** *May-early Sept* 10am-6pm daily; occasional dates in autumn. **Admission** f18.75.
Scheepsarcheologiemuseum *Vossemeerdijk 21, Ketelhaven (03210 13287).* **Open** 10am-5pm daily. **Admission** f1.50; 75c under-14s.

Friesland

Friesland, in the far north, has always been regarded by southerners as a kind of windswept barbarian outpost. It has its own dialect, a highly unusual landscape and the nearest thing to provincial nationalism you're likely to find in The Netherlands. The region used to be literally cut off because of its vast network of lakes and canals.

In summer, the lakes are packed with yachts and motor cruisers. The town of **Sneek** is the boating focus. The best way of exploring the waterways and their towns is to go on an excursion or rent a boat and stop off at the lovely little fishing towns of **Grouw**, **Terhorne**, **Heeg** and **Sloten** or, towards the northern coast, **Dokkum**. Sloten's narrow cobbled streets, illuminated bridges and high-water warning cannon make it one of the most attractive villages in Friesland. Although tiny, it's officially designated a 'city' for the purposes of the Elfstedentocht, an 11-city skating race held when it's cold enough for the waterways to freeze (*see chapter* **Sport & Fitness: Skating**).

The best feature of the province is its landscape, but the capital, **Leeuwarden**, has a picturesque centre within a star-shaped moat. Like Groningen (*see below*), Friesland is dotted with beautiful brick churches, built on *terpen* mounds to escape flooding. The best examples, such as that at **Hogebeintum**, west of Dokkum, are at the far north of the province.

The five sparsely populated **Frisian Islands** (or Wadden Islands), and the sea around them, have become the symbol of the Dutch conservation movement. Even today they are reserved more for migrant birds and a diminishing grey seal colony than for human visitors. Sadly you can't island-hop, since each island's ferry only shuttles to and from the coast (two to five times per day). Between May and September, when the tide is out, you can cross to the nearer islands by foot, provided you're with a local guide and don't mind *wadlopen* – wading up to your ankles in mud.

Terschelling, with its sixteenth-century lighthouse and old fishing villages, is the most picturesque island. **Ameland** is good for walking and cycling tours, and has a nature reserve. The biggest island, **Texel**, is in fact administered by Noord Holland and reached via Den Helder. It has two bird reserves (De Slufter and De Muy) and a seal sanctuary at the resort of De Koog. On more remote **Schiermonnikoog**, further east, local accents are thicker and cars are banned. **Vlieland**, also car-free, is the most

deserted island, which is not surprising since some of its beaches are reserved for bombing practice by the Dutch Air Force. The archipelago continues east as Germany's Ostfriesische Inseln; the resorts on **Borkum** island can be reached from Delfzijl in Groningen *(see below)*.

Further Information

Provincial & Leeuwarden VVV *Stationsplein 1, 8911 AC (058 132224).*
Dokkum VVV *Grote Breedstraat 1, 9100 KH (05190 93800).* **Open** 1-5pm Mon; 9am-noon, 1-6pm, Tue-Thur; 9am-noon, 1-9pm, Fri; 1-5pm Sat.
Hindeloopen VVV *Postbus 4, 8713 ZG (05142 2550).*
Sneek VVV *Marktstraat 18, 8601 CV (05150 14096).*

Frisian Islands

Ameland VVV *Rext van Donerwecht 2, 9163 TR (05191 2020).* **Open** 8.30am-12.30pm, 1.30-6.30pm, Mon-Fri; 8.30am-4pm Sat.
Schiermonnikoog VVV *Reeweg 5, 9166 PW (05195 31233).* **Open** 9am-1pm, 2.30-6.30pm, Mon-Sat.
Terschelling VVV *Postbus 20, 8880 AA West Terschelling (05620 3000).* **Open** 9am-1pm, 2-5pm Mon-Fri; 11am-1pm Sat; also open Fri evenings at arrival of last ferry.
Texel VVV *Groenplaats 9, 1791 CC Den Burg (02220 14741).* **Open** 9am-6pm Mon-Fri; 9am-5pm Sat.
Vlieland VVV *Hafenweg 10, 8899 ZN (05621 1111).* **Open** 9am-12.30pm, 1.30-5pm, Mon-Fri; when ferry arrives Sat, Sun.

Gelderland

Gelderland, in the east, is the largest province. Nearly a third of it is covered by the **Veluwe** (Bad Land), a 4,600 hectare (11,400 acre) stretch of forest and moorland. In the south of the Veluwe, near Arnhem, is The Netherlands' biggest national park, the **Hoge Veluwe**. Hidden among the trees, near the park's Otterlo entrance, is the fascinating **Kröller-Müller Museum**. Principally housing a bequest by the art lover Hélène Kröller-Müller, it holds an impressive number of well-known paintings, including the most important collection of Van Goghs outside Amsterdam as well as works by Mondrian and the Dutch symbolists. Outside, the woods are dotted sculptures, including pieces by Rodin, Moore, Hepworth and Giacometti.

The Dutch come to the Veluwe to walk, cycle, go camping or to stay in rented chalets in the woods, but on a slightly less grand scale than their forebears, who used to hunt deer and wild boar here. The biggest chalet in the area is undoubtedly **Paleis Het Loo**, built originally as a hunting lodge by William III in 1685-92, and the country's nearest approximation to the Palace of Versailles.

The **Betuwe** (Good Land) is the south-west region of fertile land sandwiched between the River Waal, the River Maas (Meuse) and the River Lek further north. The countryside east and towards Germany, dubbed *Achterhoek* (Black Corner), is dominated by commercial waterways.

Terschelling *is the most picturesque of the Frisian Islands.*

The number of times you'll need to cross rivers will make it obvious why Allied divisions found it so difficult to stage a surprise attack on **Arnhem**, the provincial capital, in 1944. The war cemetery and Hartenstein Villa, now the Airborne Museum, are in **Oosterbeek**, while the Bevrijdingmuseum (Liberation Museum) is in **Nijmegen**. Arnhem and the province's biggest city, Nijmegen, both have several good museums, notably Arnhem's excellent **Nederlands Openluchtmuseum**, an open-air collection of folklore (open Apr-Oct daily; NS rail excursion available). The best thing about both cities are their imposing Gothic churches and riverside views. Nijmegen's church survived the city's almost total destruction by Allied bombs in World War II.

Further Information

Provincial VVV *Postbus 142, 6860 AC Oosterbeek (085 332033).* **Open** 8.30am-5pm Mon-Fri.

Arnhem & Zuid Veluwe VVV *Stationsplein 45, 6811 KL (085 420330).* **Open** 9am-5.30pm Mon-Fri, 9am-4pm Sat.

Nijmegen VVV *St Jorisstraat 72, 6511 TD (080 225440).* **Open** 9am-6pm Mon-Fri; 9am-4pm Sat; *Jul, Aug* 11am-3pm Sun.

Hoge Veluwe National Park *entrances at Schaarsbergen, Otterlo and Hoenderloo (Visitor Centre 08382 1627).* NS rail excursion/bus from Arnhem (late Jun-early Aug). **Open** park 8am-5pm daily; Visitor Centre 10am-5pm daily. **Admission** f7.50 per person; free under-6s; f7 per car.

Kröller-Müller Museum *Hoenderloo, Hoge Veluwe (08382 1041).* NS rail excursion 37. **Open** 10am-5pm Tue-Sat; 11am-5pm Sun. **Admission** park f7; f3.50 under-12s; *museum* f7; f3.50 under-12s.

Paleis Het Loo *Amersfoortseweg, Apeldoorn (055 212244).* NS rail excursion 51. **Open** 10am-5pm Tue-Sun. **Admission** f10; f8 children, over-65s.

Groningen

All roads lead to the city of **Groningen**, the far north-eastern province's capital and namesake. This isn't surprising when you discover that it has generated six centuries of local wealth, first as a member of the Hanseatic League and then as the only grain market for miles around. The province's history is explained in the **Groningen Museum** (open Tue-Sun), also noted for its exhibitions of modern art.

In the capital, bone up on the history of inland shipping at the Noordlijke Scheepvart (Northern Shipping) Museum. The exhibits cover everything from the local transportation of bricks to the world-wide wanderings of the Dutch East India Company. It's housed in the thirteenth-century Gottischhuis; next door, in the equally old Canterhuis, is the Tabacologisch (Tobacco) Museum. The symbol of Groningen's good fortune is the capital's fifteenth-century Martinikerk. The six-tiered church tower has a carillon and can be climbed for fine views.

The lush agricultural landscape that you can see from the Martini tower is sprinkled with eighteenth-century *kop-romp* ('head-trunk') farmhouses, a combination of tall, stuccoed villas and wide barns built for heavy harvests. They can best be seen in the Westerwolde district bordering Germany, particularly lining a five-kilometre (three-mile) street at **Bellingwolde**, near **Winschoten**.

However, the real glory of the province is its rural churches. Unusual, beautifully proportioned and generally with high, saddleback towers peeping over a ring of trees, they're seen to best effect in the morning mist or under a thick blanket of snow. Many are to be found in tiny villages, whose circular shape betrays their origins as *terpen* mounds. You can see some wonderful examples in a 70-kilometre (44-mile) loop north-east of Groningen city. Begin the tour with the church at **Garmerwold**, a typical *tour de force* in brick, with geometric designs outside and sixteenth-century frescos inside. Move on past the chapel of a former Benedictine monastery at **Ten Boer** to **Stedum**, where the church sits astride a mound, surrounded by a moat. The church at **Loppersum** has well-preserved frescos and the one at **Appingedam** sits in the marketplace of the attractive town centre, next to an arcaded town hall of 1630. Skirt north up the coast, passing the churches at **Bierum**, **Spijk** and **Uithuizermeeden**, to **Uithuizen**. This town has a church with a twelfth-century tower and one of the loveliest, but least visited, country houses in The Netherlands, the fortified fifteenth-century **Menkemaborg** (Feb-Dec 10am-noon, 1-5pm, daily). Return to Groningen via **Het Hogeland** open-air museum at Warffum (Apr-Nov 10am-5pm Tue-Sat; 1-5pm Sun) or the circular villages of **Kantens** and **Middelstum**, each built round a *terp*.

Further Information

Provincial & Groningen VVV *Naberpassage 3, 9712 JV (050 139700).*

Appingedam VVV *Blankenstein 2, 9901 AX (05960 24488).* **Open** 10am-6pm Mon-Thur; 10am-6pm, 7-9pm, Fri; 9am-noon Sat.

Uithuizen VVV *Hooftstraat 11, 9981 AA (05953 4051).* **Open** *Apr-Oct* 2-5pm Mon; 10am-5pm Tue-Fri; 1-4pm Sat; *Nov-Mar* 2-4pm Mon, Sat; 10am-noon, 2-4pm, Tue-Fri.

Winschoten VVV *Stationweg 21A, 9671 AL (05970 12255).*

Limburg

This undulating southern spur of Dutch territory, wedged between Belgium and Germany, is the antidote to all those clichés about The Netherlands being a flat country. For a taste of its countryside, aim for the valley of the **Geul**, a small stream which drives water-wheels and clatters past black and white half-timbered farmsteads. The valley is dominated by **Valkenburg**, a fortified town with prehistoric caves and Roman catacombs, and is dotted with picturesque villages such as **Schin op Geul**. Nearby **Heerlen** has remarkably complete Roman baths in its Thermen Museum (closed Mon). Try not to miss the strangely peaceful, pink and white town of **Thorn** close to the Belgian border.

Maastricht, the provincial capital, is notably un-Dutch in character. Its eleventh-century, Romanesque Basilica of St Servatius is – unusually – built of stone and is most reminiscent of Rhineland churches, with its vividly painted and gilded north portal. Walk the length of the remaining southern ramparts at Maastricht for a breathtaking view of the river and the city's oldest building, the Romanesque Basilica of Our Lady.

Maastricht is a wonderful town to wander about in; make for the tiny streets jostling around the Markt, many of whose shops sell *Limburgs vlaai*, a fruit tart often eaten around **carnival** time as a special treat before Lent (*see also below* **Noord Brabant**). The French influence has turned Maastricht into the gastronomic capital of The Netherlands, a fact celebrated in the last week of August, when restaurateurs set up tents and stalls on Urijthof Square for public tastings, the so-called *preuvenement*.

Almost as rewarding, both gastronomically and culturally, is **Roermond**. The part-Romanesque, part-Gothic Munsterkerk was built in 1220; nine years later the impressive tombs of the Count of Gelderland and his wife were installed. Local antiquities and works by artists from the town are exhibited in the Gemeentemuseum, alongside displays on PJH Cuypers, architect of Amsterdam's Rijksmuseum, whose house this was.

Further Information

Provincial VVV *Postbus 811, 6300 AV, Valkenburg (04406 13993)*. **Open** 8.30am-12.30pm, 1.30-5pm, Mon-Fri; 10am-noon Sat.
Heerlen VVV *Honingmanstraat 100, 6411 LM (045 716200)*. **Open** 9am-5.30pm Mon-Fri; 9am-4pm Sat.
Maastricht VVV *Kleine Straat 1, 6211 ED (043 252121)*. *NS rail excursion 39*. **Open** *Sept-Jun* 9am-6pm Mon-Sat; *Jul, Aug* 9am-7pm Mon-Sat; 11am-3pm Sun.
Roermond VVV *Markt 24, 6041 EM (04750 33205)*. **Open** *Oct-Mar* 9am-5pm Mon-Fri; 9am-2pm Sat; *Apr-Sept* 9am-6pm Mon-Fri; 9am-4pm Sat.
Valkenburg VVV *Th Dorrenplein 5, 6301 DV (04406 13364)*. *NS rail excursion*. **Open** *Apr-Jun* 9am-6pm Mon-Fri; 9am-5pm Sat; 10am-2pm Sun; *Jul, Aug* 9am-6pm Mon-Sat; 10am-5pm Sun; *Sept* 9am-5pm Mon-Fri; 9am-1pm Sat; *Oct-May* 9am-5pm Mon-Fri; 9am-1pm Sat.

Noord Brabant

Noord Brabant, bordering Belgium in the south, was one of the last provinces to renounce support of Spain during the Dutch Revolt at the turn of the

*There are two bird reserves and a seal sanctuary on **Texel**, the largest of the Frisian Islands. See page 258.*

seventeenth century and one of the most reluctant to forget its Burgundian past. Consequently, its character has been shaped to a large extent by its Catholic population, who in 1867 commissioned PJH Cuypers and G van Swaay to build a replica of Rome's St Peter's Basilica in **Oudenbosch**, east of Breda. Five centuries earlier, and with a better result, the **Cathedral of St Jan** was built at **'s-Hertogenbosch**. It is the only real example of pure Gothic architecture in the country.

Den Bosch, as the provincial capital is known, was the birthplace of Hieronymous Bosch and there's a statue of the painter in the marketplace. It is one of the two main Dutch centres of **carnival** (the other is Maastricht). Each February or March before Lent, residents spend a fortune in beer, bands and false noses and career around town holding up traffic. The carnival atmosphere can be sampled all year round at fantasy park **De Efteling** (*see chapter* **Children & Parents**).

The city of **Eindhoven** is dominated by the industrial multi-national Philips, whose football club, PSV Eindhoven, has come a long way since it was the factory team (*see chapter* **Sport & Fitness**). An electric bulb works was founded here in 1891 by Dr AF Philips, whose statue is on Stationsplein. The **Van Abbe Museum** (open Tue-Sun) houses a collection of major modern art which is of such size it can't all be exhibited at once. Art lovers should also head a few miles north to **Nuenen**. Van Gogh's family lived in the vicarage there and displays of memorabilia have made it something of a centre of pilgrimage; a memorial to the painter stands in Op den Bergh Park. Towards the German border are the nature reserve of **De Groote Peel**, and the National War and Resistance Museum at Overloon (*see chapter* **World War II**).

If you prefer to be out of doors, head west to the wilderness of the **Biesbosch** tidal estuary, north of **Breda**, a shopping town whose main sight is the Grote Kerk. You can take boat excursions through the Biesbos (reed forest) from the fortress town of **Geertruidenberg**. Vintage car enthusiasts would also enjoy the nearby **Nationaal Automobiel Museum** (01621 85400, open April to September). Downstream is another fortified city, **Willemstad**, built in 1565-83 by William the Silent to safeguard the choppy Hollandsch Diep waters. South towards Antwerp in Belgium is the ancient town of **Bergen Op Zoom**, once the most fortified of Dutch cities, now a characterful market town.

Further Information

Provincial VVV *Postbus 3259, 5000 DG Tilburg (013 434060)*. **Open** 9am-5pm Mon-Fri.

Bergen Op Zoom VVV *Beursplein 7, 4611 JG (01640 66000)*. **Open** 9am-6pm Mon-Fri; 9am-5pm Sat.
Breda VVV *Willemstraat 17-19, 4811 AJ (076 222444)*. **Open** 9am-6pm Mon-Fri; 9am-5pm Sat.
Eindhoven VVV *Stationsplein 17, 5611 AC (040 449231)*. **Open** 10am-5.30pm Mon; 9am-5.30pm Tue-Fri; 9am-4pm Sat.
's-Hertogenbosch VVV *Markt 77, 5211 JX (073 123071)*. **Open** *Sept-May* 9am-5.30pm Mon-Fri; 9am-4pm Sat; *Jun-Aug* 9am-5.30pm Mon-Fri; 9am-5pm Sat.

Overijssel

Randstad residents might look upon Overijssel, due east of Amsterdam, as being in *tukkerland* – out in the sticks – but they're happy to holiday in the province over the IJssel river (hence its name). Crisscrossed by long, winding rivers and 400 kilometres (249 miles) of canoe routes, the province is superb for watersports and is dotted with holiday homes and hikers' cabins; the VVV even provides self-drive, horse-drawn carts, which you can sleep in.

Most visitors head for the **Lake District**, comprising the **Weerribben** and **Wieden** districts. Between the two runs the road linking **Steenwijk** and **Blokzijl**, both fortified towns, the latter with a marina in its old harbour. Dominating Wieden is the huge **Beulaker Wijde/Belter Wijde** lake, bordered by **Vollenhove**, a Zuider Zee port until the Northeast Polder was drained; **Zwartsluis**, where paintings dating from the seventeenth century, when it was Fortress Zwartsluis, still hang in the town hall; and the watersports centre of **Wanneperveen**, with its splendid thatched farmsteads. Almost completely hidden among the reedlands are the villages of **Belt Schutsloot** and **Giethoorn**, where the residents get around mostly by boat, the buildings being individually marooned, with only boats and foot bridges to connect them. On the second and third weekends of August the Jazz Inn and Blues Inn music festivals are staged on a platform in the lake, and a procession of flower-decked boats takes place the following Saturday.

Tracing the boundary of the province up the IJssel you reach **Kampen**, which has a wealth of historic buildings and a particularly beautiful waterfront. Up-river is **Zwolle**, which like Kampen was a Hanse town and retains its star-shaped moat and bastions. In the town hall, parts of which date from 1448, is an imposing *schepenzaal* (elders' meeting chamber), a feature found only in Overijssel. The rococo former *stadhouder*'s palace now houses the Provinciaal Overijssels Museum. Boats leave for the lakes from Zwarte Water. Where the IJssel enters the province is the major city of **Deventer**. Known for *Deventer koek* honey gingerbread and the domed tower of St Lebuinuskerk, the city has some attractive houses on Brink square and in the old Berg Quarter.

Almost every town in Overijssel has a summer carnival. **Raalte** holds its harvest festival in the third week of August (Wed-Sat); vehicles parade through **Lemelerveld** covered in flowers during *Bloemen Corso* (early August); and sheepdogs herd sheep around **Hellendoorn** during its sheep market around 14 and 15 August. It's on special market days (Wednesdays, late July to early August) and on Sundays that you're most likely to see people in traditional costume at **Staphorst**, just north of Zwolle. Many of these strictly Protestant locals also inter-marry and shun the modern world, banning vaccinations, cars on Sundays – and cameras. This *lintdorp* (ribbon village) – or *weendorp* (peat village) – is nearly 12 kilometres (7½ miles) long; it swallowed up settlements along canals dug in peat, and incorporates farmhouses decorated in unique colour schemes. The community has retained a rigidly religious lifestyle centred on its countless Dutch Reformed Churches.

East along the River Vecht from Zwolle and surrounded by woods is the superb fishing centre of **Ommen**. Collect a fishing licence from the post office and ask about the best baits and fishing spots in the first-class tackle shop, Beste Stek (Vrijthof 1; 05291 54972). Hotel de Zon, on the river bank, is favoured by fishermen swapping angling stories. Stretching south are the **Salland Hills**, which rise to 81 metres (266 feet) at Holterberg, south of Nijverdal, where there's fun to be had at **Hellendoorn Adventure Park**.

The district stretching up to Germany is **Twente**, dominated by the province's biggest city, **Enschede**. Rebuilt after a fire in 1862, its main draws are Los Hoes, a textile industry museum, and the Rijksmuseum Twente, which displays modern art. Some of Twente's surviving Saxon farms can be seen on an NS day excursion (which includes travel in a horse-drawn covered waggon), or on a six-day cycle tour (March to October) organised by the provincial VVV, who can forward luggage from hotel to hotel. Some of the finest farms are concentrated around **Ootmarsum**, a knot of narrow streets lined with timber buildings, and **Denekamp**, with its thirteenth-century sandstone church and Natura Docet natural history museum. These two Catholic towns celebrate Easter with tree felling, street processions, ritual chanting and bonfires.

Further Information

Provincial VVV *Postbus 500, 7600 AM Almelo (05490 18767)*. **Open** 8.30am-5pm daily.
Enschede VVV *Oude Markt 31, 7511 GB (053 · 323200)*. **Open** 10am-5.30pm Mon; 9am-5.30pm Tue-Fri; *Sept-May* 9am-1pm Sat; *Jun-Aug* 9am-5pm Sat.
Giethoorn VVV *on a boat, Beulakerweg, 8355 AM (05216 1248)*. NS rail excursion 48. **Open** *Jun-Aug* 9am-noon, 1-6pm, daily; *Apr, May, Sept* 10am-noon, 1-5pm, Mon-Sat; *Oct-Mar* 10am-noon, 1-5pm, Mon-Fri.
Ommen VVV *Markt 1, 7731 DB (05291 51638)*. **Open** 9.30am-5pm Mon-Fri; 10am-5pm Sat; 2-5pm Sun.
Zwartsluis VVV *Stationsweg 32, 8064 DG (05208 67453)*. **Open** 8am-6pm Tue-Sat.
Zwolle VVV *Grote Kerkplein 14, 8011 PK (038 213900)*. **Open** 9am-5.30pm Mon-Fri; 9am-4pm Sat.

Utrecht

If you go anywhere in The Netherlands by land, the chances are you'll go through the city of Utrecht, the country's main rail and road junction, just south of Amsterdam (*see chapter* **The Randstad**). Earlier travellers, who came down the Lek river, chose the province in AD863 as the location for Europe's largest trading post, Dorestad. It is the site of present-day **Wijk-bij-Duurstede**, which still has many ancient buildings. In either direction along the Lek, old towns such as **Rhenen**, **Amerongen** and **Culemborg** remain virtually unchanged.

Water is Utrecht's chief asset. Between Amsterdam and Utrecht are the 2,500 hectare (6,200 acre) **Loosdrechtse Plassen**, and smaller **Vinkeveense Plassen**. These fan-shaped lakes have narrow strips of land radiating into them and are now used mainly for fishing and watersports. The area groans with private wealth,

The cathedral tower looms over the city of **Utrecht**.

A masterpiece of the De Stijl movement: the **Rietveld - Schröder House** *in Utrecht. See page 255.*

as the many villas dotted around the picturesque old villages of **Oud-Loosdrecht, Westbroek** and **Breukeleveen** testify. A few kilometres away in Noord Holland are **Hilversum**, home of Dutch television, and the mini-Hollywood at **Laren**. For a taste of more ancient privilege, wander down the Vecht, which flows north between the *plassen*. It's The Netherlands' prettiest navigable river, overshadowed by iron bridges, grand, decaying estates at **Loenen, Vreeland** and **Breukelen**, and the province's ubiquitous castles (*see chapter* **Excursions in Holland: Castles**).

In the eastern half of the province, water makes way for a large wooded area, ostensibly for recreational purposes but dominated by danger signs as walkers constantly risk stumbling onto military firing ranges. **Soestdijk** is home to the country's former queen, now Princess Juliana, and at **Austerlitz**, Napoleon's army built a huge sand pyramid purely because they had nothing else to do at the time. Best of all, though, is **Amersfoort**, a beautifully-preserved medieval town set in a ring of canals on the edge of the Leusder Heide heath.

Further Information

Provincial VVV *Postal enquiries only to Europalaan 93, 3526 KP Utrecht (030 801100)*.
Amersfoort VVV *Stationsplein 9-11, 3800 RK (033 635151)*. **Open** 9am-6pm Mon-Fri.
Utrecht VVV *Vredenburg 90, 3511 BD (063 4034085)*. NS rail excursion 62. **Open** 9am-6pm Mon-Fri; 9am-4pm Sat.
Wijk-bij-Duurstede VVV *Markt 24, 3961 BC (03435 75995)*. **Open** 1-4.30pm Mon; 10am-noon, 1-4.30pm, Tue-Fri; 10am-4pm Sat.

Zeeland

This collection of islands in the river delta bordering Belgium has a famous maritime past and distinctive Zeeland traditions which were preserved by its isolation. But in January 1953 massive storm floods swept away old buildings and farms, brutally launching the province into

the twentieth century. Salt water damage and tide-marks, seen halfway up columns in the medieval churches of **Kruiningen** (on the isthmus to Beveland Island) and **Brouwershaven** (on Schouwen Island), are the only reminders of the perennial threat of flooding – eliminated, the Dutch hope, by the **Delta Works**. The world's biggest flood barrier, it keeps the sea under control and reduces the cost of coastline maintenance. It was completed in 1986, after 30 years of construction costing f14 billion. The revolutionary technology is explained at **Delta Expo** on Neeltje Jans, an island halfway along the Ooster Schelde Dam.

Changes in tide movements have not affected the main activity of oyster and mussel catching. Seafood is available all over Zeeland, but the best hauls of the day usually find their way to restaurants in **Yerseke** (a town near Kruiningen named after the Dutch for oyster). In season (September to April) you can take a tour of the oyster beds.

In the Middle Ages, Zeeland grew fat on cloth and wool trade with England and France. Indeed the English still know the port of **Vlissingen** as Flushing. It's the birthplace of the heroic Admiral de Ruyter (*see chapter* **Decline & Fall**), whose statue in the Rotunda surveys the dramatic seascape. Among the local artefacts in the Stedelijk Museum is a copy of De Ruyter's portrait by Ferdinand Bol; the original is in Zeeuws Museum in the provincial capital, **Middelburg**, alongside tapestries depicting local sea battles. Although bombed in 1940, Middelburg has a charming circular centre parcelled within star-shaped fortifications, now landscaped. Like **Goes**, it owed its prosperity to medieval trade with England.

Over the Westerschelde estuary is **Zeeland Vlaanderen** (Flanders). From there it's a short hop over the Belgian border to the beautiful cities of Antwerp, Gent and Bruges (*see chapter* **Beyond Amsterdam: Crossing the Border**).

Just north of Middelburg is the most beautiful town in Zeeland, **Veere**, where elegant flèche spires and the towering Church of Our Lady can be seen across the flats for miles. The churches in the province are worth a tour in themselves. Many were used as lighthouses for ships at sea. The churches at **Kapelle, Zoutelande** and **'s-Heer Arendskerke** are among the biggest and best.

Further Information

Provincial & Middelburg VVV *Markt 65, 4330 AC (01180 33000)*. **Open** 8.30am-1pm, 1.30-5pm, Mon-Fri. NS rail excursion 4 (includes Walcheren miniature town). Goes VVV *Stationsplein 3, 4461 HP (01100 20577)*. **Open** *Apr-Sept* 1.30-5pm Mon-Fri; 10am-noon Sat; *Oct-Feb* 1.30-4pm Mon; 10am-12.30pm, 1.30-4pm, Tue-Fri; 10am-noon Sat.

Veere VVV *Oudestraat 28, 4351 AV (01181 1365).*
Open *Sept-Jun* 11am-3pm Mon, Tue, Thur, Sat; *Jul, Aug* 10am-5pm daily.
Vlissingen VVV *Nieuwendijk 15, 4381 BV (01184 12345).* *Sept-Jun* 9am-5pm Mon-Fri; 9am-1pm Sat; *Jul, Aug* 9am-6pm Mon-Sat; 1-5pm Sun.
Yerseke VVV *Kerkplein 1, 4401 ED (01131 1864).*
Open 2-4pm Mon; 10am-4pm Tue-Fri; 10am-noon Sat.
Delta Expo *Oosterschelde Dam, on Route N57 (01115 2702).* **Open** *Apr-Oct* 10am-5pm daily; *Nov-Mar* 10am-5pm Wed-Sun. **Admission** *high season* f13; f10 under-12s, over-65s; *low season* f10; f7.50 under-12s, over-65s.

Fighting the Sea

Everything you see in the Dutch landscape is affected by its relationship with the sea. Over half the country is below sea level, so without flood defences, at high tide most of the the major towns and cities and two thirds of the population would be underwater: all of Holland, Zeeland and Flevoland; most of Friesland, Groningen and Utrecht; and parts of Gelderland and Overijssel. The Zeeland flood of 1953 (*see under* **Zeeland**) illustrated the threat, and the Dutch are willing to spend upwards of f50 billion per year just to maintain the 450 kilometres (280 miles) of sea defences. There are yet more barriers against river flooding.

Man-made alterations to the countryside began in around AD1000 with Friesland's *terpen* (mounds), on to which the population would scramble during floods (for examples, *see under* **Friesland** and **Groningen**). Early settlers devised ways of 'winning' land by linking *terpen* via raised walls (dikes). The enclosed land was drained to make a polder, the excavated ditch inside the dike became a canal (*gracht* in town, *sloot* in the country) and freshwater rivers were used to flush salt out of the soil. All rural landscape matches this pattern, and street plans of towns (Amsterdam, Rotterdam) follow original polder divisions. Windmills, such as those at Kinderdijk (*see chapter* **Excursions in Holland: Traditions**), were built to speed up the continuous draining required, later to be replaced by steam, then electric pumping stations (for example, **De Blocq van Kuffeler**, Flevoland).

The first large-scale draining scheme (1848-52) was the Haarlemermeer, an 180 square-kilometre (70 square-mile) lake, now the site of Schiphol Airport. The polder system literally 'made' The Netherlands: it increased the size of the country (almost doubling it over the past millennium); formed freshwater basins; improved drainage; reduced the length of the coastline to make it more manageable against flooding; and made direct road links possible. The A7 links Noord Holland and Friesland, via the **Afsluitdijk**, which enclosed the former Zuider Zee in the most ambitious reclamation project of all (1927-1968).

Land for agriculture and new towns was created first on the Wieringermeer polder (1932), then on the North-east Polder (1942) and Flevoland (1968), a total of 1,650 square kilometres (637 square miles). In the process it formed the freshwater IJsselmeer and the recreational Randmeren (ring of lakes) between Flevoland and the mainland. The battle against the sea seemed all but won following the completion of the **Delta Works** in 1986 and the storm surge barrier at **Krimpen aan der IJssel**, near Rotterdam.

The sense of common purpose in fighting sea has had profound social effects; *see chapter* **Beyond Amsterdam**. Yet the Dutch are now resisting this perpetual driving force of their history and national psyche. The last planned Zuider Zee polder, the 600 square-kilometre (232 square-mile) **Markerwaard**, has been suspended. There are fears that it threatens ecology, poses unacceptable financial risks to the state, and that it may not even be needed. However, Amsterdam still plans to drain part of IJ Meer to create a new eastern suburb.

But the fight against the sea isn't over. The Dutch are now having to contemplate a threat to the entire future of the country they've handbuilt: the greenhouse effect. The sea level is already rising at the rate of 12-20 centimetres (5-8 inches) a century and dikes are being raised. But scientists and the government admit this will not compensate for any effects of global warming and are studying contingency plans to find a permanent solution. The most bizarre idea is to inject sulphuric acid (a plentiful waste product of Dutch industry) into the limestone layer deep below the surface. A chemical reaction would then form expanding gypsum and raise the country slightly. Apparently, it's not as crazy as it sounds.

Survival

Amsterdam is a small, welcoming city, and English-speakers have a particularly easy time, but in any foreign land it's important to have essential names and addresses at your fingertips. From emergencies to irritations, the answers are overleaf.

Survival

Practical information on surviving in the city: how to cope with emergencies, phone home, or have a bath.

Communications

Telephones/PTT Telecom

Public phone boxes are scattered throughout the city. The kiosks are mainly glass with a green trim and have a green and white *ptt telecom* logo. There are both coin-operated and card phones. The coin boxes take 25c, f1 and f2.50 coins. Phonecards are available from post offices and phone centres (*see below*), priced f5, f10 or f25.

The procedure for **making a call** is as follows: Listen for the dialling tone (a low-pitched hum), insert money – a minimum of 25c, or in some cases 50c – dial the appropriate code (none required for calls within Amsterdam), listen for the dialling tone to return (usually with a higher pitched hum), then dial the required number. A digital display on public phones shows the credit remaining, but only wholly unused coins are returned. Phoning from a hotel room is more expensive.

International phone calls:
The code is 09 (remember to wait for a new dialling tone before dialling the country code). International calls can be made from all phone boxes. The time for **off-peak rates** for international calls is generally 6pm-8am Monday to Friday (the USA gets an hour less, 7pm-8am), and all day on Saturday and Sunday. **European countries** are not counted as international by the Dutch phone system and so there are no off-peak rates for them. For more information on off-peak rates, phone international directory enquiries (*below*).

Telephone directories can be found in post offices and phone centres (*see below*). When phoning information services, taxis or train stations you may hear the recorded message, '*Er zijn nog drie (three)/twee (two)/een (one) wachtenden voor u.*' This tells you how many people are ahead of you in the telephone queuing system.

Emergency phonelines are listed under **Emergencies** (*page 267*); help phonelines are listed under **Help and Information** (*page 270*). The following operator services are open 8am-10pm daily.

Directory Enquiries 06 8008
International Operator 06 0410
International Directory Enquiries 06 0418

Phone Centres

If you have a number of phone calls to make, and little change, use a phone centre. They can be found in all tourist areas (for example Damrak, Kalverstraat and Leidsestraat) and some are more expensive than others. We list two of the largest.

Telehouse
Raadhuisstraat 46-50, C (674 3656). Tram 1, 2, 5, 13, 14, 17. **Open** 24 hours daily. **Credit** AmEx, DC, MC, TC, V.
As well as being a convenient place to make international phone calls, Telehouse offers fax, telex and telegram services. The cost of sending a **fax** ranges from f5.25 for one page (25c per additional page) to f14.75 for one page (f9.25 per additional page). You can arrange to have a fax sent to you at Telehouse on 626 3871 or 626 5326, at a cost of f5. The sender must include your name and telephone number with their fax, and Telehouse will phone to inform you of its arrival. The **telex** service costs 15c-f5.30 per minute to send, plus f10 operator charges, and f5 to receive. The number is 11101 TELEH NL. For **telegrams**, *see below*.

Teletalk Center
Leidsestraat 101, IS (620 8599/fax 620 8559). Tram 1, 2, 5. **Open** 10am-midnight daily. **Credit** AmEx, DC, MC, V.
The cost of sending a **fax** from here is f5 plus standard telephone charge, which drops in off-peak hours. It costs f3.50 to receive a fax here, however long the document, and photocopying costs 25c per page of A4 paper.

Telegrams, Telex and Fax

Telegrams can be sent from phone centres or post offices for a basic charge of f17.50, plus 45c-f1.10 per word (including address and signature). For **telex** and **fax** facilities, *see above* **Phone Centres** and *chapter* **Business**.

Post/PTT Post

Post offices and letterboxes are spread throughout Amsterdam. The logo for the national postal service is *ptt post* (white letters on a red oblong). **Post offices** are generally open from 9am to 5pm Monday to Friday. Here you can weigh letters, buy stamps and postal orders, send telegrams and send letters by express post. For post destined outside Amsterdam, use the *overige* slot. The **postal information phoneline** is 06 0417 (8am-8pm Mon-Fri; 9am-1pm Sat).

Stamps
At the time of writing, it costs 70c to send a postcard from Amsterdam anywhere in Europe (90c to the USA) and 90c for letters weighing less than 20g. To send post elsewhere prices vary according to weight and destination. Stamps (*postzegeten*) can also be bought with postcards from many tobacconists and souvenir shops.

Main Post Office
Singel 250, C (556 3311). Tram 1, 2, 5, 13, 14, 17, 21. **Open** 8.30am-6pm Mon-Wed, Fri; 8.30am-8pm Thur; 9am-noon Sat. **No credit cards.**

In addition to usual services, facilities here include: phones, directories, photo-booths, a wall-map of Amsterdam, stamp machines, counters where you can buy packaging for parcels, and a counter for collectors' stamps and commemorative stationery.

Post Restante
Post Restante, Hoofdpostkantoor ptt, Singel 250, 1012 SJ, Amsterdam, Netherlands.
If you're not sure where you'll be staying in Amsterdam, people can send your post to the above address. You'll be able to collect it from the main post office (*above*) if you produce ID such as a passport or driving licence with photo.

Centraal Station Post Office
Oosterdokskade 3, C (555 8911). Tram 1, 2, 4, 5, 9, 13, 16, 17, 24, 25. **Open** 8.30am-9pm Mon-Fri; 9am-noon Sat. **No credit cards.**
This is the parcels post office. Only this and the main post office (*above*) deal with parcels. Despite its name, it is in fact a five-minute walk east of Centraal Station.

Foreign Newspapers

For the American Discount Book Center *see chapter* **Students**; for the Athenaeum Nieuwscentrum and WH Smith, *see chapter* **Shopping: Books**. Most newsagents have a selection of foreign papers: the two below are particularly well-stocked.

AKO
Rozengracht 21, IW (624 5369). Tram 13, 14, 17. **Open** 8am-8pm Mon-Fri; 10am-6pm Sat, Sun. **No credit cards.**

Kiosk *Centraal Station, Stationsplein 13, C (627 4320). Tram 1, 2, 4, 5, 9, 13, 16, 17, 24, 25.* **Open** 6.30am-10.45pm daily. **No credit cards.**
Two of the best-stocked branches of this large chain. Others are dotted around the city.

Bruna
Leidsestraat 89-93, IS (622 0578). Tram 1, 2, 5. **Open** 9am-9.30pm daily. **No credit cards.**

Disabled

The most obvious difficulty people with mobility problems face in The Netherlands is negotiating the winding cobbled streets of the older towns. Poorly maintained and broken pavements are also widespread and canal houses, with their narrow doorways and steep stairs, can also present access problems. On the positive side, the pragmatic Dutch don't have preconceptions about people with disabilities and any problems are generally solved quickly and without fuss.

Most of the large museums have reasonable facilities for wheelchair users but little for the blind and hard of hearing. Most cinemas and theatres, too, have an enlightened attitude and are accessible, some with assistance. Throughout the Guide, we list establishments that claim to have wheelchair access. It's advisable to check in advance and to be specific about your needs.

Emergencies

Emergency Switchboard
(0611)
This 24-hour switchboard deals with ambulance, fire and police emergencies.

Central Medical Service
(664 2111)
A 24-hour medical and dental service, referring callers to a duty doctor or dentist. Operators can also give details of chemists open outside normal hours.

Lost credit cards
Report lost or stolen credit cards on the following 24-hour numbers:
American Express *(642 4488)*
Diner's Club *(557 3407)*
Mastercard *(010 20 70789)*
Visa *(660 0600)*

Rape & sexual abuse
TOSG *(612 7576)*
A helpline for women who are victims of rape, attack, sexual harassment or threats. Open from 10.30am-11.30pm daily.

Blijf-van-m'n-lijf-huis (Don't Touch My Body House) *(620 1261 9am-5pm; 638 7636 5pm-9am)*
Women being abused will be referred to a safe house.

The **Metro** is accessible to wheelchair users who 'have normal arm function', except for the Waterlooplein station which has no lifts. There is a **taxi service** for wheelchair users (*see chapter* **Getting Around**). Most **trams** are inaccessible to wheelchair users and the high steps may also pose problems for those with limited mobility; however new trams on the following routes should be accessible by wheelchair: 1, 2, 5, 6, 10, 16 and 24.

NS (Nederlandse Spoorwegen), the national railway network, produces a booklet called *Rail Travel for the Disabled*, plus timetables in braille, available from all main stations. There is wheelchair access to refreshment rooms and toilets at all stations. If you need assistance to board a train, phone 030 331 253 between 8am and 4pm Monday to Friday, at least a day in advance.

The Netherlands' Board of Tourism and the VVV (*see chapter* **Essential Information**) produce brochures listing accommodation, restaurants, museums, tourist attractions and boat excursions with facilities for the disabled.

Gehandicaptenoverleg Amsterdam

Keizersgracht 523, 1016 DP; IS (638 3838). Tram 1, 2, 5, 16, 24, 25. **Open** *9am-5pm Mon-Fri.*
This organisation campaigns to improve facilities for the disabled. The information literature is in Dutch, but the staff speak English. Phone for local information and advice.

Drugs

It's widely known that the Amsterdam authorities have a relaxed attitude towards **soft drugs** such as cannabis. Possession of up to 28g (1oz) of cannabis, though technically still an offence, is generally regarded as a misdemeanour for which you're unlikely to be prosecuted.

There exist numerous coffee shops (*see chapter* **Cafés & Bars**) where the drug is openly sold over the counter. It's extremely unwise to buy drugs on the street: at best you'll be ripped off; at worst, made ill or poisoned. You can buy the best hash in smaller, backstreet coffee shops. Some of these produce their own extra-strong homegrown grass (skunk), or buy hash directly from importers.

It's not acceptable to smoke everywhere in Amsterdam; a certain amount of discretion is required. Many bars and all tea houses will not tolerate the practice and eject any offenders. Similarly, outside Amsterdam, public consumption of cannabis is highly unacceptable.

Foreigners found with any amount of hard drugs, especially heroin, should expect prosecution. Organisations offering help and advice to users have become increasingly restricted in their ability to help foreigners with drug-related problems – government subsidies are generally aimed at helping nationals. Visitors caught dealing in drugs are likely to be prosecuted and repatriated pretty swiftly.

If you are suffering from the ill effects of too much cannabis, go to a hospital outpatients' department or see a doctor, who will be well-used to dealing with the problem. There are two **helplines** that offer advice and information on drug and alcohol abuse: 570 2335 (drugs) 570 2325 (alcohol); they are both open between 9am and 5.30pm Mon-Fri.

Embassies and Consulates

The VVV offices have comprehensive lists of embassies and consulates. Most countries have their embassies in The Hague. Unless otherwise stated, if only a consulate is listed then it will deal with all visa enquiries and other problems.

American Consulate General

Museumplein 19, OS (664 5661/679 0321). Tram 3, 5, 12, 16. **Open** *1.30-5.15pm Mon-Fri.*

Australian Embassy
Carnegielaan 12, 2517 KH, Den Haag (070 310 8200).
Open 9am-12.30pm, 1.15-5.15pm, Mon-Thur; 9am-12.30pm Fri.

Belgian Consulate
Drentestraat 11, OS (642 9763). Bus 40, 60, 158, 173.
Open 9am-2pm Mon-Fri.
Deals with visa enquiries and documentation for Belgians in Utrecht, North Holland and Flevoland.

Belgian Embassy
Lange Vigversberg 12, 2513 AC, Den Haag (070 36 44 910). **Open** 9am-noon, 2-4pm, Mon-Fri.
Deals with all other visa enquiries.

British Consulate General
Koningslaan 44, OS (676 4343; visa enquiries 675 8121). Tram 2, 6. **Open** 9am-noon, 2-3.30pm, Mon-Fri.

British Embassy
Langvoorhout 10, 2514 ED, Den Haag (070 36 45 800). **Open** 9am-1pm, 2.15-5.30pm, Mon-Fri.

Canadian Embassy
Sophialaan 7, 2514 JP, Den Haag (070 361 4111).
Open 9am-1pm, 2-5.30pm, Mon-Fri.

Eire Embassy
Dr Kuyperstraat 9, 2514 BA, Den Haag (070 63 0993).
Open 10am-12.30pm, 2.30-5pm, Mon-Fri.

Federal Republic of Germany Consulate
De Lairessestraat 172, OS (673 6245). Tram 16. **Open** 9am-noon Mon-Fri.

French Consulate
Vijzelgracht 2, IS (624 8346). Tram 6, 7, 10, 16, 24, 25. **Open** 9am-1pm Mon-Fri.

Italian Consulate
Herengracht 609, IS (624 0043). Tram 4. **Open** 9am-12.30pm Mon-Fri.

New Zealand Embassy
Mauritskade 25, 2514 HD, Den Haag (070 346 9324).
Open 9am-12.30pm, 1.30-5.30pm, Mon-Thur; 9am-12.30pm, 1.30-5pm, Fri; *visa enquiries* 9am-12.30pm Mon-Fri.

Portuguese Consulate
Willenskade 18, 3016 TL, Rotterdam (010 411 1540).
Open 9am-3.30pm Mon, Wed-Fri; 1-7.30pm Tue.

Spanish Consulate
Frederiksplein 34, OS (620 3811). Tram 3, 4, 6, 7, 10.
Open 9am-2pm Mon-Fri.

Swiss Consulate
Johannes Vermeerstraat 16, OS (664 4231). Tram 16.
Open 10am-noon Mon-Fri.

Health

For **emergency services and medical or dental referral agencies** *see page 267* **Emergencies**.

In the case of minor accidents, try the outpatients' departments at the following hospitals (*ziekenhuis*), all of which are open 24 hours a day and offer first aid facilities.

Academisch Medisch Centrum
Meibergdreef 9, OE (566 9111; 566 3333). Bus 59, 60, 61, 62, 120, 126, 158.

Boven IJ Ziekenhuis
Statenjachtstraat 1, OE (634 6343). Bus 34, 36, 37, 39.

VU Ziekenhuis
De Boelelaan 1117, OE (548 2318). Bus 23, 48, 64, 65, 173.

Lucas Ziekenhuis
Jan Tooropstraat 164, OW (510 8911). Bus 19, 47, 80, 82, 97.

Onze Lieve Vrouwe Gasthuis
1E Oosterparkstraat 179, OE (599 9111). Tram 3.
The most central, though some say the worst, outpatient department.

Dentists

For a dentist (*tandarts*), phone the Central Medical Service (*see page 267* **Emergencies**).

AOC
Wilhelmina Gasthuisplein 167, OW (616 1234). Tram 1, 2, 3, 5, 6, 12. **Open** 8.30am-10pm Mon-Fri; 8.30am-5pm Sat; 1-6pm Sun. **Credit** (minimum f50) AmEx, DC, MC, V.
Emergency dental treatment is unlikely to cost more than f150.

Prescriptions

Chemists (*drogisterij*) sell toiletries and non-prescription drugs such as aspirin and cold remedies, as well as tampons and condoms. They are usually open between 9.30am and 5.30pm Monday to Saturday. For prescription drugs you will have to go to a pharmacy (*apotheek*), usually open 9.30am to 5.30pm Monday to Friday.

If you need a chemist or pharmacist outside these hours phone the **Central Medical Service** (*Centraal Dokters Dienst*) on 664 2111 (24 hours daily) or consult the daily newspaper *Het Parool* which publishes details of which *apotheek* are open late that week. Details are also posted at local *apotheeks*.

Special Clinics

AIDS Helpline
(freephone 06 022 2220). **Open** 2-10pm Mon-Fri.
A free national helpline with English-language advice, information and counselling for those concerned about AIDS and related problems. Booklets (in English) on safe sex are also available from COC (*see chapter* **Gay Amsterdam**).

GG VD Clinic
Groenburgwal 44, C (555 5822). Tram 9, 14. **Open** 8.30am-5pm Mon-Fri.
Free and confidential advice and treatment on sex-related problems and sexually transmitted diseases. Phone first, as there are various walk-in clinics with changing times and an appointments system. There are also men- and women-only clinics.

HIV Positive Line
(664 2466). **Open** 1-4pm Mon, Wed, Fri; 8pm-1.30pm Tue, Thur.
A telephone information and helpline.

SAD
Eerste Helmersstraat 17, 1054 CX; OW (685 3331).
Tram 1, 2, 3, 5, 6, 7, 10, 12. **Open** 7-9pm Fri, Sat; 2-3pm Sun.
The Foundation for Additional Services (SAD) has a regular weekend clinic offering VD and HIV-testing for gay men. On other days, consultation is by appointment only.

Contraception and Abortion

Condomerie Het Gulden Vlies
Warmoesstraat 141, C (627 4174). Tram 1, 2, 4, 5, 9, 13, 16, 17, 24, 25. **Open** 1-6pm Mon-Fri; noon-5pm Sat. **No credit cards.**
Condoms for all occasions. *See chapter* **Shopping**.

Polikliniek Oosterpark
Oosterpark 59, OE (693 2151). Tram 3, 6. **Open** 9am-5pm Mon, Wed, Fri.
Information and advice on contraception and abortion. Abortions are carried out although non-residents without appropriate insurance will be charged from f520 for the operation. The process is prompt and backed up by sympathetic counselling.

Rutgersstichting
Aletta Jacobshuis, Overtoom 323, IW (616 6222). Tram 16. **Open** by appointment 9am-4pm Mon-Fri. **Consultation** fee f30. **No credit cards.**
Staff at this family planning centre can help non-Dutch visitors with prescriptions for contraceptive pills, morning-after pills and condoms, IUD fitting and cervical smear tests (with prompt results). Prescription costs vary; none are free.

Help and Information

VVV (tourist office) *(06 340 340 66).* **Open** 9am-5pm daily. *See also chapter* **Essential Information**.
Transport information: GVB *(06 9292).* **Open** 8am-11pm daily. *See also chapter* **Essential Information**.
Time (06 8002).
Weather (06 8003).

Help Phonelines

Alcoholics Anonymous
(686 5142). **Open** 24-hour answerphone.
Phone and leave a message on the answerphone and a counsellor will ring you back.

Crisis Helpline
(616 1666). **Open** 9am-3am Mon-Thur; 24 hours Fri-Sun.
A counselling service, comparable to the Samaritans in the UK and Lifeline in the USA, for anyone with emotional problems, run by volunteers. English isn't always understood at first, but keep trying and inevitably someone will be able to help you.

Legal and Immigration

Legal Advice Centre/Bureau Voor Rechtshulp
Spuistraat 10, C (626 4477). Tram 1, 2, 5. **Open** 1-4pm Mon; 9am-noon Tue-Fri.
Funded by the Ministry of Justice, this centre has qual-ified lawyers who give free legal advice on matters of tenancy, social security, immigration (residence permits), insurance, consumer complaints and disputes with employers. Staff will assess whether they can help you and then refer you to the nearest of their four offices.

Legal Advice Line
(548 2611). **Open** 9am-5pm Mon-Thur; 9am-1pm Fri.
You can get free advice on this phoneline from student lawyers, who offer a relaxed, friendly service. They deal mainly with civil law queries and problems, but will occasionally be able to help with minor criminal law matters. Most speak excellent English.

Libraries

You'll need to present proof of residence in Amsterdam if you want to join a library (*bibliotheek*) and borrow books. However, in the public libraries (*openbare bibliotheek*) you can read books, newspapers and magazines, without membership or charge. For university libraries, *see chapter* **Students**.

American Institute
Plantage Muiderstraat 12, OE (525 4380). Tram 9/Metro Waterlooplein. **Open** 10am-4pm Mon, Wed, Fri.

British Council Library
Keizersgracht 343, IW (622 3644). Tram 1, 2, 5, 7, 10. **Open** 10am-4.30pm Mon-Fri.

Centrale Bibliotheek
Prinsengracht 587, IW (523 0900). Tram 1, 2, 5, 7, 10. **Open** 1-9pm Mon; 10am-9pm Tue-Fri; 10am-5pm Sat.
Anyone is welcome to use this, the main public library, for reference purposes. There is a variety of English-language books and newspapers and a small coffee bar. *Wheelchair access with assistance.*

Left Luggage

There is a manned left-luggage counter at Schiphol Airport, open 7am-10.45pm daily. The charge is f3 per item per day. There are also lockers in the arrival and departure halls, costing f3 (small), f5 (large) per day. Inside Amsterdam, there are lockers at Centraal Station.

Lost Property

For the sake of insurance, it's wise to report **lost property** (*gevonden voorwerpen*) to the police as quickly as possible; for the central police phone number, *see below* **Police and Security**. Should you lose your passport, inform your embassy or consulate as well. If you lose anything at the Hoek van Holland ferry terminal or Schiphol Airport contact the company you're travelling with, as there are no central lost property depots at either of these points. To report lost credit cards, *see page 267* **Emergencies**.

Centraal Station
NS Lost Property Information, Stationsplein 15, C (557 8544). Tram 1, 2, 4, 5, 9, 13, 16, 17, 24, 25. **Open** 5am-1am daily.

Even the police favour pedal-power in Amsterdam.

Items found on trains are kept here for ten days and then sent to *NS Afdeling Verloren Voorverpen, Daalsedijk 4, 3500 HA, Utrecht.*

GVB Head Office
Prins Hendrikkade 108-114, C (551 4911). Tram 1, 2, 4, 5, 9, 13, 16, 17, 24, 25. **Open** 9am-4pm Mon-Fri.
Report here for any item lost on a bus, Metro or tram. If reporting a loss from the previous day, phone after 2pm to allow time for the property to be sorted.

Police Lost Property
Waterlooplein 11, C (559 8005). Tram 9, 14. **Open** 11am-3.30pm Mon-Fri.
Try here for any items lost in the streets or parks. It's always advisable to report any loss to the police station in the same district as they generally hold items for a day or so before sending them on here.

Pets

To bring cats and dogs into The Netherlands you must have rabies vaccination certificates. There are no restrictions for other common domestic pets, but it is wise to check before bringing them over. Protected animals and live-stock cannot be brought into The Netherlands without clearance. Remember that you'll face your own country's regulations if returning with an animal.

If your animal is ill while here, consult one of the numerous **veterinary surgeries** (*dierenart-sen*) listed in the Yellow Pages (*Gouden Gids*), where you can also find details of cat and dog **ken-** nels (*dierenpensions*). In an emergency, you could even call out an animal ambulance.

Dierenambulance Stichting Centrale
Hoogte Kadijk 61, IE (626 1058/24-hour emergency line 626 2121). **Open** *for emergencies* 24 hours daily.
If you take pity on an injured animal in the street, for f25 this unique ambulance service will collect and treat it. Staff also attempt to find the owner or a new home. If it's your own animal, you must pay both the f25 plus the cost of treatment and boarding.

Dierenopvancentrum
Polderweg 120, OE (665 1888/93 6494). Tram 9. **Open** 10am-1pm, 2-4pm, Mon-Sat.
This particularly good animal hospital and sanctuary offers comprehensive veterinary services. You can also board cats and dogs here for between f8 and f18.50 per day.

Police and Security

The Dutch police are under no obligation to grant a phone call to those they detain (they are entitled to hold people for up to 6 hours for ques-tioning if the alleged crime is not too serious, 24 hours for serious matters), but they will phone the relevant consulate on behalf of a foreign detainee.

If you are a victim of theft or assault, report to the nearest police station. In the case of a serious incident or an emergency, phone the **emergency switchboard** on **0611** and ask for the police.

Hoofdbureau Van Politie (Police Headquarters)
Elandsgracht 117, IW (559 9111). *Tram 7, 10*. **Open** 24 hours daily.

Locksmiths

Amsterdam Security Center
Prinsengracht 1097, IS (671 6316). *Tram 4*. **Open** *for emergencies* 24 hours daily. **Credit** AmEx.
The cost of calling a locksmith varies depending on the area. To get into a car will cost between f65 and f85; into a house f85 to f125. After midnight prices rise and you can expect to pay a minimum of f135.

Religion

Catholic
St John and St Ursula *Begijnhof 30, C (622 1918)*. *Tram 1, 2, 5, 4, 16, 24, 25*. **Open** 10am-6pm Mon-Sat. **Services** *Dutch* 9am, 5pm, Mon-Fri; 9am Sat; 10am Sun; *English* 12.15pm Sun; *French* 11.15am Sun.
A small and serene chapel in the peaceful Begijnhof.

Papegaai *Kalverstraat 58, C (623 1889)*. *Tram 4, 9, 14, 16, 24, 25*. **Open** 10am-4pm Mon-Sat; 9am-1.30pm Sun. **Service** *Latin* 10.30am, 12.15pm, Sun.

Christian Scientist
First Church of Christ Scientist *Richard Wagnerstraat 32, OS (662 7438)*. *Tram 5, 24*. **Services** *Dutch* 10.30am Sun; *English* 8pm Wed.

Dutch Reformed Church
Oude Kerk *Oudekerksplein 23, C (625 8284/624 9183)*. *Tram 4, 9, 16, 24, 25*. **Open** *Mar-Oct* 11am-5pm daily; *Nov-Feb* 1-5pm Fri-Sun. **Services** *Dutch* 11am Sun.

Westerkerk *Prinsengracht 281, IW (624 7766)*. *Tram 13, 14, 17*. **Open** 10am-4pm Mon-Sat. **Services** *Dutch* 11am Sun.

Episcopal Church
English Episcopal Church *Groenburgwal 42, C (624 8877)*. *Tram 9, 14*. **Open** for services only. **Services** *English* 10.30am, 7.30pm, Sun.

Jewish
Liberal Jewish Community Amsterdam *Jacob Soetendorpstraat 8, OS (642 3562)*. *Tram 4*. **Open** *office* 9am-5pm Mon-Thur; 9am-3pm Fri. **Services** 8pm Fri; 10am Sat.
Times may vary so phone first to check.

Orthodox Jewish Community Amsterdam *PO Box 7967, Van der Boechorstraat 26, 1008 AD; OS (646 0046)*. *Bus 69, 169*. **Open** 9am-5pm Mon-Sat; 9am-3pm Fri.
Information on orthodox synagogues and Jewish facilities in Amsterdam. Phone first for an appointment.

Muslim
THAIBA Islamic Cultural Centre *Kraaiennest 125, OS (698 2526)*. *Metro Gaasperplas*. **Prayer** 12.30pm, 3pm, 4.35pm, 6.35pm, daily.
Times vary, so phone for details of prayer times and cultural activities.

Quaker
Religieus Genootschap der Vrienden *Vossiusstraat 20, OS (679 4238)*. *Tram 1, 2, 5, 6, 7, 10*. **Open** for services only. **Service** 10.30am Sun.

Reformed Church
English Reformed Church *Begijnhof 48, C (624 9665)*. *Tram 1, 2, 5*. **Open** *May-Sept* 2-4pm Mon-Fri. **Services** *English* 10.30am Sun; *Dutch* 7pm Sun.
The main place of worship for the English-speaking community in Amsterdam.

Russian Orthodox
St Nicolaas *Utrechtsedwarsstraat 5A, OS (622 5385)*. *Tram 4*. **Open** for services only. **Services** 5.30pm Sat; 10.30am Sun.
Services on the first and third weekends of the month are mainly in Slavonic languages, mainly Dutch on the other weekends.

Salvation Army
National Headquarters *Oudezijds Voorburgwal 14, C (520 8408)*. *Tram 4, 9, 16, 24, 25*. **Open** 9am-5pm Mon-Fri.
Phone or drop in for information on Salvation Army Citadels in Amsterdam.

Washing and Cleaning

Baths and Showers

Opening times for the showers and baths (*badhuis*) listed below tend to fluctuate, so phone before setting out.

Fronemanstraat 3
OE (665 0811). *Tram 9*. **Open** 12.30pm-7am Mon; 10am-1.30pm, 4-7pm Tue; 10am-4.30pm Wed, Thur; 12.30-6pm Fri. **Cost** f2 per shower.
Bring your own towel.

Marnixbad
Marnixplein 5-9, OS (625 4843). *Tram 3, 10*. **Open** *for baths or showers* 4-7pm Mon-Fri; 10am-6pm Sat. **Cost** f2.50 per shower; f3.50 per bath.
The best place in town for a wash; there's a bar to relax in afterwards, and towels can be hired.

De Warme Waterstaal Sticht
Da Costakade 200, OW (612 5946). *Tram 3, 7, 12, 17*. **Open** 1-9pm Tue; 10am-5pm Sat. **Cost** f2.50 per shower; f4.50 per bath.
Take a towel with you.

Launderettes

A comprehensive list of launderettes (*wassalons*) can be found in the Yellow Pages (*Gouden Gids*). For the reliable Clean Brothers chain and dry-cleaners, *see chapter* **Services**.

Travel and Driving

For details of rail travel, *see chapter* **Getting Around**.

Driving and Breakdown

It's advisable to join a **national motoring organisation** before arriving in The Netherlands. These provide international assistance booklets, which not only explain what to do in the event of a breakdown in Europe, but also offer gener-

al information on continental motoring. To drive in The Netherlands you'll need a valid national driving licence, although the Dutch motoring club, **ANWB** (*see below*) and many car hire firms favour an **international driving licence**, available from branches of national motoring organisations. In Britain, take your full licence and a passport photo to a branch of the AA or RAC and they will process it in minutes.

Major roads are usually well-maintained and clearly sign-posted. Motorways (which have traffic lights) are labelled 'A'; major roads 'N'; and European routes 'E'.

Some points to note: the Dutch drive on the right; drivers and front-seat passengers must always wear seatbelts; speed limits are 50kmh (31mph) within cities, 80kmh (50mph) outside, and 120kmh (75mph) on motorways; be wary of cyclists; trams will not give way to cars in most circumstances.

To bring your car into The Netherlands you'll need an international identification disk, a registration certificate, proof of the vehicle having passed a road safety test in its country of origin, and insurance documents.

Royal Dutch Touring Club (ANWB)
Museumplein 5, OS (673 0844; 24-hour emergency line 06 0888). Tram 2, 3, 5, 12, 16. **Open** 8.45am-5pm Mon-Fri; 8.45am-noon Sat. **Credit** AmEx, DC, foreign currency, MC, TC, V.
If you haven't already joined a motoring organisation,

you can enrol here for f90.70, which covers the cost of assistance should your vehicle break down. It will cost you more if you wait until you need the emergency services. If you're a member of a foreign motoring organisation, you're entitled to free help providing you can present membership documents. You may find emergency crews don't accept credit cards or cheques at the scene; be sure to ascertain the method of payment when you phone.

Spare parts
Bergam Automaterialen *Kalfjeslaan 25, Amstelveen, OS (643 0321). Bus 170, 171, 172.* **Open** 8.30am-6pm Mon-Fri; 9am-4pm Sat. **No credit cards.**
Dick's Car Clinic *Groenmarktkade 5, OW (626 3217). Tram 3.* **Open** 8.30am-5.30pm Mon-Fri. **No credit cards.**
If you think you can fix it yourself, try one of these. Phone first to check they've got the part you need.

Parking and Petrol

Parking space is at a premium in central Amsterdam – you're unlikely to find space on the streets. Illegally parked cars get clamped or towed away. There are no 24-hour **car parks** (*parkeren*, indicated by a white 'P' on a blue square), but after 7pm you can park at some meters free, and after midnight parking in uncovered car parks is also free. Below we list a selection of central car parks where you're more likely to find a space during peak times.

De Bijenkoorf *Beursplein, Damrak, C.* **Open** 8am-midnight Mon-Sat. **Admission** f1.25 first half hour; f2.50 per half hour following.

Europarking *Marnixstraat 250, IW (623 6694)*.
Open 6.30am-12.30am Mon-Thur; 6.30am-1.30am Fri,
Sat; 7am-12.30am Sun. **Admission** f1.75 per hour.

Museumplein (uncovered),*OS (671 6418)*. **Open** 8am-
8pm daily. **Admission** f3 per hour Mon-Sat; free Sun.

Prinsengracht 540-542 *IS (625 9852)*. **Open**
7.30am-4.30pm Mon-Fri; 3pm-5.30am Sat; 6pm-4.30am
Sun. **Admission** f3 per hour.

In the city limits the main **24-hour petrol sta-
tions** (*benzinestation*) are at:
Sarphatistraat 225, *IE*
Marnixstraat 250, *IW*
Spaarndammerdijk 218, *OW*

Clamping

Amsterdam's wheel-clamp (*wielklem*) teams are swift to
act and show little mercy. If you outstay your allotted
time at a meter (usually about f2-f4 per hour) you'll be
clamped. A yellow sticker on the windscreen informs you
where to go to pay the fine (f121). Once you've paid,
return to the car and wait for the traffic police (information on 523 3115) to remove the clamp. Happily, this service is prompt. If you park illegally (double-parking, for
instance), your car will almost certainly be towed away.
It'll cost at least f121 to reclaim it from the pound if you
do so within 24 hours, and about f250 otherwise. Take
your passport and enough cash or personal cheques to
pay the hefty fine. Credit cards are not accepted.

Car Hire

Dutch car hire (*auto-verhuur*) companies generally expect at least one year's driving experience
and will want to see a valid national driving licence
and passport. Unless stated otherwise, each company will require a deposit through an international credit card, and you'll need to be over 21.
International companies are considerably more
expensive than local ones. Other firms are listed
in the Yellow Pages (*Gouden Gids*). Prices given
below are for the hire of the cheapest car available at the company office at time of writing, not
including insurance.

Adam's Rent-a-Car

Nassaukade 344-347, OW (685 0111). *Tram 7, 10, 17*.
Open 8am-9pm Mon-Sat. **Credit** AmEx, DC, MC, V.
Hire for a day costs from f65; the first 100km are free,
and after that the charge is 35c a kilometre.

Avis

Nassaukade 380, OW (683 6061). *Tram 10*. **Open**
7.30am-9pm Mon-Fri; 7.30am-4pm Sat, Sun. **Credit**
AmEx, DC, MC, TC, V.
Prices start at f119 per day, including unlimited mileage
and insurance.

Budget

Overtoom 121, OW (612 6066). *Tram 1, 6*. **Open**
7.30am-7pm Mon-Fri; 8am-4pm Sat; 9am-1pm Sun.
Credit AmEx, DC, MC, V.
Hire costs start at f190 per day, unlimited mileage and
insurance included. You'll need a credit card to pay the
deposit plus passport as ID, and you must be over 23.

Diks

Van Ostadestraat 278-280, OS (662 3366). *Tram 3, 4*.
Open 8am-7.30pm Mon-Sat; 9am-12.30pm, 8-10pm,
Sun. **Credit** AmEx, DC, MC, V.
Prices start at f41 per day plus 41c per km.

Europcar

Overtoom 51-53, OW (618 4595). *Tram 1, 6*. **Open**
7.30am-6pm Mon-Fri; 8am-4pm Sat; 8am-noon Sun.
Credit AmEx, DC, MC, V.
Hire charges rise from f277.88 per day, inclusive of
unlimited mileage and insurance.

Hertz

Overtoom 85 OW (612 2441). *Tram 1, 6*. **Open** 8am-
6pm Mon-Thur; 8am-7pm Fri; 8am-4pm Sat; 9am-2pm
Sun. **Credit** AmEx, DC, MC, V.
Prices start at f134 per day, including unlimited mileage
and insurance.

Kasper and Lotte

Van Ostadestraat 232, OS (671 0733). *Tram 3, 4*.
Open 8am-7.45pm Mon-Sat. **Credit** AmEx, DC, MC, V.
Including unlimited mileage and insurance, prices start
at f108 per day.

Discount Travel

Budget Air

Rokin 34, C (627 1251). *Tram 4, 9, 16, 24, 25*. **Open**
9.30am-5.30pm Mon-Fri; 10am-3pm Sat. **Credit** AmEx,
DC, MC, V.
Low-cost fares to world-wide destinations with discounts
for students, young people and senior citizens.

Budget Bus

Rokin 10, C (627 5151). *Tram 4, 9, 14, 16, 24, 25*. **Open**
9.30am-5.30pm Mon-Fri; 10am-4pm Sat. **Credit** MC, V.
This agency sells bus tickets for Europe and Morocco,
with discounts for students.

NBBS

Dam 17, C (620 5071). *Tram 1, 2, 4, 5, 13, 14, 16, 17,
24, 25/Leidsestraat 53, IS (638 1736)*. *Tram 1, 2, 5*.
Both **Open** 9.30am-6.30pm Mon-Fri; 10am-3pm Sat.
No credit cards.
Low cost flights to world-wide destinations, with discount
travel for students and young people, and a Eurotrain discount for under-26s.

Travel Express

Rokin 38, C (626 4434). *Tram 4, 9, 14, 16, 24, 25*.
Open 10am-5pm Mon-Fri. **No credit cards.**
Travel Express arrange bus travel to European destinations. There are also 'bike' buses – buses with space
allocated for bicycles – to some locations in the summer, package trips to London by air and flights to
Paris.

Hitch-Hiking

The spots listed below are good places to start
a journey out of Amsterdam.

The Lift Centre

Nieuwezijds Voorburgwaal 256 (622 4342).
Helpful service based in the centre of town. A single trip
to Paris costs f30, payable to the driver (registration costs
a standard f7.50). Phone for details.

Starting points

Direction The Hague and Rotterdam: at the access
to the motorway, between RAI rail station (terminus of
tram 4) and the RAI congress building on Europa
Boulevard.
Direction Utrecht: by the corner of Rijnstraat and
President Kennedylaan (terminus of tram 25).
Direction Arnhem and Germany: Gooise Weg, close
to Amstel rail station.

Index

This edition revised and updated in consultation with Paul Andrews, Karen Seekings, Howard Shannon

Features in this guide were written and researched by: Introduction Hélène Vlessing. **Essential Information** Julie Sinclair-Day; Ellen Sinke. **Getting Around** Julie Sinclair-Day; Ellen Sinke. **Sightseeing** Abi Daruvalla; Julie Sinclair-Day; Tjaart Thorn; *Collapsing Houses, Hofjes* and *Houseboats* Jon and Sara Henley. **Amsterdam by Area** Ellen Sinke; *Leidseplein* Michael Cooper; *The Museum Quarter* Bambi Bogert; *The Red Light District* Robin Pascoe; *The Jordaan* Jonette Stabbert; *Waterlooplein & The Plantage* Robin Pascoe; *De Pijp* Michael Cooper; *The Port* David Post. **The Canals** Jon Henley. **Amsterdam by Season** Abi Daruvalla; Tjaart Thorn. **Accommodation** Karen Seekings; Julie Sinclair-Day. **Early History** Sophie Marshall. **War & Reformation** Sophie Marshall. **The Golden Age** Sophie Marshall. **Decline & Fall** Sophie Marshall. **Between the Occupations** Sophie Marshall; *The Amsterdam School* Philip Cornwel-Smith. **World War II** Kees Neefjes. **Post-war** Mark Fuller. **Amsterdam Today** Sara and Jon Henley; Mindy Ran. **Green Issues** Sara Henley; Mindy Ran. **Restaurants** Karen Seekings. **Cafés & Bars** Jon Henley; Desmond Rouse. **Shopping** Lyn Ritchie; Karen Seekings; Jonette Stabbert. **Services** Jonette Stabbert. **Galleries** Femke van Dongen; Mari Shields; Ellen Sinke. **Museums** Judi Seebus; Ellen Sinke. **Media** Paul Andrews. **Children & Parents** Mindy Ran; Marieke Sjerps. **Clubs** Paul Jay; David Pepper; Karen Seekings. **Dance** Ariejan Korteweg; Lisa Sove. **Film** Chris Fuller; Jac Goderie; Howard Shannon. **Music: Classical & Opera** Rose Anne Hamilton; Tom Samilijan. **Music: Rock, Folk & Jazz** Karen Seekings; Maz Weston. **Sport & Fitness** Jeroen van den Berg; Ellen Sinke. **Theatre** Lisa Sove; Bert Verheij. **Early Hours** David Pepper. **Business** Jon Henley; Tjaart Thorn; *additional research* Julie Sinclair-Day. **Gay Amsterdam** Pip Farquharson; Kees Neefjes; Mindy Ran. **Students** Eric Buchanan; Kees Neefjes. **Women's Amsterdam** Mindy Ran; Marieke Sjerps. **Beyond Amsterdam** Ann Campbell-Lord; Pip Farquharson; *Crossing the Border* Ailsa Camm. **Excursions in Holland** Ann Campbell-Lord; Pip Farquharson; Lyn Ritchie. **The Randstad** Ailsa Camm; Pip Farquharson. **The Provinces** Ailsa Camm; Pip Farquharson; *Overijssel* Eric Nicholls. **Survival** Mindy Ran; Julie Sinclair-Day.

The Editors would like to thank the following people and organisations for help and information:
Charles Godfrey-Faussett; the staff at Amsterdam University Faculty of History.

Photography by Julian Anderson except for:
Dave Swindells page 178; **Ben van Duin** page 181; **The Netherlands Board of Tourism** pages 250, 252, 253, 254, 257 258, 259, 262, 263, 264.

Maps

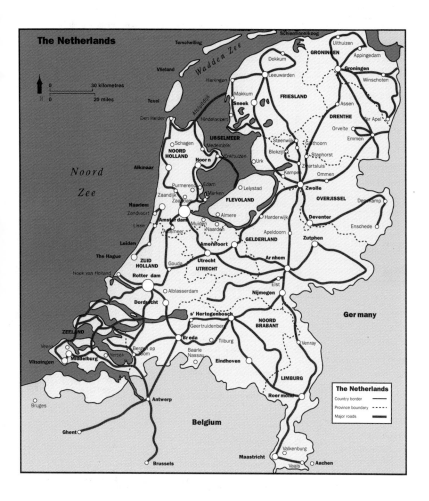

The Netherlands

Noord Zee

0   30 kilometres

0   20 miles

N

Schiermonnikoog

Terschelling

Wadden Zee

Uithuizen

GRONINGEN

Dokkum   Appingedam

Vlieland

Groningen

Leeuwarden

Winschoten

Harlingen

Makkum

FRIESLAND

Texel

Sneek

Assen

Den Helder

DRENTHE

Ter Apel

Hindelopen

Orvelte

Schagen

IJSSELMEER

Steenwijk   Giethoorn

Emmen

NOORD HOLLAND

Medemblik

Blokzijl

Staphorst

Hoorn

Enkhuizen

Urk

Alkmaar

Kampen   Zwartsluis

Ommen

Purmerend   Edam

Lelystad

Zwolle

Zaandijk

Marken

FLEVOLAND

OVERIJSSEL

Denekamp

Zaandam

Haarlem

Almere

Harderwijk

Deventer

Zandvoort

Enschede

Lisse

Amsterdam

Muiden

Apeldoorn

Leiden

Naarden

GELDERLAND

Zutphen

Aalsmeer

Amersfoort

The Hague

ZUID HOLLAND

Gouda

Utrecht

UTRECHT

Arnhem

Hoek van Holland

Rotterdam

Elst

Alblasserdam

Nijmegen

Dordrecht

Germany

s'Hertogenbosch

Geertruidenberg

NOORD BRABANT

ZEELAND

Breda   Tilburg

Veere

Bergen op Zoom

Venray

Yerseke

Baarle Nassau

Middelburg

Eindhoven

Vlissingen

LIMBURG

The Netherlands

Antwerp

Roermond

Country border

Bruges

Province boundary

Major roads

Ghent

Belgium

Valkenburg

Maastricht

Vaals   Aachen

Brussels

AMSTERDAM CITY MAP

THEATERS

- **A** BELLEVUE
- **C** CARRÉ
- **D** CONCERTGEBOUW
- **E** MUZIEKTHEATER
- **F** NIEUWE DE LA MAR
- **G** STADSSCHOUWBURG

MONUMENTS

- **1** BEGIJNHOF
- **2** KONINKLIJK PALEIS (ROYAL PALACE)
- **3** MAGERE BRUG
- **4** MONTELBAANSTOREN
- **5** MUNTTOREN
- **6** NATIONAAL MONUMENT
- **12** SCHREIERSTOREN
- **14** WAAG

CHURCHES

- **7** DE NIEUWE KERK
- **8** NOORDERKERK
- **9** OUDE KERK
- **10** PORTUGESE SYNAGOGE
- **11** KOEPELKERK
- **13** ST. NICOLAASKERK
- **15** WESTERKERK
- **16** ZUIDERKERK

OTHER OBJECTS OF INTEREST

- **A** ARTIS (ZOO), PLANETARIUM
- **B** HORTUS BOTANICUS
- **H** HEINEKEN (BREWERY)

MUSEUMS

- **1** ALLARD PIERSON MUSEUM
- **2** AMSTELKRING MUSEUM 'OUR LADY IN THE ATTIC'
- **3** AMSTERDAMS HISTORISCH MUSEUM
- **4** ANNE FRANKHUIS
- **5** BIJBELS MUSEUM
- **6** NEDERLANDS FILMMUSEUM
- **8** VAN GOGH MUSEUM
- **9** JEWISH HISTORICAL MUSEUM
- **10** 'T KROMHOUT WERFMUSEUM
- **14** REMBRANDTHUIS
- **15** RIJKSMUSEUM
- **16** NEDERLANDS SCHEEPVAART MUSEUM (MARITIME MUSEUM)
- **17** STEDELIJK MUSEUM
- **18** NEDERLANDS THEATER INSTITUUT
- **19** TROPEN MUSEUM (TROPICAL MUSEUM)
- **20** MADAME TUSSAUD'S
- **22** MUSEUM WILLET-HOLTHUYSEN
- **24** UNIVERSITEITSMUSEUM

MARKETS

- **1** ALBERT CUYPSTRAAT, GENERAL, 9 AM-5 PM, MON-SAT
- **2** DE LOOIER, ANTIQUE MARKET, 11 AM-5 PM, MON-THUR, SAT, SUN
- **3** BLOEMENMARKT, FLOWER MARKET, 9 AM-5 PM, MON-SAT
- **4** BOERENMARKT, FARMER'S MARKET, 10 AM-3 PM, SAT
- **5** KUNSTMARKT, ART MARKET, APRIL-OCT, 11 AM-6 PM, SUN
- **6** OUDEMANHUISPOORT, BOOK MARKET, 10 AM-4 PM, MON
- **7** POSTZEGELMARKT, STAMP MARKET, 1-4 PM, WED, SAT
- **8** WATERLOOPLEIN, FLEA MARKET, 10 AM-5 PM, MON-SAT
- **9** KUNSTMARKT, ART MARKET, APRIL-DEC, 10 AM-6 PM, SUN

W INFORMATION OFFICE AMSTERDAM TOURIST OFFICE

∞ RAILWAY STATIONS

M METRO

⇄ PUBLIC TRANSPORT INFORMATION/TICKETS

P PARKINGS

⟲ CANAL TRIPS

⊠ POST OFFICE

⚕ POLICE

B THEATERS

4 MUSEUMS

15 MONUMENTS, CHURCHES

G OTHER OBJECTS OF INTEREST

2 MARKETS

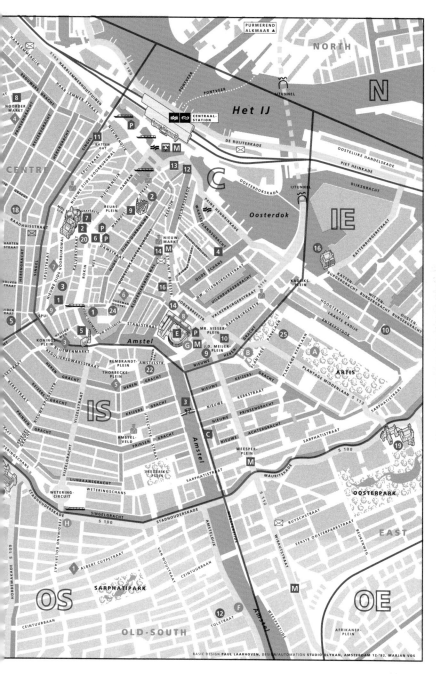

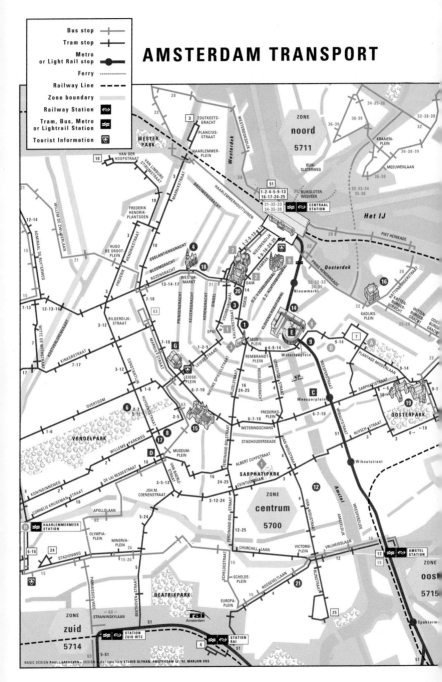

AMSTERDAM TRANSPORT

Bus stop
Tram stop
Metro or Light Rail stop
Ferry
Railway Line
Zone boundary
Railway Station
Tram, Bus, Metro or Lightrail Station
Tourist Information

BASIC DESIGN PAUL LAARHOVEN • DESIGN AUTOMATION STUDIO OLYKAN, AMSTERDAM 12 '92, MARJAN VOS